Anatomy of Authoritarianism in the Arab Republics

By examining the system of authoritarianism in eight Arab republics, Joseph Sassoon portrays life under these regimes and explores the mechanisms underpinning their resilience. How did the leadership in these countries create such enduring systems? What was the economic system that prolonged the regimes' longevity, but simultaneously led to their collapse? Why did these seemingly stable regimes begin to falter? This book seeks to answer these questions by utilizing the Iraqi archives and memoirs of those who were embedded in these republics: political leaders, ministers, generals, security agency chiefs, party members, and business people. Taking a thematic approach, the book begins in 1952 with the Egyptian Revolution and ends with the Arab uprisings of 2011. It seeks to deepen our understanding of the authoritarianism and coercive systems that prevailed in these countries and the difficult process of transition from authoritarianism that began after 2011.

JOSEPH SASSOON is an associate professor and Al-Sabah Chair in Politics and Political Economy of the Arab World at Georgetown University. He has published extensively on the Middle East. His recent publications include *Saddam Hussein's Ba'th Party: Inside an Authoritarian Regime* (Cambridge University Press, 2012) and *The Iraqi Refugees: The New Crisis in the Middle East* (2009).

D0912749

Anatomy of Authoritarianism in the Arab Republics

JOSEPH SASSOON

CAMBRIDGE
UNIVERSITY PRESS

University Printing House, Cambridge CB2 8BS, United Kingdom

One Liberty Plaza, 20th Floor, New York, NY 10006, USA

477 Williamstown Road, Port Melbourne, VIC 3207, Australia

4843/24, 2nd Floor, Ansari Road, Daryaganj, Delhi - 110002, India

79 Anson Road, #06-04/06, Singapore 079906

Cambridge University Press is part of the University of Cambridge.

It furthers the University's mission by disseminating knowledge in the pursuit of education, learning and research at the highest international levels of excellence.

www.cambridge.org
Information on this title: www.cambridge.org/9781107618312

© Joseph Sassoon 2016

First published 2016

A catalogue record for this publication is available from the British Library

ISBN 978-1-107-04319-0 Hardback
ISBN 978-1-107-61831-2 Paperback

To Rachey

Contents

Tables

Acknowledgments

During the years of research and writing this book, I amassed a large debt of gratitude to many people and a few organizations. Georgetown University, my new academic home, has been a wonderful and supportive place for me and I feel fortunate to be at the Center for Contemporary Arab Studies. Osama Abi-Mershed, the director of the Center, Rochelle Davis, and Fida Adely are friends and colleagues who provided help and advice on many levels.

Many colleagues have read chapters and provided excellent suggestions: Eugene Rogan, Michael Willis, Gretchen Helmke, and Rochelle Davis. Furthermore, I benefited from discussing the project with a number of colleagues, among them Martin Dimitrov and Dina Khoury, particularly at the early stages.

Another organization that I am indebted to is the Woodrow Wilson Center for International Scholars. During the academic year 2014–15, I was given a fellowship, which allowed me to write the book in the most congenial atmosphere possible for scholars. I would like to thank Haleh Esfandiari and Robert Litwak for their help and encouragement. The Library team at the Center is a dream team for every researcher: Janet Spikes, Katherine Wahler, and Michelle Kamalich. A great advantage of being at the Center is the presence of other fellows and scholars who provide invaluable suggestions. I would like to thank in particular Robert Worth, Max Rodenbeck, and Roya Hakakian for their wonderful friendship and support.

Alissa Walter accompanied this project from its genesis. Her knowledge of the region and Arabic, her organizational skills, her research capabilities, and her dedication are truly the envy of any academic. I thank her profusely for her help. Special thanks are due to Virginia Myers for help with editing the book in the early stages.

The team at Cambridge University Press has been wonderful. I would like to thank in particular my copy-editor, Mary Starkey, for her superb editing, commitment to the project, and attention to detail.

Special thanks are due to the many Tunisians whom I interviewed while researching the transition chapter who were generous with their time and shared their thoughts about the past and the future.

Friends and family were once again a source of encouragement. In particular I would like to thank my childhood friend Terry Somekh, whose interest in the work at every stage continuously drove me forward, my mother, who never ceases to support me, my daughter Rachey, to whom this book is dedicated, and finally to Helen. Her tremendous encouragement, technical help in the final stages of the manuscript, her proofreading, and most importantly her love and friendship are always a source of inspiration and comfort.

Notes on transliteration

For most Arabic names and words, this book uses a modified transliteration system based on the guidelines of the *International Journal of Middle East Studies* (*IJMES*). In the interest of making Arabic terms accessible to non-specialist readers, I have only included diacritical marks for the Arabic letters *ayn* (') and *hamza* ('). Otherwise, Arabic letters have been transliterated according to the *IJMES* system with diacritical markings omitted.

Two important exceptions have been made to this system. First, correct transliteration can have the unfortunate effect of rendering famous names unrecognizable, changing, for instance, Gamal 'Abd al-Nasser to Jamal 'Abd al-Nasir or Béji Caïd Essebsi to Baji Qa'id al-Sabsi. Thus, for heads of state *only* I have broken with the *IJMES* system and have instead used spellings that are more easily recognizable. For presidents from North Africa, where French is widely spoken, I have used the common French rendering of names. For the others, I have used common English spellings. A list of the names of Arab presidents can be found in Table 3.1.

Second, a small number of the memoirists examined in this book published their writings in English or French, in addition to Arabic. In these cases, I consistently used the authors' own preferred English or French spelling of their names, rather than using a "correct" transliteration of their names according to the *IJMES* system, even when referring to their writings in Arabic. This applies to authors such as Mohamed Mzali, Ahmed Mestiri, and Khalid Nezzar.

Glossary and abbreviations

amin shurta	deputy inspector
amin sirr	party secretariat
amn al-dawla	state security organization
al-amn al-ijtimaʿi	security for social affairs
al-amn al-qawmi	national security
badal	fee for military exemption
dawla amniyya	state dominated by security services
dhikrayat	memories
diwan	presidential offices
hiwar	dialogue
al-Ikhwan al-Muslimun	Muslim Brothers
infitah	"opening," economic liberalization policy
jihaz al-amn al-khass	special security organization
jihaz al-mabahith	investigation bureau
jihaz al-mukhabarat al-ʿamma	general intelligence directorate
khaliyya	party cell
al-mabahith al-ʿamma	general investigative directorate
majlis al-nuwwab	chamber of deputies
majlis al-shaʿb	people's council
al-makatib al-ʿaskariyya	military bureaus
masirat hayat	autobiographies
mudhakkirat	memoirs
mukhabarat	intelligence services
qasr al-nihaya	"palace of the end," an Iraqi prison
al-qiyada al-qutriyya	regional command
risala	message
wazir awwal	prime minister in North Africa
yawmiyyat	diaries

Abbreviations

FLN	Front de Libération Nationale (National Liberation Front) – Algeria
NDP	al-Hizb al-Watani al-Dimuqrati (National Democratic Party) – Egypt
PSD	Parti Socialiste Destourien (Constitutional Socialist Party) – Tunisia
RCD	Rassemblement Constitutionnel Démocratique (Democratic Constitutional Rally) – Tunisia
SSO	Special Security Organization – Iraq

Map of the eight Arab republics

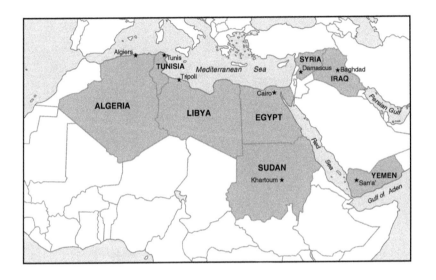

Introduction

Five years after the uprisings that swept through the Arab republics in 2011, it is hard to argue that the people in these countries are faring any better than before, except in the case of Tunisia. All eight republics – Algeria, Egypt, Iraq, Libya, Sudan, Syria, Tunisia, and Yemen – have long been characterized as authoritarian regimes. This book seeks to deepen our understanding of the authoritarianism and coercive systems that prevailed in these countries, and such knowledge is also critical to making a successful transition to a more open and free society.

The failure and collapse of countries such as Libya or Yemen, and Syria's protracted civil war, suggest that the demise of authoritarianism in the region is perhaps remote. Western observers' misunderstanding of the uprisings was partly due to their lack of awareness of how authoritarian regimes operated. Many were propelled by a wave of enthusiasm that engulfed not only local people but also scholars and commentators. A salutary lesson can be drawn from the continuing research into Latin American and Eastern European regimes where authoritarianism has been perpetuated in spite of their apparent transition to democracy. This underlines the importance of detailed and accurate analysis of the inner workings of these powerful and pervasive systems.

When researching my previous book (*Saddam Hussein's Ba'th Party: Inside an Authoritarian Regime*), which was based on the archives of the Ba'th Party regime in Iraq (which ruled from 1968 to 2003), I kept asking whether the other Arab republics were similar or not to Iraq and to each other. To answer that question, I would ideally have to examine the archives of other authoritarian Arab regimes. Unfortunately, they are inaccessible to any researcher. Consequently, I turned to memoirs written by those who were embedded in the system: political leaders, ministers, generals, security agency chiefs, party members, and businessmen close to the center of power. I also examined memoirs of people who were on the outside: political opponents of these regimes

1

and political prisoners. I hoped that a combination of the two groups – insiders and outsiders – would help in the endeavor to learn about the coercive tyrannies of the Arab world in spite of being unable to tap into their closed archives. Secrecy was, of course, the norm in these regimes and dissent was severely punished, so reliable information is not readily available. As Lisa Anderson explains, one of the dimensions of autocracy is that "neither rulers nor their subjects have reliable access" to information that would allow proper decision making.[1] Memoirs, however, can partially bridge the gap by revealing the inner functioning of organizations such as the military or the security forces. Even more importantly, we gain insights into the thinking of the leaders of these countries and their relations with their associates.

This book addresses a myriad of questions. How did the different regimes operate? What was the role of the ruling party in countries with a multi-party system, like Tunisia and Egypt? To what extent were repression and violence used, and how did the security services control opposition and co-opt other influential groups such as labor and student unions? How was the executive branch structured, and how were decisions made? Was Saddam Hussein's personality cult similar to or different from that of Hafiz al-Asad in Syria or Habib Bourguiba in Tunisia? How did economic planning differ? And how did these regimes tackle their economic problems?

The book is thematic, rather than allocating a chapter to each republic. It does not intend to be a historical review of events, but zooms in on certain episodes and trends through the prism of memoirs. It begins in 1952 with the Egyptian Revolution and ends with the Arab uprisings of 2011, with a final chapter devoted to the difficult process of transition from authoritarianism that began after 2011.

The monarchies of the Arab world, like Saudi Arabia, Jordan, Morocco, Kuwait, and other Gulf countries, are excluded for several reasons. First, it would have been too ambitious to include them all in one book. Second, in some monarchies such as Saudi Arabia, political parties do not exist, and it is very problematic to compare their government structure to the republics. Finally, while numerous political

---

[1] Lisa Anderson, "Authoritarian Legacies and Regime Change: Towards Understanding Political Transition in the Arab World," in Fawaz A. Gerges (ed.), *The New Middle East: Protest and Revolution in the Arab World* (New York: Cambridge University Press, 2014), p. 48.

memoirs have been written in Morocco and Jordan, few have emerged from Saudi Arabia and the Gulf.

Among the Arab republics, Lebanon was not covered because of its particular political structure, and it lacks many of the elements of authoritarian Arab regimes. Palestine was also not included, since most of the country still toils under occupation, and while aspects of the Palestine Liberation Organization (PLO) are similar to other republics, it is nevertheless an anomaly. Iran, an obviously authoritarian republic, is excluded because it is not an Arab state, and its political system is somewhat unique compared to those of its regional neighbors.

Certain disciplines, such as anthropology and literature, have drawn widely on memoirs from the region, yet memoirs are less commonly used as a primary source in modern history and politics, especially in studies of the Arab world. Historians of other regions have been quicker to recognize the value of memoirs as a primary source. Given the lack of archival sources in the Arab world, however, memoirs could become an essential tool in our study of these countries. Significantly, the governments that came to power in Tunisia after the fall of Ben 'Ali in 2011 refused to open the national archives, fearing that this could lead to upheavals in the country. One report indicated that files were burnt in several Tunisian ministries. In Libya, the archives are still supposedly intact; it is not clear which side controls them.[2] Even in those authoritarian countries around the world that have opened their archives, as in Russia, scholars regularly complement their work by poring over memoirs to examine the undercurrents in society and how those who were on the inside (or outside) perceived the regime.

Because excellent work has already been published about the Arab world and authoritarianism, to a certain extent this allows us the "luxury" of studying memoirs to complete the picture of political history. The present book draws on more than 120 memoirs from the eight republics, as well as recently published testimonies from Tunisia. These testimonies, which began to be collected after the uprising there, give remarkable insights into the hidden world of prisons and torture endured by the many opponents of the previous regime, regardless of their political or

---

[2] 'Abd al-Jalil al-Tamimi (ed.), *Dawr al-qasr al-ri'asi fi al-nizam al-Nufimbiri* [The role of the presidential palace in the November regime] (Tunis: Tamimi Foundation for Scientific Research and Information, April 2014), no. 41, pp. 15–16. The November regime refers to November 1987 when Ben 'Ali took over the presidency in a bloodless coup.

religious beliefs. No doubt there are memoirs that I have either missed or could not access, but among those that I read, the all-important questions I addressed are who wrote them, when and where they were published, and who their primary audience was. For instance, questions about the reason why so many Egyptian generals wrote their memoirs will be addressed in a number of chapters to underline the actual significance of publishing their memoirs. In addition, a large assortment of scholarly studies in Arabic, English, and French have supplemented this study.

There is no doubt that memoirs have significant drawbacks, and these are detailed in Chapter 1. Many were written after their well-placed authors had left their positions, and sometimes their country. What authors of memoirs remember, and why, changes over time, and all these aspects are shaped by the politics of memory. Regrettably, the memoirs studied here are not divided equally among the eight countries. From Sudan we have very few, while from Egypt there is an abundance from a parade of political actors. Needless to say, the book to some extent reflects this, but I have attempted to compensate by taking a thematic approach.

I have chosen to focus primarily on how authoritarian systems operated internally within each of the eight republics. Many memoirs are centered on major events such as wars or peace negotiations, and relations with the United States or the Soviet Union. Interesting as these topics are, they shed little light on internal dynamics. Also, these memoirs do not explore the role of the superpowers in the region in strengthening the durability of the regimes internally.

Other limitations of this collection of memoirs have affected the content of this book. For example, very few women in politics wrote memoirs or were written about. This is due, in large part, to their exclusion from key positions of power. In contrast, many biographies of "famous women" were published in the twentieth century celebrating their achievements, but unfortunately they do not fit the scope of this book.[3] Second, almost no memoirs of labor movement members or student union leaders were found that focus on authoritarianism and its implications for these movements. As a result, I could not examine issues of gender, education, or labor in great depth, and these are

---

[3] For a comprehensive study of these biographies, see Marilyn Booth, *May her Likes be Multiplied: Biography and Gender Politics in Egypt* (Berkeley: University of California Press, 2001).

mentioned only when referred to by authors. Regrettably, a project such as this cannot encompass every major aspect of authoritarian systems or how all segments of society were profoundly affected.

The history of authoritarianism in these eight republics stretches back before 1952.[4] As provinces of the Ottoman Empire they suffered from tyranny, and then, as colonies of the British, French, and Italians in the late nineteenth and early twentieth centuries, all were governed by authoritarian systems. When they became independent republics, they inherited remnants of despotism as well as limited institutional capacity. Many scholars have analyzed the problems of authoritarianism in the region in eloquent terms. Prominent among them was 'Abd al-Rahman al-Kawakibi (1848–1902), a Syrian official and journalist who vehemently opposed Sultan 'Abd al-Hamid, one of the most tyrannical rulers of the Ottoman Empire. In a short but succinct treatise titled *The Characteristics of Despotism and the Death of Enslavement*, al-Kawakibi discusses the various implications of despotism. He details the intertwining of tyranny on the one hand, and wealth and corruption on the other, and does not mince his words:

If tyranny were a man who wanted to talk about himself, he would say: "I am evil, my father is injustice, my mother is offense, my brother is treachery, my sister is misery, my father's brother is harm, my mother's brother is humiliation, my son is poverty, my daughter is unemployment, my homeland is ruin, and my clan is ignorance, my country is destruction. As for my religion, honor and life they are money, money, money!"[5]

Al-Kawakibi addresses his essay to the youth, so they could learn about the far-reaching impact of tyranny before it is too late, "before despotism annihilates the last remnants of vitality in them." Fearing reprisal, he says that his booklet is not about a particular ruler but is a discussion of a general phenomenon. (This theme recurs in many of the memoirs studied here, even those published long after the rulers have died or been ousted.) Written more than a century ago, al-Kawakibi's emphasis on the

[4] For a survey of authoritarianism in the Arab world, see Zuhair Farid Mubarak, *Usul al-istibdad al-'Arabi* [The origins of Arab despotism] (Beirut: al-Intishar, 2010).
[5] 'Abd al-Rahman al-Kawakibi, *Taba'i' al-istibdad wa masari' al-isti'bad* [The nature of tyranny and struggle against enslavement] (Cairo: Iqra' Foundation, 2013), p. 64. Translation of the quote is from Sami A. Hanna and George H. Gardner, *Arab Socialism: A Documentary Survey* (Salt Lake City: University of Utah Press, 1969), p. 218.

importance of good governance and the destructive effects of despotism apply equally today to many of the eight republics. He discusses the connection of despotism with religion, science, glory, wealth, morality, education, and progress. Each chapter of his book details those interactions; for instance, he argues that "political despotism is inseparably tied to religious despotism," and that "despots, assisted by the clergy, take on for the common people the powers, attributes, and the very names of God."[6] Defining despotism, he asserts that it is dehumanizing and demoralizes a whole society, and adds: "It is unaccountable, unlimited, arbitrary, self-serving, and exclusive rule. It is served by the coercive military power of the ruler and the incapacitating ignorance of the ruled."[7] In fact, al-Kawakibi's treatise is an excellent introduction to authoritarianism in the Arab world. He manages to cover all the main features of tyrannical rule and its devastating effects on both the individual and society.

Authoritarianism is not solely a product of the Arab region or entrenched in its culture. Many revolutionaries around the world, from Mao in China to Kenyatta in Kenya, never fulfilled their promises of equality or democracy, and after coming to power they were mostly interested in staying there. Many of the characteristics and policies of authoritarian Arab regimes were learned or copied from other regimes, beginning with the Soviet Union and Nazi Germany in the 1930s, and continuing with the military dictatorships of Latin America and Asia.

Time and again, the role of the leadership and the centrality of decision making by the presidents are emphasized here. But as two scholars put it: "The declaration of absolutism, however, is never true. No leader, no matter how august or revered, no matter how cruel or vindictive, ever stands alone."[8] Hence, apart from focusing on leadership, the book looks at the other main components of authoritarianism: party, military, security services, and an economic cronyism that is dependent on the leadership.

Needless to say, there is a wide variety in history, politics, and economics among these countries, but the book strives, first of all, to find

---

[6] Al-Kawakibi, *Taba'i' al-istibdad*, pp. 24–40. Translation was taken from Khaldun S. al-Husry, *Three Reformers: A Study in Modern Arab Political Thought* (Beirut: Khayats, 1966), p. 63. For an interesting discussion of al-Kawakibi's book and views, see pp. 55–112.

[7] See Suzanne Kassab, *Contemporary Arab Thought: Cultural Critique in Comparative Perspective* (New York: Columbia University Press, 2010), p. 37.

[8] Bruce Bueno de Mesquita and Alastair Smith, *The Dictator's Handbook: Why Bad Behavior is Almost Always Good Politics* (New York: Public Affairs, 2011), p. 2.

common features or dissimilarities. Second, I examine the role of coercive organizations such as the military and security services, and whether that role changed over time. Third, I explore what kinds of institutions were established and what their legacies are going forward. Obviously, this is very pertinent to the chances of a successful transition from despotism. Fourth, I raise the more hypothetical question of whether authoritarian rule might return to these republics. Will institutions like the oppressive security services continue to act as before, and will the new leaders reinstate a cult of personality to serve their needs and ambitions? By investigating an extensive collection of memoirs and testimonies from across these countries, the book will answer those questions judging from how those on the inside (and to some extent from the outside) perceived these systems and described their functionality.

The book will argue that the eight republics have far more in common than was previously envisaged. Variation in degrees of repression or denial of freedoms is an important distinction among them, but does not alter the final picture. Attitudes toward violence differed; some countries engaged in public hangings or assassination of political opponents, while others abstained from such activities. However, all the republics used systematic torture in their prisons, and the structure of their coercive apparatuses did not differ much. The systems of repression they created or "strengthened" after coming to power were quite comparable; all penetrated their societies by planting informants at every level, including in the high echelons of power to ensure the loyalty of the elites. Leadership was characterized by its centrality, and the decision-making process was in the hands of the leader with a small cohort of advisers. But it would be a mistake to imagine that these regimes could sustain power for such a long period without the critical assistance, to varying degrees, of ruling parties, security services, and the military. Economic management varied widely among those countries, but all leaders ensured that their economic cronies and networks of support would continue to support the regimes in return for financial benefits.

The book is divided into seven chapters. Chapter 1 discusses political memoirs as a source of information for studying the Arab world. It looks at memory and interrelated issues, and appraises the positives and negatives of studying these relatively neglected memoirs for political analysis of the region. In a general manner, the different genres of memoirs are categorized. The lack of personal diaries in the region was striking, and is surely due to the state of fear that prevailed. Understanding the reasons for writing memoirs, the expectations of their authors in publishing them, and what they included or omitted are all important in understanding the personalities of these political actors.

Chapter 2 deals with the ruling party and governance from the perspective of these memoirists. Some of these republics, such as Iraq and Syria, had a one-party system, while others, like Egypt and Tunisia, had multi-party systems. But there were also countries like Libya, whose leadership annulled political parties and parliament and created its own unique system. Through the memoirs of party members, parliamentary opponents, and ministers, the chapter analyzes the substantial role of ruling parties in perpetuating the regimes. While the triangular relationship between the leadership, the party, and the bureaucracy differed from one republic to another, the overall structure of governance did not vary widely, except in the case of Libya.

Chapter 3 focuses on one of the core organizations in authoritarian regimes: the military, which had been a vital factor in the histories of these nations since they gained their independence from the colonial powers Britain, France, and Italy. Most of the leaders had a military background, to which they remained connected. Military conflicts and civil wars had immense political ramifications for these republics, except in Tunisia, whose leadership managed to keep the army out of politics. Armed conflicts allowed the authoritarian regimes to stay in power longer by rallying the population around them and subjugating their opposition. Yet in spite of the prominence of the military, this chapter will convey how, once the military leaders became presidents, their relationship with the military was not always harmonious. An insight is gained by looking at the lives and careers of military officers through the memoirs they authored, which mostly indicated the cohesiveness of these institutions.

Chapter 4 dwells on the role of the security services, which were a cornerstone in establishing these regimes and ensuring their durability. Heads of security services in almost all the republics wrote memoirs, mostly to justify their actions. Once again we find many common characteristics. Among them was the fact that all the regimes, without exception, used imprisonment, torture, and trials as a means of coercing the opposition in all its shapes and forms. Furthermore, all these regimes feared the influence of religion and felt threatened by religious movements. Memoirs of political prisoners portray the extreme suffering of anyone who opposed or was suspected of opposing the regime, and document the extent of violence meted out to opponents and their extended families. The chapter also reveals how these societies were deeply penetrated by informants, whose numbers swelled dramatically in most republics. While the mass of information they gathered was colossal, this did not guarantee that it was properly analysed or efficiently used; a case in point was the assassination of Egyptian president Anwar al-Sadat, where the information was available but the follow-up was flawed.

Chapter 5 discusses economy and finance. It is clear from memoirs that economic issues were not high on the leaders' agenda unless facing a crisis. The majority of leaders focused on staying in power, and decisions related to military and foreign affairs were far more important in their eyes. Hence, most memoirs only delved slightly into economic issues, but they still convey information about decision making and the role of certain prominent businessmen. One feature was that leaders in most of these republics were not interested in stemming corruption. Corruption began to gather momentum in the late 1970s, and became embedded in the political and bureaucratic systems of these countries, which in turn benefited the economic elites and strengthened their alliance with the political leadership.

Chapter 6 analyzes leadership and the cult of personality. Leaders of the Arab republics shared many personality traits, particularly those who held power for a long time. Each had a deep belief in himself and in his elevated role toward his country and people. Many believed they were carrying a divine *risala* (message) to their people. As they were surrounded mostly by yes-men and sycophants, this conviction intensified over time. Escaping assassination attempts and overcoming internal resistance strengthened their determination and self-belief. Memoirs clearly highlight another common characteristic: the lack of trust in anyone or anything. While the leaders demanded utter loyalty from those close to them, and cherished it, they were not always loyal to their friends or to those who helped them early in their careers. For instance, Gamal 'Abd al-Nasser, Mu'ammar al-Qaddafi, and Saddam Hussein removed most of the men who were alongside them when they assumed power.

Biographies and autobiographies of leaders underline that they changed with time. Events such as wars impacted them; assassination attempts and betrayals by those close to them changed their views and attitudes. Several became old and sick, which altered their behavior and decision making. Many observers overlook the contribution of the cult of personality to leadership, or accord it little weight, but the evidence is that this was, and remains, an important tool in the political armory of authoritarianism and was skillfully used by some leaders. It placed them above recrimination or reproach and made it extremely hard to resist their ideas or decisions.

The final chapter addresses the burning issues that continue to confront these republics on their troubled path of transitioning from authoritarianism post-2011. Because only a few memoirs discuss this, the chapter engages in comparisons with other parts of the world to understand this process. For Tunisia, the only country that is truly undergoing a transition, I interviewed senior people from the previous regime, as well as current politicians, academics, and businesspeople to gain an insight into current issues and challenges. The chapter examines three facets of transition: governance and state–religion relations; economic problems and corruption; and confronting the past. The chapter also asks if Iraq after 2003 could become a case study of post-authoritarianism among these republics. I argue that in spite of the vast differences between Iraq and the other republics that witnessed uprisings, lessons can still be learned from Iraq post-Saddam Hussein. Comparative studies show that when political change is not accompanied by substantial economic change, there is a risk of reversion on the political front, as old vested interests can regain control over the political process.

As for dealing with the history of these regimes, it is argued here that genuine transition cannot take place unless there is reconciliation with the past. The coercive security apparatus that existed in the Arab region, not dissimilar from other parts of the world, has to be analyzed and understood. The testimonies of political prisoners recently collected and published in Tunisia augur well for its future in that regard. It has become clear that the scars of the past that remain after decades of tyranny and terror cannot be obliterated or ameliorated until we more fully comprehend the complexities of these despotic and damaging regimes.

Finally, it is hoped that this book will encourage other researchers to make greater use of memoirs in understanding the anatomy of authoritarianism in the Arab states, at least until their archives are made available.

1 | *Political memoirs in the Arab republics*

The practice of writing biographies and autobiographies has a long history in both Western and Arabic civilizations. Historians have been challenged by the subjectivity of personal memoirs since the days of chronicling the Romans. Commenting on the task facing historians of England, Benjamin Disraeli wrote: "Generally speaking, all the great events have been distorted, most of the important causes concealed, some of the principal characters never appear, and all who figure are so misunderstood and misrepresented that the result is a complete mystification."[1] Yet, given the lack of archival resources, the recollections gathered in memoirs of all types can help bring the past to life in remarkable ways. As one eminent historian put it:

> We historians, too, have to go back and immerse ourselves into that same "conceptual climate," to reconstruct what people – leaders and led alike – knew up to that point, the memories and experiences that shaped their fears, expectations and mentalities.[2]

Elie Kedourie's seminal study about Arab political memoirs in the 1970s stated: "That they apologize, or palliate or embellish or suppress, in no way diminishes the value of what they write."[3] From ancient times, those engaged in political life recorded their deeds and accomplishments in personal memoirs. The motivation for "presenting one's life" was seen as an "act of thanking God and for others to emulate."[4] As Judith Tucker observes about the role of biographies in the Middle East:

---

[1] Benjamin Disraeli, *Sybil, or the Two Nations* (Oxford: Oxford World's Classics, 2008), p. 15.

[2] Peter Hennessy, *Distilling the Frenzy: Writing the History of One's Own Times* (London: Biteback Publishing, 2012), p. 19. Lord Hennessey is the Attlee Professor of Contemporary British History at Queen Mary College, University of London.

[3] Elie Kedourie, *Arabic Political Memoirs and Other Studies* (London: Frank Cass, 1974), p. 178.

[4] Dwight F. Reynolds (ed.), *Interpreting the Self: Autobiography in the Arabic Literary Tradition* (Berkeley: University of California Press, 2001), p. 3.

The meaning of an individual life can thus be sought in its impact, for good or ill, on the past and present. It is here that biography and history are joined together as mutual influences, through their shared understanding of human agency and of the extent to which the meaning of an individual life is to be grasped only in the context of a community informed by a past, inhabiting a present, and anticipating a future.[5]

Some modern historians in the Arab world looked to memoirs as an important research tool. One Egyptian scholar who examined memoirs of Egyptian politicians over a period of ninety years argues that they constitute an integral part of researching the country's political history. He rejects the notion that "non-objective" sources such as recollections, diaries, and memoirs are less valuable than "objective" sources such as archives, party manifestos, laws and regulations.[6] Political memoirs fall within the comprehensive camp of historiography. "Memoirists, for all their inherent focus on the personal, emulate the principal functions of historiography in attempting to describe past events and conditions, to explain the causes of these events and to interpret their meaning."[7]

'Abd al-'Azim Ramadan in his study categorizes memoirs in Egypt according to the party membership of their authors (al-Wafd Party, the Muslim Brotherhood, etc.), and then another group about the July 23, 1952 Revolution. He pinpoints some of the incongruities and advises against relying on the writers' dating of specific events.[8] Another scholar who made extensive use of Egyptian memoirs is Hazem Kandil, whose book about the Egyptian military utilized memoirs effectively to illustrate the relations between different generals and within the Egyptian leadership.[9]

Political memoirs examined extensively in this book suffer from certain deficiencies. The politics of remembering are invariably complicated:

[5] Judith Tucker, "Biography as History: The Exemplary Life of Khayr al-Din al-Ramli," in Mary Ann Fay (ed.), *Auto/Biography and the Construction of Identity and Community in the Middle East* (New York: Palgrave, 2001), p. 17.

[6] 'Abd al-'Azim Ramadan, *Mudhakkirat al-siyasiyyin wa al-zu'ama' fi Misr, 1891–1981* [Memoirs of politicians and leaders in Egypt, 1891–1981] (Cairo: al-Watan al-'Arabi, 1985), pp. 13–20.

[7] George Egerton (ed.), *Political Memoir: Essays on the Politics of Memory* (London: Frank Cass, 1994), p. 348.

[8] For a list of memoirs not examined by Ramadan, see Ramadan, *Mudhakkirat al-siyasiyyin*, appendix 2, pp. 224–30.

[9] Hazem Kandil, *Soldiers, Spies, and Statesmen: Egypt's Road to Revolt* (New York: Verso, 2014).

"What is remembered and what is forgotten, and why, change over time. Thus remembering has a politics."[10] Consequently, the portrayal of political life holds many hazards for researchers: the act of recounting major events, the experience of political activity, the presentation of certain major events, are all challenging to the historian. Yet as this book shows, memoirs can open avenues for understanding the authors' countries.

Numerous historians, philosophers and psychologists have long debated the issue of memory and of "subjectivity versus objectivity in history."[11] A study about autobiographies in the Levant remarked that autobiography is similar to a novel: reminiscing about the past also needs one's imagination.[12] A Syrian Ba'thist general and former deputy minister, Walid Hamdun, begins his book in an unusual fashion, telling readers: "I had difficulty in writing my memoirs, particularly anything related to chronology and remembering events and names, but I overcame that, thanks to God, due to the purity of my mind and my brain powers."[13] According to Nikolaos Van Dam, one of the few writers who drew extensively on political memoirs when researching the Syrian Ba'th regime, Hamdun writes about events that he was not part of, and Van Dam quotes Mustafa Talas, a minister of defense for more than three decades, who said that Hamdun's book contains exaggerations and mistakes.[14] Yet, as Van Dam correctly states, the book is still useful in providing an insider's view of his party comrades. Van Dam analyzes some other famous memoirs published by prominent Syrians and Ba'th Party leaders such as Talas.[15] He outlines the difficulties of describing events from different angles when authors do

---

[10] Sidonie Smith and Julia Watson, *A Guide for Interpreting Life Narratives: Reading Autobiography*, 2nd edn. (Minneapolis: University of Minnesota Press, 2010), p. 24.

[11] See, for example, the enormous work by Paul Ricoeur, *Memory, History, Forgetting*, translated by Kathleen Blamey and David Pellauer (Chicago: University of Chicago Press, 2004), pp. 333–42.

[12] Mahir al-Sharif and Qays al-Zarli, *al-Siyar al-dhatiyya fi Bilad al-Sham* [Autobiographies in the Levant countries] (Damascus: Dar al-Mada, 2009), p. 17.

[13] Walid Hamdun, *Dhikrayat wa ara'* [Memories and opinions] (Damascus: Walid Hamdun, 2007), p. 11.

[14] Nikolaos Van Dam, *The Struggle for Power in Syria: Politics and Society under Asad and the Ba'th Party*, revised 4th edn. (London: I. B. Tauris, 2011), p. 152.

[15] Ibid., pp. 145–57.

not even agree on the dates or details of events. Nevertheless, he stresses that these memoirs contain "valuable detailed elements about Syrian history under Baʿth rule."[16]

Before evaluating the memoirs used in the present book, it is important to note that in spite of their sizeable number, one genre noticeably absent is that of personal diaries, which can capture daily or weekly events with greater accuracy. Prior to the rise of authoritarianism, diaries were written in the Arab world, and some scholars have done interesting work on these memoirs.[17] The lack of diaries in a region gripped by authoritarian rule is comparable to what prevailed in the Soviet Union. Jochen Hellbeck observes that diaries thrived in pre-revolutionary Russia, but became almost extinct in the post-revolution climate of terror and fear. "Given the omnipresence of state repression in totalitarian systems, only exceptional persons risk keeping diaries impelled by conscience or a concern for posterity."[18] One can safely assume that almost no politician in these Arab republics would dare keep a diary describing, for example, meetings of the ruling party or the cabinet. The number of those in the inner circle who were being watched, arrested, ousted, or exiled was high enough to plant fear into the hearts of most politicians. Even when I obtained the personal diary of a Baʿthist, it turned out to be an "official" diary itemizing the agenda discussed in the weekly meetings of a party cell in Iraq. In some instances, an author would call their book a diary, but in fact it was written long after the event and was never in diary form. For example, the powerful story of a prisoner in Syria headlined *Diary of a Voyeur* was in fact written years after the dramatic events took place.[19]

Political memoirs in the Arab region rarely include biographies written by, and about, women. This stems from the fact that very few women were in power, and, apart from some ministers, no women were in high positions in the military, security services, or in a real leadership capacity. Those in positions of power rarely wrote about

[16] Ibid., p. 157.
[17] See, for example, Kimberly Katz, *A Young Palestinian's Diary, 1941–1945: The Life of Sami ʿAmr* (Austin: University of Texas Press, 2009).
[18] Jochen Hellbeck, *Revolution on my Mind: Writing a Diary under Stalin* (Cambridge, MA: Harvard University Press, 2006), p. 3.
[19] Mustafa Khalifa, *al-Qawqaʿa: yawmiyyat mutalassis* [The shell: the diary of a voyeur], 2nd edn. (Beirut: Dar al-Adab, 2010).

their experiences after they left politics. Numerous memoirs, particularly those about the presidents of Iraq and Yemen, accentuate the masculinity of these leaders to create an aura of respect. This assertion of authority and masculinity applies not only in the Arab world but also in other parts of the world such as Russia.

In spite of the drawbacks of memoirs, they are still an excellent source. They definitely provide an interesting source of information from different points of views; they shed light on relationships within the executive branch; and uncover for us many intriguing stories that secondary sources such as newspapers never review. Hannah Arendt concluded that "true understanding has hardly any choice" but to accept these personal statements, given that "self-understanding and self-interpretation are the very foundation of all analysis and understanding."[20] Politicians felt that they "owe [it] to history to present an account of their careers."[21] Intriguingly, there is also some consistency in the information provided in many of these sources, whether in Algeria, Syria, Tunisia, or Egypt, which adds to our understanding, for instance, of the workings of the security services.

It is possible to group the political memoirs used in this book into six categories, although they are by no means comprehensive of every political memoir in the Arab world. Political biographies in the region are diverse, and some are hard to classify within a genre because of the different techniques used by authors to describe their experiences.[22] Various memoirs of ambassadors are not included here as their emphasis was on international relations, which is not the focus of this book. For instance, one Yemeni memoir deals with the author's ambassadorial appointments and Yemen's relations with Britain and neighboring countries during the 1940s and 1950s. It could

---

[20] Hannah Arendt, "On the Nature of Totalitarianism: An Essay in Understanding," in Hannah Arendt (ed.), *Essays in Understanding, 1930–1954* (New York: Harcourt, 1994), pp. 338–39.

[21] See, for example, the introduction by Mohamed Mzali, who served as prime minister under Bourguiba in the 1980s, in Mohamed Mzali, *Un premier ministre de Bourguiba témoigne* [A prime minister of Bourguiba testifies] (Paris: Jean Picollec, 2004), pp. 11–14.

[22] One textbook about autobiography finds sixty genres of Life Narratives. See Smith and Watson, *A Guide for Interpreting Life Narratives*, appendix A, pp. 253–86.

therefore be useful for those writing the history of Yemen, but is less relevant here.[23]

Specific event biographies

Most common within this type of memoir are recollections about events such as war or assassination attempts. Generals, particularly Egyptian ones, have been prolific in writing about the defeat of 1967 and the military victory of 1973. Similarly, Egyptian senior members of the security services produced a spate of memoirs about the assassination of President Anwar al-Sadat. As Chapter 3 makes clear, military leaders were not willing to take the blame for the crushing defeat of 1967. Some blamed 'Abd al-Hakim 'Amr, who was then the chief of staff, while others held the political leadership responsible – Egypt's president, Gamal 'Abd al-Nasser. On the other hand, many generals claimed to be an integral part of the Egyptian military victory of 1973, and wanted their audience to be aware of their contribution. The memoirs do not elaborate in detail what happened militarily at the end of the 1973 War, which in essence ended with the Israeli army threatening Cairo and Damascus. The focus is mostly on the brilliant crossing of the Suez Canal by Egyptian troops, which took the Israelis by total surprise and caused them serious casualties. An example of a general involved in these wars is Muhammad 'Abd al-Ghani al-Jamasi, who was one of the architects of the 1973 War. A serious and dedicated soldier, al-Jamasi never mentions that the tide turned against the Egyptians in the second part of the war, even though he is very candid about military developments. He is bitter about being pushed out of his job when he was one of the main engineers of the victorious crossing, but insists that he is not critical of anyone, and is simply sketching how things developed in the period before 1967 until the end of the 1973 War.[24] Other wars widely written about are the Iran–Iraq War, the Iraqi invasion of Kuwait, and the Yemen War.

Many memoirs about particular events were written long after they took place, when those involved felt free to write. One example is the

---

[23] Najib Abu 'Izz al-Din, *'Ishrun 'aman fi khidmat al-Yaman* [Twenty years in the service of Yemen] (Beirut: Dar al-Bahith, 1991).

[24] Muhammad 'Abd al-Ghani al-Jamasi, *Mudhakkirat al-Jamasi: Harb Uktubir 1973* [al-Jamasi's memoirs: The October 1973 War] (Paris: al-Sharqiyya Publishing, 1990).

memoir by the Iraqi ambassador to Washington during the invasion of Kuwait. Although written five years after Saddam Hussein's fall and seventeen years after the First Gulf War, the author admits that he still does not have the answers to what he sees as fundamental questions: Was Kuwait a ploy by the Americans to trap Saddam Hussein? Was Saddam Hussein in cahoots with the American administration to allow the United States to get control of oil fields? What was the role of the Zionist lobby in the invasion of Kuwait?[25] These questions, raised by a veteran diplomat and sociology graduate, are more akin to conspiracy theories. Some accounts of events are more balanced; for instance, a senior Egyptian officer describes the Yemen War in the mid 1960s, and how Egypt found itself in a quagmire. He believes that newspapers and official documents are not enough to give a complete picture of history, and that his memoirs can contribute to this.[26]

Among specific event memoirs that could be included are the stories of incarceration. In the Arab world, powerful testimonies in this genre have been published. Political prisoners desperately want the outside world to recognize their suffering and to tell the public what really happened inside the prisons. "Contemporary narratives of witness often record the struggle of incarcerated subjects with dehumanizing systems and the forging or preserving of identity under duress."[27] These ex-prisoners "use the realm of memory as a form of cultural resistance."[28] In one rare case in Algeria there are two memoirs, one about a prisoner depicting life in prison and the other by General Khalid Nezzar, who was in charge of the prisons for political prisoners (the main prison was named after the general, who masterminded the fight against the Islamists).[29] These two memoirs present such a

---

[25] Muhammad al-Mashshat, *Kuntu safiran lil-'Iraq fi Washintun: hikayati ma'a Saddam fi ghazu al-Kuwait* [I was Iraq's ambassador in Washington: my story with Saddam during the invasion of Kuwait] (Beirut: Arab Institute for Research and Publishing, 2008), p. 30.

[26] Salah al-Din al-Hadidi, *Shahid 'ala Harb al-Yaman* [Witness of the Yemen War] (Cairo: Madbuly Publications, 1984), p. 11.

[27] Smith and Watson, *A Guide for Interpreting Life Narratives*, p. 134.

[28] Sune Haugbolle, "The Victim's Tale in Syria: Imprisonment, Individualism, and Liberalism," in Laleh Khalili and Jillian Schwedler (eds.), *Policing and Prisons in the Middle East: Formations of Coercion* (London: Hurst, 2010), p. 223.

[29] Lyes Laribi, *Dans les geôles de Nezzar* [In the dungeons of Nezzar] (Paris: Paris–Méditerranée, 2002); Khalid Nezzar, *Mudhakkirat al-Liwa' Khalid Nezzar* [Memoirs of Major-General Khalid Nezzar] (Algiers: al-Shihab Publishing, 1999).

contrast that they enhance our understanding of that troubled period in Algeria in the 1990s by shedding light on the war against Islamists and the life of prisoners.

One compelling prison memoir is by a Communist Party member in Syria who paid a heavy price for his membership: sixteen years in prison. He reflects that his book is somewhat out of the ordinary because it cannot be part of prison literature; it is not a sociological research of incarceration, or a biography of a prisoner, or a document of the regime's policies. His aim is to demystify life in prison by focusing on the triangular relationship between the prison, the prisoner, and the imprisoner. Having spent most of his youth in prison, he argues that the most important factor for surviving prison experience is a technique he calls *al-sajin al-mustahbas* (the prisoner who "embraces" the prison). The author's concept is that the prisoner should accept his life in prison, make it his home, and not live in a permanently tense state awaiting or longing for release. He admits, however, that this idea can work best for young bachelors who do not have young families dependent on them emotionally and economically.[30]

Another Syrian prisoner raises the issue of memory and forgetting; its author refused to dwell on his life in prison for fourteen years after his release. "I tried to bury the story of my prison in the ruins of memory." His efforts failed; psychologically, he could not free himself from the demons of the period. He emphasizes, however, that he is not writing to inform us about details of the imprisonment system, and he reveals the absorbing fact that once prisoners were released in countries like Syria or Iraq, they were forbidden to say they were ex-prisoners or to divulge any information about their imprisonment or interrogation. Indeed, his book avoids any dates, names, and places in order not to break "security secrets." He thus titles it, *Stories from an Imaginary Memory of a Real Prisoner*.[31]

A fascinating account of imprisonment is given by the prominent Egyptian feminist Nawal al-Sa'dawi. She wrote a play in Arabic about her time in prison, and her memoirs were translated into English. Her story is very similar to those of many in the Arab world who were

---

[30] Yasin al-Hajj Salih, *Bilkhalas, ya shabab: 16 'aman fi al-sujun al-Suriyya* [Salvation, young men: sixteen years in the Syrian prisons] (Beirut: Dar al-Saqi, 2012), pp. 9–10, 148.

[31] Lu'ay Husayn, *al-Fiqd: hikayat min dhakira mutakhiyyala li-sajin haqiqi* [The loss: stories from an imaginary memory of a real prisoner] (Beirut: al-Furat, 2006), pp. 10–11.

arrested for opposing the regime or because they were thought to be a "threat" to the authoritarian system. Describing this state of affairs, al-Sa'dawi explains: "Everything in our country is in the hands of the state and under its direct or indirect control, by laws known or concealed, by tradition or a by a long established, deeply-rooted fear of the ruling authority."[32] She attempts to understand why people did not openly write about or act upon the beliefs or opinions that they expressed in small and closed meetings. Her succinct answer, echoing those in many countries around the world is: "Fearing servility, people become servile."[33]

Autobiographies (*masirat hayat*)

Many of these autobiographies begin with the authors recounting their childhoods, details about their families, their neighbors, and the country's history during their formative years. Yet, in a study about autobiography, one essay underlines that "strictly speaking, autobiography is not a recollection of one's life." It is "an artifact, a construct wrought from words."[34] Autobiography does not necessarily show us the objective stages of a life and career, but "reveals instead the effort of a creator to give the meaning of his own mythic tale."[35]

The wide collection of Arabic memoirs ranges from presidents to businessmen. It includes those by Egyptian president Sadat, Tunisian prime minister Mohamed Mzali, Yemen's president 'Abd al-Rahman bin Yahya al-'Aryani, and Egyptian businessman 'Uthman Ahmad 'Uthman. Even lesser-known personalities wrote lengthy autobiographies. A good example is Mansur al-Atrash, who was a Syrian minister in 1963 and a member of the regional and national bureaus of the Syrian Ba'th Party. His autobiography of almost 500 pages describes his childhood, education, travels, political struggles, times in prison, and official jobs, and offers an insight into the second tier of the executive branch who lived under these regimes and were part of the

---

[32] Nawal el-Saadawi, *Memoirs from the Women's Prison*, translated by Marilyn Booth (London: Women's Press, 1986), p. 3.
[33] Ibid.
[34] Barrett J. Mandel, "Full of Life Now," in James Olney (ed.), *Autobiography: Essays Theoretical and Critical* (Princeton: Princeton University Press, 1980), p. 49.
[35] Georges Gusdorf, "Conditions and Limits of Autobiography," in Olney (ed.), *Autobiography*, p. 48.

machine. Interestingly, he calls his autobiography *The Condemned Generation*, which he believes describes the lives of many of his compatriots.[36]

Autobiographies attempt to construct life and its stages through the eyes of the authors.[37] "Those who tell the stories, rule the world."[38] There is a strong tendency to verbosity, and political autobiographers seldom suffer from lack of confidence. Their books are characterized by idealization of issues, pontification, flattery, and distortion. Rarely are mistakes admitted or responsibility taken for disastrous decisions. One senior Iraqi who occupied many senior positions, Tawfiq al-Suwaydi, asserts that even when "I was young I began to think on a higher plane than my peers. Unlike them, I rebelled against many traditions and criticized the stagnation and rigidity that had come to have such a hold on the Arab East."[39] Most of these authors felt compelled to write mammoth tomes detailing even the most mundane questions, and adorned their memoirs with long titles. The president of Yemen's autobiography fills two volumes; the Egyptian businessman Sayyid Mar'i, who later became a minister and the secretary-general of the Egyptian ruling party under Sadat, produced a three-volume memoir, while the biographies of both al-Suwaydi and Muhammad Hadid, Iraq's minister of finance after the 1958 Revolution, are more than 500 pages. This is not just an Arab phenomenon; a review of the

[36] Mansur Sultan al-Atrash, *al-Jil al-mudan: sira dhatiyya* [The condemned generation: an autobiography] (Beirut: Riyad al-Rayyis Books, 2008). Al-Atrash died in 2006 and the biography was completed by his daughter Rim, who informs us in the preface that she promised her father she would finish the manuscript if he died before publication.

[37] For a general discussion, see Robert Folkenflick (ed.), *The Culture of Autobiography: Constructions of Self-Representation* (Stanford: Stanford University Press, 1993).

[38] This quote has been recently popularized by Jonah Sachs in his book *Winning the Story Wars* (Cambridge, MA: Harvard Business Review Press, 2012) and by Shane Snow in his TEDx talk, "Those Who Tell Stories Rule the World," August 11, 2014, available at www.youtube.com/watch?v=Asm2Ad49cyI. The origin of the quotation is unclear, having been attributed to both Plato and to Hopi Native Americans. Though it is commonly used to refer to the power of stories to compel political or consumer action, it can also be used to illustrate the powerful influence that the political narratives in these memoirs have in shaping memories about the legacies of authoritarian regimes.

[39] Tawfiq al-Suwaydi, *My Memoirs: Half a Century of the History of Iraq and the Arab Cause*, translated by Nancy Roberts (Boulder, CO: Lynne Rienner, 2013), p. 55.

500-page autobiography of Leon Panetta, former head of the CIA and secretary of defense, commented that "Panetta's self-confidence is blunt and seemingly without limits ... in a fifty-year career, there seems to be almost nothing Leon Panetta got wrong."[40]

In a "l'état c'est moi" (I am the state) syndrome, presidents perceived their lives as synonymous with their countries. As Sadat put it in his prologue: "This is the story of my life, which is at the same time the story of Egypt since 1918 – for so destiny has decreed. I therefore tell my story in full, not merely as the President of Egypt, but as an Egyptian whose life has been intimately bound up with that of [Egypt's] life."[41] This was the image he had of himself since childhood. In other words, it is less a historical analysis than the writer's careful creation of his mythical tale. Biographies of presidents were an essential component in establishing their cults of personality (see Chapter 6). Apart from those written by the leaders themselves (no doubt with professional help), some were penned by journalists at the behest of the regime, or by a close associate of the leader. Hardly ever did these biographies carry any negative images of the leaders; on the contrary, they attempted to show their humble origins, their hard work and determination to serve their countries, and the many obstacles they overcame while performing their duties. Sometimes biographies targeted different audiences; for instance it is clear that Sadat directed his book *In Search of Identity* mainly to a foreign audience after the signing of the peace agreement with Israel, and attempted to show himself as a liberal politician that the West could rely on and do business with.

Tunisian prime minister Mzali offers an interesting glimpse into what drives politicians to write biographies:

I think that every politician is accountable before his society and history, to present a testimony of his public life. He must present, at some point in his life, some kind of a balance, the most sincere and objective as possible. I owe the truth to my fellow countrymen and also to historians.[42]

Another senior Tunisian politician is very honest about autobiographies: "This kind of literature is tough and carries many dangers,

---

[40] Michael Tomasky, "How to Become Eminent in Washington," *New York Review of Books*, December 4, 2014, pp. 26–28.

[41] Anwar el-Sadat, *In Search of Identity: An Autobiography* (London: Collins, 1978), p. 1.

[42] Mzali, *Un premier ministre*, pp. 11–12.

particularly for a writer like myself who is not a professional writer."
Yet, like his compatriot Mzali, he felt a strong urge to present a
"testimony to history" about his life and work.[43]

Senior politicians and military generals took care to explain the aims of
their books to their audience. One such author is Kamal Hasan 'Ali, who
held senior positions in military and politics under all Egyptian presidents, and was war minister, head of intelligence, and prime minister. He
gives ill-health as the reason for writing his memoirs, and then asserts:

> I did not intend these many pages to be simply an autobiography, or memoirs
> depicting personal or political events. My intention is to have a historical and
> an analytical record of an era in the twentieth century that is filled with wars
> and critical events. I fully believe that we cannot segregate between our
> personal and public lives and the turbulent historical developments.
> Therefore these pages will communicate to you about me and they will tell
> you about Egypt![44]

A somewhat provocative thought about autobiographies comes from
another prominent Egyptian, Khalid Muhyi al-Din. While he called his
book in Arabic *And Now I Speak*, it was translated into English as
Memories of a Revolution. In his introduction entitled "No
Introduction" he tells us: "Yes, this is not an interlocution. Papers,
memoirs or diaries are in themselves introductions to events and to the
speaker. To be more exact, they are attempts to present the author's
vision of events. Hence, the presentation of an introduction is unnecessary." He confesses that staying silent haunted him, but he promised
himself to "fulfill my obligation to Egypt and its people by writing what
I knew to reveal the whole truth."[45]

---

[43] Ahmed al-Mestiri, *Shahada lil-tarikh: dhikrayat wa ta'mmulat wa ta'aliq hawla fatra min al-tarikh al-mu'asir li-Tunis wa al-Maghrab al-Kabir (1940–1990) wa thawrat 2010–2011* [Testimony to history: reminiscences, reflections, and commentaries about a period in the contemporary history of Tunisia and the Greater Maghreb (1940–1990) and the revolution 2010–2011] (Tunis: al-Junub Publishing, 2011).

[44] Kamal Hasan 'Ali, *Mashawir al-'umr: asrar wa khafaya sab'in 'aman min 'umr Misr fi al-harb wa al-mukhabarat wa al-siyasa* [Life's deliberations: secrets and mysteries of seventy years of Egypt's life in war, intelligence, and politics] (Cairo: al-Shuruq Publishing, 1994), p. 17.

[45] Khaled Mohi el-Din, *Memories of a Revolution: Egypt 1952* (Cairo: American University in Cairo Press, 1992), pp. 1–2. For his Arabic publications, see Muhyi al-Din.

A recurrent theme among many of these autobiographers is that they hesitated for a long time before putting down their recollections, but the call to serve their nations or convey their experiences impelled them to write. Sayyid Mar'i, for instance, informs us that he dithered about whether to write his memoirs, but was convinced by his friends and colleagues that he was among those rare politicians who were active in three different eras: during the monarchy; in the period after the 1952 Revolution; and after what he terms the May 1971 Revolution (called the Corrective Movement and launched by President al-Sadat to purge Nasserists, and beginning the distancing of the country from the Soviet Union). He promises his readers authenticity in presenting his life as he lived it, and announces that Egypt's readers are smarter than its writers and would detect any fallacy in portraying past events.[46]

Memoirs of work and public service

Unfortunately, such memoirs mostly lack detailed biographical information about the subjects' childhood, upbringing, and families. Many of their writers were ministers, heads of security services, and a few technocrats. Some, however, straddled two categories. Kamal al-Janzuri occupied many ministerial jobs in Egypt, and at one point became prime minister. He published two volumes simultaneously, one of them autobiographical, detailing his childhood, his education in the USA, and his meteoric rise in the government.[47] The other was about his involvement in Egypt's economic development.[48] One Egyptian reviewer harshly criticized al-Janzuri for not exposing any of the financial corruption or economic cronyism that prevailed in Egypt while he was minister of planning or prime minister. The reviewer believed that al-Janzuri's modus operandi was to be compliant in order to last as long as possible as prime minister. The review cites some episodes to show that al-Janzuri was acquiescent and

---

[46] Sayyid Mar'i, *Awraq siyasiyya* [Political papers], 3 vols. (Cairo: al-Maktab al-Misri al-Hadith, 1978), vol. I: *Min al-qarya ila al-islah* [From the village to reform], pp. 5–7.

[47] Kamal al-Janzuri, *Tariqi: sanawat al-hilm, wa al-sidam, wa al-'uzla: min al-qarya ila ria'sat majlis al-wuzara'* [My path: years of dreams, confrontation, and isolation: from the village to head of the cabinet] (Cairo: Dar al-Shuruq, 2013).

[48] Kamal al-Janzuri, *Misr wa al-tanmiya* [Egypt and development] (Cairo: Dar al-Shuruq, 2013).

accommodating not only to President Hosni Mubarak, but also to those in his inner circle.[49]

Prominent in this category were heads and deputy heads of security services, and senior officers from intelligence agencies in the various republics. Several reasons lie behind this phenomenon: they wrote their versions of history to justify what happened under their command, to settle political scores with their adversaries, predecessors or political competitors, or simply to present their achievements. These three factors apply to many generals and politicians as well. Scoring political points is an essential element. A rare admission comes from a Syrian politician who was a member of parliament and a minister in the early 1960s: "I do not want to plead innocence that politics did not impact my writing of these memoirs." He then proceeds to inform us of how politics impacted the daily life of politicians in numerous fashions.[50] The memoir of Khalid Nezzar, who was minister of defense in Algeria and in charge of fighting the Islamists during the 1990s, is a typical example of attempted self-justification. He recounts his hostility to certain policies and senior politicians whom he believed not only failed to uproot Islamic fundamentalism but also "connived" with the Islamic Front to increase their power.[51]

Egyptian heads of security were prolific in writing accounts of their service, and their messages are remarkably alike. They all hesitated to pen their recollections, but the call of duty, the sense of purpose in sharing their experience, and the critical times that the country was going through led them to write to show the courage of the security services. Salah Nasr, who headed Jihaz al-Mukhabarat al-'Amma (the General Intelligence Directorate) for ten years (1957–67), wrote a series of memoirs about his work and the challenges that faced the revolution. He admits that it was hard, but says that he tried his best not to settle political scores with his enemies, although they dominated his thinking.[52] Another memoirist is Hasan Tal'at, who headed

---

[49] Bilal Fadl, "al-Dawla al-Misriyya "al-mukhawwakha" kama ra'aha kahinaha al-a'zam" [The "peachy" Egyptian state as its grand priest perceived it], January 11, 2015, available at www.madamasr.com/ar/opinion/politics/.

[50] 'Abd al-Salam al-'Ujayli, *Dhikrayyat ayyam al-siyasa: al-juz' al-thani min kitab lam uktab juz'uhu al-awwal ba'd* [Memories of the days of politics: the second volume of a book whose first volume has not been written] (Beirut: Riyad al-Rayyis: 2000), p. 252.

[51] Nezzar, *Mudhakkirat al-Liwa' Khalid Nezzar.*

[52] Salah Nasr, *Mudhakkirat Salah Nasr: thawrat 23 Yuliyu bayn al-masir wa al-masir* [The memoirs of Salah Nasr: the July 23 revolution between the

al-Mabahith al-'Amma (the General Investigative Directorate) and was among those ousted by Sadat in May 1971. He emphasizes that information is the key to victory over any enemy, and gives details of his work as a detective and how he climbed the ladder of his agency.[53]

An interesting facet of this hesitation by authors comes from Hasan Abu Basha, who held many senior positions in al-Mabahith al-'Amma and as minister of interior. He informs us that he resisted publishing memoirs because all his life he worked away from the limelight and never discussed the details of his assignments. However, under "pressure from friends and colleagues," he accepted the task "to write my testimony to history as a patriotic duty to uncover the truth surrounding the many historical events of the country."[54] Another "hesitator" is a senior Syrian intelligence officer who methodically gives three reasons for his qualms about writing memoirs and four reasons for finally deciding to go ahead. He felt that he was inexperienced in writing, that he was not a historian, and that history is an art with its own rules and customs. He also felt misgivings about naming some of those involved in events because they were still alive. On the other hand, the push factors were encouragement from friends and expert writers, the knowledge that information was not a personal property but belonged to the nation, outrage from reading distorted accounts of the events he had lived through, and finally, wishing to correct inaccurate and biased histories of Syria and the Arab world.[55]

A very similar message comes from two senior Sudanese officers who worked in the national security agencies. In their own words, they had been programmed throughout their careers to keep secrets, and to treat everything they read and heard as confidential. Hence the process of writing had to overcome this ingrained training. Their mission was supposedly not only to defend the men working in those agencies, but

---

journey and the destiny], vol. I (Abu Dhabi: Ittihad Publishing, 1986), pp. 7–8.

[53] Hasan Tal'at, *Fi khidmat al-amn al-siyasi, Mayu 1939–Mayu 1971* [In the service of political security, May 1939–May 1971] (Cairo: al-Watan al-'Arabi, 1983).

[54] Hasan Abu Basha, *Mudhakkirat Hasan Abu Basha fi al-amn wa al-siyasa: Yanayir 1977, Uktubir 1981, Ramadan 1987* [Memoirs of Hasan Abu Basha in security and politics: January 1977, October 1981, Ramadan 1987] (Cairo: al-Hilal Publishing, 1990), p. 11.

[55] Fawzi Shu'aybi, *Shahid min al-mukhabarat al-Suriyya 1955–1968* [Witness from the Syrian intelligence 1955–1968] (Beirut: Riyad al-Rayyis, 2008), pp. 10–14.

also to clarify and expose the truth.[56] It is rare to have a biography by two co-workers, and it is the only one included here that is not aided by a ghostwriter or journalist.

Iraqi generals followed in the steps of Egyptian generals and published numerous volumes about the Iran–Iraq War and the invasion of Kuwait. Some of these are good sources for military historians; a balanced one full of details and maps is by Ra'ad Majid al-Hamdani, a staff lieutenant-general in the Republican Guards who had participated in all Iraq's military conflicts since 1973. Another example is by Brigadier-General Najib al-Salihi about the invasion of Kuwait, the First Gulf War, and the uprisings in northern and southern Iraq in 1990–91. While these books lack childhood memories, we get a good understanding of their military backgrounds and their relationships with the top Egyptian or Iraqi leadership.[57]

A different type of work-related memoir is one describing the labor movement and its struggles in Tunisia by Habib Achour, who played a leading role in the Union Générale Tunisienne du Travail (UGTT) even before the country gained its independence from France. This is the type of memoir from which one can truly learn a great deal about the history of the labor union, its structure, its relations with successive governments before and after independence, and details about the various strikes that it launched throughout the forty years spanned by the book.[58]

Some technocrats who were involved in relatively low-level politics seemed to be similarly driven to write long memoirs describing their life's work and achievements. An Iraqi petroleum engineer describes in minute detail the development of the oil refineries and gas production in Iraq. Given that he could not write a diary, the author asks for forgiveness for any distortions in his tome. He informs us that anyway memories do not

[56] Muhammad 'Abd al-'Aziz and Hashim Abu Ranat, *Asrar jihaz al-asrar: jihaz al-amn al-Sudani 1969–1985* [Secrets of the secret organization: the Sudanese security services 1969–1985] (Khartoum: 'Izzat Publications, 2008), p. 12.

[57] Ra'ad Majid al-Hamdani, *Qabla an yughadiruna al-tarikh* [Before history leaves us] (Beirut: Arab Scientific Publishers, 2007); Najib al-Salihi, *al-Zilzal: madha hadatha fi al-'Iraq ba'd al-insihab min al-Kuwait? Khafaya al-ayyam al-damiyya* [The earthquake: what happened in Iraq after the retreat from Kuwait? Mysteries of the bloody days] (London: al-Rafid Publications, 1998).

[58] Habib Achour, *Ma vie politique et syndicale: enthousiasme et déceptions, 1944–1981* [My life in politics and unions: enthusiasm and deceptions, 1944–1981] (Tunis: Alif, 1989).

stay the same, and this is why we cherish them. He claims that he wrote his book in gratitude to those who taught him, and for Iraqi youth in particular and Arab youth in general who would like to work in the petroleum industry, and for his family and friends. He also wants to prove that his generation has served the nation and paid its dues, and only in reading memoirs such as his, those "without conscience" would find that there were many achievements.[59] His subtitle, *More than Memoirs and Less than History*, reflects the theme of many writers that their books are not history, but rather a sketch of certain aspects of the history they lived through or chose to focus on.

Other memoirs in this category describe relations with the leadership, but mostly place the emphasis on their sphere of work. An example is two memoirs by two senior Iraqi Ba'th members who worked in high positions in the country's economic hierarchy. They reveal in detail their relations with senior Iraqi officials, principally the two men who ran the country after the rise of the Ba'th Party to power in 1968: Ahmad Hasan al-Bakr, who was president from 1968 to 1979, and his vice president, Saddam Hussein. This kind of memoir serves three purposes: it provides information about economic planning and decisions during the late 1960s and throughout the 1970s; it portrays the personalities of Bakr and Saddam and their leadership styles; and, of course, provides details about the subjects of the memoirs.[60] The interaction between senior officials and ministers with their leaders allows authors in this category not only to write about the leader, but also to cast a positive light on themselves. In the above-mentioned Iraqi memoirs about the authors' relationships with Bakr and Saddam Hussein, the focus was more on their own ministries and the mode of operation in the economic arena. A derivative of this style is found in the numerous memoirs, particularly in Egypt, of the authors' relationships with Nasser or Sadat, but with much more emphasis on the activities and functioning of the leader rather than on their own ministries. Amin Huwaydi's memoir about Nasser, for

59 Sa'ad Allah al-Fathi, *Min burj al-takrir: akthar min dhikrayat wa aqall min tarikh* [From the tower of a refinery: more than memories and less than history] (Amman: al-Ayyam Publishing, 2014), pp. 5–6.
60 Jawad Hashim, *Mudhakkirat wazir 'Iraqi ma'a al-Bakr wa Saddam: dhikrayat fi al-siyasa al-'Iraqiyya, 1967–2000* [Memoirs of an Iraqi minister with al-Bakr and Saddam: reflections on Iraqi politics, 1967–2000] (Beirut: al-Saqi Publishing, 2003); Fakhri Qadduri, *Hakadha 'ariftu al-Bakr wa Saddam: rihlat 35 'aman fi Hizb al-Ba'th* [This was the way I knew al-Bakr and Saddam: a journey of 35 years in the Ba'th Party] (London: Dar al-Hikma, 2006).

instance, shows how he treated his ministers, what took place in the cabinet, and Nasser's dealings with parliament.[61] Another good example is Murad Ghalib's memoir of his experiences with Nasser and Sadat. Ghalib was one of the very few civilians connected to the Free Officers who launched the 1952 Revolution, and occupied numerous ambassadorial posts before being appointed minister of foreign affairs. While the book is really more about the author, it still exposes the functioning of these regimes under two different presidents. Ghalib is more open about writing memoirs, and warns us:

I kept asking myself if one could be neutral. Is there absolute neutrality? Whatever a person believes in neutrality, at the end of the day he is a human being who loves and hates and is affected by those who treated him well and those who mistreated him. One has to be objective ... but I admit that one is writing under the influence of his unconscious. Therefore I confess the subjectivity of my objectivity.[62]

A final example is a recent memoir that appeared in English about Mubarak and the revolution from Abdel-Latif el-Manawy, the man who oversaw Egypt's state television between 2005 and 2011, including the eighteen days of the revolution that toppled Mubarak. Again, while the memoir's title is about Mubarak, in essence most of it is devoted to the action and policies of el-Manawy himself.[63]

Staged memoirs and biographies written by others

In this category, there was an "official" involvement of someone else in producing the memoirs either in the form of presenting questions to the subjects or, as in most other cases, discussing with them the topics covered in the memoirs. Typically, a journalist or professional writer presents questions to the subject, and long and detailed answers then follow. One could assume this was prearranged between the two sides, as it makes it easier for the politician or senior officer to respond to rather than engage in solitary writing. In a way, it also relieves the subject of the

---

[61] Amin Huwaydi, *Ma'a 'Abd al-Nasser* [With 'Abd al-Nasser] (Cairo: al-Mustaqbal Publishing, 1985).

[62] Murad Ghalib, *Ma'a 'Abd al-Nasser wa al-Sadat: sanawat al-intisar wa ayyam al-mihan* [With 'Abd al-Nasser and al-Sadat: years of victory and days of tribulation] (Cairo: Ahram Center for Publishing, 2001).

[63] Abdel-Latif el-Manawy, *Tahrir: The Last 18 Days of Mubarak: An Insider's Account of the Uprising in Egypt* (London: Gilgamesh, 2012).

biography from calling it an autobiography, thus avoiding the accusation of historical or chronological inaccuracy; and permits them a choice of topics on which to focus, rather than feeling obliged to explain in detail events they might prefer to skim over or avoid.

One such example is the biography of an Egyptian general, Muhammad Fawzi, who was involved in the 1967 defeat and the subsequent War of Attrition (1969–70). The journalist tells us that Fawzi's life can be summed up in one word: the "building" of the army and the country. While there are no tough or embarrassing questions for the general, the book does contain a wide range of interesting information about the 1967 War, the historical commission set up to investigate the defeat, and relations with Nasser and Sadat. Even so, few details can be gleaned from Fawzi's description of his clashes with Sadat that led to his imprisonment.[64]

A second example is the book about the Tunisian prime minister Mohamed Mzali. Written as an interview with a French journalist (and a year later translated into Arabic), it is largely structured around themes: party, democracy, economy, and of course relations with Bourguiba.[65] Twenty years after this set-up biography, Mzali published a detailed personal autobiography referred to above.[66]

A final example of this style is a *hiwar* (dialogue) conducted with thirty-five ministers and senior Egyptian officials. While the book gives us valuable information about the inner circle and their backgrounds, the author uses too much flattery and somewhat embellishes their contributions. Of most interest is a dialogue with two female ministers that provides a significant insight into their high qualifications and work as ministers. Given the scarcity of senior women in power, and hence of their biographies, these two dialogues help to fill a vacuum.

Unlike the staged memoirs, biographies written by others do not necessarily mean that the subject or his family cooperated with the

---

[64] 'Abdullah Imam, *al-Fariq Muhammad Fawzi: al-naksa, al-istinzaf, al-sijn* [Lieutenant-General Muhammad Fawzi: the setback, the attrition, the prison] (Cairo: Dar al-Khayyal Publishing, 2001).

[65] Mohamed Mzali, *La Parole de l'action: conversation avec Xavière Ulysse* [The talk of action: conversation with Xavière Ulysse] (Paris: Publisud, 1984). The Arabic translation was Muhammad Mzali, *Hadith al-fi'l* [The talk of action] (Tunis: Tunisian Society for Publications, 1985).

[66] Mzali, *Un premier ministre*.

biographer, especially if it was written after his death. There are even
negative biographies; a key example is the one about Shams Badran,
who was a principal actor in the Egyptian military before and during
the 1967 War. He also headed the *mukhabarat* and was actively
involved in suppressing the Muslim Brotherhood under Nasser.
Although the book is prejudiced against Badran, it still contains interesting information about him and his relationships with the Egyptian
leadership (particularly Nasser and his chief of staff during the 1967
War, 'Abd al-Hakim 'Amr), and the numerous plots by the Muslim
Brotherhood. The author obviously researched in depth and interviewed many of the other political actors at that time.[67] Famous people
such as Badran attract many journalists wanting to sell biographies of
well-known politicians. One journalist, who wrote a biography of
Badran, tracked him down in Plymouth, England where he was living
with his family, conducted a detailed interview and wrote the book
about him. But the author wanted to hype up his work, so he added to
the title Nasser and Su'ad (a reference to the actress Su'ad Hosni), and
Sadat and Hamat (a reference to an attractive young radio announcer,
Hamat Mustafa). The problem with this kind of memoir is that sensa-
tionalism overshadows the many items of valuable information about
Badran and his era.[68] However, one could argue that even rumors can
be a tool in understanding the political history by allowing us to weave
together the material of the past. Rumors inform us about what people
believed about their leaders, or what people were interested in even if
they were not true. Montaigne wrote that rumors had a power in
shaping history, adding that: "Each man can make his profit of it
according to his understanding."[69]

Although the majority of works of this type were written by journalists or writers who focused on biographies of important people or
sensational cases, some were written by associates of the politicians,
as it gave them a chance to highlight their own involvement. A case in

---

[67] Hamada Husni, *Shams Badran: al-rajul alladhi hakama Misr* [Shams Badran:
the man who ruled Egypt] (Beirut: Beirut Library, 2008).

[68] Hamdi al-Husayni, *Mudhakkirat Shams Badran: asrar al-hayat al-khassa
li-Nasser wa Su'ad, al-Sadat wa Hamat* [Memoirs of Shams Badran: the secrets
of the private lives of Nasser with Su'ad, Sadat with Hamat] (Cairo: al-Nakhba
Publishing, 2014).

[69] Michel de Montaigne, *Religion and Philosophy*, vol. II of *Montaigne's Essays in
Three Books* (London: n.p., 1743), p. 97.

point is the book by Béji Caïd Essebsi, who was a minister under Habib Bourguiba and became president in the 2014 elections. The biography was written in French and later translated into Arabic. It is a clear example of the usefulness of memoirs: it gives us an account of the relationship within the Tunisian leadership before and after independence, of Bourguiba the man, his wife, and their relations with those in the inner circle, and finally a discussion of some of the crises and topical questions that faced the country.[70]

Biographies of notable men written after their death and with the cooperation of their families tend to suffer from exaggeration; one case is a biography of General 'Abd al-Mun'im Riyad, who was killed in 1969 during the War of Attrition between Israel and Egypt. The author assures us that his small volume "displays the details of the genius life of that remarkable man whose death as a martyr stirred the emotions of his whole nation towards the victory on the 6th October 1973."[71] A more balanced, but still biased, biography is that of the Shi'i leader 'Abd al-Majid al-Khu'i, who was killed in Najaf in April 2003. The author, a close friend, informs us that the book's main purpose is the "why" of his killing and by whom. The book amply illustrates, although from a Shi'i point of view, the circumstances prevailing in Iraq prior to the US-led invasion and the turbulent days that followed.[72]

Another posthumous biography is that of Field Marshal Muhammad Abu Ghazala, written by a journalist who penned similar biographies. Once again, we encounter descriptions ranging from great to genius about Abu Ghazala: "There are a few who make history ... and among the great leaders was the human leader, the strategic thinker ... Field Marshal Muhammad 'Abd al-Halim Ghazala." While the memoir has relevant material about the general, it omits the tensions that

---

[70] Béji Caïd Essebsi, *Habib Bourguiba: le bon grain et l'ivraie* [Habib Bourguiba: the wheat and the chaff] (Tunis: Sud Editions, 2009). The Arab translation was Béji Caïd Essebsi, *al-Habib Bourguiba: al-muhimm wa al-ahamm* [Habib Bourguiba: the important and the more important] (Tunis: Dar al-Junub Publications, 2011).

[71] Muhammad Muhammad al-Jawadi, *al-Shahid 'Abd al-Mun'im Riyad: sima' al-'askariyya al-Misriyya* [The martyr 'Abd al-Mun'im Riyad: the finest of the Egyptian military] (Cairo: al-Atibba' Publishing, 1984), p. 55.

[72] Ma'ad Fayyad, *Zahira sakhina jiddan: al-qissa al-haqiqiyya li-qatl al-Sayyid 'Abd al-Majid al-Khu'i* [A very hot afternoon: the true story of the killing of Sayyid 'Abd al-Majid al-Khu'i] (Baghdad: Dar al-Huda, 2007).

prevailed between Mubarak and Abu Ghazala (see Chapter 3). In
fact, the author devotes three pages to discussing the position that
was created for Abu Ghazala under Mubarak as special assistant to
the president, and accentuates the high relevance of this appointment
without even hinting at other undercurrents.[73] This could be partly
explained by the book's publication while Mubarak was still in
power, and it highlights a negative feature of some of these memoirs:
sycophancy on the one hand; and burying significant data about the
life and work of the subject on the other. Other writers have complained about indirect censorship; for example, the author of a book
profiling eight officers who had worked with Nasser was later banned
in Egypt, because he had claimed that Sadat did not want books that
glorified Nasser and his era, especially in the first few years after
coming to power.[74]

An additional retrospective memoir was written about General
Ahmad Isma'il thirty-nine years after his death and forty years after
the end of the October 1973 War in which he played an important role.
A member of his family openly admits the reasons why it took so many
years before they allowed a journalist to research the general's papers
and write a memoir with the help of the family:

(1) The outbreak of the January 25 Revolution that afforded freedom
    and democracy to every citizen.
(2) Upon requests from journalists, we discovered hand-written
    important papers written [by the general].
(3) On many occasions we [the family] found out there was little
    knowledge about the role of the Field Marshall Ahmad Isma'il in
    the October War.[75]

These above points highlight some of the obstacles in publishing contemporary political memoirs of politicians after their leaving their jobs.

---

[73] Amira Fikri, *al-Mushir Muhammad 'Abd al-Halim Abu Ghazala: masirat
      hayat* [Field Marshal 'Abd al-Halim Abu Ghazala: a life journey] (Cairo:
      al-Jumhuriyya Publishing, 2010), pp. 143–45.
[74] Husayn Qadri, *'Abd al-Nasser wa alladhin kanu ma'ahu* ['Abd al-Nasser and
      those who were with him] (Cairo: al-Jumhuriyya Publishing, 2007).
[75] Majdi al-Jilad, *Mushir al-nasr: mudhakkirat Ahmad Isma'il wazir al-harbiyya fi
      Ma'rakat Uktubir 1973* [The marshal of victory: memoirs of Ahmad Ismail,
      minister of war in the October 1973 War] (Cairo: Nahdat Misr Publishing,
      2013), pp. 7–8.

Autobiography in the third person

There are few works written by political figures who wrote their life story in the form of a novel. One exception is Saddam Hussein, who wrote a semi-autobiographical novel called *Men and a City*. The hero in his novel is called Hussein, but in the introduction he tells readers that they will encounter a knight whom history had not seen before (a good example of the masculinity referred to above). A significant drawback is that dates are not exact, and it is sometimes hard to distinguish between fact and fiction. On the other hand, authors such as Saddam Hussein must have felt more comfortable using this device, although it was an open secret that he was the author. In fact, his book is more illuminating about his childhood and upbringing than the official biographies written about him later by journalists or professional writers.[76] Some activists and literary figures such as Nawal al-Sa'dawi and Hisham Matar have used this genre effectively. In writing a play depicting her life in prison, al-Sa'dawi managed to portray in a powerful manner the inner thinking and feelings of the women prisoners.[77] Matar portrayed the disappearance of his father in a moving story and detailed his family's life in Libya under a tyrannical regime.[78]

Before concluding this chapter it is important to highlight some general features of many of the memoirs examined in this book. One is that the timing and place of publication of memoirs give us information about the circumstances of writing and about the author himself. In a memoir of the head of Nasser's presidential offices, Mahmud al-Jayyar, written by a third party, the author does not inform us how he managed to get these "records," and the book is presented as though written by al-Jayyar himself. Apart from

---

[76] Saddam Hussein, *Rijal wa madina: riwaya li-katibiha* [Men and a city: a novel by its author] (Baghdad: Ministry of Culture, n.d.). A typical "ordered" biography is Amir Iskander, *Saddam Hussein: The Fighter, the Thinker, and the Man*, translated by Hassan Selim (Paris: Hachette Réalités, 1980). For more details about the significance of Saddam's novel and the information gleaned from it, see Joseph Sassoon, *Saddam Hussein's Ba'th Party: Inside an Authoritarian Regime* (Cambridge: Cambridge University Press, 2012), pp. 163–64.

[77] Nawal el-Saadawi, *al-Insan: ithnay 'ashr imra'a fi zinzana* [The human: twelve women in a cell] (Cairo: Madbuly Publishing, 2005).

[78] Hisham Matar, *Anatomy of a Disappearance* (New York: Dial Press, 2012). His other novel is *In the Country of Men* (New York: Dial Press, 2006).

illustrating the relations between Nasser and those close to him, he also accuses Sadat of avarice and corruption. Yet the book was published ten years after the death of Sadat, and intriguingly, published in Damascus by the Talas Publishing Company, which was connected to Mustafa Talas, the Syrian defense minister, and the proceeds of the book sales were allocated to the schools of the martyrs' children in Syria.[79]

This key aspect about power and the publication date of memoirs is remarkably relevant. We have dozens of books about Nasser and Sadat from almost every possible viewpoint: military, political, social, and economic. However, there is a paucity of memoirs by Mubarak's close associates detailing his life and leadership in spite of the fact that he was in power for three decades. This will probably change, as it did in Libya. In Egypt, members of the Muslim Brotherhood published numerous memoirs after the toppling of Mubarak and their victory in the first elections in 2012. These books not only detailed their suffering in the torture chambers of the regimes, particularly those of Nasser, but also highlighted the "critical" role played by the Brotherhood in the 1952 Revolution, in order to emphasize its historical contribution as a revolutionary movement.[80] Likewise, a number of informative or staged memoirs of senior Libyans have been published since the end of the Qaddafi regime and are referred to here.

A second facet is fear and censorship. One could safely assume that even those who were in exile in Europe or the USA would not take the personal risk, or expose their extended family in their home country, to the consequences of publishing a memoir about the functionality of the regime, the abuses committed by the authorities, and their relationships with the president while he was still alive. A few writers discussed the aspect of fear; Muhsin al-'Ayni, who was prime minister in Yemen a number times during the late 1960s and the 1970s, and then ambassador in

[79] Sulayman al-Hakim, *al-Jayyar yatadhakkar: sijil dhikrayat Mahmud al-Jayyar mudir maktab Gamal 'Abd al-Nasser* [al-Jayyar remembers: record of memories of Mahmud al-Jayyar, bureau chief of Gamal 'Abd al-Nasser] (Damascus: Talas Publishing, 1991).

[80] See, for example, Sulayman al-Hakim, *'Abd al-Nasser wa al-Ikhwan: bayn al-wifaq wa al-shiqaq* ['Abd al-Nasser and the Brothers: between harmony and rift] (Cairo: Jazirat al-Ward, 2010).

many countries, ponders the reasons for his hesitation and expresses some of the malaise of the region:

I hesitated in writing as many do not read, and those who read would love to read what they agree with, and if they read something different, they would not be willing to think about new ideas, or to forgive the author. Many of those in public offices prefer to be silent, and if they wrote something with significance, they made sure it would be published only after their death.

I know I did not please anyone but in fact I angered everybody. I blame those who demanded that I write my memoirs, but what did they expect me to say?[81]

A different example of censorship comes from a series of recollections published by Salah Salim, who was a member of the council set up after the 1952 Revolution and who assisted in the ousting of Muhammad Neguib. Salim became the editor of *al-Sha'b* (The People) newspaper and began serializing his memoirs in 1956. The first part was titled "Why I resigned from the Revolutionary Council and the Cabinet?" After thirty installments (mostly dealing with the relations between Egypt and Sudan), the memoirs ceased to appear. Although the newspaper gave no reason, it was assumed that some of the revelations were embarrassing to the leadership, and hence there were concerns that Salim would place Nasser in an uncomfortable position, especially with regard to his Sudan policy.[82]

A third aspect of all these writings is, of course, that of *dhakira* (memory). Some writers titled their books as *dhikrayat* (memories) rather than *mudhakkirat* (memoirs), possibly to give themselves some flexibility in what they wrote. Given the lack of *yawmiyyat* (diaries), many apologize in their introductions that they could not remember precise dates, specific events, or what exactly took place during meetings that were being written about years and sometimes decades later. Some authors use the word memory in their titles but with certain modifications; in one instance a memoir of a senior Tunisian official who worked closely with

---

[81] Muhsin al-'Ayni, *Khamsun 'aman fi al-rimal al-mutaharrika: qissati ma'a bina' al-dawla al-haditha fi al-Yaman* [Fifty years of shifting sands: my story in building the modern state in Yemen] (Beirut: al-Nahar Publishing, 2000), pp. 9–11.

[82] 'Abd al-Raziq 'Abd al-Raziq 'Isa (ed.), *Mudhakkirat al-sagh Salah Salim* [Memoirs of the listener Salah Salim] (Cairo: Egyptian Institution for the Book, 2013), pp. 11–12. This memoir is unusual in having footnotes and proper documentation about the history of relations between Sudan and Egypt.

Bourguiba and was general secretary of the Arab League from 1979 to 1990 is titled *Lights from Memory*.[83]

One repercussion of the Arab uprisings is the rediscovery of national memory in Tunisia. As the national archives remain closed even after the revolution, many Tunisians are starting to record their testimonies about events that took place under the authoritarian rules of Bourguiba and Ben 'Ali, the latter in particular. For the first time, testimonies of those who opposed the previous regime or were under arrest (and tortured) are presenting new accounts of those bleak days that will become invaluable for anyone interested in the history and politics of Tunisia in the absence of official records.[84] Undoubtedly, multiple memoirs from such Tunisians will be published in the next few years, and reservations will again be raised about the accuracy of the contents. Work has been done to explore collective memory, and how the memory of a group is sustained and conveyed to future generations.[85] Hopefully, as Tunisians feel able to write and express themselves freely, we will see more diaries written by politicians and senior officials that will become a resource for the next generation of historians.

Conclusion

A wide range of genres of memoirs was discussed in this chapter. One scholar has argued that "most autobiography is too personal to be of value, either as literature or as a source of information."[86] As Egerton indicated, "there are powerful temptations to relegate political memoirs beyond the pale of scholarly attention." But he adds thoughtfully:

---

[83] Al-Shadhili al-Qulaybi, *Adwa' min al-dhakira: al-Habib Bourguiba* [Lights from memory: Habib Bourguiba] (Tunis: Dimitir, 2014). This is another example of a book that could be useful for understanding Tunisia's Arab and foreign relations.

[84] See, for example, 'Abd al-Jalil al-Tamimi (ed.), *al-Mu'aridun al-siyasiyyun tahta al-ta'dhib fi Tunis: 'abr sijillat al-dhakira* [The political opponents under torture in Tunisia: through records of memory] (Tunis: al-Tamimi Foundation for Scientific Research and Information, December 2013), no. 29. Further references to these testimonies are in Chapter 7.

[85] See, for example, Paul Connerton, *How Societies Remember* (New York: Cambridge University Press, 1989).

[86] William C. Spengemann, *The Forms of Autobiography: Episodes in the History of a Literary Genre* (New Haven: Yale University Press, 1980), p. 190.

While much of such self-recordings serves only the cause of apologia, it is nevertheless true that our knowledge of many facets of human history, ancient and modern, would be massively impoverished without the memoirs generated by the political actors themselves.[87]

The importance of the human factor is well demonstrated by one memoir describing the relations between Egypt and Libya, and it shows how memoirs can contribute to our understanding of political leaders, their behavior, policies, and ambitions. The author, an Egyptian ambassador to Libya, exposes some of the idiosyncrasies in the personalities of Sadat and Qaddafi. "It is amazing how fateful decisions were profoundly influenced by emotional, temperamental and personal considerations."[88] Another valuable feature is the graphic accounts in many of these memoirs about the childhoods and family lives of influential political actors, thus allowing us to understand their environment and what impacted them. From countless memoirs we get an insight into the authors' personal stance and what they are attempting to show. For example, army generals in Egypt and Iraq who felt a strong compulsion to disassociate themselves from military defeats or associate themselves with victories wrote copious memoirs to highlight their achievements and defend themselves against criticism. Undoubtedly, writing memoirs gives the writer certain powers that those who abstained from writing would not enjoy. "The man who writes about himself and his own time is the only man who writes about all people and all time."[89]

Ignoring or not taking political memoirs seriously is not applicable only to the Arab world. A recent study of the Northern Ireland conflict highlights this lacuna in understanding the complexities of this conflict.[90] The following chapters draw extensively on the rich information that the memoirs of political leaders, generals, heads of security, party members, political opponents, political prisoners, activists, and businessmen can provide about the anatomy of authoritarianism in these eight republics.

---

[87] Egerton (ed.), *Political Memoir*, pp. 2–3.
[88] Salah el-Saadany, *Egypt and Libya from Inside, 1969–1976: The Qaddafi Revolution and the Eventual Break in Relations*, translated by Mohammad el-Behairy (London: McFarland & Co., 1994), p. vii.
[89] George Bernard Shaw, "The Sanity of Art," in *Major Critical Essays*, introduction by Michael Holroyd (Harmondsworth: Penguin, 1986), p. 312.
[90] Stephen Hopkins, *The Politics of Memoir and the Northern Ireland Conflict* (Liverpool: Liverpool University Press, 2013).

2 | Party and governance

Authoritarian politics are shaped by two factors: a conflict between the ruler and the ruled, defined as "the problem of authoritarian control," and a conflict between the ruler and his partners in power, termed "the problem of authoritarian power-sharing."[1] In the Arab republics, as part of solving the first "problem," the regimes relied on the autocracy of their hegemonic parties to sustain their rule. In two countries, Syria and Iraq, there were single-party systems, while in Egypt, Tunisia, and Algeria it was called a multi-party system, but in reality these definitions of single or multi are superfluous because the ruling party in all these republics behaved in a more or less similar fashion. In fact, after independence, Algeria and Tunisia began with a single party and then moved to what was portrayed as multi-party rule.[2] In most republics, there was a structure of two interlocking pyramids: the state and the party, ruled with substantial overlap between the two, allowing the state to control and monitor the party. This is very similar to the classic communist model.

Although the dictatorial regimes in single-party countries occasionally included other groups or factions, this never constituted a true multi-party system, which was apparently not an impediment to any of the regimes that hosted regional conferences for Arab parties.[3]

---

[1] Milan W. Svolik, *The Politics of Authoritarian Rule* (New York: Cambridge University Press, 2012), p. 2. The author argues that the basic features of authoritarian rule such as institutions, policies, and the survival of leaders are shaped by these twin problems.

[2] For a theoretical discussion of political parties and single-party systems, see Samuel P. Huntington, *Political Order in Changing Societies* (New Haven: Yale University Press, 2006); Clement H. Moore, "The Single Party as a Source of Legitimacy," in Samuel P. Huntington and Clement H. Moore (eds.), *Authoritarian Politics in Modern Society: The Dynamics of Established One-Party Systems* (New York: Basic Books, 1970), pp. 48–72.

[3] Jennifer Gandhi, *Political Institutions under Dictatorship* (New York: Cambridge University Press, 2008), pp. 36–39. The regimes under the Ba'th rule

Damascus twice hosted such a conference under the auspices of Bashar al-Asad, and no irony was intended in the document issued by the second conference declaring that "democracy and political pluralism are the exemplary means for the conduct of relations between the ruler and the ruled, and in building the state's institutions."[4]

In Libya, about two years after the coup d'état that brought him to power, Mu'ammar al-Qaddafi announced the formation of the Arab Socialist Union as a single-party system styled after its Egyptian counterpart. Two years later, this ill-equipped party was abandoned when popular committees were created to encourage the masses to participate in the system.[5] The leadership wanted to create a society without a parliament or governing party, based on Qaddafi's philosophy, as laid out in his *Green Book*, that "the party is the contemporary dictatorship. It is the modern dictatorial instrument of governing. The party is the rule of a part over the whole."[6] Asked how he wanted history to remember him, Qaddafi replied: "For having implemented direct democracy in my country. For having enabled my people to rule themselves, without government, without members of parliament, without representatives."[7] However, in the other republics that did not heed Qaddafi's advice, the leaders of the dominant parties were able to mobilize large sections of the population and demand their loyalty, which in turn allowed them to rule for decades.

This chapter will discuss how these parties were structured; how and whom they recruited; their political activities; their connections with other organs of the state such as the security services; and how they

in Iraq and Syria on a number of occasions "invited" other factions and parties, such as the Communist Party, to be part of a "national front."

4   Rihab Makhal, "Tarikh al-mu'tamarat al-qawmiyya" [History of the regional conferences], in Muhammad Jamal Barut (ed.), *al-Ahzab wa al-harakat wa al-tanzimat al-qawmiyy fi al-watan al-'Arabi* [Nationalist parties, movements, and organizations in the Arab world] (Beirut: Center for Arab Unity Studies, 2012), p. 917. The general conference for Arab parties began to meet on a yearly basis in 1996. This large study of about 1,100 pages spans all the parties in the Arab world, and has interesting articles about some of the smaller ones.

5   Ronald Bruce St. John, "Libya's Authoritarian Tradition," in Noureddine Jebnoun, Mehrdad Kia, and Mimi Kirk (eds.), *Modern Middle East Authoritarianism: Roots, Ramifications, and Crisis* (New York: Routledge, 2014), pp. 127–30.

6   Mu'ammar al-Qaddafi, *The Green Book* (Tripoli: Public Establishment for Publishing, n.d.), p. 11.

7   Muammar Gaddafi with Edmond Jouve, *My Vision* (London: John Blake, 2005), pp. 87–88.

dealt with opposition parties. By examining governance and the role of senior officials and ministers, we can gain an insight into an important pillar of the authoritarian system. Drawing on memoirs of party and parliamentary members, opposition politicians, and senior government officials, it becomes clear that the ruling party played a critical role in the durability of these regimes, and was the vital link that allowed the state to exercise its power.

Structure and ideology

In these republics, the mass-mobilizing parties emerged from "the impact of imperial powers' policies on traditional elites' sociopolitical standing."[8] The patron–client relationship that developed allowed collaboration between different groups of society, and empowered the state to exercise control over not only the educational and legal systems, but also over the religious establishment. These authoritarian regimes could not transform society by simple bureaucratic methods, and thus "people have to be mobilized, different groups integrated, opposition contained."[9] The ruling party was the instrument that provided "a political setting for mediating elite disputes and preventing elite defections to the opposition."[10] Indeed, with the exception of Libya, the party system became a critical tool used by the leadership of these states to sustain their longevity. Even in countries such as Algeria, where the army was the dominant force, the party was pivotal in controlling the country. After Chadhli Bendjedid became president of Algeria in 1979, he realized the need to strengthen the ruling party in order to penetrate and control the army, so he appointed one of his loyal aides as the party's secretary-general.[11]

---

[8] Michele Penner Angrist, *Party Building in the Modern Middle East* (Seattle: University of Washington Press, 2006), p. 32.

[9] Roger Owen, *State, Power and Politics in the Making of the Modern Middle East*, 3rd edn. (New York: Routledge, 2008), p. 27.

[10] Jason Brownlee, *Authoritarianism in an Age of Democratization* (New York: Cambridge University Press, 2007), p. 42.

[11] Riyad Saydawi, *Sira'at al-nukhab al-siyasiyya wa al-'askariyya fi al-Jazai'r: al-hizb, al-jaysh, al-dawla* [Political and military clashes of the elites in Algeria: the party, the army, the state] (Beirut: Arab Institute, 1999), p. 49. Bendjedid was a senior officer in the Algerian army and stayed on as president until he was persuaded by the military to resign in January 1992.

Ruling parties underwent many changes and transformations. In Egypt, al-Hizb al-Watani al-Dimuqrati, known in English as the National Democratic Party (NDP), evolved in 1976 on the heels of al-Ittihad al-Ishtiraki (the Socialist Union), and before that it was called al-Ittihad al-Qawmi (the National Union). Egypt's three presidents prior to the revolution of 2011 (Gamal 'Abd al-Nasser, Anwar al-Sadat, and Hosni Mubarak) were integral elements of the ruling party's inner circles.[12] Similarly, in Tunisia in 1964, the Neo-Destour was officially renamed Parti Socialiste Destourien (PSD) (Constitutional Socialist Party), and in 1989 its name was changed to Rassemblement Constitutionnel Démocratique (RCD) (Constitutional Democratic Rally) to underline Tunisia's so-called multi-party system. Other parties were utterly transformed, such as the Front de Libération Nationale (FLN) in Algeria, from its origins as a group fighting French colonialism. But in essence it remained more of a network of different groups within the power structure than a fully fledged political party.[13]

Although the structure of the ruling parties differed from one republic to another, the one important common denominator was centralization, which inevitably led to the top of the pyramid: the president. In Iraq and Syria, the president also functioned as the party secretariat (*amin sirr*) in charge of the regional command (*al-qiyada al-qutriyya*), which, in turn, was the executive body in charge of party operations in every town and village.[14] In Syria in June 2003, the regional command issued a directive reiterating that "the party leader

---

[12] Rabab el-Mahdi, "The Democracy Movement: Cycles of Protest," in Rabab el-Mahdi and Philip Marfleet (eds.), *Egypt: The Moment of Change* (New York: Zed Books, 2009), p. 88. Interestingly the term "party" was not used in the first two decades after the 1952 Revolution in order to avoid division and obscure the lack of a national purpose. See Maye Kassem, *Egyptian Politics: The Dynamics of Authoritarian Rule* (Boulder, CO: Lynne Rienner, 2004), p. 51.

[13] Michael J. Willis, *Politics and Power in the Maghreb: Algeria, Tunisia and Morocco from Independence to the Arab Spring* (New York: Columbia University Press, 2012), pp. 122–24.

[14] For details about the structure in Iraq, see Sassoon, *Saddam Hussein's Ba'th Party*, pp. 34–38; for Syria, see Souhaïl Belhadj, *La Syrie de Bashar al-Asad: anatomie d'un régime autoritaire* [The Syria of Bashar al-Asad: anatomy of an authoritarian regime] (Paris: Belin, 2013), pp. 139–44; Raymond Hinnebusch, *Syria: Revolution from Above* (New York: Routledge, 2002), pp. 76–83. Apart from the structure, the book has statistics on the occupations of members as of 1980 and 1984.

provides direction, planning, supervision, and control of the general policy."[15] Already in 1971, a slogan of *qa'id al-masira* (the leader of the march) was announced for the party leader and began to be heavily promoted by the regional command of the Syrian Ba'th Party among its party cadres.[16] Remarkably, the pyramid structure in the multi-party countries was very comparable; the RCD in Tunisia had President Zine al-'Abidine Ben 'Ali at the top of the pyramid, just as the Syrian Ba'th had Asad.[17] In Iraq, Syria and Tunisia, the bottom of the pyramid was the *khaliyya* (cell), while in Egypt it was the unit, followed by the division or center, then the province, and at the top was the party secretariat and the political bureau.[18] In Egypt, the president of the republic was the head of the party and there was no distinction between the presidency and the party in terms of policy.

In Iraq, Syria, and Tunisia, the ruling party reached into every aspect of life. As the formal ideology of parties such as the Ba'th diminished (see below), the party's main function was to be the eyes and ears of these regimes. A diary of a party member in Iraq indicates that the activities of the cells and divisions of the party spanned a variety of tasks: security; organizing seminars and conferences to spread the word of the Ba'th; cultural activities and political education. Every week, the cells around the country listed cultural; political; organizational; military; criticism and self-criticism; and miscellaneous topics on their agendas.[19]

---

[15] Directive 408–409 issued on June 15, 2003, is quoted in Belhadj, *La Syrie de Bashar al-Asad*, p. 141.

[16] Munir al-Hamash, "Hizb al-Ba'th al-'Arabi al-Ishtiraki fi Suriya (1953–2005)" [The Arab Socialist Ba'th Party in Syria (1953–2005)], in Barut (ed.), *al-Ahzab wa al-harakat*, p. 140.

[17] Steffen Erdle, *Ben Ali's "New Tunisia" (1987–2009): A Case Study of Authoritarian Modernization in the Arab World* (Berlin: Klaus Schwarz, 2010), annex 4a, 4b, pp. 504–05. See also Zuhair al-Muzzafir, *Min al-hizb al-wahid ila hizb al-aghlabiyya* [From the single party to the majority party] (Tunisia: Sanbakit, 2004), p. 104.

[18] Al-Hizb al-Watani al-Dimuqrati, *Ru'ya li-mustaqbal Misr: watha'iq al-Mu'tamar al-'Amm al-Thamin lil-Hizb al-Watani al-Dimuqrati wa tashkilat al-hizb* [A vision of the future of Egypt: documents from the Eighth General Conference of the National Democratic Party and the structures of the party], September 15–17, 2002 (Cairo: al-Jumhuriyya Publishing, 2002), p. 23.

[19] A diary of Bayji branch given to the author which details, in handwriting, the weekly agenda and comments of the participants (ranging from seven to twelve in number).

One difference between the two Ba'th parties in Iraq and Syria in comparison to the ruling parties in the other republics is the concept of self-criticism, a practice borrowed from the Communist Party whereby members had a duty to criticize their own activities and roles. A Syrian Ba'th Party report emphasized the importance of criticism and self-criticism as "one of the basics of the internal system of the party," which helped to guarantee proper coordination and discipline in dealing with members.[20] In Tunisia, Béatrice Hibou argues that the main function of RCD was not security, but "the minute network of surveillance of the country constitutes one of central modalities." While this is a subtle difference compared to the two Ba'th parties, Hibou confirms that apart from the police, "the bodies of the RCD are indisputably the most significant and most systematic means of surveillance."[21] In fact, the party "functioned as a mechanism of social control at all levels of society," and neighborhood watch committees were created by the party to monitor Islamists' activities.[22]

In Egypt, although the political activities, recruitment, and promoting of the NDP programs and policies were the main functions of the different organizations of the party,[23] in reality, members were also asked from time to time to keep an eye on someone or to report activities in campuses and offices. It is difficult, in the case of Egypt, to determine the exact demarcation between the party and the security services, but senior ministers, particularly the minister of interior, were usually members of the political bureau, the executive body of the NDP. According to Robert Springborg, in the elections of 1986, Minister of Interior Zaki Badr addressed numerous party meetings "railing against the opposition and lauding his audience for their activities in cementing alliance between the party and the popular bases."[24] Hasan Abu Basha, who occupied the post of minister of

---

[20] Hizb al-Ba'th al-'Arabi al-Ishtiraki, *Hawla al-dimuqratiyya al-markaziyya* [About centralized democracy] (Damascus: Cultural Bureau and Party Preparatory Publications, n.d. (1970s)), p. 7.

[21] Béatrice Hibou, *The Force of Obedience: The Political Economy of Repression in Tunisia*, translated by Andrew Brown (Cambridge: Polity, 2011), pp. 86–87.

[22] Noureddine Jebnoun, "Ben Ali's Tunisia: The Authoritarian Path of a Dystopian State," in Jebnoun et al. (eds.), *Modern Middle East Authoritarianism*, p. 110.

[23] Al-Hizb al Watani al-Dimuqrati, *Ru'ya li-mustaqbal Misr*, p. 23.

[24] Robert Springborg, *Mubarak's Egypt: Fragmentation of the Political Order* (Boulder, CO: Westview Press, 1989), p. 155.

interior and was for many years in charge of Egypt's security forces, confirms the deep relations between the ministry and all political parties, but argues that the role of the minister was "to supervise all political forces, ensure that they follow the legal path, and abide by the rules that govern the society."[25]

Irrespective of which country, recruitment was a core function of all the ruling parties. Some parties that originally had a more ideological base used their teachings and principles to attract new cadre. For instance, the Iraqi Ba'th Party had a special school called Madrasat al-I'dad al-Hizbi (Party Preparatory School), to groom those destined for higher positions, and to instruct them in the intellectual and ideological aspects of party philosophy.[26] Recruitment of youth, the educated, and women was a high priority for most parties. In countries such as Egypt and Tunisia, joining the party was not onerous: the candidate had simply to declare that he or she was not a member of another party and that they believed in the principles of the ruling party. In Syria and Iraq, there was more monitoring, and forms to complete, as the Ba'th was very security conscious, and apart from the lowest level of party membership, known as *mu'ayyid* (sympathizer), promotion was more rigorous.[27] By 1992 the Iraqi Ba'th had a clear slogan: "Let us capture the youth, so we can capture the future."[28] Iraqi documents from the 1990s show that in some major branches the percentage of those aged below thirty-five reached over 50 percent, while that of women members topped 40 percent.[29] In Syria, the proportion of women among party activists ranged from 29 to 31 percent, and Syrian data indicated that by 2004 the number of young members had reached almost 67 percent.[30]

---

[25] Abu Basha, *Mudhakkirat Hasan Abu Basha fi al-amn wa al-siyasa*, p. 151.
[26] For a comprehensive discussion of Madrasat al-I'dad al-Hizbi, see Joseph Sassoon, "The Iraqi Ba'th Party Preparatory School and the 'Cultural' Courses of the Branches," *Middle Eastern Studies*, vol. 50, no. 1 (2014), pp. 27–42.
[27] For the requirements to join the Egyptian NDP, see al-Hizb al-Watani al-Dimuqrati, *Ru'ya li-mustaqbal Misr*, p. 47; for the Iraqi Ba'th, see Sassoon, *Saddam Hussein's Ba'th Party*, chapter 2.
[28] Sassoon, *Saddam Hussein's Ba'th Party*, pp. 54–55.
[29] See, for example, Salah al-Din branch in *Ba'th Regional Command Collection* (BRCC), 174-3-2, 1992; and a report from one section in Baghdad to Party Headquarters, November 11, 2002, BRCC, 004-5-6.
[30] Belhadj, *La Syrie de Bashar al-Asad*, p. 149.

It would be wrong to assume that the Ba'thification process in Syria diminished with the rise to power of Bashar al-Asad after his father's death. A documentary investigating the issue of flooding related to the building of the Euphrates dam clearly shows the deep penetration of the Ba'th even in small villages and towns. Living in a valley near the Euphrates River, one tribal head and his family were all connected to the party. The headmaster in the local school, himself a senior party member, was in charge of ensuring that the students joined the different youth groups of the party. In his words, it was critical that "the principles of the Ba'th are planted in every child, so the child would love freedom, socialism, and Arab unity [the party's motto]."[31] Almost identical to Iraq, emphasis was laid on what was termed *tala'i' al-Ba'th wa jil al-mustaqbal* (the avant-garde of the Ba'th and the future generation).[32] Interestingly, all the students in the village had to wear military uniforms, an idea that Asad copied from North Korea.

In Egypt, the eighth conference of the NDP in 2002 called for expanding the role of women in society by increasing the membership of women, and of youth in general, in order to modernize the country.[33] In Tunisia, party reports showed that 30 percent of members were women, and the RCD was proud to announce that many academics and professors from different universities joined the party after November 7, 1987 (when Ben 'Ali, then minister of interior, seized power from Habib Bourguiba, the founding father of the Republic after its independence from France), having previously boycotted the party. One report indicated that 2,772 university professors had joined the RCD by 2003, and underlined that 29 percent of party members had tertiary education.[34]

There is no doubt that many young and educated people joined these parties because of their political beliefs, but the majority joined simply for economic reasons, knowing that promotions and

---

[31] Omar Amiralay (dir.), *Tawafan fi bilad al-Ba'th* [Flood in the country of the Ba'th], a film produced in Syria and France in 2003. The producer admits that he decided to make the film after his first movie supported the Ba'th modernization plans that led to the building of the dam and the flooding of small villages. The film was chosen as one the best 100 Arabic movies in the 2013 Dubai Film Festival.

[32] For a discussion on children and youth under the Iraqi Ba'th Party, see Sassoon, *Saddam Hussein's Ba'th Party*, pp. 268–73.

[33] Al-Hizb al-Watani al-Dimuqrati, *Ru'ya li-mustaqbal Misr*, pp. 111–19.

[34] Al-Muzzafir, *Min al-hizb al-wahid*, p. 79.

government jobs were more widely available to party members. Whether in Tunisia, Syria, or Iraq, it was almost impossible for a non-member of the ruling party to join the military, the police, or the security forces. Furthermore, party members predominantly filled senior positions in government, the judiciary, and academic institutions. Essentially, this became a fundamental part of the rewards system that, in turn, guaranteed a significant increase in membership, and, more critically, a high quality of cadre that the leadership could rely on. Thus the party was no longer about ideology, but more about a cooptation that allowed these regimes to indirectly control the population at large, in particular the young and educated, of whom the leadership was naturally wary.

As Hinnebusch points out, careerism was an important motivation in recruitment to the ruling parties in Egypt and Syria, although his research conducted in the early 1980s shows that in Syria many young men and women were attracted to careers through their association with the Ba'th because of their low social status.[35] Intriguingly, a recent report about the Communist Party in China showed similar trends: while there was no real zeal for the party's ideology, many university students were rushing to join it because "public-sector employers usually prefer party members and often require membership for better positions."[36] No wonder, then, that membership swelled dramatically; in Tunisia, based on the statistics of the RCD, Hibou claims that there were almost 2 million members out of a population of 10 million, a high number indeed compared to many other countries.[37] In Iraq, for instance, internal documents of the Ba'th indicated a total membership by 2002 of about 4 million out of a population of roughly 25 million.[38] Belhadj, quoting Syrian reports, posits that there were 2.4 million members in the Syrian Ba'th by 2005 (out of a population of roughly

[35] Raymond A. Hinnebusch, "Party Activists in Syria and Egypt: Political Participation in Authoritarian Modernizing States," *International Political Science Review*, vol. 4, no. 1 (1983), pp. 84–93. This study is based on a small survey sample of youth recruits and was conducted among recruits to the Syrian Ba'th Party and the Egyptian Wafd Party.

[36] "Students and the Party: Rushing to Join," *Economist*, February 22, 2014, p. 38.

[37] Hibou, *The Force of Obedience*, p. 86 and fn. 24, p. 309. A Tunisian study confirms this number and claimed that in 2001 there were 2.3 million. See al-Muzzafir, *Min al-hizb al-wahid*, p. 102.

[38] Sassoon, *Saddam Hussein's Ba'th Party*, appendix II, p. 286.

18 million) but only 547,000 were active.[39] A major caveat in all this data is that the vast majority was in the lower levels of the pyramid and joined the party either under duress or to enjoy the benefits of belonging to a ruling party.

Ideology played a more important part in the 1970s and 1980s compared to the following three decades. Some ruling parties, in particular the Ba'th, had strong ideological beginnings, and although it changed its policy over time, its fundamentals and motto (Arab Unity, Freedom, and Socialism) remained intact, at least on paper. A good example of lackluster ideology is recounted by one of Egypt's ministers. In 1976, he recounts, when Sadat decided to transform the Arab Socialist Union, the original focus was to be more on socialism, and hence the new party was called Hizb Misr al-Ishtiraki (Egypt Socialist Party). But within a short period Sadat changed his views and did not want a party defined as socialist, and thus the new NDP was created. Amazingly, all the senior ministers and most of those in the first party emigrated to the new party headed by the president, and no one thought it bizarre to switch a party and its ideology so swiftly.[40] Some members of ruling parties, whether due to opportunistic considerations or a genuine belief in their party's ideology, wrote extensively about the reasons they joined the ruling parties. One such description is by Dr. 'Abd al-Mun'im Sa'id, an Egyptian academic, who presents four reasons for joining the NDP: (1) more freedom than those who belong to other parties, given that the NDP was the right platform for discussions and exchange of ideas; (2) the fact the NDP was very strict in collecting fees from its members (120 Egyptian pounds, equivalent to US$20 in the mid 2000s), which according to Sa'id reduced opportunism in the party, and furthermore, the numerical rise of the youth within party ranks; (3) the NDP had a clear policy toward Israel, the USA, and the West, which was important as Egypt was in a region where sectarianism and fundamentalism were on the rise; and (4) the NDP, after long internal travail, had come to the conclusion that the only way to rid Egypt of its poverty was to focus on human development and Egypt's

---

[39] Belhadj, *La Syrie de Bashar al-Asad*, p. 397, fn. 44.
[40] 'Abd al-Wahhab al-Burlusi, *Kuntu waziran ma'a 'Abd al-Nasser* [I was a minister with 'Abd al-Nasser] (Cairo: Arab Mustaqbal Publishing, 1992), pp. 114–15.

resources.[41] Unfortunately, Dr. Sa'id does not present a thorough analysis of these four 'push' factors. Indeed, a review of ideological discussions and writings of some party members in those republics is far from impressive. Few of the party conferences delved in detail into theoretical and ideological issues, although many of the important topics were actually raised. For instance, the fourth annual conference of the NDP, which took place in September 2006, emphasized that the "National Democratic Party does not monopolize constitutional amendments and welcomes dialogue with all parties." The head of the Committee for Citizenry and Democracy Politics had on its agenda themes such as equilibrium between the different powers of the state; a reexamination of the relationship between the executive and judicial authorities; more independence for the judiciary; and increasing local governance in order to reduce the centralization of power.[42] Needless to say, all those significant questions remained as ideas without any serious discussion, and definitely without implementation.

In Tunisia, some of the RCD's philosophy and ideas remained strictly on paper, such as democracy and equality among citizens. In other areas, however, there was indeed significant progress such as modernization, increased literacy, and more rights for women.[43] Overall, the RCD became "largely devoid of ideology, but it retained the system of patronage."[44] In Iraq, an analysis of the Ba'th Party's preparatory school's curricula clearly shows how ideology lost its allure by the late 1980s and was replaced by the personality cult of President Saddam Hussein; instead of having the recruits focusing on the ideology of the founder, Michel 'Aflaq, and writings about socialism, the teaching shifted to the writings and speeches of "the great leader Saddam Hussein."[45] In Syria, Ba'th ideology and party writings were vague and

---

[41] 'Abd al-Mun'im Sa'id, *Islah al-sasa: al-Hizb al-Watani wa al-Ikhwan wa al-libraliyyun* [Reform of governance: the National Party and the Brothers and liberals] (Cairo: Nahdat Misr Publications, 2010), pp. 93–96.

[42] Al-Hizb al-Watani al-Dimuqrati, *al-Mu'tamar al-Sanawi al-Rabi'* [The Fourth Annual Conference], September 19–21, 2006, minutes of the meetings of the conference (Cairo: n.p., 2006), pp. 118–19. The head of the committee was Dr. Mufid Shihab.

[43] For an example of a detailed discussion of the ideas and policies of the RCD, see Tariq al-Qayzani, *al-Hizb al-Dimuqrati al-Taqaddumi* [The Progressive Democratic Party] (Tunisia: Dar Muhammad for Publishing, 2011).

[44] Jebnoun, "Ben Ali's Tunisia," p. 110.

[45] Sassoon, "The Iraqi Ba'th Party Preparatory School."

had many meanings and interpretations. One scholar argues that this was intentionally done to "incorporate disparate groups into a nation-state, minimizing conflict and promoting consensus."[46] For instance, a party report discussed in detail *al-dimuqratiyya al-markaziyya* (centralized democracy), but a thorough reading of this publication shows it is mainly about party discipline and "creating a deep foundation for the popular structure and party activities."[47] In fact, the regional command was worried about the vagueness of discussion and uninspiring style of the political activities, attributing it mostly to the "weakness of the intellectual effort, and the continuation of nebulous and incomplete ideology, which in turn is leading the apparatus to hesitate and reduce the confidence of the party cadre."[48] Similar to Iraq, the personality cult of President Hafiz al-Asad in Syria dominated its ideology and, with the passage of time, overshadowed the fundamental ingredients of the party's philosophy.

Weak, or even a lack of, ideology was one of the reasons for the waning of ties between the upper and lower echelons of these parties. As one ex-member of the Central Committee of the PSD lamented after five years as a senior party member:

Among the members of the Central Committee in charge of the political bureau, those at the top of the pyramid, see no alienation between their thinking and the thinking of the rank and file of the party ... When one of them declares and announces their protests about marriage, abortion, pregnancy, and inheritance, I asked myself: does this senior person have the same culture and civilization of the [Tunisian] people?[49]

This member's seniority did not help him when he heard, to his utter disbelief, an announcement during a large party meeting that he had withdrawn his candidacy for the Central Committee.[50] Throughout the Arab republics, the pyramid structure of power allowed a small group of people to make decisions, which were communicated to the central

[46] Lisa Wedeen, *Ambiguities of Domination: Politics, Rhetoric, and Symbols in Contemporary Syria* (Chicago: University of Chicago Press, 1999), p. 40.

[47] Hizb al-Ba'th, *Hawla al-dimuqratiyya al-markaziyya*, p. 13.

[48] Al-Qiyada al-Qawmiyya, *Nidal al-Ba'th: watha'iq Hizb al-Ba'th al-'Arabi al-Ishtiraki* [The struggle of the Ba'th: documents of the Arab Socialist Ba'th Party], vol. IV: *1955–1961* (Beirut: al-Tali'a Publishing, 1964), p. 207.

[49] Al-Munji al-Ka'bi, *Mudakhalat 'udu bil-Lajna al-Markaziyya* [Interjections of a member of the Central Committee] (Tunis: al-Kitab Publishing, 1986), p. 57.

[50] Ibid., p. 6.

committee or politburo of the ruling parties. These were disseminated down the line all the way to the lowest echelons, rarely with any discussion, and mostly without any explanation. The absence of ideology combined with the lack of unity of purpose (apart from staying in power and reaping the associated rewards) must have contributed to the inability of these ruling parties to keep the population under control by 2011. The paralysis of the Syrian Ba'th Party in the 2012 elections can be partly explained by the violence spreading in the country, but also by its inability to counter opposition and regain popular support for the regime. This weak connection between the leadership and the party cadre was already highlighted in the late 1970s, at the time of an internal crisis in the Syrian Ba'th Party, and it was recommended to "review the relationship between the party and the leadership in a way that guarantees a truthful leadership of the party."[51] Four decades later, it became obvious that this recommendation was never properly implemented.

Opposition parties

An important function of any ruling party is to attract the masses to its principles and make sure that other parties or factions cannot draw people away or, even worse, mobilize them. Within the single-party republics, there were opposition parties that were sometimes incorporated into the system, but more often they were harassed and prevented from functioning. The Communist Party in Iraq was a good example of how the Ba'th regime made an alliance with an opposition party, only to trap it, execute many of its members, and reduce its influence dramatically.[52] Other republics, particularly Egypt and Tunisia, allowed a multi-party system to exist on the clear understanding that elections would not lead to a change of regime. Opposition parties were

---

[51] Hizb al-Ba'th al-Arabi al-Ishtiraki, *al-Haraka al-Tashihiyya: min al-Mu'tamar al-Qawmi al-'Ashir al-Istithna'i ila al-Mu'tamar al-Qawmi al-Thalith 'Ashir* [The Corrective Movement: from the Extraordinary National Tenth Conference to the Thirteenth National Conference] (Damascus: Cultural Bureau and Party Preparatory, 1983), p. 15. The Corrective Movement took place in November 1970 when Hafiz al-Asad seized power. For more details on those events, see Van Dam, *The Struggle for Power in Syria*, pp. 65–74.

[52] For a comprehensive analysis of this alliance and the events, see Tareq Y. Ismael, *The Rise and Fall of the Communist Party of Iraq* (Cambridge: Cambridge University Press, 2008).

also dominated by their leaders, and as Willis points out, "control and manipulation of political parties by the power-holding elites is perhaps the fundamental feature of political parties in Algeria, Tunisia and Morocco."[53] It is not my intention here to analyze why these elections took place[54] or why some countries allowed a multi-party system versus those with a single party, or why some switched from a single-party system to a multi-party-system.[55] Rather, to give a flavor, the chapter turns to memoirs to understand how the opposition parties viewed themselves, and how the ruling party perceived them. In the next section on parliaments, I will examine how some opposition parties functioned, again through the lens of some of those who were on both sides of the political divide.

An insight into pluralism and opposition is gained from the memoirs of Ahmad Fathi Sarur, an ex-minister who also headed the Egyptian parliament for a decade. He revealed how the opposition leader was chosen: Sadat met with Mustafa Kamil Murad, a member of the Egyptian parliament and head of a small opposition party, and informed him that he was being appointed as head of the opposition:

The reality behind the appointment of the head of opposition by an oral order from the president of the republic was not haphazard but intentional. The idea was that the opposition complies with what the president

---

[53] Michael Willis, "Political Parties in Maghrib: The Illusion of Significance?" *Journal of North African Studies*, vol. 7, no. 2 (2002), p. 4. This article is the first of a two-part article. The second one is "Political Parties in the Maghrib: Ideology and Identification, a Suggested Typology," *Journal of North African Studies*, vol. 7, no. 3 (2002), pp. 1–28.

[54] For an analysis of elections in Egypt, see Lisa Blaydes, *Elections and Distributive Politics in Mubarak's Egypt* (New York: Cambridge University Press, 2011); for analysis of elections in North Africa, see Lise Storm, *Party Politics and the Prospects for Democracy in North Africa* (Boulder, CO: Lynne Rienner, 2013). For further analysis of Egypt's 2010 elections and elections in the region since 2010, see Ellen Lust, "Elections," in Marc Lynch (ed.), *The Arab Uprisings Explained: New Contentious Politics in the Middle East* (New York: Columbia University Press, 2014), pp. 218–45.

[55] Many works discuss this issue, for a reference to a few of these, see, for example, Mona el-Ghobashy, "Governments and Oppositions," in Michele Penner Angrist (ed.), *Politics and Society in the Contemporary Middle East* (Boulder, CO: Lynne Rienner, 2010), pp. 29–47; Baghat Korany, "Restricted Democratization from Above: Egypt," in Baghat Korany, Rex Brynen, and Paul Noble (eds.), *Political Liberalization and Democratization in the Arab World*, vol. II: *Comparative Experiences* (Boulder, CO: Lynne Rienner, 1998), pp. 39–69; Angrist, *Party Building in the Modern Middle East*, pp. 54–72.

determines along the basics and principles of how the freedom of the media is prescribed, freedom that is bound by those principles [of the regime].[56]

Supporters of the regime obviously had a different interpretation of political parties and freedom of the press in Egypt. One professor of communications, in his study of the political press from 1981 to 2005, argued that "in reality the political system during the era of President Muhammad Hosni Mubarak emphasized democracy as an untouchable source that provides legitimacy." The author later quoted a Mubarak speech of September 18, 1985: "Democracy is the free press that provides a true mirror for society and expresses its dreams and hopes, and speaks its truth." The president also called for a "free press that encourages criticism, defends the rights of the subjugated and oppressed, and not be a tool for subjugation and oppression."[57] Almost every opposition party published a newspaper expressing its views, but this was somewhat insignificant as many of these parties lacked any real popular support. In fact, one author observed that most of the opposition press was "for sale to the highest bidder," and contended that this "political prostitution" was happening under the guidance of the High Council for Newspapers. He further asserted that one of the reasons why Nasser was against political pluralism was his conviction that many of the opposition parties would become agents for other factions or countries.[58]

A fairer analysis of the situation was presented by Rif'at al-Sayyid, who argued: "We do not have a free multi-party system," because political parties required a license that was in the hands of the Committee of Political Parties. He confessed that although he was in opposition, he could not name the fourteen opposition parties that operated in the late 1990s, because "these groupings represent nothing in Egyptian politics and have no standing whatsoever with the Egyptian

[56] Sawsan al-Jayyar, *Fathi Sarur wa al-barlaman: asrar wa i'tirafat* [Fathi Sarur and the parliament: secrets and confessions] (Cairo: Arab Press and Publications, 2002), p. 22. Sarur was head of the Egyptian parliament from 1990 until 2001. Before that he was minister of higher education. For detailed analysis of pluralism in Egypt, see Noha el-Mikawy, *The Building of Consensus in Egypt's Transition Process* (Cairo: American University Press, 1999).
[57] Shiyam 'Abd al-Hamid Qutb, *Mustaqbal al-sahafa al-hizbiyya fi Misr* [The future of the party press in Egypt] (Cairo: Dar al-'Alam al-'Arabi, 2010), p. 132.
[58] 'Abd al-'Azim Ramadan, *al-Sira' al-ijtima'i wa al-siyasi fi 'asr Mubarak* [The social and political clash in Mubarak's era], vol. VII (Cairo: al-Hay'a al-Misriyya lil-Kitab, 1995), pp. 45–49.

people."[59] This charade continued in spite of the fact that those involved, both on the regime and the opposition sides, clearly recognized that there was no true multi-party system in the country. Explaining why these opposition leaders or at least some of them accepted the situation, al-Sayyid explained:

We use the little freedom we have in order to demand the introduction of true democratic measures and in order to get the people and the rulers to learn and appreciate the value and necessity of democracy. We are trying to effect the transition to democracy gradually, step by step. We do not despair because we believe that a fundamental right of our people is to have a true democratic system.[60]

The former head of parliament conveyed in his memoirs how the regime was annoyed with him on multiple occasions for allowing opposition parties to express their views without first obtaining permission from higher sources.[61] Relations between the regime and the opposition in Egypt changed considerably during Mubarak's era, in contrast to the two previous presidencies of Nasser and Sadat. As Ellen Lust-Okar explains, Mubarak, unlike Sadat, allowed "more opposition groups to participate in the formal system while simultaneously keeping important groups on the fringes."[62] In spite of having clear laws about establishing new parties, the Egyptian authorities barred the granting of licenses with a variety of bizarre excuses. For instance, one opposition leader recounts that in 2003, a document signed by hundreds of supporters presented an application to create a new party only to be denied on the grounds that "the new party's program is not dissimilar from other parties."[63]

Pluralism in Tunisia was approached in two stages; in November 1983, two parties were legalized, in addition to the already recognized

[59] Mark C. Kennedy (ed.), *Twenty Years of Development in Egypt (1977–1997), Part 1: Economy, Politics, Regional Relations,* Cairo Papers 20th Anniversary Symposium, vol. 21, monograph 3 (Cairo: American University Press, Fall 1998), p. 77. Al-Sayyid was part of al-Tajammu', a group of three opposition parties with a socialist platform created in 1975.

[60] Ibid., p. 80.   [61] Al-Jayyar, *Fathi Sarur wa al-barlaman,* pp. 7–8.

[62] Ellen Lust-Okar, *Structuring Conflict in the Arab World: Incumbents, Opponents, and Institutions* (New York: Cambridge University Press, 2005), p. 140. See the list of major political forces under Sadat in the 1970s, and under Mubarak during the 1980s and 1990s, pp. 191–201.

[63] Ayman Nur, *Sajin al-hurriya: Ayman Nur yaktubu min khalf al-aswar* [The prisoner of freedom: Ayman Nur writes from behind walls] (Cairo: n.p., 2006), p. 8.

Communist Party. Then in 1987, with the toppling of Bourguiba and the rise of Ben 'Ali, the door was opened to other parties. In essence, the regime admitted that it could not represent all Tunisians, but inserted enough safety valves to ensure that the RCD would continue to dominate. The regime defined the "duty" of the opposition to represent other groups or factions that were not involved with the ruling party.[64] Intriguingly, even before the 1987 opening up to a multi-party system, those in charge, such as Mohamed Mzali, who was appointed prime minister and secretary-general of the Destour Party in 1980, claimed that in fact the one-party system was not dictatorial:

Some are trying to confuse us by [arguing] that the one party system necessarily means an absolutist regime based on control or dictatorship, and that democracy is limited to multi-party system … But in Tunisia the Socialist Destour Party is not just a single party … It coexisted with the Tunisian Communist Party to the end in 1962 and granted it a permit to operate in 1981 … In Tunisia, Bourguibism as a system proved its efficacy, and the march [to democracy] has to be gradual.[65]

One scholar suggested that there were three types of opposition in Tunisia: clientelistic opposition approved by the regime; legal opposition; and illegal opposition. The first two categories had direct and indirect connections with the regime, while the third consisted of Islamist or leftist groups.[66] Overall, the modes of opposition in most of the authoritarian states in the Arab world are similar; another scholar observed that these modes "oscillate on a range between regime-loyal opposition at one end, and anti-system opposition at the other."[67]

In Algeria, the move from a single party to multi-party system was prompted by riots that swept the country in late 1988. By early 1989, "associations of a political nature were allowed to be formed." As Michael Willis explains, "the real reason behind [President] Chadli's

[64] For detailed analysis of these safety measures, see Erdle, *Ben Ali's "New Tunisia"*, pp. 295–300.

[65] Mzali, *Hadith al-fi'l*, pp. 350, 354. Mzali's views are presented in a question-and-answer format, although there is no interviewer named.

[66] Larbi Chouikha, "L'Opposition à Ben Ali et les élections de 2004," in *L'Année du Maghreb, 2004* (Paris: CNRS Édition, 2006), pp. 365–66.

[67] Holger Albrecht, "Political Opposition and Arab Authoritarianism: Some Conceptual Remarks," in Holger Albrecht (ed.), *Contentious Politics in the Middle East: Political Opposition under Authoritarianism* (Gainesville: University of Florida Press, 2010), pp. 21–22. This edited volume has other interesting articles on opposition in the Arab world from different perspectives.

decision to reform lay, as ever, in the complex internal politics of the Algerian regime." This related to the internal battles within the FLN and Chadli's maneuvering to deprive the party of its monopoly, so that he could be seen "as a president above party politics."[68] It is safe to argue that two factors have impacted political life in Algeria since its independence in 1962: the FLN and the army (see next chapter); and the *pouvoir* (power) was mostly in the hands of the generals.[69] In spite of the numerous parties that competed in the pluralistic elections, data indicate that only the FLN "established stable roots in society."[70] One interesting consequence of pluralism in Algeria was the rise in numbers of teachers and civil servants participating in elections, given their political activism; in the 1990 elections more than 36 percent of those elected as heads of local councils on behalf of different parties were teachers.[71] Coopting this group confronted the regime from time to time with some security issues, because of the lack of linkage between teachers and the main pillar of the state, the army.

Opposition from Islamists was seen as a serious threat to these republics (see Chapter 4). Members of the Muslim Brothers (al-Ikhwan al-Muslimun) in Egypt and Syria were hounded, and their organization suppressed and outlawed for long periods. Their participation in the Egyptian parliament is discussed below, but suffice to say that part of the "process of deliberalization" that took place in Egypt and other republics was in response to what was perceived as a threatening force. The net result was that the process led to "the erosion of positive and negative liberties alike."[72] Mubarak's regime thwarted the danger by "usurping the space of political Islam."[73] In Tunisia, opposition

---

[68] Willis, *Politics and Power in the Maghreb*, pp. 130–31.

[69] For an interesting discussion of Algeria's elite, see Isabelle Werenfels, "Algeria: System Continuity through Elite Change," in Volker Perthes (ed.), *Arab Elites: Negotiating the Politics of Change* (Boulder, CO: Lynne Rienner, 2004), pp. 173–205.

[70] Storm, *Party Politics*, pp. 134–36.

[71] Nasir Jabi, *al-Jaza'ir: al-dawla wa al-nukhab, dirasat fi al-nukhab, al-ahzab al-siyasiyya wa al-harakat al-ijtima'iyya* [Algeria: the state and the elites, a study in elites, political parties and social movements] (Algiers: al-Shihab Publications, 2008), p. 92.

[72] Eberhard Kienle, "More than a Response to Islamism: The Political Deliberalization of Egypt in the 1990s," *Middle East Journal*, vol. 52, no. 2 (Spring 1998), p. 220.

[73] Lust-Okar, *Structuring Conflict in the Arab World*, p. 145.

members, whether communists or Islamists, were harassed, and sometimes imprisoned and tortured.[74]

In Iraq, Saddam Hussein believed that with the fall of communism,
Iraq's youth were attracted to Islam as an ideology and he was
frustrated that the weakening Ba'th ideology was not appealing to the
young and educated. An important fact was that Saddam Hussein, not
unlike other leaders of the republics, was in essence secular, and thus
felt that the party should "oppose the politicization of religion by the
state and within society."[75] In 1986, during a meeting held in Baghdad
with senior Ba'th members from Arab countries, Saddam Hussein
expressed views about Islamists and the Muslim Brothers that later
became a basic tenet in the other secular republics:

They [Islamists] consider any country, including Iraq that does not accept
their logic and teaching, as non-Islamic. They ask: in an Islamic country, is
there a [belly] dancer on television? And their answer is absolutely no.
    In the final analysis, I do not think it is wise to clash with them as the
religious tendency in the Arab world [is increasing], if we have the possibility
to avoid them. This religious movement in the Arab world is the most
dangerous. We have a state and a system, and if they reach power, this
would be a threat to our regime and party.[76]

Amazingly, almost three decades later, another Arab leader, Egypt's
President 'Abd al-Fattah al-Sisi, reiterated the same concept and some
of Saddam Hussein's words: "Their [the Muslim Brothers'] ideological
structure makes confrontation with us inevitable. The ideological
structure of these groups is that we are not real Muslims, and they
are real Muslims."[77] This "confrontation" or clash of ideologies with
the Brotherhood was repeated in other republics, such as Syria and
Tunisia.

---

[74] For fascinating testimonies of the regime's opponents, see al-Tamimi (ed.),
al-Mu'aridun al-siyasiyyun tahta al-ta'dhib fi Tunis.
[75] Saddam Hussein, *Nazra fi al-din wa al-turath* [A glimpse into religion and
tradition] (Baghdad: al-Huriyya Publishing House, 1980), p. 7. For Saddam's
views about the Muslim Brotherhood, see Sassoon, *Saddam Hussein's Ba'th
Party*, p. 260.
[76] Audiotape of a meeting between Saddam Hussein and Arab Ba'th members,
Baghdad, July 24, 1986, *Conflict Records Research Center* (CRRC), National
Defense University (NDU), Saddam's Tapes, SH-SHTP-A-001-167.
[77] David D. Kirkpatrick, "Egypt's New Autocrat, Sisi Knows Best," *New York
Times*, May 25, 2014. The journalist is quoting from a television interview with
General Sisi.

Islamism was one of the reasons, but not the only one, that all these regimes became less tolerant of the opposition. Both Egypt and Tunisia stifled these Islamic opposition groups, and fought by every means to reduce their power and appeal to the electorates. Each ruling party wanted to increase its majority, even though this majority was already overwhelming: in the Egyptian elections of 1990, 79 percent of the parliamentary seats went to the NDP. But by 1994, this majority had strengthened to reach 94 percent. According to Joshua Stacher, only five opposition parties were capable of taking part in Egypt's political life under Mubarak, while many other parties were "frozen" by the government.[78] His accurate conclusions were that parties opposed to the regime were weak organizations. "They are autocratically run, easily fragmented, and incorporated into the cooption and patronage networks of Mubarak's Egypt."[79] Similar conclusions could be easily reached about Tunisia and other multi-party systems in the Arab republics.[80] One study of opposition parties in Egypt showed how they were deprived of financial resources and thus were unable to communicate with the masses, particularly in the rural areas. Furthermore, these parties were traditional, did not attract the youth, and recycled old slogans in their parliamentary campaigns.[81]

The question that begs itself is why these authoritarian regimes made such efforts to ensure a multi-party system if they had an overwhelming majority for their ruling parties. Many scholars covering different regions of the world have studied this question. The answer, to borrow from a study on Mexico, is that such regimes wanted to show invincibility and to prove to the masses that they had no other viable choices.[82] There are two other reasons: first, the need to show the West, and particularly the United States, that these regimes were on

---

[78] Joshua A. Stacher, "Parties Over: The Demise of Egypt's Opposition Parties," *British Journal of Middle Eastern Studies*, vol. 31, no. 2 (November 2004), pp. 215–33. The five parties were al-Wafd, al-Ahrar, al-'Amal, Tajammu', and the Nasserist.

[79] Ibid., p. 232.   [80] See, for example, Chouikha, "L'Opposition à Ben Ali."

[81] Hala Mustafa, "Mu'asharat wa nata'ij intikhabat 1995" [Indicators and results of 1995 elections], in Hala Mustafa (ed.), *al-Intikhabat al-barlamaniyya fi Misr, 1995* [The parliamentary elections in Egypt, 1995] (Cairo: al-Ahram Political and Strategic Studies Center, 1997), p. 41. The study contains a wide range of analysis and field studies from several governorates.

[82] Beatriz Magaloni, *Voting for Autocracy: Hegemonic Party Survival and its Demise in Mexico* (New York: Cambridge University Press, 2006). See also Blaydes, *Elections and Distributive Politics in Mubarak's Egypt*.

the path to democracy, as elections, rightly or wrongly, became synonyms for democracy. Second, the leaders of these regimes, after numerous years in power, became increasingly delusional and believed their own propaganda. A documented instance is that even in the most authoritarian republic, Iraq, Saddam Hussein considered referendums a high priority in spite of having no competition, since he was the only contender. In fact, a supermajority was not enough, as the president insisted on getting 100 percent, and told his inner cabinet that with "some more explanation" all the people of Iraq would have voted for him.[83]

While the regimes in the so-called multi-party systems struggled with opposition parties, legal and illegal, single-party countries such as Iraq and Syria had a different kind of competition: they had to ensure that their Ba'th and not the "other Ba'th" would gain the upper hand. The two regimes had been in conflict since they rose to power, in part because of "the desire of the Syrian rulers to monopolize Ba'thi legitimacy."[84] They waged both open and secret wars against each other to ensure the dominance of their own faction of the party, even though it had the same founder and, in essence, the same ideology.[85] In countries such as Iraq, Syria, and Libya, repression did not allow any proper channel for a legal opposition.

Parliaments

In the multi-party systems, and even in single-party systems, parliaments functioned to show the world that democracy existed in these countries. As Nathan Brown eloquently states: "Parliaments [in the Arab world] constitute a public sphere but not a tool for political

---

[83] Sassoon, *Saddam Hussein's Ba'th Party*, p. 176.

[84] Eberhard Kienle, *Ba'th v. Ba'th: The Conflict between Syria and Iraq 1968–1989* (London: I. B. Tauris, 1991), p. 170.

[85] For interesting details of how this competition took shape, see Dafi al-Jam'ani, *Min al-hizb ila al-sijin 1948–1994: mudhakkirat* [From party to prison, 1948–1994: memoirs] (Beirut: Riyad al-Rayyis Books, 2007). Jam'ani, a Jordanian, joined the Ba'th Party in his youth and later became a member of the military committee of the Jordanian Ba'th politbureau. He progressed to become a member of the Syrian Ba'th regional command, but was arrested after Hafiz al-Asad's "Corrective Movement" and kept in prison for twenty-three years.

accountability."[86] A good portrait of these parliaments or what was known, in certain countries, as *majlis al-sha'b* (the people's council) was given by Sarur, the head of the Egyptian parliament:

The People's Council ... did not represent anything as it was an outcome of the Arab Socialist Union and every member is lost, not knowing whether he is obliged to debate, to think, to call [officials] to account, or reconcile. He [the member] heard about democracy and imagined it as simply attending sessions, listening to statements given for the official record, and then clapping at certain times. On other occasions, the applause amplifies and turns into cheering to make it a historical or a unique event.[87]

Intriguingly, many of the observers of the Egyptian parliament concur on how things were conducted, unless they were intrinsically part of the government machine. An Egyptian journalist who studied parliamentary activities from 1995 to 2000 commented:

The role of Majlis al-Sha'b within the legislative sphere is reduced to approving legislation presented by the government and passing it without any major amendments, due to the overall majority of the National Democratic Party.[88]

However justified that criticism is, the fact remains that at least there were discussions and debates, and sometimes opposition parties in parliament did play a positive role. Furthermore, there were a few members within the ruling party who believed in pluralism and allowed a freer debate of issues. On the other hand, in single-party regimes such as Syria, memoirs and studies of parliamentary life are reduced to several pictures of the president, the chair of *majlis al-sha'b*, a list of the rules and regulations enacted, and a roll call of various committee representatives, etc.[89] In Hafiz al-Asad's world, democracy was somewhat abstract and did not refer to elections and parliaments. In one of his speeches he defined democracy: "The

---

[86] Nathan J. Brown, "Bumpy Democratic Routes to Dictatorial Ends?" in Jebnoun et al. (eds.), *Modern Middle East Authoritarianism*, p. 35.

[87] Al-Jayyar, *Fathi Sarur wa al-barlaman*, p. 17.

[88] Sawsan al-Jayyar, *Majlis nuss al-layl: ru'ya suhufiyya jari'a: barlaman 1995–2000* [The midnight council: a brave journalistic insight: the parliament of 1995–2000] (Cairo: Arab Agency for Media and Publications, 2000), p. 151.

[89] A typical memoir of this kind can be found in Muhammad Shakir As'id, *al-Barlaman al-Suri fi tatawwurihi al-tarikhi* [The Syrian parliament and its historical development] (Damascus: al-Mada Press, 2002).

formula of democracy is not a commodity that can be imported from a
country of another. It is, however, the framework under which citizens
practice their rights and duties according to their local circumstances."
He then added that democracy is a cultural matter inciting man to
create and give.[90]

Creating a majority for the NDP in Egypt was comparable to the
process that took place in Tunisia. Erdle explains the composition of
the two houses (upper and lower) of the Tunisian National Assembly
and shows that in practice 80 percent of seats of the lower house were
reserved for the RCD, and the system ensured that a big majority for
the RCD existed in the upper house. His conclusion could apply to
other republics with parliaments: "no real parliamentarization of
political life," nor a "real change in the overall power relations between
the different components of the political system, nor in the everyday
working conditions for members of parliament."[91]

Who were the members of parliament? Egypt has the largest number
of members' memoirs and studies compared to other countries in the
region. In one such study, eighteen members (elected to parliament in
1990) are presented: their background, their campaigns, the parliamentary issues they focused on, and their political careers in their own
words.[92] Although all are shown in a positive and rather obsequious
light, one can still learn about the daily life of parliamentarians. Many
argue that the main reason behind their standing for elections was their
desire to serve the people, *'ata' dhati* (self-giving), but while doing so
they had to face opposition from other representatives, as well as
unscrupulous measures taken against them to ensure that they were
coopted into the system. One member tells the story of how he once
uncovered a scandal in a village in Port Sa'id, which led the governor of
Port Sa'id to use his relatives in the intelligence services to scrutinize the
members of parliament who were investigating the scandal and cast
aspersions on their characters.[93] Conflicts between the regime and
members or potential candidates were common; another member in
this collection had the "honor" of having the shortest stint in

---

[90] Adel Reda, *A Reading in Assad Thinking* (Cairo: Akhbar al-Yawm, n.d.),
p. 182.
[91] Erdle, *Ben Ali's "New Tunisia"*, pp. 164–65, 169.
[92] Jalal al-Sayyid, *Tajribati al-barlamaniyya* [My parliamentary experience]
(Egypt: n.p., n.d). The book seems to have been published in the early 1990s.
[93] Ibid., pp. 59–64. The member of parliament referred to was Mahmud Subh.

parliament. After he was elected with a large majority, newspapers published stories about his tax evasion, and in a relatively swift and efficient manner other members voted to oust him. It was, according to this biography, a typical story in the Egyptian parliament, where it was unclear who was wronged or who was wrong.[94] Another member was an ex-police officer, Mamduh al-Jawhari, who served for twenty-four years in the police force but decided to move into politics. He claims that he studied the platforms of all the parties and discovered that the programs of the Wafd and NDP were closest to his opinions, as "one had roots in the past and the other in the present." So he chose NDP, and seems to have been more assertive than many of his peers about the role of the parliament:

In spite of my admiration for Dr. Fathi Sarur the head of Majlis al-Sha'b for allowing freedom of expression for members, I am not satisfied until now. The basic function of the Majlis is to legislate and supervise, and yet this is not done. After all, most of the legislation and its amendments come from the government, when it should be by the Majlis and its members. Similarly most questions and requests for investigations and probing issues are left without any positive results. It could be due to the weakness of the member [raising the topic], but I blame the supermajority that consistently supports the government ... I believe the government should be chosen by the party and not vice versa, and then the Majlis should be charged with supervising and overseeing [the government's actions].[95]

One member was a total contrast to al-Jawhari; Mahmud al-Sharif came from an aristocratic family that had been represented in the Egyptian parliament since 1930. Although four of its members were already in parliament during the monarchy, more took their seats beginning in 1957. Al-Sharif talks about his family's traditions and how they always seemed to have good relations with whoever was in power, but at the same time to "represent the people."[96]

Not all those in the collection of biographies were members of the NDP; the head of the opposition in the early 1990s, Khalid Muhyi al-Din, was included. Nonetheless, he was part of the establishment as a Nasserist involved with the earlier national assemblies, one of the three members who opposed the Camp David Agreement between Egypt and Israel, and again one of the few who called for a halt to the

[94] Ibid., pp. 37–47. The member was Badir al-Din Khitab representing the NDP.
[95] Ibid., pp. 97–102.   [96] Ibid., pp. 109–14.

war against Iraq after its invasion of Kuwait.[97] A final example from
this collection is an independent member who represented the Suez
region in a few parliaments, but was pushed aside when different
governments were not happy that he and other independents raised
sensitive issues, such as the increase in prices of staple foods in 1977.
Overall, the focus of the independent members was mostly on social
and economic issues.[98]

When the Muslim Brothers were allowed to participate in the elections, or when its leadership decided not to boycott the elections, its
members played a role in parliament and wrote about it. In the 2000
elections, seventeen representatives won seats (representing 3 percent
of the total 454 members). A memoir was written by one of these
members, Muhammad Jamal Hishmat, a doctor who was teaching at
Alexandria University, who began his political activities at the age of
sixteen, and in 2000 became a member of parliament for the next five
years. In his book, he reviews the accomplishments of the Muslim
Brothers in the political, economic, and social spheres.[99] Cases of
political liberties, and issues emanating from emergency rule, dominated the Brothers' agenda. They were among the fiercest critics of
Mubarak's relations with Israel and continually attacked the presence
of the Israeli Academic Center in Cairo, accusing it of being "a den of
spies." In addition, they were interested in educational and cultural
themes and attempted to introduce Islamic-slanted reforms. Other
subjects also aroused their fury: the annual selection of Miss Egypt, a
competition they abhorred and regarded as totally opposed to Islamic
values. They also defended the right of twenty-four women broad-
casters who were banned for wearing the hijab.[100] When they raised
sensitive aspects of security, such as torturing members of the Brothers,
the Ministry of Interior tended to brush aside their complaints by
denying that acts of torture were committed by the authorities.[101]
Even when they were not in parliament, the leaders of al-Ikhwan
wrote prodigiously and deliberated about a wide variety of subjects.
One such example is 'Umar al-Talmasani, who occupied an important

---

[97] Ibid., p. 124.   [98] Ibid., pp. 115–19. The member was Faruq Mutawalli.
[99] Muhammad Jamal Hishmat, *Mudhakkirat na'ib min Misr: sharaf al-niyaba 'an
        al-sha'b wa 'azmat al-tajriba* [Memoirs of a representative from Egypt: the
        honor of representing the people and the grandeur of the experience] (Cairo: al-
        Wafa' Publishing, 2006), pp. 34–59.
[100] Ibid., p. 121.   [101] Ibid., pp. 61–62.

role in the Brothers' leadership. He reminisces about his political struggles, his incarceration, his marriage and views of women. He was honest enough to admit how jealous he was, to the extent that for the first seventeen years of their marriage his wife did not walk in the street, was not allowed to use public transport, and was taken everywhere by car. "I was too jealous even from the rays of the sun that might shine on her, or the wind that might touch her clothes. I did not allow her to visit me in prison for the first ten years out of the seventeen years I was imprisoned, envious that the prison guards or some of my fellow prisoners would see her."[102] He argued that his attitude toward women did not represent disdain for women; and claimed that, on the contrary, his respect for women was unrivaled, as he vehemently believed in the equality of men and women according to the teachings of Islam.[103]

One element that becomes clear from descriptions of the workings of Egyptian parliaments was that to operate successfully as a member, a person needed to be connected in one way or another to a minister. Thus, a major complaint of independent or opposition members was that their queries and efforts to maneuver the government bureaucracy mostly failed, as they did not possess a direct – or indirect – line to a minister.[104] However, lack of success in achieving parliamentary goals was not entirely due to the government and its policies; many of the members did not attend parliament and its committees, and one author contends that apart from the opening session each year, no session had a full quorum.[105] Excesses by members of parliament were another impediment; embezzlement, *wasta* (influence and nepotism), profiteering, and favoritism all contributed to a lackluster mode of operation. Intriguingly, few MPs who wrote their memoirs discuss these practices in detail, and sometimes referred to them only when they were attacking their "enemies" in parliament. In fact, a report by the *majlis al-sha'b* in 1996 referred to this problem, claiming that "These excesses that the last elections [1995] witnessed are basically due to the [actions of]

---

[102] 'Umar al-Talmasani, *Dhikrayat la mudhakkirat* [Memories not memoirs] (Cairo: Islamic Press and Publications, 1985), p. 18.
[103] Ibid., pp. 21–22.
[104] For details on this issue, see al-Jayyar, *Majlis nuss al-layl*, pp. 313–15.
[105] Ibid., pp. 311–12.

representatives and their supporters, and not because of the regime
or its institutions."[106]

As for the role of women in parliament, once again we have more
data on the Egyptian parliament than on any other Arab parliament. A striking feature about the 1979–84 parliament, which had
thirty-four women representatives, was that fourteen of them never
addressed the parliament or stood on the podium throughout their
five-year terms. Others, on the other hand, were extremely active,
raised numerous topics and questioned the government on important problems.[107] A second salient feature is the high level of
education and experience of women members compared to their
male counterparts.[108] A third is that some members were married
to other high officials; for instance the very active 'Inayat al-Zaid
was married to the governor of a province, and in the 1984–87
parliament she reduced her active participation because she felt that
her criticism of the government was putting her husband in an
awkward position.[109]

Women were also part of the opposition and, as will be seen later,
were imprisoned and tortured for their religious or political beliefs.
Zainab al-Ghazali, an activist in the Muslim Brotherhood and head of
the Muslim Ladies Group, was coaxed into joining the Arab Socialist
Union under Nasser, but was later imprisoned and humiliated, and
suffered terribly. Her relationship with the regime began to deterio-
rate after she refused a request from the ruling party "to take your
banners and go to the airport to welcome the President [Nasser]
home."[110] From that point on, Nasser's security agents were on her
case: her office was raided, her files confiscated, and eventually she
was imprisoned.[111]

---

[106] *Al-Taqrir al-istratiji al-'Arabi, 1996* [The Arabic strategic report, 1996] (Cairo:
al-Ahram Center for Political and Strategic Studies, 1996) p. 383.

[107] Muhammad al-Tawil, *al-Mar'a wa al-barlaman: taqyim al-tajriba al-barlam-
niyya lil-mar'a al-Misriyya* [Woman and parliament: an assessment of the
parliamentary experience for the Egyptian woman] (Cairo: al-Nada
Publishing, 2001), p. 179.

[108] Ibid., p. 203.   [109] Ibid., p. 207.

[110] Zainab al-Ghazali, *Return of the Pharaoh: Memoir in Nasser's Prison*,
translated by Mokrane Guezzou (Leicester: Islamic Foundation, 1994), p. 10.
Al-Ghazali recounts how she met Hasan al-Banna, the leader of the Ikhwan;
her pledge of allegiance to the Brotherhood; and her strong religious beliefs in
spite of her horrendous experience under the Nasserist regime.

[111] Ibid., pp. 12–14.

The participation of these opposition parties in different parliaments in the republics was dictated by several factors mostly out of their control. Stacher suggests that the "Egyptian state under Mubarak was far more influential in determining *how* [italics in the original] the Brothers participated than were the Brothers themselves."[112]

Different pictures emerge from the other republics, Libya, Algeria, and Sudan. In Libya, Qaddafi in his *Green Book* concluded that parliaments are irrelevant:

A parliament is originally founded to represent the people, but this in itself is undemocratic, as democracy means the authority of the people and not authority acting on their behalf. The mere existence of a parliament means the absence of the people, but true democracy exists only through the participation of the people, not through the activity of their representatives.[113]

According to one scholar, Algeria's political class, unlike that in Tunisia, was not focused on constitutional issues. The 1996 constitution was a step in the right direction, but the national assembly remained weak with "very limited prerogatives" which allowed governments to be unaccountable to parliament.[114] In Sudan, one massive 500-page memoir by a presidential candidate in the 2010 elections describes in detail the four elections held in the country since its independence in 1956, under so-called multi-party systems, while ignoring the six elections that took place under the military regime between 1963 and 1982. To underscore the fragmentation of the system, sixty-six parties competed in the 2010 elections, making it almost impossible for voters to truly understand each one's political platforms, and many of them were small and frankly irrelevant. The author underlines the corruption that prevailed: buying votes by representatives of the ruling party, Hizb al-Mu'tamar al-Watani (National Conference Party) which paid 5,000 Sudanese Pounds (roughly $800) to each voter who would swear to vote for the party.[115] In other words,

---

[112] Joshua Stacher, "Conditioned Participation: The Mubarak State and Egypt's Muslim Brothers," in Jebnoun et al. (eds.), *Modern Middle East Authoritarianism*, p. 184.

[113] Al-Qaddafi, *The Green Book*, p. 7.

[114] Hugh Roberts, *The Battlefield Algeria 1988–2002: Studies in a Broken Polity* (New York: Verso, 2003), p. 209.

[115] Hatim al-Sirr Sakinjo, *al-Sudan: ra'is ma'a iqaf al-tanfidh: tajribati ma'a intikhabat 2010* [Sudan: president with no implementation: my experience

elections in Sudan and the ruling party's victories were analogous to those in the other republics discussed above. Another observer commented that "the multiple cleavages in Sudanese society preclude the establishment of a stable democracy and ensure that any political system will be fragile."[116] The NDP in Egypt perfected the system of distributing "gifts" on election days, but, as one young Egyptian writes in utter astonishment, representatives were around poll stations in the first free elections after the uprising engaged in distributing cash for purchasing votes in the same manner as before the revolution.[117]

It is evident that elections and parliaments were simply tools for the ruling parties and the regimes to justify ruling their countries. Thus, it is important to examine how the governance of these states functioned, and what those who participated thought and wrote about it.

Governance

The authoritarian republics developed a large management apparatus, and at the apex of the hierarchical pyramid was a small number of trusted and loyal individuals on whom the leadership relied. In some cases, the leaders did not want even their ruling party to become too dominant and therefore competitive with the center of power. Springborg believes that Mubarak did not push the NDP forward because of his fear that "it will develop a will of its own or serve as a platform on which talented, aspiring political leaders could demonstrate their abilities."[118] Hence the reliance on this bureaucratic apparatus, which rewarded loyalty and was relatively easier to control and manipulate than other arms of the state. The Tunisian politician Mzali discussed the criteria for choosing his staff. While ostensibly

with the 2010 elections] (Cairo: al-Ward Library, 2011), p. 185. Hatim al-Sirr literally can be translated as "the Judge/Protector of the Secret," a title given to this candidate by his party, al-Hizb al-Ittihadi al-Watani (Democratic Unionist Party).

116 Ann M. Lesch, "Democratization in a Fragmented Society: Sudan," in Korany et al. (eds.), *Political Liberalization and Democratization in the Arab World*, vol. II, p. 203.

117 Mirette Baghat, "Memoirs of an Egyptian Citizen," in Nasser Weddady and Sohrab Ahmari (eds.), *Arab Spring Dreams: The Next Generation Speaks Out for Freedom and Justice from North Africa to Iran* (New York: Palgrave Macmillan, 2012), pp. 53–57.

118 Springborg, *Mubarak's Egypt*, p. 155.

focusing on creativity and integrity, he reiterated: "I would like to give full attention to a noble quality that goes beyond simple devotion, and is one of the dearest and most powerful spiritual qualities, and that is loyalty."[119] Indeed, loyalty is the most essential factor for being close to the leadership, and in many places, such as Iraq, loyalty was far more critical than tribal affiliation or even family connections. Another senior Tunisian politician describes how loyalties were defined: *La lil-wila'at illa li-Bourguiba* (No allegiance but to Bourguiba).[120] In other words, allegiance and devotion to a president and his authority were above everything else. Under Ben 'Ali, the state bureaucracy in Tunisia preserved three features developed by the Bourguibian regime: centralization; strong and overlapping ties with the RCD; and a leading role in public life.[121]

To better understand how those on the inside saw matters, it is worthwhile perusing some memoirs that assess their authors' role in government and recount their relationship with the country's leaders. In Egypt, ministers were appointed according to the wishes of the president.[122] 'Abd al-Wahhab al-Burlusi explains how Nasser, during a meeting of the Arab Socialist Union, called him and offered him the post of minister of health. After he accepted, the Ministry of Higher Education became vacant, and without consulting al-Burlusi, another presidential decision rescinded the original offer of minister of health so that he could become minister of higher education. For both appointments very little deliberation took place, not least with the prospective candidate.[123] Another senior Egyptian politician, Khalid Muhyi al-Din, who occupied many important roles after the 1952 Revolution that toppled the monarchy, bemoans the fact that it had already become clear in 1953, first with Muhammad Neguib, the senior general who led the revolution, and then with Nasser, who dislodged Neguib and kept him under house arrest, that both men were intent on creating a small committee, later called Majlis Qiyadat al-Thawra

[119] Mzali, *Hadith al-fi'l*, p. 347.
[120] Al-Ka'bi, *Mudakhalat 'udu bil-Lajna al-Markaziyya*, p. 39.
[121] Erdle, *Ben Ali's "New Tunisia"*, pp. 149–50.
[122] An interesting analysis with many examples of the different ministries in Egypt can be found in Springborg, *Mubarak's Egypt*, chapter 5: The System of Political Control, pp. 134–81.
[123] Al-Burlusi, *Kuntu waziran ma'a 'Abd al-Nasser*, pp. 72, 78.

(Revolutionary Command Council), that would concentrate power in its hands. Muhyi al-Din also blames the Muslim Brothers for petitioning against a parliamentary system and allowing political parties to operate freely.[124] He recounts the inner conflicts within the Egyptian leadership in the early 1950s, and how Nasser, after displacing Neguib, continually reiterated to his senior colleagues the two choices available to them: "Either absolute democracy, or a policy of discipline and revolution. Either utter freedom and giving up our role, or allowing the Revolutionary Council to resolutely exercise all its powers."[125] Reading Muhyi al-Din's memoirs leaves us with no doubt that Nasser was intent on becoming authoritarian in his governance, and that he laid the foundations for repression and denying civil liberties (see Chapter 4).

Al-Burlusi, however, judges Nasser otherwise; in his two years as a minister in the mid 1960s, he believed that Nasser was a good listener and open to other ministers' ideas and suggestions. "Nasser was not a dictator as some people think. He was polite, strict, clear and honest. He understood what was discussed and then made his decisions. Sometimes he would revise his thinking and explain his ideas." The problem, in al-Burlusi's opinion, was that other ministers always consented to his views, thus creating an atmosphere of dictatorship.[126] Tharwat 'Ukasha has a totally different view of Nasser: during the cabinet meetings, Nasser would ask for ideas and suggestions on how to improve matters, but 'Ukasha felt that in reality there were no deep debates about the crux of issues. He also describes the conflicts within the government apparatus, which began expanding during this period and created an overlap of responsibilities.[127] As minister of culture and information, he strongly believed that these two ministries should be split and that there is a central distinction between information and culture. In spite of his efforts and a number of conversations with

---

[124] Khalid Muhyi al-Din, *Wa al-'an atakallam* [Now I speak] (Cairo: Ahram Center for Translations and Publications, 1992), pp. 212–13. Muhyi al-Din was a member of the Revolutionary Command Council and later became head of the leftist Nasserist faction.

[125] Ibid., p. 302.

[126] Fathi Radwan, *Fathi Radwan yarwi li-Dhia' al-Din Bibars asrar hukumat Yuliyu* [Fathi Radwan recounts to Dhia' al-Din Bibars the secrets of the July government] (Cairo: al-Ma'rifa Publishing, 1976), pp. 225–26.

[127] Tharwat 'Ukasha, *Mudhakkirati fi al-siyasa wa al-thaqafa* [My memoirs in politics and culture], vol. II (Cairo: al-Hilal Publishing House, 1990), p. 132.

Nasser, 'Ukasha reached the conclusion that the differences between the two men were wide, and he tendered his resignation. While in London for medical treatment, he found out that two senior assistants in his ministry had been arrested. Furious, he returned to Cairo to learn that the reason for the discontent with him and his senior staff was the accusation that these two men were passing on jokes about Nasser to his brother, who lived in London.[128]

Needless to say, the faults in governing the country did not lie with just one man, and the ministers definitely carry some culpability for failure. In a sardonic portrayal of ministers in Egypt, a book about 'Amru Musa informs us:

The ministerial job in Egypt carries expansive influence in all the corridors of power within the state. It is a golden key to enrich one's self, and to utterly enjoy the honor and popularity [of the position]. Protocol dictates that a minister must be extremely elegant and stylish, beginning with his shoes all the way to the chair he sits on. The uniform of his secretary, the ministry building, the make of the car driven by his chauffeur [all are important].[129]

Discussing 'Amru Musa's career, the book highlights an intriguing point about those in senior positions in the Foreign Ministry, claiming that since the end of the 1970s "the secret code in the Egyptian diplomacy is that Israel managed with dexterity and canniness to topple many of the most gifted men in Egyptian politics," including three foreign ministers: Muhammad Ibrahim Kamil, Butrus Butrus Ghali, and 'Amru Musa, because of their opposition at one point or another to close ties with Israel, or for what the Israelis characterized as their intransigence during the negotiations between the two sides.[130]

Egyptian ministers were mostly drawn from a relatively small circle of well-educated men and women, retired senior military and police officers, and numerous people who spent their lives in the government bureaucracy or in running governorates. These men and women were, throughout their careers, mostly connected to the top echelons of the regime. In a fascinating and very pro-regime book, that could even be

[128] Ibid., pp. 139–40.
[129] Shihab Nasir, *'Amru Musa: al-malaffat al-sirriyya* ['Amru Musa: the secret files] (Cairo: Center for Arabic Civilization, 2001). Musa was a foreign minister in Egypt from 1991, secretary of the Arab League for the next ten years, and a presidential candidate in the 2011 elections that were won by Muhammad Morsi from the Muslim Brotherhood.
[130] Ibid., pp. 26–27.

seen simply as propaganda, a journalist interviews and details the lives and careers of thirty-three men and two women working close to President Mubarak. Only one out of this group was appointed from the outside, a scientist who spent her life in research and science, while the rest were from the inner circle and spent their careers climbing the ladder to get near the president.[131] Interestingly, the journalist was told by Dr. Venice Kamil Jawdat, who was appointed as minister for scientific research, that she never joined any political party, but she quickly added that the "NDP is the most moderate party; it is a respectable party with fine ideas attempting to develop Egypt forward, and if I was offered a party to join, I would choose the National Democratic Party."[132] Many observers have rightly concluded that the formal structure of the government and the state did not change to any great extent during the almost six decades following the 1952 Revolution.[133]

Running the two vital organs of the state in these regimes, the military and the security forces (see the next two chapters) was critical, but suffice to say here that in countries such as Egypt, the management of the Ministry of War, throughout its numerous military conflicts (in Yemen, and against Israel) was nothing short of cataclysmic. One startling example is the decision making during the period preceding the Six-Day War in June 1967, when Shams Badran was minister of war. Badran, one of the Free Officers who participated in the 1952 Revolution, was later tried for his incompetence in preparing the armed forces for the 1967 War. The problem was not just inefficient management; corruption, nepotism, and lack of real interest in the burning issues all contributed to the calamity that shook the country after a few days of war.[134]

A few words are in order about governance in Libya, given its fundamental differences from other authoritarian regimes: In the mid 1970s, Qaddafi's philosophy, as expressed in the *Green Book*, was

[131] Nura Rashid, *Rijal hawla al-rai's: hiwar ma'a shakhsiyyat hamma* [Men around the president: dialogue with important personalities], vol. I (Cairo: Egyptian Institution for the Book, 1997). Another minister who was relatively outside the circle is Faruq Husni, who was appointed minister of culture. Prior to his appointment, he spent most of his career in the art world, except for a short stint as head of the technical bureau in the Ministry of Culture and later the head of the Egyptian Academy for Art in Rome. See pp. 111–25.

[132] Ibid., p. 267.   [133] See, for example, Kassem, *Egyptian Politics*, p. 43.

[134] Husni, *Shams Badran: al-rajul alladhi hakama Misr.*

based on the creation of a *jamahiriyya* (state of the masses) to replace the "normal" state in other countries. As a result, revolutionary committees were formed to supervise the running of this new state; they were charged with enforcing Qaddafi's ideology and to "circumvent the hierarchy of decision-making processes of almost all state institutions (with the exception of the oil sector and the armed forces)."[135] As Roger Owen points out, a large bureaucracy with an expanding army and security forces continued to operate in this new system, where the people were supposed to rule and not the state.[136]

Conclusion

The function of the ruling party in the Arab republics, whether in single-party or multi-party systems, was to ensure the durability of these authoritarian regimes. When elections took place in countries such as Egypt and Tunisia, history showed that these hegemonic parties managed to control the elections and to assure their own dominance. Opposition parties in these countries were weak and fragmented, but accepted the system of parliament, and of "managed" elections, because, as Jennifer Gandhi put it:

For the potential opposition, assemblies and parties provide an institutionalized channel through which they can affect decision-making even if in limited policy realms. For incumbents, these institutions are a way in which opposition demands can be contained and answered without appearing weak.[137]

Indeed, as Magaloni showed in the case of Mexico, elections can be used by these regimes as a way "to regularize payments to their supporters and implement punishment to their enemies, among both the elite and the masses, so as to induce them to remain loyal to the regime and to have a vested interest in its survival."[138] Unfortunately, the masses in these republics not only accepted this structure, but also

---

[135] Hanspeter Mattes, "Formal and Informal Authority in Libya since 1969," in Dirk Vandewalle (ed.), *Libya Since 1969: Qaddafi's Revolution Revisited* (New York: Palgrave Macmillan, 2008), p. 67. For a more detailed historical analysis of the *Green Book* and the revolution, see Dirk Vandewalle, *A History of Modern Libya* (New York: Cambridge University Press, 2006).

[136] Owen, *State, Power and Politics*, p. 55.

[137] Gandhi, *Political Institutions under Dictatorship*, p. xviii.

[138] Magaloni, *Voting for Autocracy*, p. 19.

had to play a role in sustaining it. A good example was Algeria, where the tentacles of the FLN helped to secure for 'Abd al-'Aziz Bouteflika, the incumbent president, about 85 percent and 90 percent of the votes in the 2004 and 2009 elections respectively. It is impossible to conclude how much of this high percentage is due to election fraud or to large mobilization of the population.

In the single-party systems such as Syria and Iraq, cooptation through the Ba'th Party was essential for their durability, and they did not need or care to show the world that they had an electoral system. Democracy and freedom, in their philosophy, were to be exercised as members of the Ba'th, and the party was open to all.

It has been shown here that the common denominators among the ruling parties, whether in single- or multi-party systems, are numerous. For example, the structure of centralization, not only of the party, but also of the governance mechanism, was common to all. The overlapping of the ruling party with the other arms of the state, particularly the security services, was robust in many of these countries. For the leadership, the challenge was, in David Art's words, that "Dictators must craft coercive institutions that can deal with threats without undermining support for the regime. They must also not allow these institutions to become alternative power centers."[139] And that is exactly what happened in these republics for more than three decades: their leaders managed to create a centralized and overlapping system that allowed institutions such as the ruling party to thrive and expand, but not to an extent that could threaten them. They did the same with another institution, the military, as shown in the next chapter.

---

[139] David Art, "What do We Know about Authoritarianism after Ten Years?" Review article, *Comparative Politics*, vol. 44, no. 3 (April 2012), p. 362.

3 | The military

The military has played a key role in the history of the Arab republics since their independence from Britain and France, and no institution impacted the history of the region more than the army. The armies were the pride of these republics, regarded as one of their most important institutions, and valued for their inclusiveness in opening their doors to young educated men without too much prejudice about their socio-economic status. Historically, the structure of the armies was modeled on that of their European colonizers who helped to establish them.

The first part of this chapter will look at the military and politics; the second part, at military conflicts and their economic impact; the third section will focus on how the armies themselves were both feared and watched; and the fourth part will examine the lives of soldiers and officers. As in other chapters, the availability of memoirs has largely dictated the discussion, and once again there is a preponderance of Egyptian memoirs over those from other republics.

Military and politics

The role of the military in the Middle East has been discussed at length both before and after the Arab uprisings of 2011.[1] The purpose here, in

---

[1] The luxury of being able to focus on these memoirs has been made possible by the multiple scholarly studies of the army in the Arab world. Among those: Owen, *State, Power and Politics*; Barry Rubin and Thomas A. Keaney (eds.), *Armed Forces in the Middle East: Politics and Strategy* (London: Frank Cass, 2002); Stephanie Cronin, *Armies and State-Building in the Modern Middle East: Politics, Nationalism, and Military Reform* (New York: I. B. Tauris, 2014); Eliezer Beeri, *Army Officers in Arab Politics and Society*, translated by Dov Ben-Abba (New York: Praeger, 1979). For a general discussion of the topic, see Eric A. Nordlinger, *Soldiers in Politics: Military Coups and Governments* (Englewood Cliffs, NJ: Prentice Hall, 1977). Vast studies on the different aspects of the role of the army in specific countries of the region have also been published, some of which will be referred to in the discussion about specific republics.

essence, is to examine the role of the military through the prism of the actors themselves, and to understand civil–military relations as perceived by officers, politicians, and local observers.

After gaining independence from their British and French colonizers, four countries became monarchies (Egypt, Iraq, Libya, and Yemen), while the other four declared their independence as republics (Algeria, Sudan, Syria, and Tunisia). The tumultuous period from the 1950s to the end of the 1960s witnessed the demise of the monarchies, as well as multiple coups d'état in the republics. The new leaders of the eight republics were all military men, except for Tunisia (see Table 3.1), and "the armed forces were highly politicized and rulers generally failed to control them."[2] In the 1980s, the regimes learned the art of coup-proofing by creating structures that would minimize the possibility of a takeover by a small group of officers and prevent coups d'état.[3] The military experience of their presidents, who rose to their positions due to the army's dominance, enhanced these regimes. The only exception was Saddam Hussein in Iraq; not only was he not a former soldier (he was rejected by the Military College), but as a party man he was suspicious of army officers and regarded them as a "family" that needed to be penetrated and controlled.[4]

In each republic, the period immediately after independence was characterized by a focus on military recruiting, training, and purchasing weapons. This led to a different kind of dependency on the previous colonizers, and the issue of armaments and military industries continues to play a significant part in the economies and politics of the state. Initially, army generals strove to build a cohesive, apolitical, modernizing, and dependable force. Some argued that the original army leaders were not properly trained for their mission, and the legacy left behind by Britain and France only complicated their undertaking.[5] As Muhammad Hadid, who held many senior positions in Iraq, recounts

---

[2] Barry Rubin, "The Military in Contemporary Arab Politics," in Rubin and Keaney (eds.), *Armed Forces in the Middle East*, p. 1.

[3] James T. Quinlivan, "Coup-proofing: Its Practice and Consequences in the Middle East," *International Security*, vol. 24, no. 2 (Fall 1999), pp. 131–65.

[4] Amatzia Baram, "Saddam Husayn, the Ba'th Regime and the Iraqi Officers Corps," in Rubin and Keaney (eds.), *Armed Forces in the Middle East*, p. 207.

[5] See, for example, the memoirs of Muhammad Suhail al-'Ashi, *Fajr al-istiqlal fi Suriya: mun'ataf khatir fi tarikhihi: khawatir wa dhikrayat* [Dawn of independence in Syria: a dangerous detour in its history: reflections and memoirs] (Beirut: Dar al-Nafa'is, 1999), p. 78.

Table 3.1 Arab leaders with military and non-military backgrounds (1952–2015)
Leaders who came to power after the Arab uprisings of 2011 are shown in italics

Country	No. of leaders	No. from military	Leaders with military backgrounds	Years	Leaders without military backgrounds	Years
Algeria	5	5	Ahmed Ben Bella	1963–65	None	
			Houari Boumediene	1965–76		
			Chadhli Bendjedid	1979–92		
			Liamine Zeroual	1994–99		
			'Abd al-'Aziz Bouteflika	1999–present		
Egypt	6	5	Muhammad Neguib	1952–53	*Muhammad Morsi*	2012–13
			Gamal 'Abd al-Nasser	1954–70		
			Anwar al-Sadat	1970–81		
			Hosni Mubarak	1981–2011		
			'Abd al-Fattah al-Sisi	*2013–present*		
Iraq	7	4	'Abd al-Karim Qasim	1958–63	Saddam Hussein	1979–2003
			'Abd al-Salam 'Arif	1963–66	Nuri al-Maliki	2006–14
			'Abd al-Rahman 'Arif	1966–68	*Haidar al-'Abadi*	*2014–present*
			Ahmad Hasan al-Bakr	1968–79		
Libya	1	1	Mu'ammar al-Qaddafi	1969–2011	None	

Table 3.1 (*cont.*)

Country	No. of leaders	No. from military	Leaders with military backgrounds	Years	Leaders without military backgrounds	Years
Sudan	7	5	Ibrahim ʿAbboud	1958–64	Ismaʿil al-Azhari	1964–69
			Sirr al-Khatim al-Khalifa	1964–65	Ahmed al-Mirghani	1968–89
			Jaʿfar Numayri	1969–85		
			ʿAbd al-Rahman al-Dahab	1985–86		
			ʿOmar al-Bashir	1989–present		
Syria	10	5	Adib Shishakli	1949–54	Hashim al-Atasi	1954–55
			[Gamal ʿAbd al-Nasser][1]	1958–61	Shuhri al-Quwwatli	1955–58
					Nazim al-Kudsi	1961–63
			Luʾay al-Atasi	1963	Nur al-Din al-Atasi	1966–70
			Amin al-Hafiz	1963–66	Ahmad al-Khatib	1970–71
			Hafiz al-Asad	1971–2000		
			Bashar al-Asad	2000–present		
Tunisia	6	1	Zine al-ʿAbidine Ben ʿAli	1987–2011	Habib Bourguiba	1957–87
					Muhammad Ghannouchi	*January 2011*
					Fuʾad al-Mubazzaʿ	*Jan–Dec 2011*
					Muhammad Munsif al-Marzouqi	*Dec 2011–14*
					Béji Caïd Essebsi	*2015–present*

Yemen	7	6	'Abdullah al-Sallal	1962–67	'Abd al-Rahman	1962–67
			Ibrahim al-Hamdi	1974–77	al-Iryani	
			Ahmad al-Ghashmi	1977–78		
			'Abd al-Karim al-'Arashi	1978		
			'Ali 'Abdullah Salih	1978–2012		
			'Abd Rabbuh Hadi	*2012–present*		

---

[1] Gamal 'Abd al-Nasser was the president of both Egypt and Syria during the Union.

in his memoirs, coups d'état and attempts to control the officers plagued these nascent republics; in Iraq, four years after its independence in 1932, army officers attempted to dislodge the government by force.[6] The epidemic of coups and uncertainty also prevailed in Syria and, as one memoir depicts, these coups fundamentally unsettled the country and convinced all parties that power and authority could not be achieved without the army.[7]

However, military control over the political system was not just an Arab phenomenon. Most developing countries suffered from the same problem, and had to deal with the capacities of the military in nation building.[8] President Nasser described this conflict in his *Philosophy of the Revolution* and explained why the military – or, as he called it, the "vanguard of the nation" – had to stay in power:

> The mission of the vanguard had not ended. In fact it was just beginning at that very hour [after the revolution]. We needed discipline but found chaos behind our lines. We needed unity but found dissension. We needed action but found nothing but surrender and idleness.[9]

In other words, there was no civilian alternative to take over because, in Nasser's view, "the men of experience" could not provide any counsel. As one observer highlighted, there was a fundamental contradiction in Nasser's philosophy; on one hand he believed that the army should be neutral and not involved in politics, but on the other hand he reiterated that "Throughout my life I have had faith in militarism."[10] Indeed, for a number of years, power in Egypt remained in the hands of the Revolutionary Council, which consisted mostly of officers, and they

---

[6] Muhammad Hadid, *Mudhakkirati: al-sira' min ajl al-dimuqratiyya fi al-'Iraq* [My memoirs: the struggle for democracy in Iraq] (Beirut: al-Saqi, 2006), pp. 151–78.

[7] Amin Abu 'Assaf, *Dhikrayati* [My memoirs] (Damascus: n.p., 1996), pp. 228–56. Abu 'Assaf was a brigadier-general in the Syrian army and played a role in opposing some of the coups that took place in the 1940s and 1950s.

[8] See, for example, Alfred Stepan, *The Military in Politics: Changing Patterns in Brazil* (Princeton: Princeton University Press, 1971).

[9] Gamal 'Abd al-Nasser, *The Philosophy of the Revolution* (Cairo: n.p., 1959), pp. 32–33.

[10] An informative and comprehensive discussion of army intervention and civil–military relations can be found in Majdi Hammad, *al-'Askariyyun al-'Arab wa qadiyyat al-wahda* [The Arab military and the case of unity] (Beirut: Center for Arab Unity Studies, 1987), pp. 161–82.

were without doubt the locus of decision making.[11] The regimes in countries such as Egypt and Algeria were not outright military dictatorships along the lines of the military junta in South America. They were more like "military-dominated states," where the officers and their civilian allies created "political systems that have benefited themselves at the expense of the rest of society."[12]

For decades, the issue of separation between the army and politics dominated thinking and writing in the Arab world. In Algeria, between 1962 and 1989, the country was ruled by the party (FLN), the army, and the bureaucracy. After 1989, the control of the military became predominant.[13] In fact, the Algerian army did not remain outside politics, as it felt the need to defend the nation from "Islamist threats." No leader in Algeria had the same paramount influence as Nasser or Asad, and an inner cabal of military men met and decided who would be the president. Khalid Nezzar, who became minister of defense in mid 1990, and therefore in charge of fighting Islamists, explained how the clique reached a decision:

When a presidency came to an end, it was imperative not to leave the president's seat empty, and unfortunately the exceptional circumstances of the country did not allow for elections. The name of 'Abd al-'Aziz Bouteflika was suggested, and after we, at the highest echelons of the military, discussed it at length, we came to the conclusion, that in spite of some hurdles, this man could fulfill the mission. We were told that he was clever and wise to the extent that would allow him to harvest what we planted. The motto "Algeria Before Anything" convinced those hesitating that whatever his [Bouteflika's] mistakes and deficiencies were in the past, he was the most suitable [candidate] given that danger was on the horizon.[14]

---

[11] For an interesting analysis of the structure of power, see Ahmad Bili, *al-Safwa al-'askariyya wa al-bina' al-siyasi fi Misr* [The military elites and the political structure in Egypt] (Cairo: General Egyptian Organization for the Book, 1993), pp. 319–27; Nasser, *The Philosophy of the Revolution*, p. 30.

[12] Steven A. Cook, *Ruling but not Governing: The Military and Political Development in Egypt, Algeria, and Turkey* (Baltimore: Johns Hopkins University Press, 2007), p. 15.

[13] For the role of the army in Algeria, see Martin Stone, *The Agony of Algeria* (New York: Columbia University Press, 1997), pp. 129–38; Werenfels, "Algeria." For a discussion of how the Algerians perceived this point, see Saydawi, *Sira'at al-nukhab al-siyasiyya wa al-'askariyya fi al-Jazai'r*, pp. 52–62.

[14] Khalid Nezzar, *Bouteflika: al-rajul wa al-hasila* [Bouteflika: the man and the outcome] (Algiers: APIC, 2003), p. 19.

In fact, as Willis demonstrates, the appointment of Nezzar as defense minister was in itself significant, as it heralded the return of the Algerian army to the forefront of politics.[15] Similar circumstances prevailed in Syria in the 1960s; when politicians made an alliance with senior officers, it backfired, and the military controlled the regime and important wings of the Ba'th Party until the rise of Hafiz al-Asad in 1971, who managed later to assert control over the army.[16]

Whether in Egypt, Syria, or Iraq, the leaders effectively subordinated the army and coup-proofed their regimes, as discussed below. But that did not mean a smooth interaction between the army and the leaders. As one senior Sudanese general explained, the name of the Sudanese armed forces was exploited by the leadership to fulfill its political aims, and if officers did not want to go along with this, they found themselves in prison or were executed. While the Sudanese general admits that all coups d'état in Sudan were engineered by the military, he claims that the army overthrew existing governments on the orders of political parties.[17] In Egypt, as in other republics, clashes between leaders and the army surfaced from time to time. General Sa'ad al-Shadhli, chief of staff between 1971 and 1973, clashed with Sadat and his minister of war, Ahmed Sadiq, over policy toward the Soviet Union, and as a result of this and numerous other disputes, Shadhli was forced out of the army.[18]

Equally, Muhammad Haykal describes how in early 1972 Sadat was unhappy with his minister of war. Ahmed Sadiq had not been his first choice, but when news reached him that the general he was planning to appoint, Muhammad Fawzi, had met with other generals and expressed his discontent with the rapprochement between Sadat and the USA, Sadat changed his mind over the appointment.[19] Intriguingly, Fawzi himself had no confidence in one of his predecessors, Shams

[15] Willis, *Politics and Power in the Maghreb*, p. 101.

[16] Munif al-Razzaz, *al-'Amal al-fikriyya wa al-siyasiyya* [Intellectual and political works], 3 vols. (Beirut: Dar al-Mutawassit, 1985). Razzaz's work is a case study in civilian–military relations in Syria during that period.

[17] 'Abd al-Rahman al-Khujli, *al-Jaysh wa al-siyasa* [The army and politics] (Omdurman: Mirghani Cultural Center, 2012), pp. 14–15.

[18] Mahmud Fawzi, *al-Fariq al-Shadhili: asrar al-sidam ma'a al-Sadat* [Lieutenant-General al-Shadhili: the secrets of clashes with Sadat] (Cairo: al-Watan Publishing, 1993).

[19] Muhammad Hasanayn Haykal, *Uktubir 73: al-silah wa al-siyasa* [October 1973: arms and politics] (Cairo: al-Ahram Institute, 1993), pp. 244–45.

Badran, who was minister of war during the June 1967 War. In his memoirs (written in the form of questions and answers) Fawzi argues that Badran's appointment by Nasser and 'Amr was a mistake, as they put trust and loyalty before experience and knowledge. According to Fawzi, Badran was totally under the influence of 'Amr and served him loyally, and his rise to the senior position was only due to Badran's position running 'Amr's office.[20] Numerous memoirs have been written about the relationship between Nasser and 'Amr and the role of Badran in the defeat of the June 1967 War; many of these analyzed and attempted to understand the bizarre relationship that existed between the Egyptian president and his chief of staff and close friend; a relationship that ended dismally at the close of the war when its management became clear. Fawzi is correct that many of the appointments had little to do with experience or talent, a common problem in authoritarian regimes where loyalty was the most precious commodity. For instance, Nasser promoted 'Amr four times between 1954 and 1958 to the highest rank of marshal without his having been in one battle. Similarly, after coming to power, Asad appointed his friend Naji Jamil to be head of the air force from 1970 to 1978, although Jamil did not even go through a pilots' course.[21] One memoir of an Iraqi senior general tells how military promotions under Saddam Hussein were based on loyalty and sycophancy toward the leader, and argued that many of these military men were poorly educated and had limited capabilities.[22]

Yet it was natural for the leaders of these new republics to turn to their military colleagues to occupy the top positions: in Libya, twelve men appointed to the Revolutionary Command Council all belonged to the armed forces.[23] In Egypt, among the political elite, a large section had a military background: during Nasser's era about 38 percent of the ministers were from the military, and in 1966, about 72 percent of

---

[20] Imam, *al-Fariq Muhammad Fawzi*, pp. 67–69.

[21] Shakir al-Nabulsi, *Su'ud al-mujtami' al-'askari al-'Arabi fi Misr wa al-Sham, 1948–2000* [The rise of the Arab military society in Egypt and Syria, 1948–2000] (Beirut: Arab Institute for Research and Publishing, 2003), pp. 152–53.

[22] Wafiq al-Samarra'i, *Hutam al-bawwaba al-sharqiyya* [Ruins of the eastern gate] (Kuwait: al-Qabas Publishing, 1997), p. 394. Brigadier-General al-Samarra'i served as head of military intelligence, but was later dismissed and exiled by the Iraqi leader.

[23] Mansour O. el-Kikhia, *Libya's Qaddafi: The Politics of Contradiction* (Gainesville: University Press of Florida, 1997), p. 39.

senior officials in the Egyptian Ministry of Foreign Affairs were ex-officers, and most of the ambassadors in Europe were retired military.[24] Under Sadat, between 1971 and until 1974, 17 percent of appointed ministers came from the military, and only after the *infitah* (economic liberalization) of 1974 did the percentage of those with military backgrounds drop to 8 percent (those with an academic or engineering education had the highest percentage, as Sadat put the emphasis on hiring ministers with technical expertise).[25] This was in contrast to Tunisia where essentially from the 1990s the percentage of ministers or ambassadors who were ex-military was minute, and in the decade 2001–10 there were none, given Bourguiba's policy of pushing the army out of politics.[26]

However, appointing military men who were close to the leadership to run the army as well as to fill other government posts did not mean fewer recriminations when failures were exposed. In fact, serious disasters such as the defeat of Egypt and Syria in the 1967 War led to a torrent of accusations and recriminations between the military and the leadership, each side attempting to show that they had acted correctly. But even when the results were not as calamitous, the leadership was swift to pass the blame to the military to protect its own position. As an illustration, a very senior Egyptian navy officer recounts in his memoirs how naval chiefs were ousted when there was a successful operation by the Israelis during the so-called War of Attrition that followed the June 1967 War and lasted almost until 1973.[27] Similarly, Saddam Hussein dismissed his generals whenever the Iranians made substantial gains during the Iran–Iraq War, which lasted eight years, from 1980 to 1988. His generals, on the other hand, felt that Saddam Hussein lacked the military education to understand strategy, and therefore made

---

[24] Husni, *Shams Badran: al-rajul alladhi hakama Misr*, p. 24.

[25] Bili, *al-Safwa al-'askariyya*, p. 364.

[26] Hicham Bou Nassif, "A Military Besieged: The Armed Forces, the Police, and the Party in Bin 'Ali's Tunisia, 1987–2011," *International Journal of Middle East Studies*, vol. 47, no. 1 (February 2015), tables 9 and 10, pp. 78–80.

[27] Muhammad 'Abd al-Rahman Ra'fat, *Dhikrayat dabit bahri* [Memories of a navy officer] (Cairo: Egyptian Organization for the Book, 2003), p. 65. The heads of the navy were dismissed after Israel landed a small force on an island at the end of 1969. The memoir covers the history of operations of the Egyptian navy from 1950 to 1980. Ra'fat was a major-general in the navy and served in all his country's wars during that period.

erroneous strategic decisions.[28] Coming from the same background or serving together as military cadets allowed these men to know each other well, but this sometimes backfired, because each side knew the strengths and weaknesses of the other. In Egypt, Nasser and Sadat managed to tame the politicized officers, but the rise of 'Abd al-Halim Abu Ghazala constituted a new threat. The relationship between Mubarak and Abu Ghazala was typical: both attended the Military College in 1949, and they became close friends. Abu Ghazala climbed the ladder and reached the top posts of chief of staff and later minister of defense, but the relationship between the two men was often strained, and by 1993 Abu Ghazala was forced to retire. Springborg compares their relationship to the one between Nasser and 'Amr – admiration and closeness, combined with exasperation and suspicion.[29] Kandil argues that Abu Ghazala was more popular with the masses than 'Amr, and "whether out of sincerity or cunning, he took the shortest and most effective route: religion."[30]

Dealing with the military varied among the republics depending on their ideology. Iraq and Syria were different in that they strove to build *jaysh 'aqa'idi* (ideological army). The Iraqi Ba'th Party documents clearly exhibit the indoctrination that took place throughout all military ranks immediately after the party took over power in July 1968. A system of "political commissars," much like that in the Soviet Union, was created under the title *al-makatib al-'askariyya* (the military bureaus), staffed mainly by party cadre to emphasize the party ideology and keep an eye on officers and soldiers who were perceived to be not fully committed to it. By the end of the 1980s, military education focused more on the Ba'th ideology, and the writings of Saddam Hussein became part and parcel of the curricula.[31] In a very similar fashion in Syria, Mustafa Talas, who was minister of defense for more than three decades, wrote explicitly about the ideological army:

---

[28] Al-Hamdani, *Qabla an yughadiruna al-tarikh*, p. 244.
[29] Springborg, *Mubarak's Egypt*, pp. 98–104. Springborg describes in detail the ups and downs of this relationship. Unfortunately, a biography of Abu Ghazala (see Chapter 1), blotted out these skirmishes: Fikri, *al-Mushir Muhammad 'Abd al-Halim Ghazala*.
[30] Kandil, *Soldiers, Spies, and Statesmen*, p. 177.
[31] For details of the indoctrination and penetration of the army, see Sassoon, *Saddam Hussein's Ba'th Party*, pp. 130–37.

The structure of the Syrian army is based on having a large segment of the working class that the previous bourgeois regimes attempted to turn into a professional army, endorsing the motto of "army out of politics," but the army was responding to the aspirations of the people and participating in the revolutionary work.[32]

As a result, the Syrian Ba'th Party decided to annul the principle of distancing the army from politics and to introduce "the ideological army, which would be not only an army for war but also for development."[33] Even in regimes not based on a single ideology, such as Egypt, "political training" became part of the curriculum at the War College after the 1952 Revolution. General Fawzi, who was in charge of the college and later became a chief of staff, contends that:

When I took over this job, I took upon myself developing what I termed as national and political awareness, stemming from the logic that the target of fighting by the armed forces is after all a political one, and whoever will be sacrificing himself for the nation has to understand the politics and be convinced by it.[34]

Tunisia, on the other hand, went in the opposite direction from the two ideological states, Iraq and Syria. As early as 1965, President Bourguiba announced that "members of the military are not free to have political opinions like ordinary citizens."[35] Their mission, he added, because of the power given to them by the state, was simply to rebut any aggression or threat to the country. In Libya, Qaddafi managed to control the army by using the popular committees, and members of local tribes, particularly his own tribe Qadhadhfa, were also given significant positions.[36] Over the years the once-powerful Libyan military not only lost its personnel and armaments, but also became more fragmented. "This progressively led to a complete transformation of the Military Forces into a Law

---

[32] Mustafa Talas, *Tarikh al-jaysh al-'Arabi al-Suri* [History of the Arab Syrian army], vol. II: *1949–70* (Damascus: Markaz al-Dirasat al-'Askariyya, 2002), p. 312. This was part of a three-volume history of the Syrian army. The first volume covered the period 1901–48, the second 1949–70, and the third 1970–2001.

[33] Ibid.   [34] Imam, *al-Fariq Muhammad Fawzi*, p. 17.

[35] Quoted in an article by Ridha Kéfi, "Les Habits neufs de l'armée" [The new clothes of the army], *Jeune Afrique*, July 13–20, 1999, pp. 24–26.

[36] For details of tribe affiliation and those in power, see Mattes, "Formal and Informal Authority in Libya," pp. 70–76.

Enforcement apparatus, which was primarily aimed to preserve Qaddafi and his opposed regime from every potential subversion of power."[37] Qaddafi, akin to some presidents in the republics, created popular militias to further reduce his reliance on the military and to ensure that these militias would be able to interfere to preserve the regime. Saddam Hussein was another leader who created a number of special armies as counterweights to the influence of the regular army.[38] The idea of militia was not his invention; it was used in Iraq in the period after the toppling of the monarchy, and again during the first Ba'th regime in Iraq in 1963. Other measures by the leadership to control and reduce the military's influence in these republics, such as monitoring the army, are discussed below.

Political–military relations differed among these republics, and underwent changes within each, in response to the efforts by dictators such as Mubarak, Asad, Saddam, and Qaddafi, who managed to rein in any opposition for decades. Yet, the military continued to play a significant role domestically in those republics in terms of employment and impact on the economy. An additional important influence of the military is that it contributed to social mobility by allowing young men to climb the social and economic ladder through military service. But its most serious impact on these countries was the wars that most republics were dragged into, and which in turn affected their economies and societies.

The military and wars

Of the eight republics discussed in this book, only Tunisia was not engaged in a war after its independence, although it officially aided Egypt and Syria in the October 1973 War. The other republics fought both internal and external wars, as their leaders perceived that "war is merely the continuation of policy by other means."[39] As well as

---

[37] Paola De Maio, "From Soldiers to Policemen: Qadhafi's Army in the New Century," *Journal of Middle Eastern Geopolitics*, vol. 2, no. 3 (2006), p. 23. See also George Joffé, "Political Dynamics in North Africa," *International Affairs*, vol. 85, no. 5 (2009), pp. 938–40.

[38] For a general discussion of special armies, see Quinlivan, "Coup-proofing," p. 141. For Iraq, see Sassoon, *Saddam Hussein's Ba'th Party*, pp. 145–52.

[39] Carl von Clausewitz, *On War* (Princeton: Princeton University Press, 1976), chapter 1, section 24.

political consequences, there were economic implications of war and military industrialization.

After the rise of the Ba'th in Iraq, the regime engaged in a number of skirmishes with Kurdish guerillas, after which came the eight-year war with Iran, followed by the invasion of Kuwait, which led to another major war against an international coalition that included other Arab republics. As Isam al-Khafaji shows, "war making has achieved such extraordinary social, cultural, ideological, and political centrality in Iraq."[40] The significance of being at war had implications for all the republics, except Tunisia. Certain wars did not impact just the republic that launched the war, but had wider ramifications for other Arab countries. A case in point was Iraq's invasion of Kuwait and the First Gulf War, whose consequences reverberated across the Arab world. One memoir written by a Sudanese former minister, who was also a former ambassador, describes the chaos that prevailed among different states once the news of the invasion broke. Countries had to decide which side they were on and what steps to follow after taking into consideration the pressure from the United States and its allies on one hand, and the public mood in their own countries on the other. At the time, the memoir's author served as Sudan's ambassador to Algeria and was a personal friend of the Kuwaiti ambassador there, but had to explain to his Kuwaiti friend, in the most diplomatic way, the reasons for Sudan's support of Iraq. Once the Gulf War began, all Arab countries were under pressure from Iraq either to be neutral or to support it.[41] Likewise, a senior official from Yemen, who was at the time an ambassador in Washington, sketches how inter-Arab relations were thrown into turmoil as a result of the invasion. Yemen, in his words, was pressured by all sides: Saudi Arabia, Egypt, Iraq, and the USA. When Yemen decided to support Iraq, it paid a heavy price: Saudi Arabia and the Gulf states forced thousands of Yemeni laborers to leave their countries, and the USA cut all aid.[42] The invasion of Kuwait in 1990 shattered any sense of unity among the Arab countries,

---

[40] Isam al-Khafaji, "War as a Vehicle for the Rise and Demise of a State-Controlled Society: The Case of Ba'thist Iraq," in Steven Heydemann (ed.), *War, Institutions, and Social Change in the Middle East* (Berkeley: University of California Press, 2000), p. 259.

[41] Hasan 'Abidayn, *Hayat fi al-siyasa wa al-diblumasiyya al-Sudaniyya* [My life in Sudan's politics and diplomacy] (Omdurman: Mirghani Cultural Center, 2013), pp. 159–61.

[42] Al-'Ayni, *Khamsun 'aman fi al-rimal al-mutaharrika*, pp. 357–60.

although it was not the first time that an individual country's strategy contrasted profoundly with the group's strategy. Issues such as how to deal with Israel and the liberation of Palestine before 1967 and then with the Occupied Territories, negotiating with Israel to recover the Egyptian territories that were occupied in 1967, all led to major splits in the region.

Wars against Israel did not create such a chasm, as most were supportive of that policy, at least in declarations and intentions. The ending of the 1967 War in a crushing defeat of the Arab side in six days had a shocking impact on the most important republic engaged in the war: Egypt. Dozens of books have been written in Egypt describing *al-hazima* (the defeat): who was to be blamed, who made the right or wrong decisions, what were the lessons of this defeat, and what role did politicians and generals play in the weeks preceding the war and during those critical six days. Many memoirs of generals and politicians focused on one big question: the relationship between 'Amr and Nasser, and who was accountable for what. For some generals, it was very clear who carried the responsibility for the defeat: not the Egyptian army, but the political leadership (i.e. Nasser), and the upper echelons of the military (i.e. 'Amr).[43] The most comprehensive book about decision making during wars and the relations between Egypt's political and military leadership is Amin Huwaydi's book, which contains diagrams and footnotes showing the flow and process of decisions taken in Egypt during 1967, the Attrition period, and the October 1973 War. Discussing his appointment, he said:

Why me specifically in these hard times? Given that I was banished from the armed forces for ten full years. What is required from me at this difficult stage I do not believe anyone in my critical position has ever faced in the past.[44]

Huwaydi analyzed the lines separating political and military leadership and argues that during 1967, the defeat belonged to "the military leadership and absolutely not to the army."[45] According to another

---

[43] 'Ali, *Mashawir al-'umr*, pp. 205–19.
[44] Amin Hamid Huwaydi, *al-Furas al-da'i'a: al-qararat al-hasima fi Harbay al-Istinzaf wa Uktubir: haqa'iq tunsharu li-awwal marra ma'a thamani watha'iq sirriyya* [The missed opportunities: decisive decisions in the Wars of Attrition and October: facts published for the first time with eight secret documents] (Beirut: Corporation for Printing and Publishing, 1992), p. 84.
[45] Ibid., p. 9.

Egyptian general, Muhammad Fawzi, who was chief of staff from 1964 until the end of the 1967 War, a secret study of the war and the reasons behind the defeat was prepared for Nasser and only 110 copies were made of it, which have never seen the light.[46] Huwaydi's memoirs, which were more structured and less personal, differed from most others, which devoted many pages discussing the relations between 'Amr and Nasser. Being comprehensive does not necessarily render it accurate or objective, particularly given that the writer was minister of war and head of the Intelligence Services, appointed immediately after the defeat in 1967. Most of the other authors wanted really to understand how and why this friendship developed, and ended tragically: did 'Amr really intend to launch a coup d'état against Nasser when he realized that he would be dismissed together with his main supporters? Did he truly commit suicide in his own bathroom, or was he killed?[47]

Five decades after those events the Egyptians are still absolutely fascinated by this saga. Barlanti 'Abd al-Hamid, an Egyptian actress who was 'Amr's mistress, and who later secretly married him, wrote a long memoir describing him as a true gentleman who devoted his life to Egypt, in spite of the numerous reports indicating that he was a playboy who spent more time on drinks and women than on military strategy. Barlanti, who had a child with 'Amr, emphasized during a television interview before her death in 2010 that her husband had been killed, since he was not the type to commit suicide.[48]

Another important war was the one in Yemen in the 1960s, which became known as Egypt's Vietnam. Supporting the revolution to overthrow the Yemeni monarchy dragged Egypt into a no-win war. As a Yemeni official wrote, after almost two-and-a-half years of war and

---

[46] Imam, *al-Fariq Muhammad Fawzi*, pp. 77–78. An annex in the book contains General Fawzi's testimony to the "History Committee" that was formed on the orders of President Sadat to investigate the 1967 War. See pp. 119–62.

[47] See, for example, Ghalib, *Ma'a 'Abd al-Nasser wa al-Sadat*. Murad Ghalib, who served as ambassador to Congo and the Soviet Union and was close to the Free Officers, devoted much space in his memoirs to what he termed "love and hate relations" between Nasser and 'Amr. See also Husni, *Shams Badran: al-rajul alladhi hakama Misr*. For an in-depth analysis of the confrontation between Nasser and 'Amr, see Kandil, *Soldiers, Spies, and Statesmen*, pp. 83–93.

[48] "Barlanti 'Abd al-Hamid ma'a Duktur 'Amru al-Laythi." For her interviews on Egyptian television, see YouTube video, 53:28, posted September 27, 2012, and 56:27, posted October 4, 2012, available at www.youtube.com/watch?v=6VNlm9Yi8Kg. Her memoirs are Barlanti 'Abd al-Hamid, *al-Mushir wa ana* [The field marshal and I] (Cairo: Madbuly Books, 1992).

destruction, and in spite of huge sacrifices by Egyptians in Yemen, it became evident that war was not the solution to the country's problems.[49] Indeed, the Yemen War was seen as one of the factors in the 1967 defeat, and in the words of one scholar "the key to the decline of Egyptian power at the height of the Cold War lies in Egypt's five-year intervention in the Yemeni civil war."[50] General Jamasi, who played a leading role in the 1973 War, discusses Egypt's five-year guerilla war in the distant territory of Yemen; he maintains that the level of military training dropped during this period and that the military leadership was too focused on this unwinnable war and neglected the Israeli front.[51] Another Egyptian general explains how the political leadership was, by early 1962, so preoccupied with the events in Yemen that the military and political leadership devoted most of their time to discussing the intelligence reports from Yemen rather than dealing with other threats. In the same memoir, the general speculates that a fundamental issue in the mismanagement of the war in Yemen (one that surely applies to other republics' management of conflicts) was the lack of separation between the military and political leaderships. Quoting Georges Clemenceau, the French prime minister at the end of World War I, that "war is too serious a matter to entrust to military men," the Egyptian general contends that what led Nasser and Egypt's leaders to be so immersed in the Yemen War were their own ambitions and desperate need for some success after the failure of the union with Syria in 1961.[52]

Another republic that was involved in a number of military adventures abroad was Libya. Qaddafi, as part of his world vision, endorsed "Africa against colonialism" and decided to expand his sphere of influence in that continent, given the lack of enthusiasm for his ideas in the Arab world. He sponsored numerous attempts to destabilize many African countries, usually after signing a bilateral cooperation agreement that allowed for a Libyan presence in those countries. Libya was entangled in Uganda (1977–78) and in Chad (1980–87), and

---

[49] Al-'Ayni, *Khamsun 'aman fi al-rimal al-mutaharrika*, p. 85. More than 50,000 Egyptians were bogged down in a guerilla war that lasted five years, 1962–67.

[50] Jesse Ferris, *Nasser's Gamble: How Intervention in Yemen Caused the Six-Day War and the Decline of Egyptian Power* (Princeton: Princeton University Press, 2013), p. 2.

[51] Al-Jamasi, *Mudhakirrat al-Jamasi*, pp. 61–63.

[52] Al-Hadidi, *Shahid 'ala Harb al-Yaman*, pp. 37, 111–12.

according to one report, more than 5,000 Libyans were killed and vast amounts of money lost in those futile military conflicts.[53]

As many of these republics engaged in wars, they needed two things: technical advice and arms. The Soviet Union provided one or both for most of these countries: Egypt, Iraq, Libya, Sudan, Syria, and Yemen. Needless to say, having foreign advisors was not always uneventful. Egypt's military relations with the Soviet Union were volatile, but the need for aid induced Egypt to accept the presence of a large number of Soviet advisors to train its army, both generally and in the use of Soviet weapons. Haykal's memoirs of the 1973 War convey the tensions that prevailed between the two countries, as Egypt insisted on more sophisticated arms and better equipment, particularly after the 1967 defeat. According to Haykal, Sadat was furious in one meeting with the Soviet defense minister and told him that Egypt was always two steps behind Israel when it came to the latest armaments.[54] But Haykal admonishes Sadat for expelling the military Soviet advisors (roughly 15,000) in mid 1972 without a quid pro quo arrangement with the USA. Likewise, Ghalib narrates in his memoirs that a historic deal was reached by General Tito, then president of Yugoslavia, with Nasser and American president Lyndon Johnson, which stipulated that if Egypt were to expel its Soviet advisors and reduce the Soviet presence in Egypt, the American administration would press Israel to return the Egyptian territories occupied in 1967.[55] Sadat, in his autobiography, argues that there were two major reasons for the expulsion: one was that the Soviets did not keep their word about supplying weapons promised to the Egyptians; and the other was that he felt that "the Soviet Union had begun to feel that it enjoyed a privileged position in Egypt – so much so that the Soviet ambassador had assumed a position comparable to that of the British High Commissioner."[56]

A Yemeni official depicts in more detail how purchasing arms and accepting advisors has many obstacles. Once a country purchases arms

[53] William J. Foltz, "Libya's Military Power," in René Lemarchand (ed.), *The Green and the Black: Qadhafi's Policies in Africa* (Bloomington: Indiana University Press, 1988), pp. 52–69. See also el-Kikhia, *Libya's Qaddafi*, pp. 113–17.

[54] Haykal, *Uktubir 1973: al-silah wa al-siyasa*, pp. 252–56.

[55] Ghalib, *Ma'a 'Abd al-Nasser wa al-Sadat*, p. 232. Ghalib, who served as ambassador in Moscow, gives details of the arms negotiations and describes Sadat's frustration with the Soviets: see pp. 172–79.

[56] El-Sadat, *In Search of Identity*, p. 231.

from another, there is an obligation to use that country's advisors and facilities to train its own officers. Al-'Ayni describes how the Yemeni government kept changing its mind about where to buy arms, and which country's advisors to use. It was advised to have Egyptian advisors, given their intimate knowledge of Soviet arms, but all this got muddled in the internal politics of Yemen.[57] Similarly, the Soviet Union stepped in when Egyptian–Libyan relations reached their lowest ebb in 1975, and signed an enormous military deal with Libya including the latest MIG jet fighters. A former Egyptian ambassador to Libya exposes the angst in Cairo on receiving the reports from Tripoli about the military deal, which the Egyptian leadership regarded as a true menace to their country.[58]

Another implication of war was, and is, the need to allocate a high percentage of national budgets to the army and to military industrialization. Many of these republics, in particular Egypt and Iraq, aspired to develop strong military industries to cement their influence and power in the region. Various studies have focused on the correlation between high military expenditure and economic growth.[59] In constant prices, the Middle East region came second in the developing world in terms of military expenditure,[60] although another study shows that Middle East and North African (MENA) countries allocated more on defense spending during the first decade of the twenty-first century than any other region.[61] While the military expenditure constituted a burden on national budgets, the army was a large – if not the largest – employer, and in countries such as Yemen defense was allocated roughly 40 percent of the 2006 budget.[62] The difference between all the republics and Tunisia is striking: Tunisia spent on average only 1.5 percent of its

[57] Al-'Ayni, *Khamsun 'aman fi al-rimal al-mutaharrika*, pp. 305–07.
[58] El Saadany, *Egypt and Libya from Inside*, pp. 147–51.
[59] For a review of the literature and discussion about it see Latif Wahid, *Military Expenditure and Economic Growth in the Middle East* (London: Palgrave Macmillan, 2009), pp. 15–45.
[60] Ibid., table 2.4, p. 35. In 2005 the Middle East overall spent roughly $63 billion, while countries in the Far East spent $120 billion, but South America spent only $20 billion.
[61] Adeel Malik and Bassem Awadallah, "The Economics of the Arab Spring," *World Development*, vol. 45 (May 2013), pp. 296–313.
[62] Adam C. Seitz, "Ties that Bind and Divide: The 'Arab Spring' and Yemeni Civil–Military Relations," in Helen Lackner (ed.), *Why Yemen Matters: A Society in Transition* (London: Middle East Institute, SOAS, 2014), p. 59.

GDP on defense spending under Ben 'Ali and had a mere 35,000 men in the military before 2010.[63]

Military expenditure was a function of the policies of the leadership in these republics; for instance, Samer Soliman shows how military expenditure in Egypt increased in the 1980s coinciding with the rise of Abu Ghazala as commander of the armed forces. Abu Ghazala was closely connected to the USA from his days as military attaché in Washington, and was known to be a staunch opponent of communism.[64] After the signing of the Camp David peace agreement between Israel and Egypt in 1978, US military aid to Egypt became an important component for the country's military. In other republics where war was a more permanent feature, such as in Iraq and Algeria, military expenditure knew almost no limits: the regimes were determined to win or at least to survive prolonged military conflicts. In Algeria, for instance, Khalid Nezzar shows how everything became secondary to the demands of the military during the long civil war in the 1990s.[65] Irrespective of its economic woes, Egypt spent an incredible amount of money during the war in Yemen, including hefty payments in cash and gold to tribal leaders to win their support against the monarchy.[66]

The need for arms acquisition while avoiding the influence of the superpowers led to the creation of an intra-regional consortium for armament production, the Arab Organization for Industrialization.[67] But Egypt also developed the business independently, and has become the most important arms producer in the region. One report reveals that more than 100,000 people were employed in the military industries in some thirty factories by the end of the 1990s,[68] an economic empire built by the Egyptian officers which Springborg dubbed

---

[63] Derek Lutterbeck, "After the Fall: Security Sector Reform in post-Ben Ali Tunisia," Arab Reform Initiative, September 2012, p. 7, available at www.arab-reform.net/after-fall-security-sector-reform-post-ben-ali-tunisia.

[64] Samer Soliman, *The Autumn of Dictatorship: Fiscal Crisis and Political Change in Egypt under Mubarak* (Stanford: Stanford University Press, 2011), pp. 82–83. Soliman's book is an excellent source about how policies changed "following the revenue trail."

[65] Nezzar, *Mudhakkirat al-Liwa' Khalid Nezzar.*

[66] Al-Hadidi, *Shahid 'ala Harb al-Yaman*, pp. 156–67.

[67] Yazid Sayigh, *Arab Military Industry: Capability, Performance, and Impact* (London: Brassey's, 1992), p. 50.

[68] Stephen H. Gotowicki, "The Military in Egyptian Society," in Phebe Marr (ed.), *Egypt at the Crossroads: Domestic Stability and Regional Role* (Washington: National Defense University Press, 1999), pp. 105–25.

"Military, Inc."[69] Of the eight Arab republics, only Egypt's military industry has made a real contribution to, and is positively involved with, the national economy. According to Springborg, Syria, Iraq (under Saddam Hussein), and Sudan came behind Egypt, but given "the fact that their economies are less developed, so the opportunities for military enterprise are necessarily fewer."[70] In such an environment, where the military has vast business interests, it was only natural that nepotism and corruption developed. An Egyptian judge recounts in his memoirs how they spread throughout the centers of power, and how embezzlement took place when 'Amr and Badran were running the army and military intelligence in the mid 1960s.[71] Nepotism in the military was also highlighted by the chief of staff during the War of Attrition, 'Abd al-Mun'im Riyad, who complained bitterly that sons and relatives of senior officers were being helped to pass the Military College exams, a phenomenon that started in the mid 1950s.[72]

Militarization and national security helped the longevity of these authoritarian regimes. In Iraq, for instance, Saddam's many wars ensured that he could use these conflicts to rid himself of any opposition and consolidate his control. Similarly, Hafiz al-Asad used the conflict with Israel as a pretext for controlling opposition, in spite of the fact that Syria did not engage in a direct confrontation with Israel after the two countries signed a ceasefire agreement at the end of the October 1973 War. For a country like Egypt, which has had a peace agreement with Israel since 1979, fighting Islamism and terrorism became the new mantra to justify a free hand in controlling the population. *Al-amn al-qawmi* (national security) became a key phrase in Egypt from the 1980s; armaments and military industrialization were seen as a cornerstone of national security against both external and

---

[69] Robert Springborg, "Economic Involvements of Militaries," *International Journal of Middle East Studies*, vol. 43, no. 3 (2011), p. 397.

[70] Ibid.

[71] Samir Fadil, *Kuntu qadiyan li-hadath al-minassa: mudhakkirat qadi min Harb al-Yaman ila ightiyal al-Sadat* [I was a judge for the Podium Event: memoirs of a judge from the Yemen War until the assassination of Sadat] (Cairo: Sphinx Publishing, 1993), pp. 46–47. The Podium Event refers to the assassination of Sadat while he was sitting on a podium during the military parade.

[72] Al-Jawadi, *al-Shahid 'Abd al-Mun'im Riyad*, pp. 40–41. Riyad was killed during the Attrition War in an Israeli bombardment.

internal enemies.[73] National security was a permanent feature in the ruling party's discussions; in the fourth annual party conference of the National Democratic Party a long session was devoted to the definition of Egypt's national security. The speaker was none other than Gamal Mubarak, the son of the president, who in 2006 was undersecretary of the ruling party and in charge of its policies. In a long speech, Mubarak junior expounded on how the leadership viewed and dealt with national security. He denied that Egypt concentrated only on domestic interests, ignoring its position in the Arab world. He emphasized that "when I speak about the Egyptian national security, I do not separate that from the national security of the region in which we live."[74] He added that for Egypt to play its leadership role, the country must have a strong army and a prosperous economy. He discussed the turmoil in the region – Iraq, Lebanon, Sudan – but insisted that the main issue facing the region was still the Palestinian question, and that without a solution to this problem, there would always be ramifications for the region's national security. He praised the president for his wisdom over the last decades that had allowed Egypt to avoid the tumultuous conditions prevailing in many countries in the region.[75]

Having a strong army was a prerequisite for all these authoritarian republics. However, as indicated, the relations between the political and military leadership were complicated. Furthermore, while emphasizing military training and armaments, these governments also feared that the military could become too powerful. As a result, the republics coup-proofed their regimes and made sure they could control the military.

Watching the guardians of the nation

Watching the military, the so-called guardians of the nation, began as soon as the republics were created. For instance, in Syria, long before the Asad dynasty came to power, the frequently changing regimes still worried about the army and opposition influence within it; in late

[73] Mahmud Khalil, "al-Amn al-qawmi: ittijahat al-tahdid wa ab'ad al-muwajaha," [National security: trends of threats and dimensions of confrontation], *al-Nasr*, no. 583 (January 1988), pp. 22–23. *Al-Nasr* is a monthly magazine published by the Egyptian Armed Forces.

[74] Al-Hizb al-Watani al-Dimuqrati, *al-Mu'tamar al-Sanawi al-Rabi'*, p. 409.

[75] Ibid., pp. 403–14.

1949, under the presidency of Hashim al-Atasi, a special Bureau for Fighting Communism was created within the army, to ensure that communism could not extend its influence among officers.[76] This trend continued in the 1960s; one officer's memoir discusses how a group of officers were discharged from their military duty because of their disenchantment with the annulling of land reform laws. Opposition movements in the army were mostly labeled "military mutiny" by the different regimes so that courts-martial could send these officers and soldiers to be executed, jailed, or banned from the armed forces.[77] This continued in the 1970s after Hafiz al-Asad came to power and realized the importance of surveillance as a tool for combating opposition. He thus established several security agencies, some of which were "focused on the senior officers' echelon in the army."[78] The two main agencies that kept a watch on the officers were Air Force Security Administration and the Military Security Department. As Eyal Zisser argued, "Asad thus succeeded in making the army a loyal and obedient watchdog."[79] These agencies created to instill fear into the hearts of all Syrians, also arrested and tortured officers suspected of opposing the regime. One memoir of a Syrian officer tells us how an officer was tortured to get the names of other officers who might have been in contact with him or, worse, shared his views.[80]

Likewise, the archives of the Iraqi Ba'th clearly illustrate how the regime was intent on infiltrating the army and monitoring its movements. Apart from the political commissars mentioned above, a plethora of intelligence and security services had the sole function of being alert to any sign of mutiny or dissension with the Iraqi Ba'th Party. By the late 1980s, each officer's political inclinations were scrutinized from when he first applied as a cadet to the Military College. Surveillance of officers was extensive;

---

[76] Yusif al-Faysal, *Dhikrayat wa mawaqif* [Memories and stances] (Damascus: al-Takwin Publishing, 2007), pp. 94–95. The memoirs of al-Faysal, a Syrian communist active in Syrian politics for a long time, is a comprehensive history of the party until mid 1966. It also gives an overview of the numerous coups that plagued Syria in the 1950s and 1960s, and the role of the Communist Party.

[77] Muhammad Ibrahim al-'Ali, *Hayati wa al-i'dam* [My life and the execution], vol. I (Damascus: n.p., 2000), pp. 63, 463.

[78] Eyal Zisser, "The Syrian Army on the Domestic and External Fronts," in Rubin and Keaney (eds.), *Armed Forces in the Middle East*, p. 120.

[79] Ibid., p. 119.
These agencies created to instill fear into the hearts of all syrians, also arrested and tortured officers suspected of opposing the regime.

[80] Hamdun, *Dhikrayat wa ara'*, p. 105. The book was self-published.

any gathering of officers outside the barracks was viewed as suspicious, and the military intelligence had no hesitation in arresting and interrogating any officer regardless of rank.[81] Generals such as al-Hamdani complained that more of the intelligence's time and resources were devoted to monitoring officers than providing information about the enemy.[82] Even in less repressive regimes such as Egypt, internal security was sometimes more of a focus than external intelligence. One observer asserts that "poor intelligence contributed to Cairo's inability to win the Yemen war."[83]

Other republics also used the system of creating overlapping security and intelligence services to ensure that no one agency became too powerful. Libya, for instance, had multiple agencies whose job it was to protect the leader Qaddafi and his family and who owed him total loyalty. Many of these agencies, as in Iraq and in Syria, were led by relatives of the leader or belonged to the small clique or tribe that he came from.[84] For most of these countries, coups were an integral part of their past, and some such as Syria and Iraq witnessed extreme instability during the 1960s. Not only in the Arab world but also on other continents such as South America and Africa, coups d'état were commonplace.[85] By the 1970s, however, the republics reached a level where coups were a rare phenomenon, except in Algeria. That does not imply a lack of attempts to overthrow these regimes, but that the surveillance and control of the army had become far more sophisticated and comprehensive.

Although there were no successful coups, there were many assassination attempts against the republics' leaders, the most successful of

---

[81] For more details about the Ba'thification of the army and what they termed the "totalitarian military" see Ibrahim al-Marashi and Sammy Salama, *Iraq's Armed Forces: An Analytical History* (New York: Routledge, 2008), pp. 105–29.

[82] Al-Hamdani, *Qabla an yughadiruna al-tarikh*, p. 93. See also Sassoon, *Saddam Hussein's Ba'th Party*, pp. 143–45.

[83] Owen L. Sirrs, *A History of the Egyptian Intelligence Service: A History of the Mukhabarat, 1910–2009* (New York: Routledge, 2010), p. 77. The book extensively covers the intelligence issues emanating from Egypt's different wars and dealing with its external enemies.

[84] Derek Lutterbeck, "Arab Uprisings, Armed Forces, and Civil–Military Relations," *Armed Forces and Society*, vol. 39, no. 1 (April 2012), pp. 28–52.

[85] Abdoulaye Saine, "The Gambia's 'Elected Autocrat Poverty, Peripherality, and Political Instability,' 1994–2006," *Armed Forces & Society*, vol. 34, no. 3 (April 2008), pp. 450–73.

which was, of course, the assassination of Egypt's President Sadat. One general in charge of military intelligence in Iraq recorded seven assassination attempts against Saddam Hussein by 1982, and there were many more in the next two decades against the president and his family.[86] Another head of Iraq's intelligence writes in his memoirs about the cooperation between Arab and foreign intelligence services to thwart any assassination attempts. When there was an assassination attempt somewhere in the world, Saddam Hussein insisted that military intelligence gathered all the information, contacted the intelligence agencies in that particular country if it was a friendly nation, and prepared a report about the lessons that could be learned. Those lessons were implemented later, whenever Saddam traveled or had meetings outside his compound.[87]

The successful assassination of Sadat on October 6, 1981 during the parade to celebrate the anniversary of the 1973 War was described in many memoirs, and the failed security precautions are further discussed in Chapter 4. But it is interesting here to look at other aspects. Kamal Hasan 'Ali was Egypt's foreign minister at the time and sat on the podium very close to Sadat. He wrote a chilling account describing how there were corpses strewn all over the podium after an Islamist, Khalid al-Islambuli, and two accomplices machine-gunned the president and some of the guests watching the military parade.[88] One book about the assassination, which claimed to have collected many documents about it, tells the life story of Khalid, a graduate from the Military College who joined the Muslim Brotherhood, and had actually been questioned by the military intelligence about his connections and meetings with Muslim groups a few days before the killing. His brother Muhammad was arrested for activities related to a banned Islamist group, and although the military intelligence decided originally to exempt Khalid from participating in the parade, a shortage of other officers led to a reversal of this decision. This changed Egypt's history. Not only did he participate in the parade, but also he succeeded in

---

[86] Barazan al-Tikriti, *Muhawalat ightiyal al-ra'is Saddam Hussein* [Attempts to assassinate President Saddam Hussein] (Baghdad: Arab Publishing House, 1982). In 1996, an assassination attempt against Saddam's son 'Uday left him paralyzed from the waist down.

[87] Al-Samarra'i, *Hutam al-bawwaba al-sharqiyya*, pp. 387–90. Saddam, it seems, was very interested to learn all the details surrounding the failed assassination attempt against President Ronald Reagan in March 1980.

[88] 'Ali, *Mashawir al-'umr*, pp. 471–76.

replacing regular conscripts with his jihadi associates.[89] Years later, a failed assassination attempt against Mubarak during a visit to Ethiopia underlined the conflict between the Egyptian regime and the jihadists and other extreme Islamists; a conflict that encompassed a bombing campaign by these groups inside Egypt and attacks on senior officials. On the other hand, as Chapter 4 will show, the Egyptian security waged their own war against the jihadists and the Brotherhood and attempted to infiltrate them, while fighting them without mercy.[90]

Islamism was, as mentioned earlier, perceived by many of the regimes as a potential threat, and a source of disruption and upheaval. Algeria represents the extreme example, fighting a civil war in the 1990s against Islamic fundamentalists that led to almost 200,000 deaths. The Sécurité Militaire (SM) managed to infiltrate the army to make sure its corps had no affiliation to the Islamists.[91] Nezzar describes in detail the fight against the Islamists, and underlines how the army managed to "cleanse" itself from the influence of what he termed "extreme Islam" that would have "pushed Algeria back to the dark ages."[92] Intriguingly, in spite of the overwhelming power of the Algerian military, coups d'état and assassinations continued in that country. However, some of these incidents were instigated by those in power; for instance, the coup d'état of January 1992 was started by General Khalid Nezzar, then minister of defense, and led to President Chadhli Bendjedid being forced to resign.[93] Willis summed up the events of early 1992 as representing "the final move by the military to the very forefront of national politics, with there being no doubt that it was the army as an institution that was now fully in control of the government and regime."[94] Undeniably, during that period Algeria was the only Arab republic where the army had complete authority; in the other republics the armies had become controlled and manipulated by the leadership.

[89] 'Adil Hammuda, *Ightiyal ra'is: bil-watha'iq asrar ightiayl Anwar al-Sadat* [Assassination of a president: documents of the secrets of the assassination of Anwar al-Sadat] (Cairo: Sina Publishing, 1986), pp. 71–80.

[90] For more details on the attempt in Ethiopia and the Egyptian Intelligence, see Sirrs, *A History of the Egyptian Intelligence Service*, pp. 169–78.

[91] Stone, *The Agony of Algeria*, p. 136.

[92] Nezzar, *Mudhakkirat al-Liwa' Khalid Nezzar*, pp. 191–206.

[93] For details of the coup, see Lyes Laribi, *L'Algérie des généraux* [The generals' Algeria] (Paris: Max Milo, 2007), pp. 110–16.

[94] Willis, *Politics and Power in the Maghreb*, p. 105.

Muslim activists continued to be a major threat for the military in most of the republics. One of Egypt's top officers asserted that it would be wrong to use the term "fundamentalist" and that the right term for the men involved with these groups should be "terrorists." In his words, no one who was strict about his religious beliefs could commit murder of innocent people, and these men were distorting the image of Islam. He called on the armed forces to ensure that no group could control the thinking of its sons.[95] In the early 1990s, numerous articles in the Egyptian army magazine were devoted to extremism, religion, and terrorism, and ways in which to combat them. Fighting the Muslim Brotherhood was high on the agenda of all Egyptian presidents, particularly Nasser and Mubarak. One Egyptian observer argues that Badran was appointed minister of war in September 1966 as a reward for his efforts in fighting Islamic extremism and arresting the important players of the Muslim Brotherhood.[96] A memoir by a military judge features numerous episodes of the arrest and trials of the Brothers, culminating in the assassination of Sadat. He describes the torture inflicted on the Brothers in Egyptian prisons, and illustrates their pride and calmness in front of their interrogators and in courtrooms.[97]

The issue of succession was another challenge to the military in many of these republics. As we have seen, nepotism was widespread among the military corps, and officers' sons had a definite advantage in getting into military colleges. In the more ideological armies of Iraq, Syria, and Libya, coming from the same tribe and the right family were key tests, as they indicated loyalty to the leadership. But there was also the issue of succession to the leader, who tended to be an army officer; Hafiz al-Asad succeeded in transferring the reins of power to his son, Bashar, who was merely a captain when he returned to Syria after the death of his elder brother. Saddam Hussein, although not an officer, had appointed himself commander-in-chief (and was convinced that he knew more about military strategy than most officers), and groomed his second son, Qusay, whom he made an officer. Mubarak wanted to bring his son, Gamal, not an officer, to succeed him, but obviously this

---

[95] "Lieutenant General Salih Halbi Meets with Members of the Armed Forces," *al-Nasr*, no. 643 (January 1993), pp. 10–11.

[96] Husni, *Shams Badran: al-rajul alladhi hakama Misr*, p. 9.

[97] Fadil, *Kuntu qadiyan*: see, for example, one episode on pp. 74–77.

did not pan out as planned.[98] One observer posited that the army abandoned the regime, as the last few years of Mubarak's rule "had incubated dissatisfaction among the high command who feared that their position was deteriorating."[99] Furthermore, they resented the rise of Mubarak's son Gamal and the prevailing corruption. Even when the senior military leadership did not favorably regard these succession efforts in different republics, it is doubtful that any general could have blocked them, as that would have meant death or exile from power.[100]

Officers and soldiers

An Egyptian proverb tells us "in kunta 'aiz ta'kul 'aish, ruh lil-jaysh" (if you want to eat bread, join the army). As mentioned earlier, the military in the Arab world was perceived as a modernizing factor and a strong institution, and armies in the region expanded considerably in the second half of the twentieth century. Was it really the desire to "eat bread," or were there other factors that played a role in the appeal of the military? In this section, we look at how soldiers and officers fared, what they expected, what they endured, and how they described their lives and careers in their own words.

Pay scales of soldiers in the Arab world are low compared to the rest of the population, and certainly in contrast to the benefits given to officers. However, lack of employment in most of these countries, limited prospects for advancement, and opportunities to see the country rather than being stuck in a village or small town all played a role in recruiting soldiers. Family ties are another important factor, especially among officers.[101] The military in some of these republics offered attractive opportunities for top students, mainly in science, to complete their studies abroad and return to work in military research. Volker

---

[98] Muhammad Abdul Aziz and Youssef Hussein, "The President, the Son, and the Military: The Question of Succession in Egypt," *Arab Studies Journal*, vol. 9/10, no. 2/1 (Fall/Spring 2002), pp. 73–88. As the article shows, in 2001 Mubarak announced that Egypt is not Syria and his son was not going to be the next president.

[99] Cronin, *Armies and State-Building*, p. 3.

[100] For a comprehensive discussion of the succession issues, see Roger Owen, *The Rise and Fall of Arab Presidents for Life* (Cambridge, MA: Harvard University Press, 2012).

[101] Family ties were also important in countries such as Brazil: see Stepan, *The Military in Politics*, pp. 14–17.

Perthes claims that salaries of science officers in Syria far exceeded what other scientists earned and, furthermore, these military scientists engaged in advanced research and development.[102] The militarization of societies intensified as a result of the numerous coups d'état in some republics, or the multiple military conflicts in which most countries were involved.[103]

There is no doubt that salaries and benefits impacted the morale of the army, and leaders were very cognizant of this. Saddam Hussein fully understood its significance, and from time to time salaries were adjusted to inflation, and benefits – principally to officers – were increased dramatically.[104] After he came to power, Sadat visited the front line with Israel and granted the military a wide range of remunerations such as tax-deduction refunds, wage increases, and more paid vacation days. According to Haykal, this undeniably raised the moral of the fighting units, who welcomed the new president and his war minister after this gesture.[105] If the military was subjected to cuts in salaries and allowances, it almost certainly led to a tense relationship between them and the political leadership, as happened in Yemen in 1968.[106]

Conscription was universal in most republics, although the length of military service varied. In Iraq and Egypt, conscripts were not released when their term ended if the country was at war. The role of conscription and whether it is a cohesive force offering national values and solidarity is moot,[107] but it is hard to see how these values could grow and flourish under autocratic rule that stifles the development of society. No wonder the average soldier mostly felt disconnected from these rulers given the way he was treated.

---

[102] Volker Perthes, *The Political Economy of Syria under Asad* (London: I. B. Tauris, 1997), p. 147.

[103] See, for example, the study about the rise of military society in Syria in al-Nabulsi, *Su'ud al-mujtami' al-'askari al-'Arabi fi Misr wa al-Sham*, pp. 131–37.

[104] See, for example, head of presidential *diwan* to Ministry of Defense, "Income for the Armed Forces," December 30, 2002, BRCC, B 001-2-3 (24).

[105] Haykal, *Uktubir 73: al-silah wa al-siyasa*, p. 227.

[106] Noel Brehony, *Yemen Divided: The Story of a Failed State in South Arabia* (New York: I. B. Tauris, 2013), p. 35.

[107] See, for example, Elizabeth Picard, "Arab Military in Politics: From Revolutionary Plot to Authoritarian State," in Giacomo Luciani (ed.), *The Arab State* (Berkeley: University of California Press, 1990), pp. 202–05.

Soldiers

Memoirs by soldiers are relatively rare, and the majority are written by Egyptians, but they do inform us of the conditions of the soldiers in some of these republics. Most were written by soldiers who had a university education, or left notes that relatives or friends later published. Remarkably, the large number of memoirs by generals and officers rarely referred to or described the life of the average soldier. The chasm between the two classes was obvious to all, and the soldiers accepted the differentiation as part and parcel of military life. One memoir written by a medical student drafted as a soldier during the War of Attrition portrays life on the Suez front during 1969. One day when he had to walk a long distance in the blazing heat, he heard a car engine. "I said to myself this must be a military jeep as only officers are allowed to use cars, and they grumble if a soldier wants to accompany them, but I was exhausted and my legs could barely carry me. The jeep did stop and I was allowed to get in."[108] The conversation among the officers in the jeep, according to the memoir, centered on food, and the captain was furious that the lieutenant had forgotten to bring beer. The memoir is very critical of how news from the war was distorted; in one skirmish with the Israelis, two soldiers from his unit were killed. Later that evening, the Egyptian news claimed a huge victory over the Israelis and boasted that there were no casualties. It is possible that this was one of the reasons the memoir was banned by the Egyptian censors when it was originally presented in 1972. It was published sixteen years later by his relatives, after the writer was killed in the War of Attrition.[109] Slapping of soldiers by their superiors was allowed, and soldiers were told at the beginning of their service to expect to be treated as second-class citizens. One soldier recounts the speech given to soldiers at the start of their basic training:

The army does not accept any complaints except in three cases, when someone takes your money, takes your 'ohda (loaned military items), or uses you as a female. Besides those three, your superior can ask you to do anything. If

---

[108] Ahmad Hajji, *Mudhakkirat jundi Misri fi jabhat Qanat al-Suways* [Memoirs of an Egyptian soldier on the Suez Canal front] (Cairo: al-Fikr Publishing, 1988), p. 24. According to the biography at the end of the memoir, Hajji graduated from the Veterinary School, and although he was posted in a suburb of Cairo he volunteered to go to the front.

[109] Ibid., pp. 72–73, 139.

you think you have been unjustly victimized, you must first perform as commanded, then you can complain if you wish.[110]

Most soldiers wanted to avoid hard work because they realized there was no reward. The philosophy of survival in the armies by ordinary soldiers was: "No work, no mistake, no punishment."[111]

Books about wars and the bravery of the soldiers are abundant; they are rarely written by soldiers, and mostly by journalists, with an introduction from a senior officer. These books glorify the bravery of the soldiers, their sacrifices, and their deep commitment to defend their country at any cost, and are rarely critical of how these wars were conducted and the heavy price paid by the soldiers.[112] Other books about specific soldiers have a political motif; one is about a soldier who acted alone in shooting tourists whom he was confident were Jews spying against Egypt. The book attempts, in a very supportive and sympathetic manner, to understand the reasons for this shooting, which centered on the soldier's hatred of Jews and his desperate need to avenge all the crimes committed, in his opinion, by Jews.[113]

Preparing soldiers for battle both physically and mentally is a long process. Egypt had to rethink its practice after the 1967 defeat. Obviously, Egypt had a significant advantage in its large and relatively young population. But this reservoir of young men had to be properly trained and equipped for the next battle. Emphasis was placed on strengthening the morale of soldiers by increasing the soldier's

---

[110] Nubar Aroyan, *Diary of a Soldier in the Egyptian Military: A Peek Inside the Egyptian Army* (Bloomington, IN: Westview Press, 2012), p. 21. Aroyan, an Armenian Egyptian, had a university education but refused to become an officer because he did not want his term of service to be extended.

[111] Ibid., p. 22.

[112] See, for example, Ahmad Isma'il Subh, '*Ubur al-mihna: mushahadat 'aya-niyya wa dirasa nafsiyya lil-insan al-Misri fi Harb Uktubir* [The tribulation of the crossing: eyewitness accounts and a psychological study of the Egyptian individual during the October War] (Cairo: Egyptian Association for the Book, 1976). The introduction for this book was by Major-General Hasan al-Badry.

[113] Muhammad Muru, *Sulayman Khatir "Batal Sina'"*: *al-jundi al-Muslim alladhi dafa' 'an karamat Misr wa jayshiha* [Sulayman Khatir "Hero of Sinai": the Muslim soldier who defended Egypt's honor and its army] (Cairo: Digest Books, 1986). The book makes no distinction between Jews and Israelis (p. 29), and the title clearly shows that the author is very supportive of the soldier's act committed on his last day of duty in 1985, which led to the death of seven tourists, among them some Israelis.

confidence in himself, his superiors, and his equipment; and correspondingly by explaining the Egyptian case to reinforce the belief in the justness of the causes for war.[114] However, confidence in superiors was fundamentally shaken after the 1967 defeat. Commenting on the state of the Egyptian soldier, the army's chief of staff during the 1967 War was blunt:

Leadership neglected its main functions ... The soldier is not guilty; he would sacrifice if you cared about him, but the relations between soldiers and officers is severed. They are two sects separated ... Those [soldiers] are poor and weak and those [officers] are strong and rich.[115]

One study underlined that military leadership in the Arab world was less cognizant about safety standards for the average soldier, which meant that soldiers were at more risk than in other regions. This in turn demoralized soldiers who were fulfilling their duty; they perceived it as another sign of lack of attention by officers to their well-being.[116] Intriguingly, even in the monthly Egyptian magazine published by Idarat al-Shu'un al-Ma'nawiyya lil-Quwwat al-Musalliha (the department in charge of the armed forces' morale), little space is devoted to the soldiers' problems and aspirations. Perusing issues of the magazine shows very few articles of this kind. One relates the horrors of the first day in the army;[117] another, written by a senior medical officer, pays tribute to the military leadership for making an HIV test compulsory for soldiers.[118] General Fawzi brings up an important issue related to training: the high rate of illiteracy among Egyptian soldiers. Nonetheless, he argues that illiteracy was not such a hindrance and that with good training and leadership soldiers could reach a certain level of competence; but obviously, illiterate soldiers were harder to train on sophisticated weapons.[119] The combined result of these various elements is that the professionalism of the armed forces declined, especially in republics such as Iraq, where the constant need for soldiers and officers led to a

---

[114] Major-General Taha al-Majdub, "al-Jaysh al-Misri ba'd Yunyu 1967" [The Egyptian army after June 1967], in Lutfi al-Khuli (ed.), *Harb Yunyu 1967: ba'd 30 sana* [The June 1967 War: 30 years later] (Cairo: al-Ahram Publishing, 1997), pp. 129–30.

[115] Imam, *al-Fariq Muhammad Fawzi*, p. 95.

[116] Al-Nabulsi, *Su'ud al-mujtami' al-'askari al-'Arabi fi Misr wa al-Sham*, p. 94.

[117] *Al-Nasr*, no. 583 (January 1988), pp. 28–29.

[118] *Al-Nasr*, no. 643 (January 1993), pp. 14–15.

[119] Al-Nabulsi, *Su'ud al-mujtami' al-'askari al-'Arabi fi Misr wa al-Sham*, p. 94.

reduction in training and attention to safety issues. Soldiers in war-torn countries faced other risks: when wars were prolonged, the ferocity of battles led to a surge in deserters. According to the memoirs of one general, the Iraqi leadership, faced with increasing numbers of soldiers deserting their units during the last few years of the war against Iran and then after the First Gulf War, decided on the macabre measure of severing part of the ear and etching a sign on the forehead of any deserter caught. According to General al-Salihi, the officer corps was shocked by this brutal measure and showed many acts of sympathy toward their soldiers, such as granting them long leaves, contrary to orders from Saddam Hussein.[120] Many conscripts in Iraq were forced to serve for periods of five years or more during the Iran–Iraq War. Desertion in other republics took place as the period of service was prolonged arbitrarily, and the soldier had no say. One Egyptian soldier recounts how his service was extended without his approval for five years instead of lasting one year, given the desperate needs of the Egyptian army after the 1967 War. This led him to desert and escape to Syria because he did not believe his service would end having met people who were forced to serve for eight years.[121]

Benefits granted by the military were an important incentive for joining up long before republican authoritarianism came into existence. The autobiography of a soldier who later became a university professor in Egypt tells how he decided to join the army in 1933 after witnessing, at the age of eleven, his family's meager furniture being confiscated because his parents were in debt to a moneylender.[122] When he joined the army, he quickly discovered that military service was only for poor families, because in the late 1930s any Egyptian family that could pay twenty Egyptian pounds got its son exempted.[123] However, the military guaranteed this man regular

[120] Al-Salihi, *al-Zilzal*, pp. 391–95. For more details on desertions, and the rewards for those informing about them, see Sassoon, *Saddam Hussein's Ba'th Party*, pp. 152–55.

[121] Aroyan, *Diary of a Soldier in the Egyptian Military*, pp. 90–3.

[122] Khalil Hasan Khalil, *al-Wasya: 'an qissat hayat al-jundi alladhi asbaha ustad-han lil-iqtisad al-siyasi bi al-jami'a* [al-Wasya: the life story of the soldier who became a professor of political economy at the university] (Cairo: Egyptian Association for the Book, 1983), pp. 7–9.

[123] *Badal*, the system that allowed conscripts the option of paying in order to avoid the military service, was gradually abolished in most republics by the 1950s.

meals and ensured that his family would receive a monthly payment from him, which alleviated their abject poverty.[124] After the 1952 Revolution, the leadership was intent on improving the lives of ordinary soldiers. An interesting pamphlet, part of a series called *Ikhtarna lil-jundi* (We chose for the soldier), written by a lieutenant-colonel with an introduction by the then chief of staff 'Abd al-Hakim 'Amr, highlights what it called the socialist achievements of the revolution for the soldier, whether he is a peasant, a manual laborer, or a clerk. It describes how the *badal* system was abolished, and how military service became an honor for all young men irrespective of their socioeconomic status. More importantly, according to the pamphlet, the revolution gave political freedom to the individual, and returned soldiering to its proud place where soldiers became respected rather than disdained by society.[125] There is no doubt that in these republics, the experience of being a soldier differed depending on the socioeconomic group to which the recruit belonged. In Egypt, it was said: "For *fellahin*, the army is a *lucanda* (hotel), free lodging, free meals. For high school students, it is a trade school. For college graduates, it is a veritable prison."[126]

Officers

Entering the Military College as a cadet before becoming an officer was not a simple matter; competition in all the republics was high, as these young men realized after their countries became independent that being an officer opened doors to progress and guaranteed a decent income. Attendance at a military college was similar to that at a university, with most of them requiring three years of study. After the rise of authoritarianism, a thorny question erupted, particularly in those countries with more emphasis on ideology. The Military College in Syria in the late 1940s and throughout the 1950s, for instance, insisted on suppressing politics within the college. As the head of the college recounts: "I was always against young men studying in this institution joining any party, because I believe that they are not mature enough, and we should

---

[124] Khalil, *al-Wasya*, p. 207.
[125] Mahmud Tantawi, *Makasib al-jundi al-ishtirakiyya* [The socialist achievements of the soldier] (Cairo: n.p., 1961), pp. 25, 50–52. See also fn. 123 for definition of *badal*.
[126] Aroyan, *Diary of a Soldier in the Egyptian Military*, p. 31.

shepherd them until they mature and are free to choose their paths."[127]
By the 1970s this had been dramatically reversed in countries such as
Syria and Iraq: a cadet needed to be a party member or intending to
become one, and the doors of these institutions were closed to the
so-called "neutrals." The Iraqi archives clearly demonstrate how the
system functioned during the last two decades of Saddam Hussein's
regime: in order to join the military or the security services, a deep and
thorough investigation of each candidate and his extended family was
undertaken to expose any potential sources of opposition to the regime.
By the 1990s, the chances of anyone not fully committed to the Ba'th
Party being able to enter those establishments were non-existent.[128]

Most memoirs mentioned in this chapter give us a glimpse, if not a
full account, of life in a military college, and the majority of authors
reminisce warmly about their years in this institution, especially those
who reached the higher echelons of the military.[129] The Military
College was, in a way, a club whose members established strong friendships and created loyalties that endured for many decades in spite of
political upheavals. A fascinating insight into the details of one class is
gained through a book about the men who graduated from the War
College with Nasser in July 1938.[130] The book's author met and
profiled 66 out of the 100 cadets who were in the class. Most of them
reached the rank of brigadier-general or major-general; many assumed
high positions in the military establishment, such as Ahmad Isma'il
'Ali, who became minister of war during the October 1973 War.
Others, who left the military, were appointed to senior positions in
the government. It is interesting to note that Nasser was number 49 out
of the 99 who graduated (at the time, officers in the air force undertook
the same course at the War College). The author investigated the
careers of the 66 graduates who were still alive in late 1970: 1 was a
government minister; 2 were deputy ministers; 2 were ambassadors; 1
was governor of a province; 6 were chairmen of companies; 21 worked
independently or were senior civil servants; 4 were still in the military;

---

[127] Al-'Ashi, *Fajr al-istiqlal fi Suriya*, p. 176.
[128] Sassoon, *Saddam Hussein's Ba'th Party*, pp. 134–37.
[129] See, for example, Fikri, *al-Mushir Muhammad 'Abd al-Halim Abu Ghazala*,
       pp. 16–21.
[130] In Egypt, unlike in other republics, the college was called the War College and
       not the Military College. Similarly, it was the War Ministry and not the Defense
       Ministry. In October 1978, Sadat ordered the name to be changed to Ministry
       of Defense.

23 were not working; and there were 6 whom the author could not trace.[131] An Egyptian who was in charge of the War College disparaged the reason given by the majority of new cadets for wanting to be an officer: "To sacrifice, to sacrifice my blood for my country."[132] This confirmed for Fawzi the need to provide those young men with a political as well as a military education.

It would be wrong to assume that once the cadets graduated and became officers they maintained strong cordial relations and behaved as a single unit or class. In fact, after they graduated, officers encountered numerous hurdles and risks apart from facing an enemy in a war. Clashes with civilians and politicians began in earnest at an early stage in those republics, but as one memoir shows, there were also conflicts within the military. A case in point was soon after the 1952 Revolution in Egypt, when young officers wanted to get rid of senior officers, or those officers belonging to the bourgeois class. As a result, more than 500 officers were relieved of their military duty on the orders of the Free Officers.[133] Young officers faced different dangers: those with "wrong" political tendencies faced severe penalties, as many regimes were more fearful of young officers or cadets than of civilians with dissenting party affiliations.[134] Many others were killed in the line of duty in the numerous wars and battles entered into by the republics.[135] But the political risks and clashes were more ferocious the higher the rank of the officer. More memoirs of senior officers and generals are available than of lieutenants and captains, and they give a good picture of the conflicts these men endured during their careers. Infighting among generals and senior politicians took place in most regimes, even in those where the cult of the leader's personality was dominant. Memoirs describing the events surrounding the June 1967 War, when every politician and general placed the blame on everyone but himself, create a detailed picture of how the military leadership acted and dealt with the political leadership. The number of Egyptian generals, chiefs of staff, and war or defense ministers who wrote their memoirs exceeds

---

[131] Qadri, *'Abd al-Nasser wa alladhin kanu ma'ahu*, pp. 28–29, 267–69.

[132] Imam, *al-Fariq Muhammad Fawzi*, p. 16.

[133] Ahmad Hamrush, *Misr wa al-'askariyyun* [Egypt and the military men], 3rd edn., vol. I (Cairo: Madbuly Library, 1983), pp. 309–25.

[134] Al-'Ali's book, *Hayati wa al-i'dam*, is an example of the issues facing a young, politically-oriented Syrian officer.

[135] See, for example, the story of one Egyptian officer, related in *al-Nasr*, no. 583 (January 1988), pp. 40–41.

those of any other country in the Arab world. In this book, reference has been made to at least fourteen memoirs written by senior officers, sometimes with the assistance of professional writers and journalists (See Chapter 1). It becomes clear from these memoirs that the relationships between senior officers were not harmonious, predominantly among generals filling the same positions, such as chief of staff, head of intelligence, or minister of war. Risks confronted them on all sides: when the 1967 War ended, the then war minister, Shams Badran, was sentenced to prison, and 'Amr committed suicide, at least officially. A very small minority of generals lost their lives in the line of duty, such as two chiefs of staff, 'Abd al-Mun'im Riyad (1967–69), and Ahmad Badawi (1978–80), who was killed in a plane crash. Some accused Sadat of a conspiracy that led to the death of Badawi and thirteen other officers in early 1981, as a result of conflicts between them.[136] Others dismissed what they described as the conspiracy theory as lunacy, arguing that it was a pure accident, and that Sadat did not need to resort to drastic measures to get rid of Badawi, as he could have done so by other means had he so desired.[137] Even when a senior officer such as al-Jamasi accepted the notion that the president had the right and the legitimate power to appoint new ministers and military leaders, he was disappointed that Sadat chose October 5, 1978, the fifth anniversary of the October War, to end al-Jamasi's military career, given that al-Jamasi was one of its architects and oversaw the successful crossing of the Suez Canal.[138]

Wrangling and strife was not, of course, just an Egyptian phenomenon. Memoirs from Iraq, Syria, and Algeria give us the same impression. In Syria and Iraq, generals were under intense scrutiny by the leadership; Saddam Hussein dispensed with generals who failed in their military mission during the eight-year war with Iran in the 1980s, but was simultaneously cautious toward those who achieved military success, and whose reputation and loyalty among soldiers increased to what he considered a dangerous level. Ra'ad al-Hamdani, a senior officer in the Iraqi army, describes the uncertainty among senior officers and the unpredictability of Saddam Hussein's

---

[136] Mahmud Fawzi, *Asrar suqut ta'irat al-Mushir Ahmad Badawi* [The secrets of the plane crash of Field Marshal Ahmad Badawi] (Cairo: al-Hadaf Publishing, 1992).

[137] 'Ali, *Mashawir al-'umr*, pp. 476–77.

[138] Al-Jamasi, *Mudhakkirat al-Jamasi*, pp. 572–73.

decisions.[139] The memoirs of other senior Iraqi officers depict a similar atmosphere, and the lack of trust that prevailed among the military leadership, as almost every senior officer wanted to be as close as possible to the president in order to protect his own position.[140] In Syria, because the Asad dynasty has continued to the present, we have fewer memoirs of generals, but other accounts underline the friction among the military elite. One memoir discusses the envy and rivalry that prevailed among the senior officers close to Asad, to the extent that the writer felt that "envy destroyed the esprit de corps."[141] Another Syrian memoir by a senior air force general covers the events of the 1967 War, but admits no culpability for the disaster that took place, and while he details the reasons for defeat, none refers to the personal liability of any senior officer. Syria, like Egypt, also hid the truth of the events from its population, and Asad was furious when one general suggested announcing the fall of Qunaytara into the hands of Israel.[142] Mustafa Talas, Syria's minister of defense and a close ally of Hafiz al-Asad, who was dismissed by Bashar al-Asad after thirty years of service, wrote three volumes on the Syrian army's history and two volumes of personal memoirs. While there is interesting biographical information about senior officers, there is no hint of the problems between the military and the country's leadership, or any analysis of the military leadership's responsibilities for the different military engagements.[143]

In Algeria, Lyes Laribi describes what he terms "la guerre au sommet" (the war at the top) among senior officers around the question of electing Bouteflika as president.[144] Clashes at the top are also

---

[139] Al-Hamdani, *Qabla an yughadiruna al-tarikh.*

[140] See, for example, al-Samarra'i, *Hutam al-bawwaba al-sharqiyya*; and al-Salihi, *al-Zilzal.* See also Sassoon, *Saddam Hussein's Ba'th Party*, pp. 137–43.

[141] See, for example, Hamdun, *Dhikrayat wa ara'*, p. 105.

[142] Muhammad As'ad Muqayyid, *Masira fi al-hayat: tarikh ma lam yu'arrikh lahu al-akharun* [Journey in life: a history that was not documented by others] (Damascus: al-Dhakira Publishing, 2005), pp. 145–47.

[143] Talas, *Tarikh al-jaysh al-'Arabi al-Suri.* His memoirs are Mustafa Talas, *Mir'at hayati* [Reflections of my life] (Damascus: Talas Publishing, 1991). A review of these memoirs can be found in Youssef Aboul-Enein, "Syrian Defense Minister General Mustafa Talas: Memoirs, Volume Two," *Military Review*, vol. 85, no. 3 (May/June 2005), pp. 99–102. Talas was retired in 2004. His son, Manaf Talas, also a senior officer with a rank of brigadier-general, defected from Syria in mid 2012.

[144] Laribi, *L'Algérie des généraux*, pp. 200–10.

related to the issue of accountability due to the lack of clarity in the relations between the leadership and the military top brass in these republics. Whenever a general was demoted or retired, he was convinced that personal issues rather than performance led to his demotion. For instance, after the 1967 War, Ahmad Isma'il was forced to retire, due to the responsibility attached to his position during the war, but after appealing to Nasser, he was reinstated.[145]

Conclusion

Military men were overwhelmingly at the helm of the republics discussed here (See Table 3.1), with the exception of Tunisia. Indeed, among the leaders who managed to survive for a long time, there was only one exception – Saddam Hussein, who did not belong to the military and had no military background. Yet his ability to control the military and to give himself the rank of field marshal in charge of the armed forces clearly show his skills in manipulating the combined system of party, army, and security services to suppress any opposition, be it civil or military.[146] All the other leaders who governed for a long time derived their strength and support from the military.

A second point clearly demonstrated here is that once these military officers took over the reins of the country, their relationship with the military establishment was not harmonious, a factor that negatively impacted the decision-making process, mainly during military conflicts. Overall, the military was not the center of decision making in those republics, although it provided the backbone for the leadership. It was the most cohesive institution within each state and provided ample rewards and benefits, especially to officers. The leaders managed to coup-proof their regimes, but most of the repression was carried out by the security services, as the next chapter shows.

A third point is that memoirs of military men show an unwillingness to take responsibility for failures that occurred under their leadership. Generals and political leaders exchanged charges of culpability, but never on a personal basis. Even when Arab countries

---

[145] Al-Jilad, *Mushir al-nasr*, pp. 48–50.
[146] For a discussion of military versus non-military leaders and the use of violence, see Gandhi, *Political Institutions under Dictatorship*, pp. 25–31.

admitted that many mistakes in strategy and execution of orders took place during the June 1967 War, no one was willing to be personally accountable.

A final point is that ideological armies such as those of Syria and Iraq were more loyal to the leadership than the non-ideological ones in countries like Tunisia and Egypt, which allowed the toppling of their presidents to take place.[147]

---

[147] See Cronin, *Armies and State-Building*, pp. 7–8.

4 | *The role of security services in the Arab republics*

A strong security apparatus is essential to the longevity of authoritarian regimes. This has been highlighted in the classic studies of single-party regimes, as well in recent research into authoritarian resilience in Eastern Europe and the Middle East.[1] The security services were without doubt the cornerstone of such regimes in the Arab republics, both in establishing them and ensuring their durability.[2] Whether in communist Europe or in the Arab world, anti-regime demonstrators realized that the ultimate defeat of the security apparatus was critical for revolutions to succeed. Each republic invested large amounts of money and effort to build loyal agencies that could withstand changes and be relied upon to uproot any opposition, real or imaginary. As a result, the number of functionaries and the network of informants expanded significantly in all these countries. Technical surveillance, such as eavesdropping and filming devices, was introduced to improve

---

[1] Hannah Arendt, *The Origins of Totalitarianism* (New York: Harcourt, Brace & Company, 1951); Carl J. Friedrich and Zbigniew K. Brzezinski, *Totalitarian Dictatorship and Autocracy* (New York: Praeger, 1961). See also Yevgenia Albats, *State within a State: The KGB and its Hold on Russia – Past, Present, and Future* (New York: Farrar Straus Giroux, 1994); and the two articles of Eva Bellin, "The Robustness of Authoritarianism in the Middle East: Exceptionalism in Comparative Perspective," *Comparative Politics*, vol. 36, no. 2 (January 2004), pp. 139–57; "Reconsidering the Robustness of Authoritarianism in the Middle East: Lessons from the Arab Spring," *Comparative Politics*, vol. 44, no. 2 (January 2012), pp. 127–49.

[2] As mentioned in the Introduction, this work is restricted to the republics for two reasons: first, the availability of more data, whether in archives (Iraq) or memoirs (Algeria, Egypt, Libya, Sudan, Syria, and Tunisia); and second, the uprising in some of these countries has helped to uncover many facets of their security services. I am sure many of my depictions could apply to some Arab monarchies, and I have made references to Oman and Iran. The *Economist* argues that the difference between the security services in the Arab republics and those of the Gulf is that the latter "are usually subtler. Surveillance is high-tech and violence is exacted in prisons, away from the public view." See "Bahrain: How the Police Recruit Radicals," *Economist*, October 13, 2012.

the efficiency and accuracy of information gathering, and to create a sense of omnipresence among the population.

Fear was a powerful tool used by these organizations to bolster their authority. The miasma of fear permeated all levels of society, although it differed from one country to another. In some countries such as Iraq, the regime was Stalinist throughout its thirty-five-year hegemony. In Syria, the levels of state repression varied from high intensity during the 1980s to a relatively lower level of repression from the mid 1990s. Even in countries like Tunisia, which projected the image of a more open society, people were always on guard against the long arm of the security services. But fear and coercion – critical as they are – constitute only one element in explaining the durability of these regimes. It is hard to believe that so many of them could last for three or four decades based simply on fear.[3] Brutality alone is not a guarantee of durability, and examples such as Cambodia show that force and fear are not the only bulwarks of entrenched political power.[4] In the Arab world, it was also the ability of the republics' leaders to establish parallel systems of fear and rewards, which Steven Heydemann has termed "networks of privilege," and to make sure that their supporters were "vested" in the system, that contributed to the long life of the regimes.[5] Furthermore, to borrow from Michel Foucault, authoritarian power also plays on people's inherent "desire for the state" and a readiness to act on its behalf. In the 1960s, the desire for stability and economic growth was paramount in the Arab world after decades of instability and stagnation.[6]

Fear is central to the continuation of authoritarianism, so once the barrier of fear was broken, the end of these regimes was nigh. Interestingly, both the communist regimes and the Arab republics, with their grasp of realpolitik, understood this principle long before

---

[3] North Korea might be an exception to the rule.

[4] Jennifer Gandhi and Adam Przeworski, "Authoritarian Institutions and the Survival of Autocrats," *Comparative Political Studies*, vol. 40, no. 11 (September 2007), p. 1280. The authors argue that despite killing almost 2 million Cambodians, Pol Pot was in power for three years before being ousted.

[5] Steven Heydemann (ed.), *Networks of Privilege in the Middle East: The Politics of Economic Reform Revisited* (New York: Palgrave Macmillan, 2004), pp. 1–34.

[6] Michel Foucault, "Méthodologie pour la connaissance du monde: comment se débarrasser du Marxisme" [Methodology for knowing the world: how to get rid of Marxism], *Dits et écrits*, vol. III (Paris: Gallimard, 1978), pp. 617–18. The strategies to cultivate "popular support" embraced social and economic policies that actually led to improvement in education, life expectancy, and the welfare system, particularly in the 1970s and 1980s.

the uprisings erupted. After the mass upheavals in the German Democratic Republic (GDR) in 1953 and in Poland and Hungary in 1956, security officials realized that they were "able to control individual attitudes and individual behavior, but could not prevent mass upheavals. Therefore a great deal of effort was channeled into the suppression of the slightest symptoms of resistance for fear they would turn into mass protest."[7] Opposition groups also realized the potency of breaking the fear barrier by launching massive operations to expose a regime's weakness and galvanize others to participate.[8]

In all these authoritarian regimes, additional controls were imposed after discovering a plot or after political or economic disturbances. Following the unexpected uprising in southern and northern Iraq in 1991 after the First Gulf War, the security services were revamped, and people close to Saddam Hussein (such as his younger son, Qusay) were entrusted with running them. The Middle East witnessed exactly the same phenomenon as Eastern Europe when the barrier of fear was breached, and the security services were unable to control the masses. As one Libyan told a journalist in early 2011: "We just want to be able to live like human beings ... I'm not even afraid any more. Once I wouldn't have spoken at all by phone. Now I don't care. Now enough is enough."[9]

The history and politics of the security apparatus in the Arab republics, similar to those in communist Europe or the military dictatorships in Latin America, are about fear, violence, betrayal, and human viciousness; but it is also a story of bravery, of the suffering of ordinary citizens, and of the human kindness showed by some. An important tactic adopted by these regimes was to involve as many people as possible in their policies of control and violence. They made sure, one way or another, that "the majority of people were somehow morally discredited, compelled to violate their own moral standards."[10] For instance,

---

[7] Krzystof Persak and Łukasz Kamiński (eds.), *A Handbook of the Communist Security Apparatus in East Central Europe 1944–1989* (Warsaw: Institute of National Remembrance, 2005), p. 8.

[8] Abu Basha, *Mudhakkirat Hasan Abu Basha fi al-amn wa al-siyasa*, p. 123. Abu Basha was appointed minister of interior after the assassination of President Sadat. In 1987 he was seriously injured in an assassination attempt by Islamists and hospitalized for many months until he recovered.

[9] Angelique Chrisafis, "Libya Protests: Gunshots, Screams and Talk of Revolution," *Guardian*, February 20, 2011.

[10] Slavoj Žižek, *Did Somebody Say Totalitarianism?: Five Interventions in the (Mis)Use of a Notion* (New York: Verso, 2001), pp. 90–91.

Saddam Hussein declared that in addition to himself, other members of the regional command of the Ba'th Party could sign death warrants for deserters. He also decreed that members of the investigative committees should themselves participate in the executions if they found the deserter guilty.[11] Thus, by involving a large number of officials, regimes in Syria, Iraq, and Algeria succeeded in widening the network of accomplices, which in turn allowed the rulers and their supporters to feel more secure in the "safety" of a large group versus a small number of executioners.

Given the availability of Iraqi archives and the extensive array of memoirs from other Arab republics, this chapter will first examine the common denominators among the security services in the Arab world, and then answer four questions on how information was collected, its usage, its contribution to the longevity of these regimes, and finally, the issue of accountability.

Common denominators

As Khalili and Schwedler point out, while policing practices in the Arab world are frequently targeted by humanitarian organizations, "the literature systematically examining the emergence of *internal* coercive institutions within the Middle East has been surprisingly sparse."[12] Other scholars have noted "the insufficient scholarly attention accorded to the Arab Security Sector" by several academic publications specializing in the Middle East.[13] With regard to Iraq, we now have an excellent source – the archives of the security services – and for the first time we are able to construct how these agencies operated, how they recruited informants, and how they utilized the gathered information. The Ba'th files hold copies of the correspondence sent to the Ba'th regional command or its branches by the four main security agencies. Furthermore, the archives have a special section of almost 2,000 files relating to Jihaz al-Amn al-Khass, the Special Security Organization (SSO), which are truly insightful.

---

[11] Sassoon, *Saddam Hussein's Ba'th Party*, p. 206.
[12] Khalili and Schwedler (eds.), "Introduction," in *Policing and Prisons in the Middle East*, p. 10.
[13] Oren Barak and Assaf David, "The Arab Security Sector: A New Research Agenda for a Neglected Topic," *Armed Forces and Society*, vol. 36, no. 5 (2010), pp. 804–24.

The SSO was the most powerful security agency in Iraq from 1980 until the US-led invasion in 2003, and was managed from the early 1990s by Saddam's younger son, Qusay. Apart from being responsible for the safety of the president and the palaces, many of the SSO's departments had the task of monitoring the loyalty of officers and employees working in various organizations affiliated with the party or the army. We also now have partial documents from the Libyan secret services that add to our understanding. For other countries such as Algeria, Egypt, Sudan, Syria, and Tunisia, this chapter relies mostly on published memoirs by heads and senior officers of the different agencies in these countries, together with memoirs of long-term prisoners who wrote extensively about how the system operated. Many new memoirs, as underlined in Chapter 1, have been published since the uprisings, and senior members of these regimes have detailed how these systems functioned.

In authoritarian regimes, in the Arab world or elsewhere, the role of the security services is remarkably similar, and they have many characteristics in common. Above all, they constitute the apparatus for coercion and control by providing the rulers with information on political, economic, and social issues among the population.[14] In fact, there are more similarities than once assumed, whether in single-party states such as Iraq and Syria or in the so-called multi-party systems that existed in Egypt and Tunisia. In all these countries, security agencies were designed to overlap, and were so structured as to ensure that no one agency would become strong enough to threaten the regime. All the countries had on average four main agencies, plus a few others that were spin-offs created for specific purposes.[15] The existence of a pervasive and oppressive internal security apparatus was well established.

---

[14] For an interesting comparison with Zaire, see Michael G. Schatzberg, *The Dialectics of Oppression in Zaire* (Bloomington: Indiana University Press, 1988), pp. 40–48.

[15] For a good description of the Libyan security organizations, see Hanspeter Mattes, "Challenges to Security Sector Governance in the Middle East: The Libyan Case," Geneva Centre for the Democratic Control of Armed Forces (DCAF), Conference Paper, July 12–13, 2004. Even in less coercive systems such as Oman, these characteristics exist. See Dale Eickelman and M. G. Dennison, "Arabizing the Omani Intelligence Services: Clash of Cultures?" *International Journal of Intelligence and Counterintelligence*, vol. 7, no. 1 (1994), pp. 4–5. It should be noted that proliferation of intelligence agencies exist also in democratic countries such as the USA.

In Egypt, it began under Nasser and continued under Sadat and Mubarak.[16] In Syria, the basis for security services that controlled all facets of life was laid during the union with Egypt (1958–61). As one memoir explains, by the late 1950s, two years after the union between Syria and Egypt, security chief 'Abd al-Hamid al-Sarraj "was in control of all affairs in the Syrian Province from administrative, political, economic, and security aspects to the extent that never before had one Syrian [had] so much power."[17] Similarly in Iraq, security services were beginning to take control of events and affect decision making in the late 1950s and early 1960s, but the difference in later years was that leaders such as Hafiz al-Asad or Saddam Hussein developed and perfected the operations of these agencies to allow them to get rid of the leaders' opponents and ensure their personal dominance to an extent not seen before.

One major study in several Arab countries focused on the structure of the Ministry of Interior as the vehicle for internal security, but rarely discussed the other, more secretive, organs.[18] It is notable that while the Arab world balked at developing regional economic integration, there was considerable dialogue and cooperation between the different republics and kingdoms on matters of security and intelligence. In all these countries, the minister of interior was a powerful position; in Egypt after the 2011 revolution, for example, it was reported that the ministry had 1.4 million employees and an estimated 700,000 informants on the payroll.[19] Even official Egyptian statistics revealed the dramatic growth in the number of employees in state security and the

---

[16] For an extensive overview of the intelligence system in Egypt, see Sirrs, *A History of the Egyptian Intelligence Service*. For the repression apparatus, see Human Rights Watch, *Behind Closed Doors: Torture and Detention in Egypt* (New York: Human Rights Watch, 1992).

[17] Nabil 'Umar, *Dhi'b al-mukhabarat al-asmar: al-bab al-sirri li-Gamal 'Abd al-Nasser* [The brown wolf of the intelligence: the secret door to Gamal 'Abd al-Nasser] (Cairo: Dar al-Fursan, 2000), p. 80.

[18] Lieutenant-General 'Abbas Abu Shama and Major-General Muhammad al-Amin al-Bushri, *al-Hayakil al-tanzimiyya li-ajhizat al-amn fi al-duwal al-'Arabiyya: dirasa tamhidiyya li-wad' haykil tanzimi muwahhad* [Organization structures of security services in the Arab world: an initial study to create a unified organizational structure] (Riyadh: Naif Arab Academy for Security Studies, 1997).

[19] Alistair Lyon, "Analysis – Egyptian Army could hold Key to Mubarak's Fate," Reuters, January 28, 2011. The estimate is based on leaked cables from US diplomats.

police: an increase from about 500,000 in 1993 to more than 640,000 by 2012–13. These statistics did not include members of the armed forces, general intelligence and military intelligence, who were estimated at roughly another 600,000.[20]

The ratio of police to ordinary citizens in a country like Tunisia was 2.5 times what it is in France and almost four times that in the United Kingdom, a ratio that spread the net of fear and constantly reminded the population of the omnipresent shadow of the authorities.[21] If these statistics are correct, then Tunisia had an even higher ratio of police to citizens than East Germany with the Stasi, where it was estimated there was one police officer for every 180 citizens.[22] Yet it should be noted that in countries such as Tunisia, Iraq, and Syria the ruling party itself acted as another layer of security, as discussed in Chapter 2. Its branches provided pertinent information due to their depth of local knowledge. In Iraq, for instance, the role of party branches was paramount in hunting down army deserters in small towns and villages, where they had better sources than the city-oriented headquarters. However, the role of the police in these republics was not identical: in Iraq, for example, police work was mostly mundane, such as robberies and civilian disputes, and in the minds of the Iraqi people they were not feared as much as the different security forces. In fact, the Iraqi Ba'th documents do not contain many details of the role of the police, and rarely refer to them in arrest cases or investigations.

In a republic such as Egypt, the connection between the police and Amn al-Dawla (the State Security Organization), or what was called Jihaz al-Mabahith (the Investigation Bureau), is far closer, and in the eyes of the public the police were to be avoided as much as state security. Both police and state security dealt with labor strikes, terrorist activities, and arrests and investigations of the Muslim Brothers, and

---

[20] 'Abd al-Khaliq Faruq, *Judhur al-fasad al-idari fi Misr: bi'at al-'amal wa siyasat al-ajur fi Misr 1963–2002* [The roots of administrative corruption in Egypt: work environment and policies of ranks and salaries in Egypt 1963–2002] (Cairo: al-Shuruq Publishing, 2008), pp. 275–77. The book gives a detailed schematic structure of the Ministry of Interior in Egypt during the 1980s (see pp. 281–82.)

[21] Hibou, *The Force of Obedience*, p. 81. Hibou mentions that the ratio in Tunisia is between 1:67 and 1:112. This is compared to France (the most heavily policed country in Europe), which has a ratio of 1:265, and in the UK the ratio is 1:380.

[22] Mary Elise Sarotte, *The Collapse: The Accidental Opening of the Berlin Wall* (New York: Basic Books, 2014), p. 9.

the lines were not always clearly defined. For example, the police were partly blamed for the assassination of President Sadat, but at the same time it was the security forces that had informants within the Brothers' organization, and were actually interrogating someone who knew about the assassination plot. In an interesting and comprehensive analysis of the role of the police in Egyptian politics, one Egyptian researcher clearly demonstrates the connection between police officers and the political echelon (appointments as governors or deputy governors of provinces), citing the numerous senior officers who rose to become minister of interior, and one (Mamduh Salim) who even reached the position of prime minister.[23] The study shows how the police interfered on a regular basis in political nominations for elections, and how they were involved in curbing labor strikes and other "threats" to national security.[24] Efforts were made in Egypt to raise police standards by opening courses and training new recruits in technical skills. Educational and cultural courses were also set up to increase literacy and specialization. According to a police officer who was well versed in these courses, these efforts were not crowned with success in part due to the educational level of the average policeman, and possibly to the low salaries they received. As a result, a new layer of policemen was created called *amin al-shurta* (deputy inspector).[25] In Egypt, not only did the police resort to physical pressure and torture, but also many of its officers used *baltajiyya* (thugs) to settle scores with political enemies or simply with individuals or neighbors who irritated them.[26] One observer ascribes the use of violence to the fact that the

[23] Muhammad Muhammad al-Jawadi, *Qadat al-shurta fi al-siyasa al-Misriyya 1952–2002: dirasa tahliliyya wa mawsu'at shakhsiyyat* [Police commanders in Egyptian politics 1952–2002: an analytical study and a biographical dictionary] (Cairo: Madbuly Publishing, 2003). The book contains detailed information about senior police officers, particularly those who reached the high position of minister of interior.

[24] Ibid., pp. 398–99, 345–50.

[25] Salim Salama Juwayli, *Taqyim al-kifaya al-idariyya wa al-mihniyya li-umana' al-shurta* [An appraisal of the administrative and technical capabilities of deputy inspectors] (Cairo: Institute for Higher Studies for Police Officers, n.d.), pp. 11–13. The book was published in the 1970s. Deputy inspector was a rank between constable and officer.

[26] Basma 'Abd al-'Aziz, *Ighra' al-sulta al-mutlaq: masar al-'unf fi 'alaqat al-shurta bil-muwatin 'abr al-tarikh* [The temptation of absolute authority: the trajectory of violence in the police relationship with the citizen throughout history] (Cairo: Safsafa Publishing, 2011), p. 63.

police force in the Arab world and other colonized states emerged after independence from colonial militaries and "were hived off national armies."[27] Certainly, the role of the local police as part of the coercive apparatus in these countries needs further investigation.

Ministers of interior in most republics, at least formally, were responsible for both the local police and security services. A number of interior ministers from different republics described in their memoirs how their ministry functioned within the government and toward its "enemies." Ministers of interior were feared across the different countries; their power and influence reached all levels. History relates that when Napoleon Bonaparte was told that his minister of interior, Joseph Fouché, was a heartless man, feared even by his own children, he responded by saying that this was the first sign that Fouché would succeed as a minister of interior.[28] Hasan Abu Basha defined in his memoir the role of the minister:

In spite of the fact that [the minister of interior] is a political appointment, its occupant because of his control of security services, represents a tool for the country and the regime to rule society. The Minister of Interior is responsible for keeping track of all political forces and ensuring that they are acting legally and within the framework of democratic elections and party activities.[29]

One Egyptian journalist who had interviewed four Egyptian ministers of interior tells us that ministers who were not feared – or, even worse, who were popular, such as Ahmad Rushdi – ended up losing their jobs. Rushdi was seen as weak when faced with the dramatic events that shook Egypt in February 1986, when security forces went on the rampage at tourist sites.[30] The violence began when several thousand military policemen stormed four large luxury hotels in the Giza district of Cairo near the Pyramids, and, as tourists ran for cover, the rioting policemen ransacked the hotel lobbies and set them alight.[31] The

27 Yezid Sayigh, "Agencies of Coercion: Armies and Internal Security Forces," *International Journal of Middle East Studies*, vol. 43, no. 3 (August 2011), pp. 403–05.
28 Muhammad Mustafa, *Kuntu waziran lil-dakhiliyya* [I was a minister of the interior] (Cairo: Akhbar al-Yawm, 1992), p. 5.
29 Abu Basha, *Mudhakkirat Hasan Abu Basha fi al-amn wa al-siyasa*, p. 151.
30 Mustafa, *Kuntu waziran lil-dakhiliyya*, pp. 177–84. The author interviewed Nabawi Isma'il, Hasan Abu Basha, Ahmad Rushdi, and Zaki Badr.
31 Margaret L. Rogg, "Egyptian Policemen Fight Troops in Revolt Set off near Pyramids," *New York Times*, February 27, 1986.

pressure on the minister holding this portfolio was reflected in the high turnover of incumbents. Although President Mubarak valued stability in his cabinet, four ministers of interior held office during the five years from 1981 to 1986. Many ascribed this to the "politicization of the role – making the minister of interior the prime defender of the ruler and his party."[32]

One interior minister in Tunisia, Ahmed Mestiri, believed that being in charge of the ministry would allow him to reform the political system by promoting channels of communication between the leadership and the citizens. Information, in his opinion, percolated upward, and the party had turned into an organ to carry out the regime's policy. He felt that he had nothing in common with his colleagues, who had no interest in introducing any democratic reforms such as limiting Bourguiba's powers or the party's hegemony.[33] In fact, mismanagement of information and centralized decision making are recurring themes; another Tunisian minister clearly underlines in his memoirs how the lack of clarity and the vague and centralized decision-making process exacerbated the problems of controlling the disturbances that took place at the outbreak of the June 1967 War.[34] While dealing with a dominant and powerful leader such as Bourguiba was difficult enough, it paled in comparison to being the minister of interior under Qaddafi. 'Abd al-Mun'im al-Huni, who was a member of the Libyan Revolutionary Command Council after the revolution, interior minister and director of intelligence from September 1970, and then prime minister from September 1971, describes the turbulent times he experienced: the constant clashes within the revolutionary council; Qaddafi's lack of trust even in his senior ministers; and the decisions he took without consulting his interior minister on issues related to security.[35]

---

[32] Springborg, *Mubarak's Egypt*, p. 148. Springborg gives detailed statistics of these turnovers, p. 147.

[33] Al-Mestiri, *Shahada lil-tarikh*, p. 213. Mestiri served only fifteen months in 1970. In 1986 he was arrested on the orders of Bourguiba for participating in a demonstration condemning the American attack on Libya.

[34] Essebsi, *Habib Bourguiba: al-muhimm wa al-ahamm*, pp. 124–31.

[35] Ghassan Sharbal, *Fi khaymat al-Qaddafi: rifaq al-'aqid yakshufun khabaya 'ahdihi* [In Qaddafi's tent: the colonel's comrades expose the mysteries of his era] (Beirut: Riyad al-Rayyis Publishing, 2013), pp. 93–159. Sharbal, a journalist from *al-Hayat* newspaper, interviewed five people who were close to Qaddafi and worked with him over a long period. In 1975 al-Huni was accused of conspiring against Qaddafi and left the country, remaining in exile for almost twenty-five years.

Control of information was mostly the duty of either the Ministry of Interior or the Ministry of Culture and Information (names of ministries differ from one country to another). Media was an important tool in the hands of these regimes and mostly was under the direct control of the state. Qaddafi's chief spokesman recounts how news bulletins were reviewed and every news item edited to ensure that they fit with the regime's policies. Journalists working for these regimes were well compensated and given certain privileges such as free travel.[36]

In spite of the considerable powers of interior ministers, the reality was that in many republics the heads of General Security and of the Special Security Forces reported directly to the president rather than to the minister. Yet, we can still see how the network of gathering information developed through the Ministry of Interior, and some ministries (as in Egypt) expanded by creating new directorates such as al-Amn al-Ijtimaʿi (Security for Social Affairs), which in essence was another arm to collect information on different aspects of society.[37] The purpose of these systems, wherever they were, was for "security reasons." The argument used by the regimes was that "the personal repression of individuals and their private affairs is aimed at ensuring public order."[38] But, as Hibou states, "the law of the stronger, that is the law of the police," and becomes "superior to other powers ... to impose its own law."[39]

A common denominator is that in the Arab world many of these organizations were originally built along the lines of the British and French security services during the colonial and mandate periods. In the Arab countries under British control, the "practical culture of intelligence apprenticeship and training passed from British to Arab personnel, despite general resentment of foreign domination."[40] After toppling the monarchies and becoming republics, most countries were heavily influenced by the Soviets or East Germans, who provided training and technical assistance to security officers from Iraq to Sudan.[41]

---

[36] ʿAbd al-Munʿim Yusif al-Lamushi, *Fi ʿahd Muʿammar al-Qaddafi: kuntu mutahaddithan rasmiyyan* [In the era of Muʿammar al-Qaddafi: I was an official spokesman] (Tripoli: al-Hadath Publishing, 2012), pp. 133–36.

[37] This directorate was unique in Egypt, and no other Arab country, according to this study, had anything similar: see Abu Shama and al-Bushri, *al-Hayakil al-tanzimiyya*, p. 120.

[38] Hibou, *The Force of Obedience*, p. 85.   [39] Ibid.

[40] Eickelman and Dennison, "Arabizing the Omani Intelligence Services," p. 2.

[41] For Sudan, see ʿAbd al-ʿAziz and Abu Ranat, *Asrar jihaz al-asrar*, pp. 26–27. For Iraq, see Joseph Sassoon, "The East German Ministry of State Security and Iraq,

In the late 1960s and early 1970s, many of these republics adopted a socialist policy and were either seen to be non-aligned or else supportive of the Soviet Bloc. As a result, technical aid and intelligence advice were provided by the Soviet Union, the GDR, and Czechoslovakia, which sent teams to train officers in interrogation techniques and, more importantly, to teach local officers about using bugging devices. However, the leading country in this field reduced its help in the 1980s because there was dismay in East Berlin about the real nature of socialism in those countries (particularly Iraq and Syria), the repression of local communists, and the East Germans' insistence on getting paid in hard currency.[42] The meticulous filing and cross-referencing found in the archives of the Iraqi security agencies are clearly reminiscent of the systems used by the Stasi. The setups of many of these organizations, whether in Iraq or Syria, had many similarities with foreign agencies such as the KGB and were indeed "a state within a state."[43]

The leaders of the Arab republics were determined to coup-proof their regimes, and relied on members of their families or clans to ensure the loyalty of the inner circle. Agency heads in Iraq and Syria belonged to a few clans; for instance, within the SSO in Iraq, the nine heads of the important departments, together with the director of Qusay's office, belonged to five different tribes and extended families.[44] In Libya, Qaddafi relied heavily on members of his tribe, the Qadhadhfa, who were entrusted with preserving the regime.[45] His cousin and two brothers were assigned to security and intelligence; others occupied sensitive jobs or were tasked with commanding the Presidential Guard.[46] However, in Iraq or Syria, while there was a reliance on the inner group of Tikritis or 'Alawites respectively, the Iraqi archives prove the falsity of the assumptions that the security services and the inner group were strictly Sunnis. In fact, many Shi'is, Kurds, and Christians served at a high level in the Iraqi agencies until the 2003 invasion. Similarly in Syria, quite a number of senior officers in the

1968–1989," *Journal of Cold War Studies*, vol. 16, no. 1 (Winter 2014), pp. 4–23.
[42] Sassoon, "The East German Ministry."   [43] Albats, *State within a State*.
[44] See Sassoon, *Saddam Hussein's Ba'th Party*, table 4, p. 106 for clan affiliation of senior specialists in the Directorate of Security Affairs in the SSO.
[45] El-Kikhia, *Libya's Qaddafi*, pp. 89–91, 151–61.
[46] Mattes, "Formal and Informal Authority in Libya," pp. 73–76.

intelligence community are Sunnis. Interestingly, while a reliance on families and clans close to the regime was essential for the preservation of power in the Iraqi, Libyan, and Syrian regimes, it was sometimes a double-edged sword, as once a particular clan was considered too powerful or dangerous, the authorities had to purge the system of all its members. In other countries such as Egypt or Sudan, the clan system did not exist, as heads of these services were diverse, and many had long careers in the army or the police before being appointed to run the security agencies.

Recruitment of officers to these agencies was more similar than has been thought. Emphasis on loyalty was paramount, and the social origins of the candidate were a significant consideration. The agencies were built on paranoia and the belief that there was an enemy lurking behind every curtain. In a fascinating interview, a former senior Egyptian security officer refers to a conversation he had with Hasan Abu Basha, an ex-minister of interior, who described the ideal security officer: "Having favorable judgment of people and being content are two virtues for human beings, but grave sins in a state security officer. This is the principle of every agency."[47] The training of security officers was comparable in all these countries. A senior Egyptian security officer, detailing the process of recruiting officers and their training, admitted that all officers were trained in beating, torture, and inter-rogation techniques of suspects, and this became a habit and "a fact of life" in these services rather than learning how to investigate properly to uncover the truth.[48] The use of torture is widespread among not only the security services in these countries but also among the local police forces. A senior Egyptian police officer and professor of law at the Police Academy ascribed the prevalence of physical intimidation to the genuine belief on the part of police officers that torturing a suspect is the most efficient way of obtaining a confession. He pointed out that many within the police force were lazy and wanted to hide their lack of investigative capabilities, and he attributed the habit of debasing sus-pects to the gratification it gave officers to exercise such control over other human beings.[49]

---

[47] Interview with Brigadier Hussein Hammuda, *al-Shuruq*, April 8, 2011.
[48] Ibid.
[49] Qadri 'Abd al-Fattah al-Shahawi, *Jara'im al-sulta al-shurtiyya* [Crimes of the police authority] (Cairo: al-Nahda Publishing, 1977), pp. 21–22.

Another common denominator among the security services in these republics is the reason for joining: in addition to rewards and the ability to extract bribes, the sense of power can be intoxicating. These agencies were omnipresent; their members felt privileged and enjoyed almost total immunity from the law. Files of the Iraqi SSO clearly indicate the number of cases where officers abused their positions purely because they had the power to do so. Whether in Iraq, Syria, or Egypt, officials approved promotions and appointments within the government bureaucracy, judicial institutions, universities, and the army. In Egypt, "the security services maintained a stranglehold on Egyptian universities approving promotions and appointments, keeping tabs on loyalties of lecturers."[50] Vetting everyone and vetoing any promotion led to an immense sense of power and self-importance, exactly as had existed in communist Europe. As one Tunisian observer states, security men became themselves the law as they realized they had the power to enter any house, arrest anyone, manipulate all laws and regulations, and interfere in elections of unions.[51] From the governments' point of view, hiring large numbers to join these agencies gave them a sense of security, as well as providing employment to loyal supporters and co-opting many others into the system. Corruption and abuse of power were natural consequences of this: memos from the Iraqi archives indicate that the leadership knew that officers exploited their positions for their own benefit, or simply used their affiliation as a tool of control and power.[52] One Sudanese security official succinctly described the relationship between such regimes and their employees:

Thus we see how the totalitarian regimes politicize the civil service. Anyone chosen to serve [the regime] is not focused on serving for the benefit of the citizen or the country because his aim is to be the loyal guard of this regime that has given him the job, the rewards, and care. Hence the official does not care if this regime was corrupt or good, but more important is that it protects him, and that this regime stays in power at any price.[53]

[50] Heba Saleh, "Egyptian Academics Strike in Fight of Campus Democracy," *Financial Times*, October 4, 2011. See also Tewfick Aclimandos, "Reforming the Egyptian Security Services," Arab Reform Initiative, June 2011, available at www.arab-reform.net/reforming-egyptian-security-services.
[51] Tawfiq al-Madini, *Suqut al-dawla al-bulisiyya fi Tunis* [The collapse of the police state in Tunisia] (Beirut: Arab Scientific Publishers, 2011), p. 138.
[52] Sassoon, *Saddam Hussein's Ba'th Party*, p. 110.
[53] Abu Hamid Ahmad Ibrahim, *Qissat kifah wa najah* [The story of struggle and success] (Khartoum: 'Izzat Publishing, 2006), p. 191.

At the same time, officers in all these security agencies were themselves under the microscope, as the Iraqi archives reveal. In Iraq, for example, the SSO was in charge of monitoring those within the services and did not hesitate to arrest and severely punish security officers suspected of disloyalty or of abuses that came to the attention of the presidency or the public.[54] A memoir by two senior Sudanese security officers portrays how, in a similar fashion to Iraq, members of the service "were under more severe scrutiny than the average citizen, given that the head of the service was perturbed by any sign that a member might take advantage of his position."[55] According to the Sudanese memoir and perhaps not surprisingly, if officers of the security services were imprisoned, they knew better than any prisoner how to manipulate and exploit the prison system to their benefit.[56] New regimes also targeted security and intelligence officials, because their loyalty was paramount; a Syrian memoir depicts how 'Abd al-Hamid al-Sarraj, who was in charge of the security organization after the union with Egypt, dismissed "all those that do not believe in unity and Arab nationalism such as those suspected of being communists, Syrian nationalists, and anyone belonging to suspicious parties connected to the Baghdad Pact."[57]

Personal conflicts and competition among the heads of the different agencies in each country played an important role in shaping the modus operandi of these services. Memoirs of Egyptian, Sudanese, Algerian, and Syrian senior officers give a clear indication of the impact of internal competition within these agencies. In Egypt, for instance, those who served under Nasser but lost their positions under Sadat were extremely harsh toward the officials who ran the security services after them and toward the new regime in general. While those who were in prominent positions under Sadat, but not under Nasser or Mubarak, portrayed the Sadat era as more open and liberal than either Nasser's era or Mubarak's.[58]

---

[54] Sassoon, *Saddam Hussein's Ba'th Party*, pp. 98–112.
[55] 'Abd al-'Aziz and Abu Ranat, *Asrar jihaz al-asrar*, p. 34.   [56] Ibid., p. 317.
[57] Shu'aybi, *Shahid min al-mukhabarat al-Suriyya*, pp. 121–22. The Baghdad Pact was created in 1955 by Britain, Pakistan, Iran, Turkey, and Iraq to strengthen regional defense and curb Soviet influence in the region.
[58] See the contrast between Tal'at, *Fi khidmat al-amn al-siyasi*, who emphasizes that he left before Sadat took over, and Fuad 'Allam, who served under Sadat. See Fu'ad 'Allam, *al-Ikhwan wa ana: min al-Manshiyya ila al-minassa* [The Brothers and I: from al-Manshiyya to the Podium] (Cairo: al-Misri Publications, 1996). Al-Manshiyya is a square in central Alexandria, and it refers to the failed assassination attempt against President Nasser by a member of the Brotherhood

Another common factor is the fear that these regimes harbored, to varying degrees, of foreigners and anything foreign. Security services in all the republics monitored their citizens' contacts with foreigners; for most of the last three decades traveling abroad required multiple permits before approval was received.[59] Fear of anything foreign, or the impact of foreigners, was not unique to the authoritarian regimes in the Arab world; Václav Havel explains that each one of those tyrannical systems "reveal[s] its most essential characteristic to be introversion."[60] In Romania under Ceaușescu, "anyone belonging to associations with links abroad" was watched carefully for any sign of "treacherous behavior."[61]

Two other characteristics common to these regimes are treated in this chapter separately due to their importance: first, all of them without exception used arrests, torture, and trials as a means of coercing all opposition; and second, they all feared religion and saw religious movements as a serious threat.

Arrests, torture, and trials

The use of force by the security agencies varied, according to one detailed study of four republics – Iraq, Libya, Syria, and Yemen – that had the highest number of people sentenced to death and hanged. Almost 2,000 of their citizens were executed between 1971 and 1985, but obviously this did not include unreported cases or those who died during torture. Furthermore, these numbers should be treated with utmost caution, as there are no official statistics and even the Iraqi archives do not give details about such numbers.[62] The arrest of anyone

in October 1954, while the Podium refers to the successful assassination of President Sadat in 1981.

[59] The Iraqi Ba'th archives contain abundant examples of how senior officials and ministers had to get permission to travel abroad even when they were attending official meetings for the Arab League or international conferences. Without exception, the SSO always made sure that these officials would be accompanied by security men to keep an eye on them.

[60] Václav Havel et al., *The Power of the Powerless: Citizens against the State in Central–Eastern Europe* (New York: M. E. Sharpe, 1990), p. 30.

[61] Dennis Deletant, *Ceaușescu and the Securitate: Coercion and Dissent in Romania, 1965–1989* (London: Hurst & Co., 2006), p. 341.

[62] Hasanayn Tawfiq Ibrahim, *Zahirat al-'unf al-siyasi fi al-nuzum al-'Arabiyya* [The phenomenon of political violence in the Arab regimes], 3rd edn. (Beirut: Center for Arab Unity Studies, 2011), pp. 158, 160.

suspected of antagonistic attitudes toward these regimes was the most widespread form of political violence against the population. These arrests did not usually attract much attention within or outside these republics, and relatively few people were aware of them (usually only family and close friends). In the prevailing atmosphere it was very easy to incarcerate anyone suspected of opposing the regime, and this ubiquitous practice gave the leadership a feeling of safety and control.

Arbitrary arrest in the middle of the night (in Egypt it was called *zuwwar al-fajr*, visitors at dawn) was widespread, as these regimes could not tolerate opposition in any form, whether by journalists, artists, students, or women activists. Some suffered torture; others had to face mock trials that manipulated the law to the regimes' requirements. Local journalists were continually harassed if they did not toe the official line. One Egyptian journalist was arrested twice, along with his brother, also a journalist. He was first arrested in 1981 for writing against Sadat's economic and foreign policies, and then in 2003, when both brothers were arrested for exposing the corruption of an official who had himself been arrested the previous week. The arrest was based on an outdated ruling that had been suspended by the attorney-general five years before the brothers were incarcerated. While it was clear there were no legal grounds for the arrests, the suffering of these two journalists, who were supported by many of their colleagues, shows the arbitrariness of the system and the irrationality that characterizes authoritarian regimes.[63]

One Egyptian artist who consistently annoyed all the leadership in Egypt was Ahmad Fu'ad Najm. The son of a police officer, he lived in an orphanage after his father's death, and his education was practical – he learned tailoring. Arrested in his early thirties for forging government forms to obtain products that he could sell at a profit, he was sentenced to three years. While incarcerated he met many of the communists whom Nasser had imprisoned. He began writing poetry in prison and soon attracted attention, including from famous writers such as Yusif al-Siba'i. His poetry is colloquial and mostly mocks the regime. Nasser had no tolerance for his poems and he was thrown back into prison multiple times. Although he initially believed that Sadat was

---

[63] Mahmud Bakri, *Ayyam fi al-sijn* [Days in prison] (Cairo: Jazirat al-Ward, 2010). The author presents details of the trial and the numerous articles written on the brothers' behalf by journalists and artists in Egypt.

more open, he wrote a poem declaring that "there is no difference between 'Abd al-Nasser and al-Sadat, nor between Haykal and 'Ali Amin [two confidants of the respective leaders]."[64] A poem scorning the visit of President Nixon to Egypt infuriated the authorities. In 1975, an officer in Amn al-Dawla prepared a statement declaring that "Ahmad Fu'ad Najm has become accustomed recently to write vernacular poetry that attacks the existing regime and its leadership, inflames citizens against the coalition of the people, and diffuses the spirit of bitterness among its listeners."[65] Najm continued to be in and out of prison under Mubarak, each time for a different period. Meanwhile his popularity increased, particularly in universities and large public gatherings. He was the archetype of an artist who fought for his values and beliefs irrespective of personal consequences. He died in December 2013, having witnessed the uprising that terminated Mubarak's rule. Similarly, a Tunisian rapper, El Général, upset the authorities when he sent a direct message to Ben 'Ali, titled "Sidi El-Ra'is" (Mr. President). His lyrics were raw and frank, but stayed relatively diplomatic. His famous lines are:

Mr. President, your people are dead
Many, today, on garbage fed
As you can obviously see what's going on nationwide,
Miseries everywhere and people find nowhere to sleep
I speak on behalf of those who were wronged and ground under feet.[66]

Women writers and activists suffered at the hands of these regimes in the same way as men. Zainab al-Ghazali's memoirs detail the suffering of women identified with the Ikhwan during Nasser's era. Sometimes they were used as sources of information, and at other times to pressure their husbands to change their views or divulge information. In Ghazali's case, both she and her husband were active supporters of the Muslim Brothers and both were jailed and persecuted.[67] However, Fu'ad 'Allam, one of the heads of General Security,

---

[64] Salah 'Isa, *Sha'ir takdir al-amn al-'amm* [The poet who annoyed state security], 2nd edn. (Cairo: al-Shuruq Publishing, 2008), p. 49.

[65] Ibid., p. 52.

[66] Nouri Gana, "Visions of Dissent, Voices of Discontent: Postcolonial Tunisian Film and Song," in Nouri Gana (ed.), *The Making of The Tunisian Revolution: Contexts, Architects, Prospects* (Edinburgh: Edinburgh University Press, 2013), p. 200.

[67] Al-Ghazali, *Return of the Pharaoh.*

commented on Ghazali's writings by claiming that "her wild imagination is the real problem" and not that she or her family were tortured.[68] This was a typical response of the security chiefs, who refused to take any responsibility for the way prisoners were treated. The prolific author and playwright Nawal al-Saʿdawi depicts in a beautifully written play, based on her personal experience, the lives of twelve women in a cell, and shows the contempt that security officers felt for religious women.[69] Religion was also a wall between Muslim and Christian inmates, as some of the more religious Muslim prisoners were unhappy about sharing a cell with Christians.[70] In Tunisia, women also suffered at the hands of the authorities; one student activist recounts how she and other female students were arrested after a demonstration in November 1995, taken to prison, beaten, and humiliated.[71]

Radwa ʿAshur, an Egyptian novelist, portrays the life of students arrested for opposing the regime and organizing demonstrations on campuses. She describes the intensity of their interrogations and the constant shuttling of the suspects from one building to another. ʿAshur believed that the authorities refrained from torturing her and the hundreds of students arrested because news of this would have reached the outside world. Nevertheless, many of her colleagues broke down due to the incessant pressure, and some even committed suicide after their release.[72] One novel that had a huge impact on a whole generation, not only in Egypt but in other Arab countries, for its dealing with the sensitive issues of imprisonment and torture is *Sharq al-Mutawassit* (East of the Mediterranean), published in the mid 1970s. It depicts the suffering of the inmates, the degradation, and the humiliation of those being interrogated and tortured.[73]

---

[68] ʿAllam, *al-Ikhwan wa ana*, pp. 193–94.

[69] Al-Saʿdawi, *al-Insan: ithnay ʿashr imraʾa fi zinzana*, p. 27. Other books by this author also depict her life and political struggles.

[70] Ibid., p. 88.

[71] Testimony of Najwa al-Ruzqi in al-Tamimi (ed.), *al-Muʿaridun al-siyasiyyun tahta al-taʿdhib fi Tunis*, pp. 87–88.

[72] Radwa ʿAshur, *Faraj* [Relief] (Cairo: al-Shuruq Publications, 2008).

[73] ʿAbd al-Rahman Munif, *Sharq al-Mutawassit* [East of the Mediterranean] (Beirut: al-Taliʿa Publishing, 1975). Munif is a Saudi national of Iraqi origin who lived in Jordan and then moved to Cairo. Later he joined the Iraqi Baʿth Party and returned to Iraq to work in the Oil Ministry. For the impact of his novel, see Husayn, *al-Fiqd*, p. 31.

An essential point for the thousands of people arrested in these republics is that their suffering did not end with being released from custody or prison. Political prisoners continued to endure discrimination from the regimes, were ostracized, and in many cases prevented from returning to normal lives. Most of those who had been in the civil service were fired from their jobs and lost their pension benefits, while those who attempted to start new business ventures were harassed by the authorities or blocked from obtaining the necessary licenses. For many, "after having come close to physical death in prison, ex-detainees experience 'social death' that is often seen to be more difficult to bear."[74]

The question of torture by the security services has been well documented by inmates and journalists. Memoirs and literary works describe in detail the torture and political trials across many of these republics. It is noteworthy how much had been written about torture, and yet it was ignored until the Arab uprisings. One of numerous examples was given by a journalist from the *Guardian* newspaper, who described in vivid terms his arrest by the security forces in Egypt after the Arab uprising had begun there in early 2011:

Cuffed and blindfolded, like my fellow detainees, I lay transfixed. My palms sweated and my heart raced. I felt myself shaking. Would it be my turn next? I had "disappeared," along with countless Egyptians, inside the bowels of the *mukhabarat*, President Hosni Mubarak's vast security-intelligence apparatus.[75]

Prisoners' memoirs are obviously insightful about the system of interrogation and everyday life in prisons. One of the most powerful was written by Mustafa Khalifa, a Syrian who endured thirteen years of imprisonment and torture. In his remarkable story, *al-Qawqaʻa* (The Shell), he tells how he was arrested at Damascus airport on returning from six years of study in France. It took him almost three weeks of torture and beatings to discover that he was suspected of being a member of the Muslim Brotherhood. Attempting to inform them that

---

[74] Béatrice Hibou and John Hulsey, "Domination and Control in Tunisia: Economic Levers for the Exercise of Authoritarian Power," *Review of African Political Economy*, vol. 33, no. 108 (June 2006), p. 189.

[75] Robert Tait, "28 Hours in the Dark Heart of Egypt's Torture Machine," *Guardian*, February 9, 2011. Tait was released as he was the holder of a British passport and an accredited journalist.

not only was he Catholic by birth, but that he was actually an atheist, had no effect, and in fact made it worse for him, as his cellmates ostracized him after his declaration. From that time on, he suffered utter isolation as a *kafir* (unbeliever) and *najs* (impure).[76]

As the days passed, a shell with two walls began to be created around me: one wall was shaped by their hatred of me; I felt I was swimming in a sea of hatred, rancor, and disgust. I tried hard not to sink in this sea. The second wall was created by my fear of them [the Muslim Brothers].[77]

This memoir is illuminating for our understanding of prison life; the regular torture and humiliation; the Syrian regime's attitude toward religion in general and to the Muslim Brotherhood in particular; and finally, the impressive organization and discipline of the Muslim Brothers inside the prison and their ability to be creative and adapt to the harsh realities. The depiction of the Muslim Brothers and their suffering is given in another memoir written by a Syrian communist, Yasin al-Hajj Salih, who describes how Tadmur prison became the "natural home" for the Brothers.[78] The torture, humiliation, courage, and adaptability of prisoners are once again graphically described. Both memoirs recount how prisoners were subjected to the most infamous tool of torture in Syria: the *dulab* (tire), whereby the prisoner was placed inside a large tire and guards would beat his feet.[79] It seems that each of the Arab republics was proud to develop its own particular brand of torture; in Tunisia, prisoners were turned on a "chicken rotisserie" while being interrogated.[80] Another method of torture

---

[76] Khalifa, *al-Qawqa'a*. Khalifa does not give details of the years of imprisonment, but one gathers that it began in the early 1980s when the Syrian regime was battling against the Muslim Brothers, and ended with the relative liberalization adopted by Hafiz al-Asad in the mid 1990s.

[77] Ibid., p. 72.

[78] Salih, *Bilkhalas, ya shabab*. Salih was arrested in December 1980 when he was a medical student and a member of the political bureau of the Syrian Communist Party and released in December 1996. Tadmur prison is in the Syrian Desert, approximately 125 miles northeast of Damascus.

[79] For more details of this system and other methods of torture in Syria, see Middle East Watch, *Syria Unmasked: The Suppression of Human Rights by the Asad Regime* (New Haven: Yale University Press, 1991), pp. 54–64.

[80] Ahmad Mana'i, *al-Ta'dhib al-Tunisi fi al-hadiqa al-sirriyya lil-Jiniral Ben 'Ali* [The Tunisian torture in the secret garden of General Ben 'Ali] (Cairo: Madbuly Bookshop, n.d.), pp. 76–77. Mana'i worked at the United Nations. He returned to Tunisia in the late 1980s and decided to form an independent party to compete in the 1989 elections. See also the testimony of Las'ad al-Jawhari:

documented in a few countries was referred to as the "menu": prisoners are offered a menu of grim styles of torture and the prisoner is forced to choose his own torture from this list which could contain extraction of fingernails, electric shocks, etc.[81] An account by a survivor of the hell of Algeria's prisons tells how, during the civil war in the 1990s, thousands of people were arrested and sentenced to execution, but were tortured for days beforehand "to extract every piece of information about their comrades."[82] Sadly, as one person who was intimate with Syrian torture writes, it seems that simple words such as chair, ladder, electricity, and lock began to mean for Arabs something different from their linguistic definitions; they became symbols of torture.[83]

In Libya, torture was not motivated by political reasons only; even civil criminals were tortured as a matter of course. A Libyan attorney-general paints a truly grim picture of the treatment of those detained, both criminal and political. When the Libyan police arrested someone suspected of forming a gang of robbers, they proceeded to tie him to a car and drag him along until he died.[84] The peak of Qaddafi's internal terror happened in Bu Slim prison and became known as the Bu Slim massacre, very similar to the Tadmur prison massacre in Syria. Bu Slim became notorious for its treatment of prisoners, along the lines of the infamous prison in Iraq called Qasr al-Nihaya (The Palace of the End), and was known as "the last stop." Describing the Libyan prison, the novelist Hisham Matar quotes a smuggled letter from his father who was imprisoned after "disappearing" in Cairo: "The cruelty of this place far exceeds all that we have read of the fortress prison of Bastille. The cruelty is everything, but I remain stronger than their tactics of oppression."[85]

"Torture in Ben 'Ali's Era," in 'Abd al-Jalil al-Tamimi (ed.), *Dirasat wa sha-hadat hawla dahaya al-ta'dhib wa al-iztihad bi-anzimat al-hukm bil-Maghrab al-Kabir, 1956–2010* [Studies and testimonies about victims of torture and repression in the Maghreb, 1956–2010], no. 25 (Tunis: al-Tamimi Foundation, 2013), pp. 205–10.

[81] It seems this method was used in Iraq, Syria, and Tunisia. Interview with an Iraqi ex-prisoner at Qasr al-Nihaya, London, March 19, 2015.

[82] Laribi, *Dans les geôles de Nezzar*, p. 10.   [83] Husayn, *al-Fiqd*, pp. 18–19.

[84] 'Ali Salim al-Fayturi, *Mudhakkirat mudda'i 'amm: shahadat 'ala 'asr al-zalam* [Memoirs of an attorney-general: testimonies about the dark era] (Tarablus: al-Ruwad Publishing, 2012), p. 41.

[85] Hisham Matar, "The Return: A Father's Disappearance, a Journey Home," *New Yorker*, April 8, 2013.

The Bu Slim massacre took place in mid 1996, when mostly Islamist prisoners began a strike inside the prison. Fearing a mutiny that could expand beyond the walls of the prison, the authorities killed almost 1,400 prisoners. Before Qaddafi was toppled, they denied the incident or claimed that only a dozen inmates were killed after attacking the guards, even though Amnesty International wrote a report in 2006 calling for the need to investigate prison deaths.[86] After the uprising, a mass grave of 1,270 bodies was found, thought to be the remains of the inmates.[87] 'Abd al-Salam Jallud, who was a member of Qaddafi's Revolutionary Council and a prime minister, recounts that in his last meeting with the Libyan leader in 1998 he raised the issue of the massacre. He says that he told Qaddafi: "The massacre of Bu Slim is the largest massacre since Hitler's." Qaddafi responded: "If I did not do this, they would have burnt Tripoli and burned you too."[88] Even someone who was in the security services claims that they only heard rumors and it was impossible to discover the truth, and the massacre became a taboo subject. For many years afterwards, families continued to bring food and clothes to their loved ones, only to have them taken by the guards as there was no one to receive these parcels.[89]

Why the torture? As mentioned earlier, many police officers and security officials believed it to be the quickest and most efficient method to obtain information. The lines between "efficiency" and sadism became blurred in most of these republics. Throughout history and in many parts of the world, certain jailers take pleasure in brutalizing their prisoners because it gives them a sense of power and superiority. One scholar of Iran argues that information is not the only reason for torture; the authorities want to obtain from the prisoners "not only confession but also political and ideological recantation."[90] He argues that torture is stopped once they recanted, unlike in Latin America, where interrogators continued to torment the prisoners to satisfy their

---

[86] Amnesty International, *Libya: Investigation Needed into Prison Deaths*, October 10, 2006.

[87] "More than 1,200 Bodies Found in Tripoli Mass Grave," BBC News, September 25, 2011.

[88] Sharbal, *Fi khaymat al-Qaddafi*, p. 52.

[89] Al-Fayturi, *Mudhakkirat mudda'i 'amm*, pp. 48–49. For more details about the massacre, see Lindsey Hilsum, *Sandstorm: Libya in the Time of Revolution* (New York: Penguin Press, 2012), pp. 99–116.

[90] Ervand Abrahamian, *Tortured Confessions: Prisons and Public Recantations in Modern Iran* (Berkeley: University of California Press, 1999), p. 4.

sadistic bent. What is remarkable is that those in power fully realized the negative implications of torture, but it was almost impossible to change the system.

Once a case of torture became well known, such as that of Mustafa Amin in Egypt under Nasser, the security services tried to pretend that only a small minority engaged in these acts. Kamal Hasan 'Ali informs us in his memoirs that he was aware of his agency's bad reputation in the eyes of the public, and that "99.9 percent of what is published, the agency has nothing to do with."[91] Another head of security, Hasan Abu Basha, discusses the sentencing of forty-four officers accused of torture in 1977. While he claims that he did not condone these acts, he wanted to underline the important point that "if extreme religion uses violence and terror, this will no doubt push the security services to some transgressions in order to stem these crimes."[92] Thus, in Abu Basha's logic, torture was the fault of the detainees, because they forced the authorities to utilize these brutal methods. In fact, the judges in a country such as Egypt knew what was taking place in the detention centers, and in some cases when they released someone for lack of proof they were told to change their decision.[93] More significant is that many of the heads of these security organizations were compensated for torturing inmates and breaking down cells of suspects; a case in point is Shams Badran, who was rewarded by Nasser and 'Amr by being appointed minister of war for imprisoning thousands of members of the Muslim Brothers, torturing them, and obtaining real and fictitious confessions while he was head of the intelligence services.[94]

Fear played an important role in the lives of prisoners. Khalifa describes how it felt every day in his cell in Syria during the first few months of his imprisonment: "I never stopped being afraid of the Mukhabarat, afraid of the military police, afraid each time I heard the keys to the door of our *mahja'* [cell], afraid of beatings, pain, and death." But even fear becomes routine as time passes, and he conveys how it felt in the later stages of his imprisonment: "Was I afraid? I do not know. I became like a stone, a piece of wood stripped of any sentiments or feelings. No more thinking, no more reaction, total

[91] 'Ali, *Mashawir al-'umr*, p. 377.
[92] Abu Basha, *Mudhakkirat Hasan Abu Basha fi al-amn wa al-siyasa*, p. 105.
[93] Fadil, *Kuntu qadiyan*, pp. 56–67.
[94] Husni, *Shams Badran: al-rajul alladhi hakama Misr*, pp. 45–54.

freeze, and an utter surrender."[95] In a way, this is what these regimes aspired to: cultivating fear not only among prisoners but also among the general population. Fear was critical to keeping the masses quiescent under the shadow of despotism. Whether in Romania or Syria, regimes actually encouraged the ubiquity of fear and the pervasive sense that the long arm of the security forces was everywhere. To spread fear, such regimes used a plethora of tools: families of suspects, public trials, and liquidating the "enemies" of the state when all other measures failed.

In all these countries, but to varying degrees, families of suspects were exploited as a means of coercing the regimes' enemies into submission. Authorities in Iraq or Algeria did not hesitate to use family members to break down the suspects and force them to make confessions. Likewise, in Stalinist Russia or Mao's China, families were considered guilty by association. In Iraq, the Ba'th, unlike previous regimes, regarded the families of opponents as legitimate targets for punishment. In 1979, less than a month after Saddam Hussein became president, a Ba'th Party document detailed measures to be taken against different family members, corresponding to the seriousness of the "crime" of resisting the regime. The memo outlined the different penalties to be applied to opponents' wives and children (male and female), to siblings of those punished (both male and female), and their nephews. These penalties included barring family members from joining the party and expelling those who were already members; rejecting their applications to military or police colleges; preventing them from receiving scholarships to study abroad; limiting their choice of universities; and finally, banning them from employment in Iraqi embassies abroad and in many government offices.[96]

In addition, families were used to exert influence over suspects and "saboteurs" during and after their interrogations, and many in northern Iraq were displaced from their homes as a punishment if a member of their families joined one of the anti-government Kurdish parties.[97] Whether in Algeria or Egypt, security forces did not hesitate to arrest family members when they raided suspects' houses, and then

[95] Khalifa, *al-Qawqa'a*, p. 70.
[96] Party Secretariat to all headquarters, "Decision," August 13, 1979, *BRCC*, 003-1-1 (290-292).
[97] See, for example, *NIDS*, Patriotic Union of Kurdistan (PUK) 013, Box 55; PUK 002, Box 005; PUK 001, Box 001; and PUK 030, Box 147.

threaten the suspects that serious harm would be done to their families if they did not confess, or to coerce the family members into informing about other relatives. In many of these countries, rape was used either to disgrace the honor of the suspect, both male and female, or at least to threaten male prisoners that their female relatives would be raped if they did not cooperate.[98]

Both public and secret trials were conducted in all those republics, using methods gleaned from other authoritarian and totalitarian regimes.[99] Public trials served the dual purpose of deterrence and instilling fear among the people. They also, indirectly, encouraged the flow of malicious information to the authorities from some members of the public. In Iraq, public trials of senior officials from the monarchy period were first conducted under 'Abd al-Karim Qasim in 1959. However, show trials began in earnest under Saddam Hussein, after the Ba'th took over in 1968, followed by public hangings of "spies." The regime used the power of television (when there was only one channel) and radio as potent instruments to bring these proceedings into nearly all Iraqi homes.[100] In Syria, almost every regime conducted these trials, as each incoming regime wanted to discredit its enemies in full public view.[101] In Libya, the revolutionary committees took over the responsibility of forming courts, whose proceedings were televised across the country. "Revolutionary committees, cloaked with the garment of revolutionary legitimacy, acted as judges, jurors, and executioners."[102] According to al-Fayturi, who

---

[98] For examples from Algeria, see Mohammed Samraoui, *Chronique des années de sang: Algérie: comment les services secrets ont manipulé les groupes islamistes* [Chronicle of the years of blood: Algeria: how the secret services manipulated the Islamist groups] (Paris: Denoël Impacts, 2003), pp. 22–24. On Egypt, see Ayman Nur and Majdi Shindi, *al-'Askari al-aswad, Zaki Badr* [The black policeman, Zaki Badr] (Cairo: Arab International Publishing Company, 1990), pp. 71–75.

[99] Friedrich and Brzezinski, *Totalitarian Dictatorship and Autocracy*, pp. 150–65. See also Paul R. Gregory, *Terror by Quota: State Security from Lenin to Stalin (An Archival Study)* (New Haven: Yale University Press, 2009), pp. 133–34.

[100] Kanan Makiya, *Republic of Fear: The Politics of Modern Iraq* (Berkeley: University of California Press, 1998), pp. 46–58.

[101] Hashim 'Uthman, *al-Muhakamat al-siyasiyya fi Suriya* [Political trials in Syria] (Beirut: Riyad al-Rayyis Publishing, 2004). The author details all the penalties corresponding to the accusations that these courts used, pp. 10–12. For example, receiving money from a foreign source that might be used against the regime incurred the death penalty.

[102] El-Kikhia, *Libya's Qaddafi*, p. 104.

acted as attorney-general of one of the districts, the committees did not seek his advice, and simply ploughed ahead in a rushed and unplanned manner.[103] These makeshift courts gained notoriety for grouping the regime's critics with perpetrators of violent acts, and over the years they tried and sentenced many opponents from different factions.[104]

A number of the regimes used the drastic measure of eliminating their enemies internally and externally by assassination. From Iraq, we know now that the Ba'th did this systematically, and all Iraqis, even those who managed to leave the country, were aware of the regime's ability to reach them wherever they were. Attempted assassinations of Iraqis took place in Europe and the Arab world, where Saddam Hussein settled accounts even with those whom he exiled. But it was not just those with power and prestige who were targeted: communist students, members of the Kurdish opposition, intellectuals, and religious leaders were all included.[105] Since the overthrow of Qaddafi, more information has come to light about these assassinations and how they were used as a weapon against the regime's enemies. For example, Mansur Kikhia, a prominent dissident, disappeared from the streets of Cairo in late 1993. 'Abd al-Rahman Shalqam, a senior Libyan who worked closely with Qaddafi's regime from 1974, at first in charge of the daily media updates, then as minister of information in the early 1980s, and later as Libya's representative to the United Nations, told an interviewer that the Egyptian security forces under 'Umar Sulayman kidnapped Kikhia and handed him over to Libyan officials. He was then airlifted to Libya where he was met by 'Abdullah al-Sanusi, the brother-in-law of Qaddafi. No final details are known about how Kikhia was murdered.[106] Another opponent of Qaddafi, 'Ali Muhammad Abu Zayd, a founding member of an opposition group, was assassinated in London in late 1995.

---

[103] Al-Fayturi, *Mudhakkirat mudda'i 'amm*, pp. 32–34.
[104] International Crisis Group, "Trial by Error: Justice in Post-Qadhafi Libya," *Middle East/North Africa Report*, no. 140, April 17, 2013, p. 12.
[105] Numerous books detail such attempts, because many of these high-profile figures were killed in Europe or Arab countries. See, for example, Sassoon, *Saddam Hussein's Ba'th Party*; Makiya, *Republic of Fear*; Ibrahim al-Marashi, "Iraq's Security and Intelligence Network: A Guide and an Analysis," *Middle East Review of International Affairs*, vol. 6, no. 3 (September 2002), pp. 1–13. Many memoirs by Iraqi senior officials also refer to these attempts.
[106] Sharbal, *Fi khaymat al-Qaddafi*, pp. 172–73.

The novelist Hisham Matar tells in a book and an article the powerful story of his father's abduction in Cairo in 1990, and describes the 1980s as "a particularly lurid chapter" in Libya's political history.[107] Qaddafi did not only assassinate Libyans; Imam Musa al-Sadr, a Lebanese Shi'a leader originally from Iraq, who was on a visit to Libya, disappeared with two companions after sharp disagreements with Qaddafi. 'Abd al-Mun'im al-Huni, an ex-chief of intelligence and minister of interior in Libya, confirms this and claims that his brother-in-law was the pilot who transported the body of Musa al-Sadr. Later, security officials killed the pilot as they feared that he might divulge information about this incident.[108] Sa'id 'Isa al-Lishani also confirms these eliminations of Qaddafi's opponents in Europe and argues that a special unit was set up to murder the regime's foes.[109] In Algeria, we have no official number of those who "disappeared" during the years 1992–97, when security services and armed militias often burned the bodies of some of the victims, hence the "disappearance" phenomenon.[110]

Religion as a threat

Religious ideas were seen as a serious menace by these republics, and regimes were apprehensive about religion spreading and its popularity, particularly with the youth. In Iraq, especially after the 1991 uprising that followed the First Gulf War, Shi'i activists and religious leaders were targeted. One of the leading activists details in his biography the many arrests, interrogations, and executions of well-known Shi'i activists during Saddam Hussein's reign.[111] The Iraqi leader's obsession

---

[107] Matar, "The Return." Matar's novel based on the abduction is *Anatomy of Disappearance*. His other novel, *In the Country of Men*, illuminates the life under fear and anxiety about the unknown.

[108] Sharbal, *Fi khaymat al-Qaddafi*, p. 103.

[109] Sa'id 'Isa al-Lishani, *Min al-dhakira: qissat kifah* [From memory: the story of a struggle] (Beirut: Bissan Publishing, 2012), pp. 86–87.

[110] See Omar Ashour, "Islamist De-Radicalization in Algeria: Successes and Failure," *Middle East Institute Policy Brief*, no. 21, November 2008; Amnesty International, "Algeria: Torture in the 'War on Terror': A Memorandum to the Algerian President," news release, April 18, 2006, available at www.amnesty.org/en/library/asset/MDE28/008/2006/en/386174b5-d43c-11dd-8743-d305bea2b2c7/mde280082006en.pdf.

[111] Salah al-Hadidi, *Qabdat al-huda: Husayn Jalukhan tarikh wa rihla* [The guiding hand: Husayn Jalukhan's history and journey] 2nd edn. (Karbala: al-Hadidi Center for Studies and Research, 2009).

with Khomeinism knew no bounds; up until his last minute in power, and even after his fall, he insisted that Iran was behind what happened to Iraq in 2003.[112] In Egypt and Syria, the Muslim Brothers were perceived for decades as the major threat to the country. Two authors describe in graphic detail how the Egyptian security service conducted its campaign against political opponents, and in particular against the Muslim Brothers, under the auspices of Zaki Badr, the minister of interior in the 1980s. They give ample evidence of how suspects were tortured, humiliated, and forced to confess to whatever the security agencies deemed necessary to frame others.[113] Fu'ad 'Allam, the security chief, recounts how in 1965 the Egyptian regime desperately needed information from members of the Brotherhood: "No one thought of torturing them [the Brothers], but the circumstances necessitated the urgency of obtaining their confessions by legitimate methods, given that we were in a race with time to save Egypt from a conspiracy whose dimensions only God would know."[114] Indeed, 'Allam in his memoirs is very proud of his "relations" with the Ikhwan spanning twenty-five years, to the extent that Egyptians associate his name with the Brotherhood whenever they discuss the subject, and he was seen as the movement's number one enemy.[115] 'Allam tirelessly attempts to depict the Brothers as duplicitous people who use religion to achieve power; in more than 570 pages, the ex-head of security describes in detail one example after the other of their "conspiracies" to control the Egyptian people, and zooms in on every incident to discredit them.

One edited volume containing memoirs of six heads of security in Egypt devotes large sections to the subject of combating the Muslim Brotherhood. Overall, they share the same contempt for the group and the vehement belief that without their tireless work, the Brothers would have taken power in the country.[116] Intriguingly, three of them were imprisoned either while they were in power or after they had left their

---

[112] See the memoir of Saddam Hussein's lawyer after his arrest by the Americans: Khalil al-Dulaymi, *Saddam Hussein min al-zinzana al-Amrikiyya: hadha ma hadatha* [Saddam Hussein from his American cell: this is what happened] (Khartoum: al-Manbar Publishing, 2009).

[113] Nur and Shindi, *al-'Askari al-aswad, Zaki Badr.*

[114] 'Allam, *al-Ikhwan wa ana*, p. 348.   [115] Ibid., pp. 28, 11.

[116] Muhammad Muhammad al-Jawadi, *Mudhakkirat qadat al-mukhabarat wa al-mabahith: al-amn al-qawmi li-Misr* [Memoirs of the leaders of intelligence and security: the national security of Egypt] (Cairo: Dar al-Khayyal Publishing, 1999).

positions: Hasan Tal'at and Amin Huwaydi after the May 15, 1971 "corrective revolution" initiated by Sadat which purged all Nasserists from positions of power; and Salah Nasr was sent to prison for his role in the "conspiracy" against Nasser led by 'Amr after the 1967 defeat.[117]

The Muslim Brotherhood suffered during the presidencies of Nasser, Sadat, and Mubarak. But overall, Nasser was the worst in his treatment of the organization, and his security chiefs were virulently intent on eradicating it.[118] Under Sadat, there was a period of four to five years where the organization enjoyed dramatic growth. This was partly due to Sadat's religious beliefs, but more because of his policy of allowing the Muslim Brotherhood to strengthen at the expense of the Nasserites. Finally, during Mubarak's era, it was almost a game of cat and mouse; at certain times the regime allowed the Ikhwan leadership to function, at other times pursued it, but permitted the lower echelons to exist and operate relatively freely. Mubarak's security apparatus realized during the 1990s that the Brotherhood was not the main threat, as it had to deal with far more extreme fundamentalism, including acts of terrorism that created havoc in the country.

In Syria, the Brotherhood and the Islamists in general were likewise seen as a major threat. It is thought that the massacre in Tadmur in 1981 was organized by Rif'at al-Asad the day after a failed attempt to assassinate his brother, President Hafiz al-Asad. Known for its harsh conditions, the Tadmur prison housed both political and criminal prisoners. It was closed in 2001 as part of the "openness" of Bashar al-Asad's regime, but reopened in June 2011. The Tadmur massacre targeted the Islamists suspected of plotting against Hafiz al-Asad, but it paled in comparison to the bloodbath of Hama. In 1982, Syrian military and security forces bombed and razed the city of Hama to rubble, killing an estimated 20,000 in order to subdue or eliminate the Islamists living there. This was the bloodiest attack carried out by an Arab leader against his people in those republics, and yet other Arab and foreign

---

[117] Salah Nasr was released by Sadat in 1974, but later faced accusations of torture from the famous columnist and journalist Mustafa Amin, who was tortured during his interrogation after being accused of spying for the USA.

[118] For a comprehensive description of the Ikhwan under Nasser, see Ahmad Ra'if, *al-Bawwaba al-sawda': safahat min tarikh al-Ikhwan al-Muslimin* [The black gate: pages from the history of the Muslim Brotherhood] (Cairo: al-Zahra' Publishing, 1989).

countries barely condemned the action, or else simply ignored it. Syrian authorities banned prayers in their detention centers in the 1980s at the height of repression against Islamists: if anyone was caught praying, he was immediately executed. Yet, as Khalifa tells us, the prisoners never missed a prayer; they developed a prayer without the *rak'a* (prostration), based on what is known in Islam as *salat al-khawf* (prayer under fear).[119] Forbidding prayers was also common in Tunisian prisons, as testimonies of prisoners indicate. Furthermore, in certain prisons, the Qur'an was banned and no prisoner had the right to receive from another prisoner a copy of the holy book.[120] Given that religion was seen as a serious threat, these regimes feared and intensely fought the Muslim Brotherhood, which was perceived as "the only potent, autonomous social force outside of regime control."[121] Thus the battle against Islamists in most of these countries was not just against an organization; it was against the idea of Islam – a powerful rival ideology – entering politics, and its ability to attract the youth.[122]

Whether in Tunisia, Algeria, or Libya, any Islamic opposition was contained by labeling it as terrorist, which meant, in essence, a free hand to deal with its supporters in the most severe way. The massacre in Bu Slim prison in Libya was along the lines of the Syrian Tadmur massacre, and Islamists were again the main casualties. No country among the eight republics massacred more Islamists than Algeria (some estimate the number during the 1990s civil war as 200,000), which used all possible methods to destroy what General Nezzar described as "the threat to Algeria's freedom, and a violation of the state's values and its revolution."[123]

In spite of the similarities between the security organizations in the Arab republics, there were nevertheless many differences, as each country had its own circumstances and peculiarities. For instance,

---

[119] Khalifa, *al-Qawqa'a*, p. 75.
[120] Al-Tamimi (ed.), *al-Mu'aridun al-siyasiyyun tahta al-ta'dhib fi Tunis*, p. 23.
[121] Holger Albrecht, *Raging against the Machine: Political Opposition under Authoritarianism in Egypt* (Syracuse, NY: Syracuse University Press, 2013), p. 107.
[122] For more details of these massacres and suffering of the Brothers, see 'Adnan Sa'd al-Din, *al-Ikhwan al-Muslimun fi Suriya, mudhakkirat wa dhikrayat: sanawat al-majazir al-mur'iba min 'am 1977 wa hatta 'am 1983* [The Muslim Brothers in Syria, memoirs and memories: the years of the terrifying massacres from 1977 until 1983] (Cairo: Madbuly Bookshop, 2010).
[123] Nezzar, *Mudhakkirat al-Liwa' Khalid Nezzar*, p. 194.

in Iraq, physical intimidation and torture was much more widespread than in Egypt or Tunisia. In Algeria, violence took a totally different form during the civil war, when the military, security services, and even the local police participated in systemic violence. In this case, the opposition, who were extreme Islamists, also used excessive violence against the regime and its civilian supporters. Many argue that imposing severe punishments on opponents and using extreme methods of violence and torture lead to radicalization and an increase in opposition in the long run.[124] In essence this is true, but at the same time there were regimes such as those of Hafiz al-Asad and Saddam Hussein, which inflicted brutal retribution on their opponents and the civilian population (Hama in Syria and southern Iraq during the 1991 uprising), and yet survived the radicalization of their opposition.

Re-examining the system

Four questions are addressed here: (1) How did state security collect information? (2) How was this information used? (3) Did the information help the durability of these regimes? (4) Who shoulders the responsibility for repression in these countries?

The task of gathering information was formidable; these regimes felt the need not only to collect information about their opponents, real or imaginary, but also to penetrate different levels of society. In fact, the security services were involved in gathering information within the armed forces, professional bodies, universities, and high schools, as well as among the cultural and intellectual elites of their countries. Determining whether an article, a novel, or a poem was directly or indirectly hostile to the political leadership meant amassing huge amounts of data. In countries such as Iraq, Libya, and Syria where the cult of personality was strong, the authorities had the additional duty of ensuring the propagation of the cult by arresting those who opposed it in writing or speeches, or who simply did not adhere to its requirements.[125] Within all these republics, the definition of who was an enemy changed from time to time; most of

---

[124] See, for example, "Bahrain: How the Police Recruit Radicals," *Economist*.

[125] In Iraq, for example, the name of the president, Saddam Hussein, could not be written without adding in parenthesis (May God Protect Him). Journalists, artists, and even Iraqi diplomats had to adhere strictly to this rule.

them strongly opposed Islamic fundamentalism, and the Muslim Brotherhood was considered an archenemy, although at certain times (for example, in Sadat's Egypt) some kind of truce was reached with the Brothers. Similarly, communists or pan-Arabists were either regarded as coalition members or as agents of imperialism and Zionism (for example, in Iraq or Syria).

The leaders of authoritarian regimes tended to feel insecure because of the frequent coups d'état in the region, and also worried about whether they were receiving comprehensive information from all parts of the country. A telling example of the lack of reliable information from areas outside the capital is the uprising of 1991, when Saddam Hussein and his regime were shocked that such an event took place, particularly in the south. The uprising, which took place at the end of the First Gulf War and the liberation of Kuwait, erupted to the total surprise of the Iraqi leadership. Typically, leaderships tended to be more worried about the elites and those close to power, such as senior army officers, religious leaders, successful business people, and well-known intellectuals or artists. This meant gathering intelligence on the inner circles, and not just the regime's opponents. Hence the insecurity of the masses was matched by the insecurity of the elites. In Iraq, for instance, the archives inform us that many departments within the SSO had the task of monitoring the loyalty of officers and employees working in various organizations affiliated with the party or the army. For example, the Directorate of Republican Guard Security focused on the loyalty of military commanders in the Republican Guard. The Surveillance and Information branch had the responsibility of watching senior Iraqi officials, and preparing files on any official prior to his or her promotion or assignment to a new senior job. An analysis of the archives and numerous memoirs of security heads leave no doubt that in many cases the watchers were themselves being watched. This is important in underlining how the insecurity of elites was established across the republics but to different degrees, and in a manner comparable to the Stalinist regimes in communist Europe and the Soviet Union during the 1950s and 1960s.

In Egypt, Nasser was very sensitive to criticism emanating from anyone powerful or popular with the public, which led to large numbers of journalists, artists, and intellectuals being placed under surveillance. Indeed, as one Egyptian security chief put it: "Nasser did not allow anyone to criticize him or anyone working with him closely. In fact, he never forgave anyone who expressed criticism of his leadership."[126] Revelations from Syria show that surveillance of senior officials in the government and the military took place and the monitoring of the elite was incessant. As one senior security official who defected argues: "Syria was built from the 1960s as a system of a *dawla amniyya* (security state) where everyone is watching everyone and everyone is spying on everyone, whether in the army, the party, the party's branches, the economy, and in fact within the society as a whole."[127]

Given this insecurity and the existence of a web of overlapping agencies, it was a direct consequence that all these regimes accumulated colossal amounts of information about their citizens. One head of General Security in Egypt, Fu'ad 'Allam, recounts how obsessive the gathering and filing of information had become, and admits that "if someone passed by me and simply said *"al-salam 'alaykum"* [peace be upon you] I would write a memo and file it. This is the correct method to safeguard our future."[128] However, the transmission of information to the leadership was often imperfect because of its sheer volume, and it was also sometimes deliberately inaccurate, or embellished to hide inefficiencies or the overstated promises made by local leaders. The more repressive the regime (Algeria, Iraq, Libya, and Syria), the less accurate the information tended to be, given that a large percentage was acquired through intimidation. So much information from diverse sources flowed to the numerous security organizations that in many cases they admitted they were arresting and interrogating the wrong people; in one memo, the director of al-Amn in Iraq urged security officers to be more thorough in their investigations before hastening to arrest innocent citizens.[129] Obsessiveness about information gathering and ensuring a climate of fear and enforced obedience led to many mistakes and the arrest of numerous innocent people. However,

---

[126] Nasr, *Mudhakkirat Salah Nasr: thawrat 23 Yuliyu bayn al-masir wa al-masir*, p. 202. Nasr published a three-volume memoir in 1999, similarly titled: *Mudhakkirat Salah Nasr*.

[127] Interview with Nawaf al-Faris, in "Barnamij bila hudud" [Program without boundaries], Al-Jazeera, December 8, 2012. Al-Faris occupied many senior positions in the Syrian security organization, including in the political branch of Latakia. He also was the governor of Latakia and Qunaytra.

[128] 'Allam, *al-Ikhwan wa ana*, p. 237.

[129] Director of Amn Arbil to all Security Officers, "Guidelines," January 2, 1983, *NIDS*, PUK 011, Box 046 (550028).

officers and heads of security were not concerned about the fate of those arrested, as they believed that this was integral to the overall strategy of ensuring the regime's dominance. During the Algerian civil war, when one security chief was asked if some of those being executed were innocent, his nonchalant reply was: "In that case they will go to heaven."[130]

Although these services gathered information, the emphasis was on internal rather than external enemies. Poor foreign intelligence contributed to Egypt's inability to win the war in Yemen,[131] and in Iraq, military intelligence sometimes even lacked detailed maps of enemy territories, because their focus was more on checking the loyalty of officers and their political leanings.[132] Given the reliance on informants and the use of coercion in gathering information, internal intelligence tended to be stronger and more comprehensive. In Libya, for instance, in 1993, the security services were aware of the army officers' conspiracy from the Werfella tribe while it was being hatched, and managed to deal a severe blow to the plot before it became a serious threat.[133] Abroad, the republics had to rely mostly on three sources: students, diplomats, or official representatives of the government. Thus the information they collected about foreign countries and agencies was relatively meager, and in fact, most of the intelligence effort targeted their compatriots living abroad in order to penetrate opposition movements at home, or to uncover plans to oppose the regime.

The regimes collected information by copious means; a primary one being surveillance through wiretapping and planting bugging devices. The Iraqi archives are abundant with examples of how the special technical department within the SSO kept a watch on the presidential palaces' employees, both at work and at home, through wiretapping and bugging.[134] The Arab Spring brought revelations of how other regimes such as Egypt functioned. In a fascinating interview broadcast

---

[130] Laribi, *Dans les geôles de Nezzar*, p. 12.

[131] Sirrs, *A History of the Egyptian Intelligence Service*, pp. 77–78.

[132] See the memoirs of a general who fought both in the Iraq–Iran War and participated in the invasion of Kuwait: al-Hamdani, *Qabla an yughadiruna al-tarikh*, p. 199.

[133] The Werfella tribe was once considered very loyal to the Qaddafi regime. For details on the plot and how Qaddafi imposed his punishment on the officers, see Alison Pargeter, *Libya: The Rise and Fall of Qaddafi* (New Haven: Yale University Press, 2012), pp. 158–61.

[134] Sassoon, *Saddam Hussein's Ba'th Party*, pp. 103–05.

on Egyptian television, a major general in the Egyptian Amn al-Dawla described in detail how his organization monitored ministers, artists, journalists, and high-ranking officials. He revealed how Nasser was paranoid about people close to him and asked the security agency to keep a watchful eye on them.[135]

A primary source for gathering information was informants, who were active in surveillance. We now know that in Iraq, very much as in communist Europe, informants were not all hapless, illiterate, or coerced into providing information.[136] A review of dozens of Iraqi informers' files shows that they came from a broad range of socio-economic and educational backgrounds.[137] One could safely assume that this is the case in the other republics. After the toppling of Ben 'Ali, one Tunisian recounted how he had filled in a form to become a "citizens' watcher" for the regime. In return for information about colleagues, friends and family, he was offered perks, and home and car loans.[138] Some informants were obviously motivated by the material and job benefits; others informed for malicious reasons against colleagues or neighbors; but many simply joined the ranks of informants to supplement their incomes. Malevolent information spiked whenever there was a political upheaval or a new regime came to power; one Sudanese official comments that when Numayri launched his coup, many arrests were made and "vicious elements" exploited the situation to settle accounts. "All one had to do was to head to the nearest police station to inform about a co-worker, a superior or a neighbor, and they would be arrested."[139] Needless to say, in all these countries a large number were coerced into informing either during interrogations or after threats made to them or to members of their families. Prisoners on the verge of being released divulged how security officers wanted them to sign an agreement of "good intentions," which

---

[135] Wa'il al-Ibrashi interviewing Taha Zaki on Dream TV, April 24, 2012. The two interviews are on YouTube, available at www.youtube.com/watch?v=oku3t0PASKo

[136] See an example of an informer given by Isam al-Khafaji in his article, "State Terror and the Degradation of Politics in Iraq," *Middle East Report*, no. 176 (May–June 1992), p. 16.

[137] Sassoon, *Saddam Hussein's Ba'th Party*, pp. 122–28.

[138] Borzou Daragahi, "In Tunisia, Ben Ali was 'Big Brother'," *Los Angeles Times*, January 15, 2011.

[139] Ibrahim, *Qissat kifah wa najah*, p. 201.

translated into a commitment to inform or report about other prisoners, and then later about their friends outside the prison.[140] Most prisoners correctly assumed that there was at least one informant in every large cell, and they were reluctant to open up until they got to know their fellow inmates intimately.

In such authoritarian regimes, there were always people who believed in the leaders' policies and hence provided information out of a conviction that they were doing the right thing. The role of informants was, however, essential; in Iraq, we know that the regime even passed a law to protect informants and give them pension rights, as well as compensation for their families in case of injury or death while on duty.[141] They were everywhere, and reinforced the impression that the Iraqi regime was ubiquitous. They gathered information not only about the enemies of the state or the economy, such as the black market and illegal trading in hard currency, but also collected rumors, which are important for such regimes to gauge public sentiment. The main focus was obviously to penetrate the ranks of enemy groups. The regimes perceived any organization or group that did not accept their authority as an enemy. In Iraq, security agencies were instructed to fight at least eight categories of enemies of the state, such as Kurds, communists, Islamists, ex-Ba'thists, etc. In Algeria, a senior member of the Sécurité Militaire (SM) recounts how the SM had agents working in the Algerian airlines, government offices, and public companies; in the cultural center in Paris; in the media; and even in mosques in Algeria or in Paris, to monitor the "enemies of the state."[142] In Egypt, the Muslim Brotherhood was a thorn in the side of the security services from Nasser's days, and thus accessing information about it was critical. Heads of Egyptian security claimed that they managed to infiltrate the Brotherhood at every level through their informants. 'Allam maintains that the security agencies knew of the attempt to assassinate Sadat three hours before it took place, as one of the senior Muslim Brothers gave them all the details.

This leads to the second question: How was all this information used? In the above Egyptian case, bureaucracy, the inability to make decisions, fear of failure, and lack of real commitment to the job all

[140] Salih, *Bilkhalas, ya shabab*, p. 18.
[141] *Al-Waqa'i' al-'Iraqiyya* (Iraqi Official Gazette), no. 2,720, July 9, 1979, pp. 785–88. An informant in Iraq was called a *mu'tamin* (trusted one).
[142] Samraoui, *Chronique des années de sang*, pp. 10–11.

combined to prevent the General Security from acting on this important information to save Sadat, in spite of having the necessary facts.[143] Whether in Egypt, Syria, or Iraq, the pyramid of power was such that officers were not willing to take risks by making decisions, and thus more repression was meted out to the population because there was no effective distinction between useful and less relevant information. Furthermore, the overlapping of agencies and duplication of work created entanglements and lack of clarity. This was not a new problem in these regimes: following the separation between Egypt and Syria in 1961, all Egyptian intelligence agencies were scouring the country to get information about the new leadership in Syria without any coordination between them, and the result was that very little of the material was pertinent by the time it was presented to the Egyptian leadership.[144] What is clear from the Iraqi archives and from Egyptian, Algerian, and Syrian memoirs is that these agencies did have information on almost every important subject, but the problem was the lack of swift interpretation and its appropriate channeling upward, and finally, the decision-making process hindered utilizing the information efficiently. Despite these failures, the prodigious volume of data allowed the security services to control the population, uncover plots against the regimes, arrest anyone suspected of resisting the system, and in countries such as Iraq they were able, together with the local branches of the party, to track down many deserters from military service during the 1980s and 1990s.

A serious concern for authoritarian leaders was the credibility of the information gathered, particularly during crises. In Iraq, we know now that Saddam Hussein's inner circle did not disclose the truth to him about many situations and events, such as the invasion of Kuwait, the 1991 uprising, and the 2003 invasion. Intelligence reports sent to the president were altered from their originals, as no one was willing to inform him how the situation had deteriorated in certain strategic areas. For example, during the First Gulf War, generals admitted to Saddam that they hid the truth from him about the Iraqi army's colossal

---

[143] 'Allam, *al-Ikhwan wa ana*, pp. 292–93, 319–27; al-Jawadi, *Mudhakkirat qadat al-mukhabarat*, p. 455; the failure to act on information or potential information was the reason for the Asyut massacre that took place on October 8, 1981, two days after the assassination of Sadat, when armed Islamic groups attacked the Amn headquarters in Asyut, killing 118 soldiers and officers.

[144] Shu'aybi, *Shahid min al-mukhabarat al-Suriyya*, p. 176.

losses.[145] Likewise, a senior Syrian intelligence officer stationed in Cairo describes how Field Marshal 'Abd al-Hakim 'Amr misinformed Nasser about the military situation on the first day of the 1967 June War.[146] Of course, if the leader, as we witnessed in Iraq and other countries, was not open to challenge or to hearing negative views, then the analysis of information presented would be even weaker and less conducive to making accurate judgments.

The third question is: was the information critical for the durability of these regimes? I think the overall answer has to be yes. Targeted repression may have been adequate for dealing with dissent in times of political stability, but it was incapable of neutralizing the opposition in times of instability, when the size of the opposition rapidly expanded. Force was used against large segments of the population rather than a cool-headed analysis of the information, a phenomenon similar to that in the Soviet Union during the Stalinist period. One memoir from Syria illustrates how easy it was for the Syrian authorities, even before the Asad dynasty, to accuse suspects of the "crime of military mutiny," which carried the death sentence, rather than carry out a proper and judicious investigation.[147] These security services in authoritarian countries looked invincible throughout most of the decades they cowed the population, and yet when uprisings took place, they were unable to prevent the overthrow of the regimes.

Many of these agencies became ossified and incapable of dealing with the type of onslaught witnessed in Tunisia, Egypt, Libya, and, more recently, Syria. Political leadership was paralyzed, and even when it received information, could not act on it. The disarray that took place in those countries very much echoed what happened in communist Europe. In an exhibition about the Stasi in Berlin, there is an audiotape of an informant calling the agency a few days before the collapse of the Berlin Wall to warn his superiors of the forthcoming demonstrations, but incredibly there was no one in the headquarters to receive this information or act upon it.[148] Likewise, documents published after

---

[145] For details of the meeting between Saddam and his military chiefs analyzing the war in Kuwait, see Sassoon, *Saddam Hussein's Ba'th Party*, p. 200.

[146] Shu'aybi, *Shahid min al-mukhabarat al-Suriyya*, pp. 197–98.

[147] Al-'Ali, *Hayati wa al-i'dam*, p. 463.

[148] Federal Commissioner for the Records of the State Security Service of the former German Democratic Republic, *Stasi: The Exhibition of the GDR's State Security Exhibition*, Berlin, 2011.

the fall of Qaddafi's regime indicate the lack of reliable intelligence received by the commanders loyal to Qaddafi, leading to endless bickering and backstabbing by the different organizations. In one document, a senior Libyan official complained about the lack of information and suggested adding more informants by forcing everyone on the payroll to spy and report on twenty neighboring families.[149] None of the Libyan documents found and published in the international press addressed the possibility that the rebellion might have broad social support.[150]

The uprisings in the Arab republics showed that the security agencies were not as omnipresent and omniscient as they were thought to be. However, their loyalty to the regime proved more enduring in Egypt, Tunisia, and, to a large extent, in Syria, in contrast to the military's. Although these regimes attempted to control their armies ideologically and politically, with the exception of Saddam Hussein they failed to do so when compared to the security forces, which remained loyal to the bitter end. This may also be the case in Syria, but it is too early to tell. Obviously, one reason is that the security forces were smaller than the armies, except in Tunisia. Furthermore, the regimes succeeded in dominating these agencies by placing their families and clans in all the sensitive jobs. Saddam Hussein, the two Asads, and Qaddafi all knew that they could rely on their security forces to stay faithful, and that it was highly unlikely that any of the security heads would attempt to usurp them.[151]

The final question, relevant to a proper transition to post-authoritarianism (see Chapter 7), is that of accountability, and whether anyone should shoulder the responsibility for repression, torture, and the creation of systems based on surveillance and distrust. When an Egyptian major-general was asked by a television interviewer after the toppling of Mubarak whether he felt remorse or

---

[149] Charles Levinson and Margaret Coker, "Inside a Flawed Spy Machine as Gadhafi's Rule Crumbled," *Wall Street Journal*, September 2, 2011, pp. 1, 10.

[150] Ibid. See also "The Tripoli Files," *Globus and Mail* (Canada), September 17, 2011, pp. F6–F7.

[151] An exception to the rule was in Iraq: in 1973, the head of the Amn, Nazim Kazzar, attempted to arrest Saddam Hussein and launch a coup d'état. Saddam, with his highly developed sixth sense, found out about the plot and began sweeping changes of the security agencies that guaranteed his total control and their utter loyalty to him and him alone.

believed he had acted immorally, he gave an answer typical of those who serve in authoritarian regimes: "Orders are orders. Either you stay in your job until retirement, as you know many secrets, or you end up in prison. The blame is with my superiors, nothing to do with me."[152] Serving the country and protecting its stability were common themes among security chiefs. In Algeria, General Khalid Nezzar, who was minister of defense and was accused of being directly responsible for torture and extrajudicial executions, does not refer specifically in his memoirs to torture or methods of interrogation, but argues that Algeria was becoming a quagmire for Islamic radicalization and that therefore it was necessary to uproot its adversaries.[153]

National security, protecting the nation and the revolution, combating terrorism, and fighting against radically destructive ideas are all factors explaining the repression and torture. If officials refused to carry out the orders of their superiors, they were threatened or dismissed from their jobs.[154] Unfortunately, most of these officials believed they had to obey orders, in the words of one Syrian security official, as "mechanical robots without thinking, discussion, or reasoning."[155] The reality, however, is that not one of those security chiefs or ministers was willing to shoulder any responsibility for the repression. This was first seen in Iraq after the fall of Saddam Hussein, when members of the Revolutionary Command Council claimed that the president took all the decisions and they were simply "obeying orders."[156] Likewise in Libya, where most of the inner group argued that it was Qaddafi and his sons who were to be blamed for all that happened in Libya over four decades.[157] Similarly, no security chief in Egypt was willing to take any share of the blame; they argued that they were fighting terrorism and that any means justified the end. Furthermore, as discussed, many of them were promoted as a result of their ferocious treatment of Islamists and other opponents of the regime.

---

[152] Wa'il al-Ibrashi interviewing Taha Zaki on Dream TV, April 24, 2012.
[153] Nezzar, *Mudhakkirat al-Liwa' Khalid Nezzar*, p. 197.
[154] See, for example, al-Fayturi, *Mudhakkirat mudda'i 'amm*, p. 18.
[155] Al-Faris, "Barnamij bila hudud."
[156] Sassoon, *Saddam Hussein's Ba'th Party*, p. 231.
[157] See Sharbal, *Fi khaymat al-Qaddafi*.

Conclusion

Authoritarianism and despotism are often based on having strong and effective security services in addition to an effective army. One exception is Tunisia, where the three arms of the police state – the ruling party, the centralized bureaucracy, and the security organs – functioned for decades without the army playing a part. The Ba'th regime in Iraq also relied more on the security apparatus than the military.

As this chapter has shown, the eight republics shared many characteristics in how their security services were structured and operated. The number and role of employees in the security agencies witnessed an enormous surge in the last three decades before the Arab uprisings. In many ways, a symbiosis developed between the leadership and the security apparatus that ensured a safeguarding of the interests of both sides. They not only succeeded in preserving the longevity of these regimes, but they also created a climate of fear and distrust that permeated every corner of society. They all employed the same approaches to controlling the masses: arrests, torture, trials, and liquidating opponents inside and even outside their countries. The arbitrariness of many of these practices left a deep wound in these societies and created a sense of uncertainty that penetrated and deeply scarred the bulk of the population. The issue of complicity with the security organizations will need to be addressed in the future, particularly in view of the consistent unwillingness to bear any responsibility for the horrific acts committed in the name of these regimes. Confronting the past and the toxic legacy of the security organizations is unavoidable for any true reconciliation, and is further discussed in Chapter 7.

The suffering of the masses in all these republics, particularly in certain sectors of society such as the Islamists, was profound, and will have repercussions for decades to come. The life of every man and woman was dictated by the power and reach of these organizations, whose employees enjoyed extensive authority and frequently abused it, for a multitude of reasons. The average individual felt that his or her life was monitored at every step by the omnipresent and omnipotent security forces. A security mechanism developed which forced complicity and was all engrossing. In the words of Václav Havel, it became a system "which permeates the entire society and is a factor in shaping it, something which may seem impossible to grasp or define (for it is in the nature of a mere principle), but which is expressed by the entire society as an important feature of its life."[158]

Some regimes utilized an additional mechanism – the cult of personality – to further control the masses and create yet another barrier to the functionality of society, as discussed in Chapter 6.

---

[158] Havel et al., *The Power of the Powerless*, p. 37.

5 | Economy and finance

Since the Arab uprising, scholars have made extensive attempts to analyze the reasons for the dramatic changes that swept across five Arab republics and indirectly impacted other republics. Economic factors undoubtedly played an important part in the dislocation of the authoritarian regimes.[1] Although economic performance in the eight republics varied dramatically, from high gross domestic product (GDP) per capita in countries such as Libya to very low GDP in Yemen (see Table 5.1), they nevertheless shared a number of characteristics.

First, during the past four decades, significant progress was made in areas such as illiteracy and life expectancy.[2] Second, an enormous expansion of bureaucracy took place and a pervasive central government apparatus dominated these republics. Third, a command economy prevailed, in which decisions made by the leadership relied on the heavily bureaucratic system.[3] Fourth, patronage of elite groups became fundamental, and many republics used economic liberalization to reinforce political control. Fifth, little or no emphasis was placed on formulating economic policy and properly running the finances. Most leaders focused more on consolidating their power, and economic management only came to the fore during national or international financial crises. As a result, the number of memoirs written by political

---

[1] See, for example, Rex Brynen, Pete W. Moore, Bassel F. Salloukh, and Marie-Joëlle Zahar, *Beyond The Arab Spring: Authoritarianism and Democratization in the Arab World* (Boulder, CO: Lynne Rienner, 2012).

[2] The median rate for illiteracy in the Middle East and North Africa (MENA) dropped from 64.6 percent to 22.9 percent between 1970 and 2001, while the median life expectancy increased over the same period from 50.6 to 70.3 years. See Massoud Karshenas and Valentine M. Moghadam (eds.), *Social Policy in the Middle East: Economic, Political, and Gender Dynamics*, United Nations Research Institute for Social Development (UNRISD) (New York: Palgrave Macmillan, 2006), pp. 25, 28.

[3] For a discussion of the command economy and other categories in dictatorship, see Ronald Wintrobe, *The Political Economy of Dictatorship* (New York: Cambridge University Press, 1998), pp. 127–44.

Table 5.1 *Economies of Arab republics pre-Arab uprisings*

Country	GDP in USD (billion)[1]	GDP per capita (USD)[1]	Size of informal economy as % of GDP[2]	Population size (million)[3]	Population below 19 in %[3]
Algeria	161.2	4, 349	31%	35.9	38%
Egypt	218.89	2, 803	32%	80.4	42%
Iraq	138.5	4, 473	65%	29.7	49%
Libya	74.7	12, 375	31%	6.1	38%
Sudan	65.6	1, 439	23%	32.9	53%
Syria	40.4	2, 065	18%	22.2	47%
Tunisia	44.4	4, 212	35%	10.5	33%
Yemen	31.7	1, 349	26%	23.2	55%

Sources for Table 5.1:
1. Statistics for GDP and GDP per capita were taken from 2010 data from the World Bank Database. Syria's statistics are from 2007, which is the last year that the World Bank Database has GDP information for Syria. http://data.worldbank.org.
2. C. Elgin and O. Oztunah, "Shadow Economies around the World: Model Based Estimates." *Bogazici University Department of Economics Working Papers*, vol. 5 (2012), pp. 1–48. The statistics pertain to 2008. www.econ.boun.edu.tr/pub lic_html/RePEc/pdf/201205.pdf Elgin and Oztunah do not have any statistics for Iraq. Statistics about Iraq's informal economy come from R. Looney, "Economic Consequences of Conflict: The Rise of Iraq's Informal Economy," *Journal of Economic Issues*, vol. 4 (2006), p. 9. http://faculty.nps.edu/relooney/Rel-JEI-06.pdf
3. United States Census Bureau, using data from 2010. *International Database*. www.census.gov/population/international/data/idb/informationGateway.php

actors and leaders centering on economic issues are more limited, and many of those discussed here belong to senior officials working in the economic ministries or to commentators who closely followed their countries' economic trajectories. It is remarkable how little attention was paid to economic affairs even by those who occupied senior positions in finance and the economy. Two examples: Ahmed Mestiri, who was minister of finance and commerce in Tunisia from 1958 to 1960, devotes only nine pages to this in his more than 350-page memoir;[4] and in 'Abd al-Rahman al-Iryani's more than 600 pages, no more than a couple are dedicated to the economy of Yemen even

---

[4] Ahmed Mestiri, *Témoignage pour l'histoire* [Testimony for history] (Tunis: Sud Editions, 2011).

though he was the president for seven years (1967–74), during which the country suffered severe economic and development problems.[5]

Apart from these common denominators mentioned, the whole region suffered from similar problems. An ex-minister of economy in Lebanon during the 1950s, who later became a financial and economic consultant for the region, summed them up: (1) a low ratio of workers to the overall population (45 percent versus 61 percent for the rest of the world); (2) high youth unemployment averaging 25 percent, although general unemployment in the Middle East is not very high compared to other regions; (3) stagnation of real wages over the last two decades; (4) growth dependent on exogenous variables (oil prices, rain, tourism, remittances, foreign aid); (5) the brain drain as a major constraint for these economies; (6) concentration of investments in certain sectors; (7) low expenditure on research and development; and (8) low regional trade and a high foreign trade deficit.[6]

This chapter will examine three topics: economic policy and its perception by government or party members; the structure of the economic classes and how this was viewed by business people and others; and the thorny issue of corruption, as reflected in memoirs and studies.

Economic policy

Many writers have dwelt on various aspects of the economic system in these republics.[7] After practicing quasi-capitalism under colonialism or independent monarchies, most regimes took the path of socialism in the 1960s, and its centralized economic planning, nationalization, and land reforms dominated economic decision making. Some opening up and liberalization of these economies followed, in part to pacify the Western world. Islamic finance also played a role, but none of these republics seriously considered adopting it as a system until the Arab uprising. As none of the systems or ideologies brought sufficient

---

[5] 'Abd al-Rahman bin Yahya al-Iryani, *Mudhakirrat al-ra'is al-qadi* [Memoirs of the president judge], vol. II (1962–67) (Cairo: Egyptian Association for Books, 2013), pp. 59, 630 and appendix 3. Judge al-Iryani died in 1998.

[6] George Qarm, "al-Iqtisad al-siyasi lil-intiqal al-dimuqrati fi al-watan al-'Arabi" [The political economy of the democratic transition in the Arab world], *al-Mustaqbal al-'Arabi* [The Arab future], no. 426 (August 2014), pp. 19–40.

[7] See, for example, the discussion in al-Razzaz, *al-'Amal al-fikriyya wa al-siyasiyya*, pp. 200–38.

success, many began adopting hybrid ideas and giving them different titles. For instance, a Tunisian prime minister labeled his country's policy "socialism with humanistic attributes,"[8] but the reality was that existing policies were slightly modified but not fundamentally changed. One Egyptian observer opined that socialism in the hands of the regime became a vehicle for the military to control the outcome of the 1952 Revolution, and to ensure that all senior economic appointments emanated from the same inner circle around the regime. Furthermore, socialism enabled the military to control the means of production, so that "socialism became a bureaucracy that served itself and not the economy."[9]

Socialism had a negative connotation among business people; President al-Iryani of Yemen recounts that when news was published in 1962 that socialist measures would be implemented, the business community took this to mean confiscation of their property and refused to bring back any money to Yemen. An interesting point is that the deputy prime minister made the announcement while he was traveling in the Soviet Union, and without much consultation or study.[10] For Ba'thist Iraq, socialism was seen as "a decisive necessity for liberating the Arab nation."[11] Both Syria and Iraq elevated socialism into one of the three mottoes of the ruling Ba'th Party.

One leader who did pay ample attention to economic issues was 'Abd al-Karim Qasim, who governed Iraq between 1958 and 1963. Evaluating the Qasim years, Muhammad Hadid, who held key economic jobs such as minister of finance under Qasim, believes that significant economic and development progress took place in spite of the political uncertainty. In his opinion, this stemmed from Qasim's personal interest in the welfare of the lower classes and his strong desire to ameliorate their conditions.[12] This cannot be said for the period that followed. Based on interviews with captured senior Iraqis after the 2003 invasion, the Iraq Survey Group concluded that the economy was Saddam Hussein's third priority after security and political management.[13] For Saddam Hussein, the economy

---

[8] Mzali, *Hadith al-fi'l*, p. 362.
[9] Ramadan, *al-Sira' al-ijtima'i wa al-siyasi*, pp. 225–26.
[10] Al-Iryani, *Mudhakkirat al-ra'is al-qadi*, pp. 59, 630 and appendix 3.
[11] Law no. 35 of 1977, in the *Iraqi Gazette*, September 14, 1977.
[12] Hadid, *Mudhakkirati*, pp. 463–69.
[13] Iraq Survey Group, *Regime Strategic Intent*, vol. I: *Comprehensive Report of the Special Advisor to the Director of Central Intelligence*, September 30, 2003, p. 18.

was simply a mechanism for allocating rewards. He believed that if there
was economic growth and prosperity, then the Iraqi people would accept
Ba'th rule even if it used *damawi* (bloody) methods.[14]

The issue of concentration of power and decision making plagued all
the republics. As the leaders accumulated more power, decision making
began to gravitate upward and the president made all-important
decisions. Maye Kassem gives an interesting example of how Nasser
became the "ultimate decision maker" in political and economic matters. In appointing the minister of industry and the first director of the
General Petroleum Company, the national oil company, both of
whom had to be highly technically qualified, Nasser also made sure
of their loyalty. As Kassem illustrates, it was made clear to the new
minister that "he would ultimately be personally accountable to the
president."[15] In other words, without presidential endorsement it was
almost impossible to be nominated for a senior position. Appointments
to top economic and financial positions in the other republics were
similar; while many leaders chose qualified and well-educated administrators to run departments, ministers were mostly appointed on
grounds of loyalty, and the authority of the leader was decisive. In
such an environment, internal politics and personal rivalries were
significant. Kamal al-Janzuri, who held many senior economic positions in Egypt, including prime minister in the mid 1990s, recounts how
he lost his job mostly because of other ministers and advisors poisoning
the relationship between him and President Mubarak. Once he lost his
ministerial position, senior officials, governors, and business people
were banned from contacting him. Al-Janzuri even claims that Cairo
made sure that no organization inside or even outside the country
would honor his work. Apart from personal rivalries, he believes that
Mubarak did not like the rising popularity of a minister who had
become known by the public as "al-Janzuri, rajul al-fuqara'"
(Janzuri, the man of the poor).[16] Intriguingly, an Egyptian economist
believes that "the years between 1986 and 2006 have been among the

[14] Saddam Hussein, *al-Mukhtarat* [The Collection], vol. III (Baghdad: Dar
al-Shu'un al-Thaqafiyya, 1988), p. 86. The collection of Saddam Hussein's
interviews and speeches fills ten volumes.

[15] Kassem, *Egyptian Politics*, pp. 14–15.

[16] Al-Janzuri, *Tariqi*, pp. 182–88. Al-Janzuri became prime minister from 1996 to
1999, and was appointed again to this role during the time of the Muslim
Brotherhood (December 2011–August 2012).

worst in the lives of the Egyptian poor, not just in the last fifty years, but perhaps in the entire twentieth century."[17]

In Tunisia, Hibou summed up the situation by positing that decisions were made not in the full cabinet, but rather in the inner cabinet and by Ben 'Ali's advisors. This was exacerbated when more legislative powers were placed in the hands of the president.[18] Another important obstacle to reaching sound economic decisions was the unwillingness of ministers to share with the leader the cost of implementing their grand designs. Mzali describes in his memoirs a cabinet meeting in 1986, in which Bourguiba gave orders to eradicate poverty after he heard there were 120,000 poor people in his country. All those present promised to execute the plan, but omitted to inform him of its substantial real cost.[19] Another example from Libya shows how decisions were reached and how plans were huge ideas rather than detailed analysis. Qaddafi's spokesman narrates a meeting in 2006 between Qaddafi and al-Baghdadi 'Ali al-Mahmudi, secretary of the General People Committee (equivalent to prime minister), in which Qaddafi asked al-Mahmudi whether by 2009, for the celebrations of the fortieth anniversary of the revolution, the country could achieve four targets: no Libyan would be poor, no Libyan without a home, no Libyan without an opportunity of employment, and no road unpaved or inaccessible. His senior official immediately responded positively but he stipulated four conditions: necessary budgets to be available, help and advice from foreign companies must be allowed, reduction of presidential interference in the government's workings, and no partial assessment during those three years. Supposedly Qaddafi accepted these conditions and promised to allocate more than $100 billion to reach those targets.[20] What happened to these grandiose schemes remains unanswered, and by the time the uprising erupted in 2011, little had been achieved.

It is not surprising, then, that in those republics the decision-making process became bureaucratic, inefficient, and cumbersome. Initiatives were fundamentally not encouraged, and taking decisions meant taking unnecessary risks that had no upside for senior officials. Interestingly, it

[17] Galal Amin, *Egypt in the Era of Hosni Mubarak 1981–2011* (Cairo: American University Press, 2011), p. 73.
[18] Hibou, *The Force of Obedience*, p. 269.
[19] Mzali, *Un premier ministre*, p. 54.
[20] Al-Lamushi, *Fi 'ahd Mu'ammar al-Qaddafi*, p. 95.

was obvious to these leaders that officials were reluctant to make judgments, because the very system they had created prevented that from happening. This dilemma is clearly illustrated in a fascinating Iraqi document issued by the presidential *diwan* (offices) marked "very urgent" that was sent to all ministers, and to government institutions such as the central bank, scientific research council, and military intelligence:

Tawjih (Guidance)

It has come to our attention that some officials in the government administration upon raising certain cases to the attention of higher authority, do not express a view nor do they suggest steps to be taken. They simply want higher authorities to make a decision or at least express an opinion. This is due either to the lack of self-confidence, or the official does not want to take the trouble to immerse himself in the case, and simply writes: "find attached . . ." This behavior is basically shirking responsibility to carry the ethical, legal, and constitutional implications of making a decision. Therefore it has been decided that unless the official expresses his opinion truthfully and clearly, cases would be returned to their sender as they would lack the necessary requirements for deciding. All officials at the level of general director and above must be informed of this guidance.[21]

It is very doubtful that this document issued sixteen years before the end of the regime contributed to ameliorating a problem that had significant implications for economic development, not only in Iraq but also for the other republics.

Political parties in these republics devoted part of their annual conferences to economic issues. Some conferences, depending on the country's circumstances, allocated more time for economic and financial discussions. For instance, Egypt's National Democratic Party conference in 1986 convened many sessions dealing with the economic crisis faced by the country at the time. Although President Mubarak declared that "this conference is for work and not for catchphrases,"[22] a report to the conference titled "The People and Production" included many lines that remained merely slogans, such as this party chose

---

[21] Presidential *diwan* to ministries and agencies, "Guidance," March 11, 1987, *BRCC*, 003-3-7 (042-3).

[22] Al-Hizb al-Watani al-Dimuqrati, *al-Mu'tamar al-'Amm al-Rabi', 20–22 Yuliu 1986* [NDP, Fourth General Conference, July 20–22, 1986] (Cairo: al-Hizb al-Watani al-Dimuqrati, 1986), p. 8.

"production and self-reliance, investing in the people and for the people, expansion via localities to achieve national growth, and focus on social and economic development."[23] Two decades later, another conference tackled the issue of unemployment; Mubarak pronounced the dictum "4.5 million jobs in the next 6 years," but again one would be hard pressed to find any serious analytical work or proposals to tackle unemployment.[24]

Some parties, such as the Ba'th, saw the economy through the prism of their ideology: the belief that socialism would lead not only to prosperity but also to Arab unity, which in turn would create favorable conditions for large and modern industries. Furthermore, the movement saw in the dissolution of the bourgeoisie in the Arab world the means to overcome the economic problems in the region.[25] Opposition parties also raised economic topics to gain popularity and influence, particularly during a crisis. One such instance was the special report issued by the Ba'th Party in Sudan about the financial crisis in 1986. The report called, first and foremost, for a national unity conference, with all parties working together to resolve the crisis; second, for a strategy to deal with agricultural problems and starvation in many parts of Sudan; and finally, to resolve the problem of inflation and assist those on fixed salaries.[26] In other words, opposition parties, like ruling parties, produced more slogans than practical solutions or solid analysis for economic problems.

Strains in economic policy also arose when ministers were not in tandem with the leaders' economic philosophy, or were not allowed to exercise real power. A case in point is that of Hazim al-Biblawi. An economist who wrote about rentierism, he was working in Abu Dhabi for the Arab Monetary Fund when he received an offer to join the government of 'Isam Sharif that was formed after the Muslim

[23] Al-Hizb al-Watani al-Dimuqrati, *al-Sha'b wa al-intaj: taqrir ila al-Mu'tamar al-'Amm al-Rabi' li-Hizb al-Watan 'am 1986* [The people and production: report to the Fourth General Conference 1986] (Cairo: al-Hizb al-Watani al-Dimuqrati, 1986), p. 4.

[24] Al-Hizb al-Watani al-Dimuqrati, *al-Mu'tamar al-Sanawi al-Rabi'*, 2006, p. 515.

[25] Al-Hamash, "Hizb al-Ba'th al-'Arabi al-Ishtiraki fi Suria (1953–2005)," p. 153. The author relies on the documents of the sixth national conference held in Damascus in 1963.

[26] Hizb al-Ba'th al-'Arabi al-Ishtiraki, *Azmat al-iqtisad al-Sudani: asbab al-azma wa tariq al-khuruj minha* [The Sudanese economic crisis: reasons for the crisis and ways to solve it] (Khartoum: n.p., 1986), p. 61.

Brotherhood won the elections in Egypt in 2011. He declined to be deputy prime minister for economic affairs, as he believed that he would not be able to influence economic decisions without actually running a ministry. After consultations with the new prime minister and senior military officers, he was offered the position of finance minister. As he did not see eye to eye with the regime, he felt "caged" during his four-month tenure in this job in 2011.[27] His experience is noteworthy from the aspect of transition, and is referred to in Chapter 7. Along the same lines, issues emanating from clashes between ministers and members of the leaders' families also affected the decision-making process. One Tunisian minister, Béji Essebsi, refutes the idea promoted by Prime Minister Mzali that there was a conspiracy against him organized by the first lady, Wassila Bourguiba, and the then minister of interior, Driss Guiga. Essebsi, who was then foreign minister, admits that Mrs. Bourguiba and Guiga were negative toward Mzali, but argues that the situation was far more complicated, and that Mzali was not cognizant of the major social changes taking place in Tunisia.[28]

Libya had a totally different system from all the other republics, instituted by Qaddafi, and it is important to see how Libyans perceived this system. In his *Green Book*, Qaddafi developed what he termed "The Third Universal Theory" about a stateless society with no need for traditional parties or parliaments. He called for the elimination of ownership, for land to be shared by everyone, and stated that "wage-workers are a type of slave, however improved their wages may be."[29] The outcome was that more power was handed to the popular committees to run industries and economic enterprises. A senior Libyan, Sa'id al-Lishani, who held many positions in the economy and industry, considers 1977 as the beginning of "destruction and chaos" once these popular committees took over the running of the economy. In his view, the period before 1977 witnessed a dramatic growth in the economy and industry, which came to a halt once these

---

[27] Hazim al-Biblawi, *Arba'at shuhur fi qafas al-hukuma* [Four months in the government's cage] (Cairo: al-Shuruq Publishing, 2012).

[28] Essebsi, *Habib Bourguiba: le bon grain*, p. 217. Essebsi was appointed as caretaker prime minister from February to December 2011 after the toppling of Ben 'Ali. For Mzali's point of view, see Mzali, *Un premier ministre*, pp. 492–95.

[29] Qaddafi, *The Green Book*, pp. 42–52. For more analysis, see Vandewalle, *A History of Modern Libya*, pp. 106–09.

committees were in control. In his memoirs, al-Lishani gives examples of how new projects for cooperation and investments with Tunisia and Kenya collapsed as a result of the committees' intervention.[30] Summing up Qaddafi's attitude toward economic policy and issues, al-Lishani describes a meeting he attended. In the presence of Qaddafi, ministers met to discuss housing issues as a result of the state takeover of buildings that were distributed to the needy without any compensation to the owners, who had borrowed from banks to construct these buildings. When one participant suggested evaluating the properties and compensating the owners after deducting the cost of loans, Qaddafi was outraged, and screamed: "These [Libyan] people are ungrateful to the grace of God, and any ungrateful [person] will receive God's wrath, and I am the wrath that was sent to these people."[31]

These authoritarian regimes used economic policy as a means of enhancing their rule, and in most countries security and economy became virtually interconnected. Hibou, in her study of Tunisia's political economy, shows clearly how Ben 'Ali's regime managed to use the economy to bolster its authority. By focusing on the Fonds de Solidarité Nationale (Fund for National Solidarity), known as 26.26 for its zip code, she illustrates how the fund was set up to eradicate poverty, and began raising funds by expropriating money from firms and business people. It was then promptly turned into an instrument under Ben 'Ali's control, which allowed him to reward those loyal to the regime.[32] In Tunisia, the regime created the myth of the economic "miracle," which became part of the machinery of repression. When economic conditions deteriorated, whether as a result of internal or international crises, these republics reacted swiftly to protect their economic systems.

Any sign of major economic discontent perturbed these authoritarian rulers, and whether it was the bread riots in Egypt (1977), the drought in Syria (2006–10), or the sanctions in Iraq (1990s), they saw signs of real danger in food shortages that might unleash popular revolt. In most of these crises, regimes tended to blame outside forces or natural causes for the shortages; during the bread shortages in Egypt in 1989, the government first attributed them to the rise in wheat prices on

[30] Al-Lishani, *Min al-dhakira*, pp. 98–102.   [31] Ibid., p. 123.

[32] Hibou, *The Force of Obedience*, pp. 193–98. See also Hibou and Hulsey, "Domination and Control in Tunisia."

the international markets. But, as scholars have underlined, the regime's policy was at fault: the change in policy after the bread riots of 1977 led to the diversion of wheat to animal fodder.[33] Timothy Mitchell demonstrates that as a result of a shift to meat consumption, the large increase in wheat imports was required not for human consumption but for animal feed.[34] In Syria, governments emphasized agricultural policy, realizing its potential and the need for a proper irrigation system.[35] Nevertheless, the drought in 2006–10 and its ramifications for the agricultural sector was one of the main reasons for the uprising. But as some experts show, it was neither population pressure nor the climate itself, but rather the "Ba'th Party's continual promotion of water-intensive agriculture" that led to drought.[36] Reports from the US embassy in Damascus in late 2008, reported by WikiLeaks, quoted a senior Syrian official warning of the dire consequences of the agricultural policy and the drought.[37]

Mismanagement of the economy and the agricultural sector were thus behind many of the problems of these regimes, but it is almost impossible to find memoirs detailing those failures, and definitely no official willing to bear any blame. One could justly argue that such economic management was not unique to the Arab republics; an investigation into other countries such as Argentina and the Philippines shows many similar traits. The Perón regime, which promised a dynamic free-market economy, ended up destroying Argentina's industrial base, and accumulating a huge external debt that future

---

[33] Yahya M. Sadowski, *Political Vegetables? Businessman and Bureaucrat in the Development of Egyptian Agriculture* (Washington: Brookings Institution, 1991), pp. 35–38.

[34] Timothy Mitchell, *Rule of Experts: Egypt, Techno-Politics, Modernity* (Berkeley: University of California Press, 2002), p. 215.

[35] For the water policy in Syria, see Marwa Daoudy, "Les Politiques de l'eau en Syrie: réalisations et obstacles" [The politics of water in Syria: achievements and obstacles], in Baudoin Dupret, Zouhair Ghazzal, Youssef Courbage, and Mohammed al-Dbiyat (eds.), *La Syrie au présent: reflets d'une société* [Syria today: reflections on society] (Arles: Actes Sud, 2007), pp. 607–15.

[36] Jessica Barnes, "Managing the Waters of the Ba'th Country: The Politics of Water Scarcity in Syria," *Geopolitics*, vol. 14, no. 3 (August 2009), pp. 15–30. Similar conclusions were reached by Francesca de Châtel, "The Role of Drought and Climate Change in the Syrian Uprising: Untangling the Triggers of the Revolution," *Middle Eastern Studies*, vol. 50, no. 4 (July 2014), pp. 521–35.

[37] See http://wikileaks.org/cable/2008/11/08DAMASCUS847.html; see also Thomas L. Friedman, "WikiLeaks, Drought and Syria," *New York Times*, January 21, 2014.

generations were encumbered with.[38] In the Philippines, Ferdinand Marcos created an authoritarian regime not dissimilar from those portrayed here and in many other studies. His economic management was along the lines of Ben 'Ali and other Arab leaders: control the population by fear and rewards, and appeal to groups that could support and sustain his regime.[39] Indeed, many of the regimes in the Arab republics maintained power by utilizing the elites and creating networks of support.

Economic classes

The formation of elites and the connectivity to authoritarianism has been explored in a number of studies.[40] As these republics realized that the state alone could not act as the main engine for growth, their regimes turned to business elites to become part of the process. Mistrust existed between these elites and the regimes, particularly after most of the ruling parties embarked on socialism and nationalization in the 1950s and 1960s. Concurrently, the regimes had to ensure that the material wealth of their elites would not translate into political power. Unfortunately, memoirs by members of those elites are scarce; so I will discuss the structure of the elites, briefly look at labor, and then at how those at the top of the business pyramid interacted with the country's leadership.

In general, economic elites proved to be very cohesive, and in Syria, for instance, this solidarity was not just in business but also within the military and diplomatic communities.[41] Second, because of this cohesion and an overall identification with the regimes, the Arab uprising

---

[38] For a discussion of Argentina, see, for example, William C. Smith, *Authoritarianism and the Crisis of the Argentine Political Economy* (Stanford: Stanford University Press, 1991).

[39] Albert F. Celoza, *Ferdinand Marcos and the Philippines: The Political Economy of Authoritarianism* (Westport: Praeger, 1997).

[40] For general studies on networks and economic reforms, see, for example, Heydemann (ed.), *Networks of Privilege in the Middle East*; for specific works on countries, Bassam Haddad, *Business Networks in Syria: The Political Economy of Authoritarian Resilience* (Stanford: Stanford University Press, 2012); Hibou, *The Force of Obedience*; Emma C. Murphy, *Economic and Political Change in Tunisia: From Bourguiba to Ben Ali* (New York: St. Martin's Press, 1999).

[41] Bassam Haddad, "Syria's State Bourgeoisie: An Organic Backbone for the Regime," *Middle East Critique*, vol. 21, no. 3 (Fall 2012), pp. 231–57.

did not emanate from the elite groups as it did in other parts of the world. As Giacomo Luciani explains, the bourgeoisie in the Arab world was "merely a client of the state," and hence "unlikely to be a force for radical change."[42] In other words, these authoritarian regimes successfully managed to enlist the elites and the middle class by providing them with enough rewards, and therefore a "deal" was struck: accumulation of wealth on the understanding that there would be no threat of utilizing this wealth to gain political power. A patron–client working relationship developed between the regimes and those groups, whereby each side understood the rules of the game.[43] This process took place even in socialist countries such as Iraq and Syria. The Ba'th documents demonstrate that by the mid 1980s Saddam Hussein had tilted toward private entrepreneurship and liberalization. As a result of the wars that the regime was engaged in, it had to focus on "mobilization of human resources" and encourage wealthy families to plow some of their assets back into strengthening the economy.[44]

In Algeria, entrepreneurs were both "agents of change and [a] means of preservation of the system." When President Bouteflika came to power in 1999, he distanced himself from the traditional triumvirate that held power: the FLN, the army, and the security services, and attempted to attract the wealthy merchants.[45] An Algerian sociologist who studied Algerian prime ministers found that their socioeconomic backgrounds were characterized by wealthy, large landowning families, or they were sons of families that had accumulated significant wealth in exile. The educated middle classes managed to have two prime ministers: one was the son and grandson of judges, the other the son of a teacher.[46] Hence, this "diversification" into the realm of business did not mean opening the way for change, and in fact in many

---

[42] Giacomo Luciani, "Linking Economic and Political Reform in the Middle East: The Role of the Bourgeoisie," in Oliver Schlumberger (ed.), *Debating Authoritarianism: Dynamics and Durability in Nondemocratic Regimes* (Stanford: Stanford University Press, 2007), pp. 169, 172.

[43] For a general discussion of the concept, see James C. Scott, "Patron–Client Politics and Political Change in Southeast Asia," *American Political Science Review*, vol. 66, no. 1 (March 1972), pp. 91–113.

[44] For more details, see Sassoon, *Saddam Hussein's Ba'th Party*, pp. 239–42.

[45] Amel Boubekeur, "Rolling Either Way? Algerian Entrepreneurs as both Agents of Change and Means of Preservation of the System," *Journal of North Africa Studies*, vol. 18, no. 3 (2013), pp. 469–81.

[46] Jabi, *al-Jaza'ir: al-dawla wa al-nukhab*, pp. 44–45.

countries the demarcation between the regime and the business elite became almost invisible. A comprehensive study of the elites in Algeria by Isabelle Werenfels shows that the Algerian elites underwent dramatic changes from the mid 1990s. Most important was the increase in the number of actors exerting influence; this was partly due to the effort to heal the effects of the civil war, and partly because many opposition members were offered a platform for the first time.[47] An interesting feature of elites is the generation gap between them and the young in Algeria. For instance, all of Algeria's presidents were of the revolution generation, and while their legitimacy stemmed from fighting French colonialism, "for most Algerians that struggle is history, not a living memory or a shared experience."[48]

Whether in Syria or Tunisia, the connection between the rulers and the business community was close, principally because rulers' families became deeply involved in business and over a couple of decades became the wealthiest people in the nation. No other country exemplifies this lack of demarcation between the rulers and their families more than Tunisia. Ben 'Ali's children from his first marriage, to Na'ima Kefi, controlled banks, communication companies, pharmaceuticals, car dealerships, and telecom companies. His second marriage, to Layla Trabulsi, led to the creation of a "dynasty" that spanned all sectors of the economy, and it was estimated that the families close to Ben 'Ali controlled almost a quarter of Tunisia's gross domestic product.[49]

Elites tend to change with leadership. This happened in Syria after the death of Hafiz al-Asad, even though his son, Bashar al-Asad, succeeded him. Bashar soon became the critical decision maker, but initially lacked the sources of power. As Perthes shows, there was a gradual change in what he termed "the Politically Relevant Elite."[50] In

---

[47] Isabelle Werenfels, *Managing Instability in Algeria: Elites and Political Change since 1995* (London: Routledge, 2007), pp. 2–3.

[48] Alan Richards and John Waterbury, *A Political Economy of the Middle East*, 3rd edn. (Boulder, CO: Westview Press, 2008), p. 89.

[49] Aidan Lewis, "Tracking down Ben Ali's Fortune," BBC News, January 31, 2011, available at www.bbc.co.uk/news/mobile/world-africa-12302659, accessed September 15, 2014; Laure Kermanach and Guillaume Guichard, "La Pieuvre Ben Ali disséquée" [The octopus Ben Ali dissected], *Le Figaro*, January 21, 2011, available at www.lefigaro.fr/conjuoncture/2011/01/21/04016-20110121ARTFIG00643-la-pieuvre-ben-alipdissequee.php.

[50] Volker Perthes, "Syria: Difficult Inheritance," in Perthes (ed.) *Arab Elites*, pp. 87–114. A discussion about the Politically Relevant Elite (PRE) is in the first chapter, pp. 1–32.

Egypt, under Mubarak, prominent businessmen and leading trade unionists were in the second circle of elites after the president, with senior NDP members, top administrators, ministers, and senior military officers.[51] A study of the Egyptian social classes clearly demonstrates how the business elites expanded their influence after Sadat's *infitah* policy facilitated private foreign investment. Two of the men closest to him were from large landowning families, and the third, 'Uthman Ahmad 'Uthman (see below), represented the new bourgeoisie outside the agricultural sector.[52] The study shows how the elites chose to invest in sectors with relatively quick returns, and in areas such as telecoms where cash yields are high. These elites managed to infiltrate the political strata and influence the leadership with regard to legislation about working hours and unions. Furthermore, by establishing strong ties to the media and national newspaper editors, they ensured a strong voice in the public arena.[53] Although unions in Egypt went on multiple strikes during the Mubarak era, the reality is that organized labor continued to be a small portion of the total workforce, as the vast majority outside the public sector worked in the informal economy. Asef Bayat argues that the economic restructuring that took place in the 1980s as a result of liberalization led to the undermining of organized labor and its ability to mobilize the workforce.[54]

As in other countries, the business elite in Sudan benefited dramatically from its close ties to the government. The ruling party tended to have its own loyal supporters, who were the major beneficiaries of financial and economic legislation. One consequence was that in the late 1980s and early 1990s, businessmen close to the regime were amassing huge wealth, purchasing foreign currencies, and then smuggling their assets out of the country to foreign banks without any further investment in Sudan.[55] This

---

[51] Gamal Abdelnasser, "Egypt: Succession Politics," in Perthes (ed.), *Arab Elites*, p. 120.

[52] 'Abd al-Basit 'Abd al-Mut'a (ed.), *al-Tabaqat al-ijtima'iyya wa mustaqbal Misr: ittijahat al-taghayyur wa al-tafa'ulat 1975–2020* [Social classes and Egypt's future: trends of changes and reactions 1975–2020] (Cairo: Merit Publishing, 2002), p. 79.

[53] Ibid., pp. 369–74.

[54] Asef Bayat, *Life as Politics: How Ordinary People Change the Middle East*, 2nd edn. (Stanford: Stanford University Press, 2013), p. 63.

[55] Hafiz Ahmad 'Abdullah Ibrahim, *al-Nukhab al-iqtisadiyya al-jadida fi al-Sudan* [The new economic elites in Sudan] (Khartoum: al-Sudan Publishing, 2007), pp. 116–17.

took place not only in the Arab republics, but also in many other authoritarian regimes where the elites did not reinvest their profits to create jobs or build for long-term growth. From a survey conducted by a Sudanese researcher, 65 percent of those asked agreed that the economic groups close to the regime were the ones who reaped the rewards of the development program in the country.[56]

The networks that connected the elites were strong. They learned how to exist with and adapt to the political demands of these authoritarian regimes, and in most republics they were a powerful lobby. But, as Diane Singerman correctly points out, building networks was not just the privilege of the wealthy elites, and "despite differences in status, wealth, education, piety, and property, people can 'work' their network to further their personal and familial goals."[57] It is these networks that enabled the vast majority of the people in these republics to withstand years of economic struggle, political repression, and violence. A case in point is the thirteen years of harsh economic sanctions imposed on Iraq after the end of the First Gulf War, when networks based on kin and family provided lifelines of support to their members. It is important to underline that while overall poverty in these republics is not as high as in many developing countries and regions, the rising poverty and the high unemployment, particularly among the youth, were and continue to be serious problems for any regime. A strong perception of inequality dominates the thinking in these republics, and part of that stems from the fact the middle class felt, in the last couple of decades, that there were fewer opportunities for socioeconomic advancement because the number of jobs outside the public sector was not really commensurate with the increase in population.[58] Unfortunately, we do not have memoirs from these groups, or from workers in the industrial or agricultural sectors.[59]

---

[56] Ibid., p. 144.
[57] Diane Singerman, "Networks, Jobs, and Everyday Life in Cairo," in Donna Lee Bowen and Evelyn A. Early (eds.), *Everyday Life in the Muslim Middle East* (Bloomington: Indiana University Press, 2002), p. 201.
[58] Brynen et al., *Beyond the Arab Spring*, pp. 227–28.
[59] While I did not find memoirs of industrial workers, there are a number of outstanding studies on this topic. See, for example, Zachary Lockman (ed.), *Workers and Working Classes in the Middle East: Struggles, History, Historiographies* (Albany: State University of New York Press, 1994), which contains both general and specific chapters relating to Egypt and Iraq; Augustus

Few scholars have written on specific personalities in the contemporary Arab world, drawing on their memoirs and interviewing them and their families. An exception is the excellent research by Robert Springborg on Sayyid Mar'i, with the fundamental theme of "What strategies and tactics, given various and constantly changing political circumstances, did Sayed Marei [*sic*] adopt to exercise and enhance his personal power?"[60] Mar'i was in a unique position, at the critical junctures of economics and politics in his country. He was a member of parliament under the monarchy, and then during the Nasser era he was the "undisputed overlord of the agricultural sector."[61] In the 1950s he cultivated his friendships with the political elite, including Nasser, and others from the Free Officers who launched the 1952 Revolution. Under Sadat, Mar'i became general secretary of the ruling party, and was both a close advisor to the president and an intimate friend, to the extent that he delivered Sadat's acceptance speech for the Nobel Peace Prize, awarded after the Egyptian president had signed the Camp David Accords. The relationship between the two men became more familial, as Mar'i's son married one of Sadat's daughters. Being so closely identified with Sadat did not help him under Mubarak, who, after coming to power, attempted to disengage himself from Sadat's management style, where "special assistants" such as Mar'i and 'Uthman Ahmad 'Uthman (see below) spoke in the name of the president without any accountability.[62]

Mar'i himself wrote a three-volume memoir that begins with his childhood, but ends abruptly in the first week of the October 1973 War with his visits to Saudi Arabia and the Gulf countries to drum up support for Egypt and promote coordination using oil as a bargaining

Richard Norton (ed.), *Civil Society in the Middle East*, vol. I (Leiden: Brill, 2005); Joel Beinin and Frédéric Vairel (eds.), *Social Movements, Mobilization, and Contestation in the Middle East and North Africa*, 2nd edn. (Stanford: Stanford University Press, 2013). For a study of labor elections in Egypt, see Fawzi Mansur (ed.), *al-Haraka al-'ummaliyya fi ma'rakat al-tahawwal: dirasat fi al-intikhabat al-naqabiyya 1991* [The labor movement in the battle of change: studies in the union elections of 1991] (Cairo: Markaz al-Buhuth al-'Arabiyya, 1994).

60 Robert Springborg, *Family, Power, and Politics in Egypt: Sayed Bey Marei – his Clan, Clients, and Cohorts* (Philadelphia: University of Pennsylvania Press, 1982), p. xv.

61 Ibid., p. xiv.

62 Thomas L. Friedman, "Mubarak Trying to Penetrate Egyptian Red Tape," *New York Times*, November 2, 1981.

tool with the USA. It is not clear why he decided to finish his book so suddenly.[63] There is no doubt that Mar'i was at the heart of events during the Sadat era. He describes how he went to the presidential palace in October 1973 to hear, in Sadat's presence, the report by the minister of defense, Ahmad Isma'il 'Ali, of Egyptian forces crossing Israel's supposedly impregnable Bar Lev line. He was then dispatched, as Sadat's representative, to update the king of Saudi Arabia and other rulers in the Gulf about the chain of events during the first week of the 1973 War.[64]

Springborg succinctly summed up Mar'i's mode of operations as a middleman "keeping his lines of communication open to the president's enemies while simultaneously cultivating good relations with the president himself."[65] Under Nasser and Sadat, Mar'i managed to exploit "his family background, party loyalty, and political commitment." In other words, he succeeded in utilizing his personal and family connections and his expertise in agriculture and food to create the almost perfect patron–client relationship. Interestingly, Springborg suggests that the case of Mar'i shows that the family in Egypt is "sufficiently cohesive and adaptable to outlive even the most adverse of political circumstances."[66] Mar'i retired from public life in 1984 and died in 1993 at the age of eighty.

Another person who epitomized combining the roles of advisor, friend, relative, and successful businessman is 'Uthman Ahmad 'Uthman. Born in Isma'iliyya, he studied engineering. As a supporter of the Muslim Brotherhood, he resented the discrimination against them under the Egyptian monarchy and moved his engineering firm to Saudi Arabia, where it flourished. He set up a company called Arab Contractors, which won a contract for building part of the Aswan Dam. Later on, Nasser nationalized the Egyptian branch of this firm, but its other offices in the Arab world continued to blossom. With Sadat's ascent to power, 'Uthman benefited dramatically from the

---

[63] Mar'i, *Awraq siyasiyya.* The first volume, *Min al-qarya ila al-islah* [From the village to reform], begins with childhood in his village and ends in 1953; the second volume, *Min azmat Mars ila al-naksa* [From the March crisis until the defeat] begins with land reforms when he was appointed minister of agriculture and land reform, and ends in a meeting of the cabinet after the 1967 defeat. The final volume, *Ma'a al-ra'is al-Sadat* [With President Sadat] begins with events in Egypt in summer 1968 and ends in October 1973.

[64] Mar'i, *Ma'a al-ra'is al-Sadat,* pp. 722–29.

[65] Springborg, *Family, Power, and Politics in Egypt,* p. 241.   [66] Ibid., p. 244.

infitah policy, and later was appointed minister of reconstruction, and then minister of housing. As with Mar'i, his son married one of Sadat's daughters and he became even more of a close advisor and friend of the president. His company won many contracts while he was a minister, and its assets reached $1.5 billion dollars, with more than 60,000 Egyptian families becoming dependent on it.[67]

In his memoirs, 'Uthman, the ambitious young entrepreneur, describes how the question "min inta?" (who are you?) always upset him and made him determined to create the largest and most successful building company in Egypt.[68] Again, like Mar'i, the family played a major role; 'Uthman was close to his brothers, who relied on one another to further their careers. The three brothers were married to three sisters from a religious family. 'Uthman admits that he was so insensitive to his wife because of his obsession with work, that even during his honeymoon he woke up very early as usual and went to the office.[69] Typical of the successful entrepreneur who started with almost nothing, 'Uthman realized that his sons could not emulate him: "I grew up in destitution, and they grew up with a golden spoon in their mouths ... I believe difficulties create men, and I have to teach them lessons in suffering in order to understand real life."[70] Years later, one of his sons sued him, and rumors abounded that his death from a heart attack was the result of stress caused by hostilities within the family.

'Uthman's company had many employees who were associated with the Muslim Brothers. This led to conflicts, first during the monarchy, and then under Nasser's regime. "I want to note for the record that the Muslim Brothers were treated unjustly when they were harassed and tortured without any reason in 1954 and again in 1965."[71] Although these views put him on a direct collision course with Nasser, he proclaimed that his relationship with Sadat strengthened after he realized that Sadat knew and respected his God. He is full of compliments for Sadat, and argues that he was the only president who restored national pride and self-confidence to Egypt after the disasters under Nasser. He assumed that Sadat benefited from an incredible foresight: "He was and still is the only human being who can see things I cannot

---

[67] Arthur Goldschmidt, *Biographical Dictionary of Modern Egypt* (Boulder, CO: Lynne Rienner, 2002), p. 221.

[68] 'Uthman Ahmad 'Uthman, *Safahat min tajribati* [Pages from my experience] (Cairo: al-Maktab al-Misri al-Hadith, 1981), pp. 87–89.

[69] Ibid., p. 110.   [70] Ibid., pp. 114–15.   [71] Ibid., p. 362.

see or comprehend, and therefore I have to be guided by his think-ing."[72] 'Uthman was an ardent supporter of Sadat's *infitah* policy and asserted that this would recreate economic life, and while dislocation might take place during such a period, this would be justified to achieve the final results. He ends his memoirs in early 1981 when he was appointed deputy prime minister for popular development. His rela-tionship with Mubarak was far from close, and articles began circulat-ing in *al-Watan* newspaper refuting 'Uthman's attacks on Nasser in his memoirs. Furthermore, the Engineers' Syndicate published a book expounding 'Uthman's misdeeds and corruption, given that he was a minister and a close advisor to President Sadat at the same time that his company was winning huge contracts.[73]

The third memoir written by a member of the elite is from Iraq, although its author, Sa'ad Allah al-Fathi, did not play the same crucial role in politics and economics as the other two. However, he was a well-educated professional who worked for the government in Iraq and was a Ba'thist from his student days, so his identification with Saddam Hussein's regime was strong enough for him to be given senior jobs and dispatched abroad. Al-Fathi was born in Mosul, earned his engineering degree at Manchester University in Britain, worked in the Ministry of Oil, became head of the Dora Refineries in 1976, and then head of the Organization for Oil Refinery and Gas Exploration in 1980. After spending a few years working in Vienna for the Organization of the Petroleum Exporting Countries (OPEC), he returned to work in the Ministry of Oil and retired in 2002. His experiences as a reserve officer in the air force during his mandatory military service are intriguing in how he describes relations among the officers and life on the bases. He recounts the details of a failed coup d'état in June 1966, when a couple of pilots from the base where he was stationed bombed the presidential palace. Both were later arrested, but after the Ba'th Party came to power one of them became head of the air force.[74] His friendship with educated Ba'thists served him well, but even he complains that the party interfered in technical issues, such as including non-qualified engineers for a training course in Czechoslovakia without consulting

[72] Ibid., pp. 458, 632.
[73] Goldschmidt, *Biographical Dictionary of Modern Egypt*, p. 222.
[74] Al-Fathi, *Min burj al-takrir*, pp. 65–88.

him as the head of the refinery.[75] In a chapter titled "Years of Fire," he describes the air attacks by Iran on Iraq's oil installations, the resulting complications, and the desperate need to find oil, from internal and external sources, for the armed forces.[76]

Al-Fathi makes it clear that no one in Iraq was safe from the Ba'th regime, even the most zealous of Ba'thists. One of his superiors, and a longtime friend of his family, 'Abd al-Mun'im al-Samarra'i, was arrested one day in 1986 by the intelligence services, and after many months of interrogation was hanged without a public trial. Later on, al-Samarra'i's son was also executed and his brother was arrested and dismissed from the army. Obviously al-Fathi was distressed, but felt he was fortunate to be in Vienna away from what he termed "the cruelty of my country."[77] Yet, in spite of this harrowing experience, al-Fathi continued to believe in the regime; he felt that Iraq was "pushed" into invading Kuwait, in a move that led it into draining its resources and capabilities. Remarkably, for an educated and well-traveled man, al-Fathi goes even further and blames Kuwait's own policy since 1986 for bringing the invasion on itself. In a 480-page memoir, he dedicates just two to the invasion of Kuwait and the First Gulf War, and then shifts quickly to a denunciation of Iran. "The Iranians in the organization [OPEC] were always working against Arabs, particularly the Iraqis."[78] He returned to Iraq to serve his country during the sanctions and in the negotiations with the United Nations over the Oil-for-Food program. He retired in April 2002, and two months later was offered a consultancy job in Amman, and thus left Iraq, not realizing he would thereafter live in exile.

Corruption

Corruption is an ancient phenomenon that plagues many countries, but in the authoritarian Arab republics it was a serious issue, which together with their other inherent problems would have ramifications for transition (see also Chapter 7). Corruption is not, of course, unique to developing or authoritarian countries; the USA had its share, such as the accounting scandals related to the oil conglomerate Enron and the telecommunications company WorldCom, which led to the demise of

---

[75] Ibid., pp. 166–67.   [76] Ibid., pp. 235–305.   [77] Ibid., pp. 343–46.
[78] Ibid., pp. 383–85.

these companies and the loss of billions of dollars by institutions and individuals.

Corruption has many repercussions. It creates an atmosphere of distrust and a widespread sense of unfairness; it reduces government functionality; and it leads to a decline in the legitimacy of the state. There are many forms of what is labeled administrative corruption: bribery, embezzlement, nepotism, and illegal enrichment. Most of the republics were cognizant of these phenomena and participated in international and regional conferences to combat it. A paper by a senior Tunisian official representing his country at a seminar organized by the Arab Administrative Development Organization in 2007 correctly attributed corruption to political factors such as interconnectivity of the ruling party and the regime, to the extent that loyalty is not to the state but to the party and the rulers.[79] The Yemeni government declared that the first step in any economic, financial, and administrative reforms has to be fighting corruption, and proceeded to promulgate laws against corruption, most of which were unfortunately not implemented.[80]

The reasons behind corruption were very similar in the different republics. An interesting aspect is that while all their leaders were authoritarian, many of the first generation of leaders who toppled monarchies or led their countries to independence from colonial powers were not corrupt, and some of them (such as Nasser in Egypt and Qasim in Iraq) lived in modest houses and died without having accumulated fortunes. That changed with subsequent leaders. "Corruption flourishes because rulers and ruling classes condone, and, often, participate in its nefarious pursuits."[81] Nasser's chief of staff, who ran his presidential office, recounts that Sadat loved luxury,

---

[79] Fathi bin Hasan al-Sakri, "Dirasa hawla usas wa asalib muqawamat al-fasad al-idari" [A study of the basics and means of combating administrative corruption], in Arab Organization for Administrative Development, *al-Fasad al-idari wa al-mali fi al-watan al-'Arabi* [Administrative and financial corruption in the Arab world] (Cairo: Organization for Arab Administrative Development, 2008), pp. 149–67.

[80] Muhammad Sadiq Isma'il, *al-Fasad al-idari fi al-'alam al-'Arabi: mafhumaha wa ab'adaha al-mukhtalifa* [Administrative corruption in the Arab world: its concepts and miscellaneous ramifications] (Cairo: Arab Group, 2014), pp. 101–07.

[81] Robert I. Rotberg, "How Corruption Compromises World Peace and Stability," in Robert I. Rotberg (ed.), *Corruption, Global Security, and World Order* (Baltimore: Brookings Institution Press, 2009), p. 20.

and appearances were important to him. Rumors circulated that he bought a villa in Manufiyya, north of Cairo, after receiving a bribe from a family he helped during the revolutionary trials of the monarchy ministers. More serious is the chief of staff's claim that he saw the stub of a large check from a Gulf family paid into Sadat's personal account. Needless to say, it is impossible to know how true these comments are coming from a very close ally of Nasser who decided to wait ten years after Sadat's death before publishing his notes.[82] However, the fact that leaders were tainted from the beginning of their rule surely added to the notion that corruption was acceptable.

In Egypt, corruption existed during the monarchy at different levels, but an important factor curtailing it significantly was the transparency of state budgets under the monarchy.[83] For instance, the budget of 1949–50 contained details not only about revenue and expenditure by ministries, but the size of army brigades, the royal family's expenses, and the salaries of senior officers and officials. After the 1952 Revolution there was less and less transparency, which successive governments ascribed to *i'tibarat al-amn al-dakhli* (reasons of national security).[84] Budget allocations to defense and internal security became ambiguous, and it is almost impossible to decipher the total allocation for salaries and rewards in these ministries.[85] Furthermore, the emergence of a large public sector created a bureaucratic elite and led to inefficiencies. An Egyptian study of government units belonging to nineteen ministries (excluding those related to defense and national security) concluded that on average, workers wasted between two to three hours a day for such reasons as delayed arrival to their offices, reading newspapers, drinking and eating, and departing earlier than they should.[86]

The bureaucratic elite, "by manipulating public sector assets, succeeded in amassing large fortunes through bribery and corruption."[87] Under Sadat, the *infitah* policy of liberalization led to a deepening of nepotism and patronage, and contracts for large state projects were

[82] Al-Hakim, *al-Jayyar yatadhakkar*, pp. 85–86.
[83] For a good background on corruption during that period, see Amin, *Egypt in the Era of Hosni Mubarak*, pp. 21–30.
[84] Faruq, *Judhur al-fasad al-idari fi Misr*, pp. 164–65.   [85] Ibid., pp. 246–47.
[86] Ibid., pp. 104–09.
[87] Nadia Ramsis Farah, *Egypt's Political Economy: Power Relations in Development* (Cairo: American University Press, 2009), p. 36.

awarded to those close to power. After Mubarak became president and consolidated his regime, corruption reached unprecedented levels: a group of oligarchs close to Mubarak controlled a large slice of the economy, and loans were given to those whom the regime wanted to keep as loyal supporters. Once corruption permeated the upper echelons, there was nothing to stop it spreading across every level of society. One Egyptian study indicates that during the 1990s, the police force opened roughly 10 million files a year (criminal, administrative, complaints, etc.), and it became almost impossible to register a complaint at a police station without paying a bribe to representatives of the police or the prosecution.[88] Another feature contributing to corruption, whether in Egypt or the other republics, is the size of the informal economy, which tends to concentrate in certain sectors such as construction. Statistics about the informal economy are unreliable and difficult to find, but indications are that in most republics it amounts to 30–40 percent of the entire economy, while in some countries such as Iraq it could be as high as 65 percent (see Table 5.1). It seems, however, that the informal economies have expanded in the last couple of decades. The "exact causes of this expansion are unclear, though persistent regional conflict, globalization, and even aspects of economic reform may play a role."[89]

An extremely detailed document on corruption in Egypt published by Kifaya (Enough), which represented a grassroots movement calling for reforms, concluded that "corruption has actually become a social law and a hidden behavior that rules the different aspects of Egyptian life." The document argues that "Egypt's state under Mubarak is an embodiment of corruption," and goes on to highlight examples from different sectors and in different ministries.[90] Although Egyptian journalists enjoyed reporting corruption cases, this did not seem to impact the behavior of the regime or bring an investigation of those claims unless a huge scandal ensued. For example, in one report the journalist detailed how those close to the regime accumulated wealth, were

---

[88] 'Abd al-Khaliq Faruq, *al-Fasad fi Misr: dirasa iqtisadiyya tahliliyya* [Corruption in Egypt: an analytical economic study] (Cairo: al-'Arabi Publishing, 2006), pp. 30–31.

[89] Brynen et al., *Beyond the Arab Spring*, p. 228.

[90] Kifaya, "Corruption in Egypt: A Dark Cloud that Does Not Vanish," 2006, available at https://docs.google.com/document/d/1rh6YoHyQopURUx2Pm2D dZfdHqofYS8R3AawzfPUkCxs/edit?hl=en.

allowed to build almost anywhere and to get whatever they wanted for the right price, and described the relationship of one minister with the business elites, and how artists were "selling themselves to rich and powerful people."[91]

"Algeria is a country sapped by corruption," said President Bouteflika in a speech he gave a few months after coming to power in 1999.[92] Since then, Algeria has continued to be marred by corruption scandals, and some even argue that it has reached such epidemic proportions that "it has become a *culture* in and of itself."[93] In the last two decades corrupt practices have become more sophisticated, spanning a complex web of syndicates and cliques of senior officers and politicians. Many Algerians have described in detail the al-Khalifa case, where corruption within this business empire, built in just over three years, straddled a bank, companies in numerous sectors, and a television channel. These commentators believe the case was not just about money laundering by the military elites, but rather "the last link in the chain of systematic corruption, where the Rafiq al-Khalifa Group engaged in buying the political decision that enabled it to siphon off public monies and allowed al-Khalifa to set up his huge group in a relatively short time."[94] One researcher estimates that by the mid 1990s the amount pilfered by the military elite, with the help of the civilian elite (senior ministers and officials), reached $26 billion. There were claims that this was the main reason that no financial audit of the state was published for twelve years, and why a number of Algerians who were willing to expose details of the many corruption incidents met their deaths in one way or another.[95] Another observer believes in

---

[91] 'Imad Nasif, *Buyut min al-zujaj: al-malaffat al-sirriyya li-fasad al-kibar* [Glasshouses: the secret files of the corruption of the powerful] (Cairo: Arab Media, 1999).

[92] Quoted in Djilati Hadjadj, "Algeria: A Future Hijacked by Corruption," *Mediterranean Politics*, vol. 12, no. 2 (September 2007), pp. 263–77.

[93] Mohammed Halim Limam, "Detailed Analysis of the Phenomenon of Political Corruption in Algeria: Causes, Repercussions and Reform," *Contemporary Arab Affairs*, vol. 5, no. 2 (April 2012), p. 253.

[94] Ibid., p. 255. See also Mohammed Hachemaoui, "La corruption politique en Algérie: l'envers de l'autoritarisme" [Political corruption in Algeria: the other side of authoritarianism], *Esprit* (June 2011), pp. 111–35.

[95] Muhammad Bashir Saffar, "al-Nukhba al-siyasiyya fi al-Jaza'ir" [The political elites in Algeria], in *al-Nukhba al-siyasiyya fi al-'alam al-'Arabi* [The political elites in the Arab world], Papers for the Third Conference for Young Researchers, Cairo, November 11–13, 1995 (Cairo: Center for Political

the strong correlation between authoritarianism and the spread of corruption in Algeria; the lack of legitimacy of the consecutive despotic regimes led to corruption becoming a means of shoring up power in the hands of the rulers.[96] As Werenfels explains, the core elite blocked any political transformation and most of the economic reforms.[97] Thus, Algeria, as one of the wealthy republics (in 2011, oil exports earned Algeria about $55 billion), has not managed to reverse its reliance on oil and gas, which is another consequence of corruption.

Hibou, in her analysis of Tunisia's political economy, highlighs two important points. First, the concept of corruption in a country such as Tunisia is problematic due to "the plurality of practices that it covers, and its vagueness." Second, embezzlement and misappropriation of funds in a direct way is repressed and punished. She argues that this contributed to Tunisia being graded by Transparency International and other international organizations as a country where the level of corruption is low.[98] Indeed, out of the eight republics discussed in this book, Tunisia was the highest ranked in 2010: 59 out of 178, above any other republic in terms of cleanliness of the system.[99] It might be true that Tunisia was graded higher due to this anomaly, but there is no denying that all these republics suffered from rampant corruption, and the rankings of Sudan and Iraq among the worst in the world, with Libya and Yemen supposedly somewhat better, was closer to reality. Biblawi discusses the issue of transparency in salaries of high officials and ministers, and narrates in his memoirs how ministers in Egypt were unhappy with him when he revealed his official salary (very low by any standard) to the media, but showed that when benefits and adjustments were added it was quite high. More intriguingly, when he attended a meeting at the Council for Petroleum Affairs, he was handed a check at

Research and Studies, 1996), pp. 99–164. Saffar used documents from the Algerian embassy in Cairo to detail the many cases of corruption.

[96] Muhammad Halim Limam, *Zahirat al-fasad al-siyasi fi al-Jaza'ir: al-asbab wa al-athar wa al-islah* [The political corruption phenomenon in Algeria: causes, effects, and reform] (Beirut: Markaz Dirasat al-Wihda al-'Arabiyya, 2011), pp. 126–30.

[97] Werenfels, *Managing Instability in Algeria*, p. 5.

[98] Hibou, *The Force of Obedience*, pp. 274–75.

[99] In the 2010 rankings, after Tunisia came Egypt (98 out of 178); Algeria 105; Syria 127; Libya 146; Yemen 146; Sudan 172; and Iraq 175. See Transparency International, "Corruption Perceptions Index 2010," available at www.transparency.org/cpi2010/results.

the end of the day for his attendance. When he expressed his surprise, he was told that this was the norm, and after he refused to accept it the money was transferred to the account of the Ministry of Finance.[100]

While Sudan has long been seen as one of the most corrupt countries in the world, its government did not pay much attention to this. For instance, in the speech about the 1998 budget presented to the National Council by the minister of finance and national economy, there was no hint about corruption or its repercussions for the country. On the contrary, the minister awarded his government high marks for its discipline in implementing economic policies, and proceeded to blame international conspiracies for seeing in Sudan a threat, because the country "is leading a unique renaissance that surely would confuse all international actors and is drawing a new map for modernity."[101]

Anthropologists assert that writing about corruption cannot be complete without storytelling. These stories are not simply case studies or examples, but rather "the bedrock on which the superstructure of analysis is often constructed."[102] The Arab uprising brought a wave of memoirs from countries such as Libya, and uncovered cases hidden in regimes such as Egypt. Al-Lishani, in his memoirs, details methods of corruption used by high officials and officers, such as creating corporations and then folding them. In the interim, the assets of the corporation were embezzled, and outside sources were blamed for the company's "bankruptcy." Another tactic was to team up with foreign contractors, who proceeded to charge more for a contract and then split the difference with the senior official.[103] Al-Lishani describes a disastrous period from the early 1980s until the collapse of Qaddafi, in which corruption, nepotism, and lack of dignity permeated every level of society. "I would not be exaggerating to state that 80 percent of the population sank in corruption, and that

---

[100] Al-Biblawi, *Arba'at shuhur*, pp. 53–57.
[101] Wizarat al-Maliyya wa al-Iqtisad al-Watani [Ministry of Finance and National Economy], *Khitab wazir al-maliyya wa al-iqtisad al-watani, mashru' al-muwazana al-'amma li-'am 1998* [Speech of the minister of finance and national economy, budget proposal 1998] (Khartoum: n.p., n.d.), p. 2.
[102] Akhil Gupta, "Narrating the State of Corruption," in Dieter Haller and Cris Shore (eds.), *Corruption: Anthropological Perspectives* (London: Pluto Press, 2005), p. 174.
[103] Al-Lishani, *Min al-dhakira*, pp. 102–03.

corruption infiltrated everywhere, and that the honest person became an oddity and avoided by the people."[104]

'Abd al-Rahman Shalqam, a senior Libyan who worked closely with Qaddafi's regime from 1974 onward, exposed some of the corruption prevailing in his country during those years. He articulates the exasperation among ministers for being unable to stem the outrageous behavior of Qaddafi's family: his daughter-in-law sent a special plane to Beirut to collect a poodle she had acquired; one daughter, 'A'isha, used two private planes to fly to London when she was due to give birth; and his son, Mu'tasim, spent $4 million at his birthday party in Europe entertaining his friends with musicians and dancers. Shalqam explains that an important point relevant to most despotic leaders is their attitude to money. In his opinion, Qaddafi was not interested in money per se, because given that he was the leader, he believed he owned Libya and all its resources. He never carried cash and simply issued orders to send a bag of money to a leader, to buy someone a house, or to send another abroad for medical treatment. In essence, "all the money belonged to him, Libya and what was in it and who was in it."[105] This critical point, where leaders felt that the country and its resources were theirs to do with as they liked, affected the functionality of the state and contributed to the rampant corruption. Qaddafi, more than any other leader of these republics, behaved in a totally irresponsible manner and squandered his country's assets on adventures elsewhere in Africa and in other parts of the world. Large sums were wasted in Chad either fighting there or in Libya's assistance to that country. Then, in order to emphasize his title, "King of Kings of Africa," Qaddafi paid bribes to different African leaders to win their approval. His foreign minister, 'Ali 'Abd al-Salam al-Triki, who replaced Shalqam at the United Nations and who also defected, recounts the astonishing amounts of energy, effort, and cash that went to finance Qaddafi's dream of uniting Africa with him as leader, and also spreading Islam throughout the continent. He believes that the Libyan leader did receive support from some of the leaders who were on his payroll and found it an easy way to enrich themselves.[106] This

---

[104] Ibid., p. 122.
[105] Sharbal, *Fi khaymat al-Qaddafi*, pp. 217, 212. Shalqam announced in front of the world's cameras in February 2012 that he was defecting, as his country's representative to the United Nations, in order to support the revolution.
[106] Ibid., interview with 'Ali 'Abd al-Salam al-Triki, pp. 262–64.

behavior is identical to Saddam Hussein's dealings with his country's finances; whenever the government allocated rewards or benefits to its employees or citizens at large, the statement was always preceded by "on the orders of the President," or sometimes, as a "gift from the leader" to his people. There was even a card inscribed "Friends of Mr. President Leader Saddam Hussein" which entitled its holders to a wide range of benefits.[107]

Conclusion

Oil shaped the economies of the republics, even those that were not large producers because of labor migration and remittances. It impacted economic policy and allowed many of these authoritarian regimes to be generous with their rewards to supporters. That in turn distorted allocation of resources, enabled economic elites to benefit dramatically, and led to an increase in corruption throughout these countries at all levels. As these republics struggle to find new political paths, they will need to address the economic and social problems that are overwhelming them.[108] Many of these difficulties, as this chapter shows, were rooted in excessive authoritarianism and the relentless focus of the leaders on preserving power. Economic policy and allocation of resources were simply turned into tools to ensure durability, rather than to tackle the complicated issues facing their countries. The lines between those in power and the business elite close to them were blurred, and as a result corruption spread. Although the relationship between the state and the elites varied immensely within these republics, it was, as seen in the three examples discussed, more of a personalized association, and arrangements between the two sides tended to be informal and exclusive.

---

[107] Sassoon, *Saddam Hussein's Ba'th Party*, pp. 208–13.

[108] For an interesting discussion of political and economic issues, see Charles Dunbar, "The Middle East Political Economy and the Arab Awakening: A Difficult Symbiosis?" in Abbas Kadhim (ed.), *Governance in the Middle East and North Africa: A Handbook* (London: Routledge, 2013), pp. 50–62.

6 | Leadership and the cult of personality

Throughout the world, including the Arab region, the cult of personality has played a significant role in authoritarian and totalitarian states, impacting them politically, economically, and culturally. In general, a cult is "an established system of veneration of a political leader, to which members of the society are expected to subscribe, a system that is omnipresent and ubiquitous and one that is expected to persist indefinitely."[1] Some leaders in the Arab republics developed a personality cult, but even those who did not utilize this device to strengthen their regimes created a sense of being unassailable. With the possible exception of Algeria, Arab leaders carefully centralized power and were the final decision makers.

This chapter will first focus on leaders in the Arab republics, in order to understand how they functioned and interacted with their institutions, ministers, and other Arab leaders. It will then explore the cult of personality and compare it to tyrannical systems outside the Arab world. The reasons for developing a cult, the methods leaders used to achieve it, the common factors among the "cult" dictators, and the implications for decision making will be examined also, concluding with remarks about leadership and the future of personality cults in the region.

Leadership

Between the Egyptian Revolution in 1952 and the Arab uprisings in 2011 there have been forty-one presidents in the eight republics under study; some were in power just for one to two years, while others managed to rule for three or four decades (see Table 3.1). Thirty of

---

[1] E. A. Rees, "Leader Cults: Varieties, Preconditions and Functions," in Balázs Apor, Jan C. Behrends, Polly Jones, and E. A. Rees (eds.), *The Leader Cult in Communist Dictatorships: Stalin and the Eastern Bloc* (New York: Palgrave Macmillan, 2004), p. 4.

these presidents hailed from a military background, and there were other similarities, particularly among those who succeeded in staying in power for a long time. They learned to contend with different constraints and to deal with conflicts and wars, albeit some of their own making; they manipulated the constellation of power to suit their needs, and some created a cult of personality.

What drove many of these leaders to become more despotic is not a simple issue; no doubt they believed as time went by that they were more capable and intelligent than their colleagues, and some of them definitely worked harder than their subordinates. What seems to have taken place was that some leaders, who originally intended to implement a more democratic system, changed their views when they realized that controlling the decision-making process would not only allow them to push ahead with their programs and ideology, but also to stay in power and overrule all opposition. Two examples of this are Tunisia's first president, Habib Bourguiba, and Egypt's second leader after the 1952 Revolution, Gamal 'Abd al-Nasser. Early in their careers both men believed in a more pluralistic approach to governance, but later shifted to dictatorship.

Ahmed Mestiri, a close associate of Bourguiba, devotes a chapter in his lengthy memoir to "the black pages" in the president's history. He argues that it would have been possible to force Bourguiba to build a state based on the rule of law and democratic institutions, but this failed because he was surrounded by "a family blanket and close associates whose influence was insurmountable."[2]

An interesting glimpse into Nasser's change of attitude is found in Khalid Muhyi al-Din's memoir. Although he was a close associate and friend of the leader, this did not protect Muhyi al-Din in the long run. He strongly believes that once Nasser had ousted Muhammad Neguib in 1954, he had no intention of following a democratic path, and later on all who opposed the Revolutionary Council, with Nasser as its new leader, were dismissed.[3] An important element in the success of these leaders and their authoritarianism is that friendship counted only to a limited degree, and became irrelevant when it threatened the rulers'

---

[2] Al-Mestiri, *Shahada lil-tarikh*, p. 326.
[3] After the 1952 Revolution, Muhammad Neguib became the prime minister, war and naval minister, and governor-general of Egypt. Between 1953 and 1954 he was the president until Nasser placed him under house arrest. See Goldschmidt, *Biographical Dictionary of Modern Egypt*, pp. 150–51.

power. Muhyi al-Din recounts his conversation with Nasser when he resigned from the Revolutionary Council after Nasser ousted Neguib in late 1954:

NASSER: What do you intend to do?

MUHYI AL-DIN: I want to resign.

NASSER: I accept, but Khalid, we are friends, but the public interest is above that. You are like honey and around you all the flies will gather, and then we will have a problem and clash. I do not want to clash with you. Therefore I prefer that you leave Egypt and go abroad.

MUHYI AL-DIN: Fine, I will go to Paris.

NASSER: Not Paris. Paris has an active leftist political movement and this will get you immersed [politically], and I don't want that. I prefer you go to a quiet place.[4]

Sure enough, Muhyi al-Din was not allowed to return to his previous role in the army and was exiled to Switzerland. As he predicted, many of the loyal officers who were identified with him were forced to leave the military within a short period after his exile. Paradoxically, part of the cult of personality was that these leaders projected images of loyalty to and affection for their friends in order to show that they were compassionate. One Syrian general who was an active member of the Ba'th Party described the leader: "Here is Hafiz al-Asad who cares about his comrades more than he cares about himself, loyal to anyone he knows, truthful in his positions and in love of his friends."[5] One psychiatrist assessing Saddam Hussein wrote that "he has a flexible conscience: commitment and loyalty are matters of circumstance, and circumstances change."[6] Muhyi al-Din's conversation with Nasser bears out this assessment. As for other authoritarian leaders, a critical key to their success in maintaining their leadership is being incessantly paranoid about everything and everyone.

---

[4] Muhyi al-Din, *Wa al-'an atakallam*, p. 317.

[5] Hamdun, *Dhikrayat wa ara'*, p. 66.

[6] Jerrold M. Post, "Saddam Hussein of Iraq: A Political Psychology Profile," in Jerrold M. Post (ed.), *The Psychological Assessment of Political Leaders: With Profiles of Saddam Hussein and Bill Clinton* (Ann Arbor: University of Michigan Press, 2005), p. 339.

Nasser's interest in power and his tendency to run the country in a non-democratic manner is also reflected in Murad Ghalib's memoirs. Nasser told Ghalib: "I have no interest in clothes or food; my only hobby is power. Power allows you to fulfill your dreams of building a strong state."[7] Obviously these leaders had many abilities and talents; Huwaydi's memoir describes how Nasser ran the cabinet and his relationship with ministers. In his opinion, Nasser had a great capacity to listen to his colleagues without interrupting or interfering, and was warm and hospitable to all his ministers. Yet, ministers usually found out about their dismissal from the cabinet through the radio or newspapers. Proposals sent to the president would be returned with one of two statements attached: "I agree" or "I do not agree," and in certain cases they were returned with a request for more information. From there, the cabinet secretariat would deal with the successful proposals.[8]

There is no doubt that all these leaders, whatever their style of governing, were interested in power, and the majority were skilled at its acquisition and retention. However, they possessed other qualities that assisted them to reach the top. One man who worked with the Tunisian president and knew him well was Essebsi. He wrote a long memoir attributing Bourguiba's commanding powers of persuasion to his self-confidence and his unshakable belief in his intellectual capabilities. Essebsi further states that Bourguiba was a voracious reader who was willing to learn from philosophers and intellectuals in all fields.[9] In fact, he says that the best depiction of Bourguiba's leadership can be found in *al-Ahkam al-Sultaniyya* (The Ordinances of Government), written by a tenth-century Iraqi jurisprudent, Abu al-Hasan 'Ali al-Mawardi. In this treatise, al-Mawardi listed seven conditions of eligibility for "supreme leadership" such as justice, ability to exercise independent judgment in crises, sound physical endurance, prudence, and undaunted courage.[10]

Many enjoyed the flexibility that power brought, and were willing to reverse decisions because they relied more on intuition than on detailed analysis and open discussion of policy issues. They had a highly

---

[7] Ghalib, *Ma'a 'Abd al-Nasser wa al-Sadat*, pp. 155–56.
[8] Huwaydi, *Ma'a 'Abd al-Nasser*, pp. 31, 5.
[9] Essebsi, *Habib Bourguiba: al-muhimm wa al-ahamm*, pp. 381–82.
[10] Abu al-Hasan al-Mawardi, *The Ordinances of Government: A Translation of al-Ahkam al-Sultaniyya wa al-Wilayat al-Diniyya*, translated by Wafaa H. Wahba (Reading: Garnet Publishing, 1996), p. 4.

developed survival instinct and consequently viewed many around them with suspicion. In many cases decisions came as a total surprise to their ministers, and even to close advisors; the style of leadership was to consult no one, or just one or two members of the inner circle.[11] 'Abd al-Salam Jallud, who until the mid 1990s was the second in command in Libya, sheds light in his memoirs on how Qaddafi treated his co-members on the Revolutionary Command Council. In essence, what the president wanted, the others yielded to him. For instance, many council members were reticent in congratulating Mubarak when he "won" the elections in the early 1990s, but Qaddafi not only decided to send him a congratulatory message, but to take most of his council members to the Libyan–Egyptian border to congratulate Mubarak in person.[12] This decision-making style is also evident in a memoir that highlights the leadership style of Egypt's President Sadat. Sadat's advisor for national security, Muhammad Hafiz Isma'il, relates:

Al-Sadat chose to be the only high "political authority" in the country, thus in charge of all critical decisions whether in politics or military strategy. That does not mean he did not listen to any counseling or that he did not seek it . . . But none of those attending [the National Security Council] meetings was interested in voting about decisions to approve a certain policy. As a result, al-Sadat was the final "decision maker" on war and peace, while the council simply provided the "pulse" of the public opinion, and then the [vehicle for] the execution of the order.[13]

Needless to say, major events affected the leaders and their decision making. Many were engaged in war, and political scientists argue that "personalist" leaders "initiate more military conflicts than non-personalist leaders."[14] As Chapter 3 shows, all the leaders, except the Tunisians, were involved in some kind of military action, either

---

[11] In Libya, the expulsion of Italian nationals came as a surprise to most of Qaddafi's advisors: see el-Saadany, *Egypt and Libya from Inside*, p. 54. In Iraq, many senior officials argue that there was no consultation about the invasion of Kuwait.

[12] Sharbal, *Fi khaymat al-Qaddafi*, pp. 57–58.

[13] Muhammad Hafiz Isma'il, *Amn Misr al-qawmi fi 'asr al-tahadiyyat* [Egyptian national security in the era of challenges] (Cairo: al-Ahram Center for Publishing, 1987), pp. 184–85.

[14] Jessica L. Weeks, "Strongmen and Straw Men: Authoritarian Regimes and the Initiation of International Conflict," *American Political Science Review*, vol. 106, no. 2 (May 2012), p. 327. Personalist leaders ensure that they are the supreme leaders and they make all final decisions.

within their own country or against another one. It seems that a peaceful status quo for some leaders was threatening, and they often felt compelled to take a military course of action.[15] In fact, some have attributed the stability and endurance of these authoritarian regimes to the dictators' defiance of an external foe, be it an actual military enemy or only a political antagonist.[16] Once these conflicts ended, the behavior of the leaders changed. For example, after the Iran–Iraq War, Saddam Hussein convinced his people that he had won the war, and, as befitting a successful military strategist, he acted in a more arrogant and confident manner. However, when the First Gulf War of 1991 ended in disaster and was followed by the uprising in the south, Saddam Hussein became reclusive and even more paranoid. A second example comes from Egypt, where one of Sadat's senior advisors argues that after the October 1973 War Sadat was a different man from the 1970–73 years, as he became far more confident and willing to take risks.[17] As Laurie Brand posits, the "victory of October" allowed Sadat to consolidate his hold on power as he "was virtually free from challenges."[18]

In Egypt, Nasser's personalist style of leadership continued with Sadat, and then Mubarak. While we have many testimonies about the first two, there is a vacuum regarding Mubarak's era, and I am confident that many will speak out now that it has ended. In the words of one Egyptian observer, Galal Amin, anyone reading the Egyptian press during Mubarak's presidency would be confused about whether the governance of the country showed strength or weakness, given that "every act was attributed to him, and every prime minister, speaker or member of parliament had to begin his speech in praise of him."[19] Indeed, the obsequiousness was not limited to the media. An academic historian at an Egyptian university wrote in his seven-volume social and political history of the country under Mubarak:

---

[15] Jessica L. Weeks, *Dictators at War and Peace* (Ithaca: Cornell University Press, 2014), p. 15.

[16] Paul Brooker, *Defiant Dictatorships: Communist and Middle-Eastern Dictatorships in a Democratic Age* (New York: New York University Press, 1997), p. 7.

[17] Isma'il, *Amn Misr al-qawmi*, p. 185.

[18] Laurie A. Brand, *Official Stories: Politics and National Narratives in Egypt and Algeria* (Stanford: Stanford University Press, 2014), p. 76.

[19] Amin, *Egypt in the Era of Hosni Mubarak*, p. 148.

The problem of the Egyptian people with Muhammad Hosni Mubarak differs from other citizens' problems with their president, since all the others could replace their president with another, but the Egyptian people cannot replace Muhammad Hosni Mubarak. This is what all loyal nationalists and progressive intellectuals realize, and know that having Mubarak in charge of the regime means simply that Egypt is fine and progressing forward, and they are well aware that if Mubarak goes, the deluge will come.[20]

Many scholars have rightly pointed out that no tyrant can govern alone and "no leader is monolithic."[21] This goes to the heart of the accountability issue, which will be discussed in Chapter 7. Suffice to say that while it is impossible to run a country alone, the decision-making process, particularly on important and sensitive subjects, becomes ossified and very dependent on one person: the leader. That does not overlook the role of the bureaucracy and the ruling party in running the country, but points to the reality that they were not making decisions, but rather preparing studies on various topics for the leader and then executing his decisions. Nowhere is this clearer than in the voluminous documents of the Iraqi regime under Saddam Hussein, and even more so from the audiotapes of meetings of the senior leadership. By the early 1980s, the Iraqi president had become the final arbiter and decision maker regarding almost all important issues in the country, supported by a parallel mechanism he created in the form of the *diwan* (presidential offices), which provided him with technical information and advice on multiple issues.[22] In Iraq, a report by the Ba'th Party politbureau and distributed to all branches, presented the "activities" of President Saddam Hussein during the year 2001. It listed the monthly activities of the president, such as the number of meetings and conferences he attended, and the "vital" decisions he took in all spheres, which left no doubt in anyone's mind about the centralized leadership.[23]

A fascinating insight into the functioning of the Tunisian leadership under Ben 'Ali comes from Muhammad Ghannouchi (no connection to Sheikh Rached al-Ghannouchi), who was *wazir awwal* (prime minister) under Ben 'Ali from 1999 to 2010, and then acting president

---

[20] Ramadan, *al-Sira' al-ijtima'i wa al-siyasi*, p. 181.
[21] De Mesquita and Smith, *The Dictator's Handbook*, pp. 1–2.
[22] For more details about the style of his leadership, see Sassoon, *Saddam Hussein's Ba'th Party*, pp. 7, 162–75.
[23] Party Political Bureau, Information and Research Department, "Activities of the President for the Year 2001," January 1, 2002, *BRCC*, 012-2-7 (060-0663).

for the first few months after Ben 'Ali fled the country. In an interview, Mr. Ghannouchi described in detail how decisions were reached and what it was like to work under an authoritarian leader. He emphasized that Ben 'Ali asked him to be in charge of economic and human development affairs as the president wanted to be in control of political and international matters. Yet, when it came to economic affairs related to the Trabulsi family (Ben 'Ali's wife and relatives), he was not allowed to see any contracts signed, as these files went directly to the president. Furthermore, when on a number of occasions the prime minister or some of his ministers voiced complaints about the unfairness of these contracts, Ben 'Ali shrugged off these complaints, and even argued that in the final analysis they contributed to the economic development of Tunisia. Ben 'Ali met with his *wazir awwal* once a week, and with his cabinet only once a month, although he would call on certain ministers to meet with him privately. According to Ghannouchi, four ministries were directly under the president: Defense, Foreign, Interior, and Justice. Ghannouchi described how the president relied on his advisors rather than his ministers. In a system similar to the one Saddam Hussein created in Iraq, the presidential *diwan* became the decision-making hub in the country.[24] The centrality of the *diwan* and the president's control of economic contracts to the Trabulsi family and other large supporters of Ben 'Ali is confirmed by a senior official who worked in the presidential *diwan*.[25]

In a number of cases, Ben 'Ali reminded his ministers that Tunisia is a presidential system and hence he is the final decision maker. Indeed, while the prime ministers met twice a week with ministers, they simply prepared recommendations for the attention of the president and his office rather than making concrete decisions. Asked why he did not resign, Mr. Ghannouchi posited that he believed reform could be achieved only from the inside, and highlighted the importance of the partnership agreement with the European Union in 1995. He strongly hoped that this agreement would alter Tunisia not only economically but also politically, given "his deep belief that harmonization with the

---

[24] Ghannouchi recounts that instead of the traditional picture that a president takes with his ministers, Ben 'Ali was photographed surrounded by his advisors. Interview with Muhammad Ghannouchi, Tunis, December 17, 2014.

[25] Testimony of al-Bashir Fath Allah in al-Tamimi (ed.), *Dawr al-qasr al-ri'asi*, pp. 105–74.

European Union principles will change the system in Tunisia, step by step."[26]

In Syria, unfortunately, we do not have archives or enough memoirs to illustrate the style of Asad's leadership to the extent that we have in Egypt, Iraq, Libya, and Tunisia. However, scholars who examined the system confirmed that without doubt, President Hafiz al-Asad was "at the helm, and that all strings of power end in his hands."[27] As in other regimes, books written in Syria about Asad depicted him as the man who was making all the decisions, politically, economically, and socially, in order to enforce the image of the commander and leader of the people.[28] In other words, whether it was Mubarak, Asad, or Qaddafi, these leaders wanted to be portrayed as the final decision makers who had the power and authority to do anything, irrespective of whether a personality cult about them existed or not.

Two important topics, which are to some extent interconnected, need to be addressed: the argument that these leaders were irrational, or some even mentally ill; and their refusal to surrender when they knew the end was nigh. Indeed, the personality traits of the ruler are critical for understanding a regime and its policy. Their backgrounds and life experiences affected their dispositions and policies. Many writers have attempted to assess the political leaders of the Arab world in the hope that it would help to configure US policy toward the region. Attempts were made to label some of these leaders, such as Qaddafi and Saddam Hussein, as insane and detached from reality because of their megalomaniac and erratic attitudes. One study of five presidents – Qaddafi, Mubarak, Ben 'Ali, 'Ali 'Abdullah Salih, and Bashar al-Asad – argues that from a psychoanalytic point of view, each of these leaders had a "narcissistic personality," and that the "narcissist not only exaggerates his own capabilities, but also tends to think of himself a god."[29] The author further argues that these leaders conformed to the "hysterical personality" type, which "fears and rejects anything that smacks of finality, inevitability."[30]

26 Interview with Mr. Muhammad Ghannouchi, Tunis, December 17, 2014.
27 Perthes, *The Political Economy of Syria under Asad*, p. 139.
28 See, for example, 'Adil Hafiz, *Hafiz al-Asad: qa'id wa umma* [Hafiz al-Asad: a leader and a nation] (Damascus: al-Markaz al-Dawli Publications, 1993). The book carries an introduction by Mustafa Talas, then the defense minister.
29 Muriel Mirak-Weissbach, *Madmen at the Helm: Pathology and Politics in the Arab Spring* (Reading: Ithaca Press, 2012), p. 3.
30 Ibid., p. 5.

Another paper compared Saddam Hussein to Adolf Hitler and Kim Jong-il, and concluded that his schizophrenia and psychotic thinking were more pronounced than in the two other tyrants.[31] In the West, particularly before the 2003 invasion of Iraq, the lines between erratic decisions and being "mad" became blurred in the minds of the public and politicians. However, as the sociologist Norbert Elias points out, "even within the framework of an extremely powerful social position" there are constraints and limits to the flexibility of the ruler. He adds: "Just because the flexibility of this position and the scope for decisions it confers are particularly large, the possibility of error, rashness and derailment, which could in the long run lead to a reduction of power, is particularly acute."[32]

A psychiatric evaluation of Saddam Hussein with a more balanced approach rightly concluded that "there is no evidence that Saddam Hussein is suffering from a psychotic disorder. He is not crazy in a psychiatric sense. By any psychological measure, he is in touch with reality."[33] Likewise in Libya, one scholar explained that Qaddafi had clear ideas when it came to foreign policy, which for him consisted of "a pyramid made up of five overlapping levels. Each level includes a number of countries and certain policy orientations."[34] In essence, Qaddafi had a deep fear of both Egypt and Algeria because of their size and military power, and he turned to Africa when the Arab world shunned him. It is unlikely that any of the eight presidents of these republics would have remained in power for so long, and been so active in war and regional politics, if they had been seriously irrational and detached from reality. However, Roger Owen believes that Qaddafi's mental state, unlike that of other presidents, changed after he came to power, and that he possibly developed some type of "psychotic personality."[35]

---

[31] Frederick L. Coolidge and Daniel L. Segal, "Is Kim Jong-il Like Saddam Hussein and Adolf Hitler? A Personality Disorder Evaluation," *Behavioral Sciences of Terrorism and Political Aggression*, vol. 1, no. 3 (September 2009), pp. 195–202.

[32] Norbert Elias, *The Court Society*, translated by Edmund Jephcott (New York: Pantheon Books, 1983), p. 23.

[33] Carroll A. Weinberg, "Saddam: A Psychiatric Opinion," Middle East Council Seminar Paper, Foreign Policy Research Institute, Philadelphia, February 19, 1991.

[34] Mary-Jane Deeb, *Libya's Foreign Policy in North Africa* (Boulder, CO: Westview Press, 1991), p. 8.

[35] Owen, *The Rise and Fall of Arab Presidents for Life*, p. 198.

Leaders, like other mortals, are influenced by their personal experiences and relations with their associates. Saddam Hussein's failure to be accepted by the Military College affected his attitude toward the officer corps. He wanted to prove time and again that although he lacked the proper military training, he was more competent than his generals in military matters. Hence, he took many decisions during the war with Iran, and again in the two Gulf Wars, that had disastrous repercussions. In Tunisia, observers attributed Ben 'Ali's inferiority complex and attitude toward culture and education to not having attended university.[36] An insider argues that Bourguiba underestimated Ben 'Ali, and after he was appointed *wazir awwal*, the countdown began. Mestiri quotes King Hasan II of Morocco, who said that once appointed, Ben 'Ali was unmovable, unlike the others.[37]

A third example, more complex and open to debate, is Nasser's affiliation with the Muslim Brotherhood before the 1952 Revolution. Memoirs from senior members of the organization leave no doubt that Nasser joined the Brotherhood and gave his *bay'a* (pledge of allegiance) to the then leader, Hasan al-Banna. The claim is that Nasser was number three in the organization, but that after the Revolution he felt empowered and popular, and hence clashed with the organization and its new *murshid* (leader), Hasan al-Hudaybi.[38] Those close to Nasser denied this vehemently and argued that he conducted talks with the Brotherhood prior to the Revolution but was not part of it. Members of the Brotherhood argued that Nasser's enmity toward the organization stemmed from this historical background, and as one knowledgeable observer told me, "those on the inside tend to be crueler when they are on the outside."[39]

This leads to another important issue: when the Arab uprising began, why did these leaders – with the exception of Ben 'Ali – refuse to surrender or to leave their countries for a safe haven? They undoubtedly believed in their ability to survive, and some, such as Saddam Hussein and Bashar al-Asad, believed that time was on their side. Relinquishing power is tantamount to surrender, which was an

---

[36] Al-Madini, *Suqut al-dawla al-bulisiyya fi Tunis*, p. 44.
[37] Mestiri, *Shahada lil-tarikh*, p. 291. The exact quote is: "celui-la il ne pourra pas l'enlever comme les autres."
[38] See, for example, an account by one of the members in al-Hakim, *'Abd al-Nasser wa al-Ikhwan*, pp. 36–41.
[39] Interview with Sami al-Arian, Washington DC, November 8, 2014.

absolute anathema to these leaders. Interestingly, long before the uprising, Bashar's father, Hafiz, gave a speech asserting that "we will not
surrender because we are with the people, and the people do not
surrender and the *umma* (nation) does not surrender. We will
never surrender because we are with God."[40] These leaders undoubtedly were, at some level, delusional, certainly with regard to their
popularity and power. Ben 'Ali most probably left Tunisia when confronted by the army's approach to the uprising and its refusal to use
force; another reason could be the fracture within the inner group,
particularly with his wife and her family, the Trabulsis.

These leaders learned from and were influenced by other leaders'
experiences. According to one report, when 'Umar Sulayman, who
headed Egypt's intelligence services, informed Mubarak that Ben 'Ali
had left Tunisia for good on his plane, Mubarak responded that Ben
'Ali "is *'abit* (stupid) man . . . how can he act in such a way? How can he
behave like that?"[41] From this response, Sulayman realized that
Mubarak would stay rather than quit the country. Ben 'Ali's departure,
and the resignation of Mubarak and his subsequent humiliation, must
have greatly influenced other leaders such as Qaddafi, Salih, and Bashar
al-Asad to believe that "it is better to shoot or kill, or at least to arrest
and imprison, than to abdicate and flee."[42] Of course, all those leaders
struggled with the eternal question of how much force to use, and
when. The French political philosopher Alexis de Tocqueville, in his
study of the French Revolution of 1789, argued that a regime is at risk
when "the burden is alleviated" after a lengthy period of oppression,
and hence loosening the grip only inspires the masses to resort to
violence to demand more changes.[43]

Another element that offers some insight into the leadership of these
republics is the relationship amongst them. No leader was more

---

[40] Hafiz, *Hafiz al-Asad: qa'id wa umma*, pp. 23–24. From a speech given by Hafiz
al-Asad on March 23, 1980.

[41] Muhammad al-Baz, *al-'Aqrab al-sam: 'Umar Sulayman jiniral al-mukhabarat
al-ghamid* [The poisonous scorpion: 'Umar Sulayman the mysterious intelligence general] (Cairo: Kanouz Publications, 2014), p. 247.

[42] Michael Slackman and Mona el-Naggar, "Embattled Arab Leaders Decide it's
Better to Fight than Quit," *New York Times*, April 28, 2011.

[43] Alexis de Tocqueville, *L'Ancien régime et la révolution* [The *ancien régime* and
the French Revolution], translated by Arthur Goldhammer; edited with an
introduction by Jon Elster (New York: Cambridge University Press, 2011),
p. 157.

cantankerous in his relationships with other leaders than Nasser. During the Yemen War, he told a large audience in 1962 that "the boots of every Egyptian soldier or officer killed are worth more than the crowns of Sa'ud and Hussein [the kings of Saudi Arabia and Jordan]."[44] He regularly attacked Iraq's leader Qasim and Jordan's King Hussein in the late 1950s and early 1960s, scornful of their policies, to the delight of his large audiences.

From the audiotapes of the Iraqi leadership we have gained remarkable knowledge on how Saddam Hussein viewed other Arab leaders. Overall, he was dismissive of them: Sadat was seen as a traitor who sold out the Arab nation. Initially, Mubarak was seen as a friend, because of Egypt's support to Iraq during its war with Iran. This changed dramatically when Egypt supported the US-led coalition in the First Gulf War, and Mubarak was labeled the traitor who cozied up to the USA and Israel. From 1990 onward, Saddam Hussein told his cabinet that Mubarak's claims to Arab leadership were nothing but a joke.[45] He referred to Qaddafi as the *majnun* (crazy) one who cannot be controlled or understood. He had tremendous respect for King Hussein, and even asked him to intervene in his serious disagreements with his older son 'Uday, who considered the king almost as an uncle who could say things that a father could not. However, in the late 1990s the relationship soured and Saddam Hussein called the Jordanian leader *al-qazam* (the dwarf). His hatred of Hafiz al-Asad knew no bounds, and intensified when Syria was one of the few Arab countries that stood by Iran in its war with Iraq, and then supported the international coalition after Iraq's invasion of Kuwait. He taunted Asad about his losses in the Golan Heights and how Syria was too scared to sacrifice for the liberation of its territories.[46]

An interesting insight into Qaddafi's relations with other leaders is gained from the new memoirs published after his fall. The Libyan and Iraqi leaders clashed throughout the 1980s and 1990s, as both believed they could fill the vacuum left by Egypt as leader of the Arab world after Sadat signed the peace treaty with Israel. Libya's support for Iran in its war against Iraq exacerbated this animosity between the two leaders,

---

[44] Speech by Nasser, December 23, 1962, available at www.youtube.com/watch?v=U11cfaw5D-s.

[45] Audiotape of a meeting of Saddam Hussein with his senior advisors, September 30, 1990, *CRRC*, SH-SHTP-A-000-671.

[46] See Sassoon, *Saddam Hussein's Ba'th Party*, p. 158.

and some Libyan officials claimed that deep hatred prevailed between Qaddafi and Saddam to the end of the Iraqi regime. According to Qaddafi's long-time foreign minister, 'Abd-al-Rahman Shalqam, Qaddafi had close relations with two leaders: Houari Boumediene of Algeria and Sheikh Zayed al-Nahian from the United Arab Emirates. He had a working relationship with Hafiz al-Asad, and of course he looked up to Nasser as his mentor. With other leaders he was mercurial and unpredictable, with no regard for protocol. Shalqam narrates how Qaddafi forced him to hand a message to King al-Hasan II of Morocco, which began by describing the king as a reactionary and an agent of imperialism.[47] Qaddafi riled leaders of other countries by calling them "son" even when he was as much as twenty years younger than them.[48] Although he was a staunch supporter of the Palestinian cause, he did not respect either Yasir Arafat or Mahmoud 'Abbas, both of whom he regarded as weak.[49] Another fascinating insight of Qaddafi's relations with neighbors is gained from a testimony by the Tunisian senior official who was in charge of the Libyan portfolio both under Bourguiba and Ben 'Ali, and lived in the Libyan capital for a long period. Having almost convinced President Bourguiba to unite their countries in 1974 after a tête-à-tête meeting, Qaddafi began meddling in Tunisia's affairs until senior Tunisians realized what had happened and pressured Bourguiba to renege on his commitment to the Libyan leader.[50] His conspiracies against Tunisia continued, particularly as it gave refuge to some of his fiercest critics.[51] While Qaddafi interfered in other Arab countries' affairs, he was generally willing to help some countries in times of need. In 1973, when Yemen was short of military equipment, a senior Yemeni official, Sinan Abu Lahum, recounts in his memoirs that he went to Cairo to ask for help, but

---

[47] Sharbal, *Fi khaymat al-Qaddafi*, pp. 234–48.
[48] Ibid., p. 180. Both the president of Tanzania and the king of Morocco complained bitterly about this to Qaddafi's foreign minister.
[49] Ibid., pp. 316–17.
[50] For more information about this incident and Qaddafi's other schemes to solidify his position in North Africa in the mid 1970s, see Hugh Roberts, "Who Said Gaddafi Had to Go?" *London Review of Books*, vol. 33, no. 22, November 17, 2011, pp. 8–18.
[51] "Testimony of Rafiq al-Shilli," in al-Tamimi (ed.), *Dawr al-qasr al-ri'asi*, pp. 16–64. According to al-Shilli, the security services discovered many conspiracies by Qaddafi and his men to unsettle the situation or even to change the regime in Tunisia.

Sadat told him that given the straitened circumstances in his country he could not afford to give any aid, and suggested that he turn to Qaddafi. The Libyan leader called Sadat and without hesitation informed him that Libya would pay for Yemen's military requirements.[52]

Relations between the leaders oscillated from strong and supportive to hostile, even including assassination attempts. Relations were principally based on each leader's interests at the time, rather than the rhetoric of Arab unity or the brotherly image they attempted to present at Arab summit conferences. In a world of realpolitik, leaders were guided by their survival instincts rather than by loyalty, akin to their behavior toward their close associates. Nasser turned for help to Saudi Arabia and Jordan in 1967, ignoring all his attacks on and mockery of these leaders in the previous couple of years.

Cult

Leader cults are ancient, and many religions feature a cultural hero whose bravery saves his people. Joseph Campbell described the mythical hero as the one who "ventures forth from the world of common day into a region of supernatural wonder. Fabulous forces are there encountered and a decisive victory is won."[53] Remarkably, this description can be exactly applied to the writings of Saddam Hussein, in which he depicted himself as the hero who saved his people from monstrous imperialist forces.[54]

A cult's main purpose is to create emotional bonds between the population and its leader by invoking historical, cultural, and sometimes religious aspects to cement that relationship. As Lisa Wedeen

---

[52] Sinan Abu Lahum, *al-Yaman: haqa'iq wa watha'iq 'ayshtuha* [Yemen: truths and documents I lived through], vol. II: *1962–74* (San'a': al-'Afif Foundation, 2006). The first volume deals with the period 1943–62. Abu Lahum is a well-known politician and tribesman who had identified with the Ba'th ideology and was in the thick of events in his country for more than five decades.

[53] Joseph Campbell, *The Hero with a Thousand Faces*, 3rd edn. (Novato, CA: New World Library, 2008), p. 23.

[54] Saddam Hussein, *Zabiba wa al-malik: riwaya li-katibiha* [Zabiba and the king: a novel by its author] (Baghdad: al-Bilad Publishing House, n.d.). This motif is repeated in his other novels, such as *al-Qal'a al-hasina: riwaya li-katibiha* [The immune castle: a novel by its author] (Baghdad: al-Huriyya Publishing House, 2001).

points out, it is hard to distinguish whether that bond is based more on fear than on an emotional commitment.[55] Another objective of the cult, whether in Eastern Europe or the Arab world, was to persuade people to identify with their leaders, and thus approve of, and comply with, their government's policies.[56] Cults, like political myths, offer "validations, legitimations, and authoritative precedents for beliefs, attitudes, and practices."[57] They shift over time to accommodate the needs of the leadership. Overall, one could argue that the more authoritarian a regime becomes, the more it tends to use the personality cult to strengthen its position. There also has to be a fertile political environment in order for a cult to develop and succeed in any country. The newly founded Arab nations, emerging from decades of colonialism, were crying out for "a founding father" who would assume the responsibilities of statehood and manage the country.[58] Some countries were plagued by economic failure and social conflict, and hence their leadership needed to strengthen their symbolic legitimation. Others, such as Iraq and Syria under the Ba'th, found that there was little appeal in their ideology and they needed to reinforce the symbolic attachment of the masses to the leadership.

How do these regimes achieve the status of a cult? It is important to underline that the cult is deliberately constructed, its mechanism is managed, and it "aims at the integration of the political system around the leader's persona."[59] Arab presidents created a cult by honing different approaches specifically to suit each leadership's legitimation strategy. Some cults did not begin until a few years after a leader had come to power, as in the cases of Hafiz al-Asad and Bourguiba,[60] while for others such as Saddam Hussein, the personality cult began even before he assumed the presidency. In fact, he orchestrated articles

---

[55] Wedeen, *Ambiguities of Domination*, p. 10.

[56] Andrea Orzoff, "The Husbandman: Tomáš Masaryk's Leader Cult in Interwar Czechoslovakia," *Austrian History Yearbook*, vol. 39 (2008), pp. 121–37.

[57] Christopher G. Flood, *Political Myth* (New York: Routledge, 2002), p. 35.

[58] Jean Lacouture, *The Demigods: Charismatic Leadership in the Third World* (New York: Alfred Knopf, 1970), p. 13.

[59] Rees, "Leader Cults," p. 4.

[60] Some authoritarian leaders such as Pol Pot in Cambodia never utilized the cult, and in fact he remained anonymous for the first few years of Khmer Rouge rule, most probably for security reasons. See Daniel Chirot, *Modern Tyrants: The Power and Prevalence of Evil in our Age* (Princeton: Princeton University Press, 1994), p. 227.

exalting himself as the young vice president in the 1970s, and promoted the need for a *qa'id* (leader).[61] The cult of personality around Bourguiba began soon after he returned from exile in 1955. As early as 1957, a book written by a French author and published by Bourguiba's party extolled the leader's qualities and declared: "Bourguiba is the founder of modern Tunisia. Bourguiba did not just create the Tunisian state, but he did give its people a patriotic spirit and a national consciousness, and led them to independence."[62] Even leaders who did not initially aspire to establish a cult later wanted to make sure that they were treated differently and with greater honor. Muhyi al-Din describes how Nasser, once he had deposed Neguib, asked other officers and colleagues with whom he worked to start calling him the president. Nor did he object that, whenever he entered or left a room, all of those present stood in respect.[63]

Single-party systems in countries like Syria and Iraq were far more effective in creating a cult by exploiting their influence over the population through their network of party branches. Such was the party's domination over the citizens that they succeeded in enforcing the cult at all levels through systematic and well-planned programs. The ideology of the Iraqi and Syrian Ba'th Party was fused with an exalted idealization of the leader, and in effect the cult became the core of the party's ideology. The preparatory school of the Iraqi Ba'th Party, which was in charge of preparing the cadre, included in its syllabus and examinations material about the leader, his writings and policies. In fact, there was very little to learn about the party's ideology and much more on Saddam Hussein personally, which indicates clearly how the cult replaced ideology.[64] But even leaders such as Ben 'Ali exploited the Constitutional Democratic Rally (RCD) to spread the rituals of his cult by involving the extensive network of party offices in almost every neighborhood in the country.[65]

Some cults were secular; others used religion to enhance their position. As the historian Richard Overy remarked: "Cults are

---

[61] Sassoon, *Saddam Hussein's Ba'th Party*, pp. 175–76.
[62] Felix Garas, *Bourguiba wa mawlad umma* [Bourguiba and the birth of a nation] (Tunis: Free Constitutional Party Publications, 1957), p. 10.
[63] Muhyi al-Din, *Wa al-'an atakallam*, p. 331.
[64] Sassoon, "The Iraqi Ba'th Party Preparatory School."
[65] Daragahi, "In Tunisia, Ben Ali was 'Big Brother'."

conventionally religious rather than political phenomena."[66] Hafiz al-Asad's cult introduced "sacred imagery" with notions of immortality;[67] Mu'ammar al-Qaddafi was described as a prophet leading his people to salvation;[68] and the historians of the Iraqi regime traced Saddam Hussein's origins to the tribe of the Prophet Muhammad and equated him to 'Ali bin Abi Talib, the Prophet's son-in-law.[69] In Iraq, the motto of the president's personal paramilitary, known as *fida'iyyi Saddam*, was: "those who swear allegiance to Saddam are swearing allegiance to God."[70] No official memo was allowed to be written in Iraq mentioning the president's name without adding in parentheses "may God protect him and bless him," in the same manner that the name of the Prophet Muhammad is followed by the phrase "God's Blessing and Peace be upon him." For both the Syrian and Iraqi presidents, a *bay'a* or oath of allegiance, which has its origins in the time of the Prophet Muhammad, was used to cement the leadership. In both countries this contract of allegiance was signed in the blood of members of the National Assembly, and was intended to be personal, binding, and lifelong.[71] While their secular regimes might not have deified Bourguiba and Ben 'Ali, the reality was that whenever their names were mentioned, they were pronounced blessed and protected by God. Almost all cult leaders were portrayed as carriers of a *risala*, a message from God to lead their people.[72]

For many of the Arab and non-Arab leaders, there was an obsessive sense that they embodied the aspirations of their people. Saddam Hussein believed that the people of Iraq "have been searching over eight hundred years" for a ruler like him who would lead them into a

---

[66] Richard Overy, *The Dictators: Hitler's Germany and Stalin's Russia* (London: Penguin, 2008), p. 120.

[67] Wedeen, *Ambiguities of Domination*, p. 35.

[68] Gaddafi with Jouve, *My Vision*, pp. 109–11.

[69] Sassoon, *Saddam Hussein's Ba'th Party*, p. 177.

[70] Kevin M. Woods and James Lacey, *Iraqi Perspectives Project: Saddam and Terrorism, Emerging Insights from Captured Iraqi Documents*, vol. V (Alexandria, VA: Institute for Defense Analysis, 2007), pp. 3–6.

[71] See Ofra Bengio, *Saddam's Word: Political Discourse in Iraq* (Oxford: Oxford University Press, 1998), pp. 74–77 and Wedeen, *Ambiguities of Domination*, p. 38.

[72] See, for example, how Saddam Hussein told one of his generals that he has a *risala*, in Sassoon, *Saddam Hussein's Ba'th Party*, p. 173. The Libyan leader is described on the cover of Gaddafi and Jouve's book as a prophet and a seer. See Gaddafi with Jouve, *My Vision*.

good life.[73] Mu'ammar al-Qaddafi was confident that he had been sent to liberate the Libyan people and bring them prosperity and self-rule.

Relying on family and clan was another tool in creating a cult and advancing the leader's image. The tactics of Arab leaders were very close to those of Ceaușescu and Kim Il-sung in how they promoted their families and began to prepare their sons for succession. Bourguiba's wife, Wassila, was herself the object of a public cult along the lines of Ceaușescu's wife.[74] And whether in Egypt, Iraq, Tunisia, or Romania, the more the regime lost its legitimacy among political elites, the more heavily the leaders became dependent on their families.[75]

Patronage and rewarding cronies are interrelated with this reliance on families and clan. For example, one reward in Iraq was the "Identity Card of the Friends of Mr. President Leader Saddam Hussein, May God Protect Him." The front of the card displayed the holder's personal details, but the back featured the headline *Imtiyazat* (Privileges), followed by seven items that included extra grades in exams for the holders of these cards and their families, acceptance of their sons to military colleges, priority when dealing with government officials, meeting the president once a year, and, last but not least, two summer suits and two winter suits given annually as a personal gift from the president. Dispensing gifts such as clothing and creating the image of a generous, kind, and caring leader is not new in the centuries-long history of kingship and leadership; contemporary leaders such as Saddam Hussein simply continued that tradition.[76] It was common practice for people in Arab countries to write to their president asking for help, usually financial assistance or judicial clemency. Petitions, appeals, and requests for meetings were all part of the concept of a compassionate and benevolent leader. Saddam Hussein was a rare exception among the many world leaders who enjoyed a personality cult, in that he would meet ordinary Iraqi citizens almost every day, and

[73] Audiotape of a meeting with the party's leadership, 1981 (no specific date), *CRRC*, SH-SHTP-A-000-571.
[74] Lacouture, *The Demigods*, p. 176.
[75] For more details on Romania and North Korea, see Chirot, *Modern Tyrants*, pp. 246–48.
[76] For an interesting discussion of the role of clothes, see Catherine Richardson (ed.), *Clothing and Culture, 1350–1650* (Aldershot: Ashgate Publishing Co., 2004).

having an audience with him was like winning the lottery, because no one left empty-handed.[77]

The cult was also directed at children and youth. Again, whether in the Arab world, the Soviet Union or North Korea, the image of the father of the nation was predominant. Children in Iraqi schools had to call the Iraqi leader *Baba Saddam* (Daddy Saddam), and implicit in this metaphor, in Wedeen's words, is "love and connection between ruler and ruled."[78] Similarly, Tunisians were known as "the Children of Bourguiba."[79] This patriarchal role placed each leader in a dominant position in the social hierarchy, and gave him even more authority to dictate policies.

Mythical images of the cult were aided by poetry, prose, and art, and in all these countries symbols and spectacles were widespread. By utilizing every medium, the arts had a significant role in expressing the systematic adulation of the leaders and presenting their heroic deeds and wise policies. Portraits of Arab leaders adorned stores, schools, government offices, and even homes. Although Mubarak did not have a cult along the lines of Saddam and Asad, after his fall in 2011 the new government of Egypt had to expunge the names and photographs of Mubarak and his wife Suzanne "from all squares, streets, schools, associations, libraries, and all entities."[80] Even a major subway station had been named after him. To further reinforce the leader's status, imagery and symbols were widely employed in medals, coins and banknotes, prizes, stamps, and of course, in the renaming of towns, streets, and institutions. Similar to Mao's China, medals and badges were more widely used by Saddam Hussein than any other cult leader in the Arab world.[81] One recurring symbol, to enhance the perception of masculinity of the leaders, was the stallion: for both 'Ali 'Abdullah

---

[77] For more details, see Sassoon, *Saddam Hussein's Ba'th Party*, pp. 177–78. Among foreign leaders with personality cults, Masaryk of Czechoslovakia was an exception in his willingness to meet ordinary citizens. See Orzoff, "The Husbandsman," p. 127.

[78] Wedeen, *Ambiguities of Domination*, p. 51.

[79] Lacouture, *The Demigods*, pp. 176–77.

[80] Mona el-Naggar, "Egypt to End the Ubiquity of Mubarak," *New York Times*, April 22, 2011. See also Owen, *The Rise and Fall of Arab Presidents for Life*, p. 195.

[81] For an interesting discourse on the use of badges in China, see Melissa Schrift, *Biography of a Chairman Mao Badge: The Creation and Mass Consumption of a Personality Cult* (New Brunswick, NJ: Rutgers University Press, 2001).

Salih and Saddam Hussein, riding a stallion to win an election or a war was an image used to exalt the heroic status of the brave leader.[82] Grandiose monuments differed widely between countries, with some like Syria having none, to the other extreme of enormous statues and symbols of Saddam Hussein scattered around Iraq, comparable to the Nazi architectural excesses in Germany.[83]

The publication of biographies was an essential part of establishing the cult; many emphasized the humble origins of the leaders and their affinity to the people. Some of the biographies were written "on order" by professional journalists, such as that by Amir Iskander about Saddam Hussein.[84] Others were produced by loyal associates or senior ministers, but were not full biographies.[85] Neither category tended to show the leader in a negative light; in fact, rarely can anything wrong or negative be detected about their lives and conduct, particularly if they were still alive, or, as in Syria, if their legacy continued through their successors.[86] A third category was quasi-biographies written after the death of a leader, and some discussed his wrong policies and negative traits. This was particularly true in Egypt under Sadat and then Mubarak.[87]

Most of these presidents came from lower-middle-class families and had managed to climb to the top of the ladder; their biographies thus emphasized their connection to the people as a leader who was from them and for them. As indicated, these biographies depicted the leaders as outstanding in everything they had achieved or would achieve in the future. One such history of the "leader and commander of the people"

[82] For the image of the Yemeni president, see Lisa Wedeen, *Peripheral Visions: Publics, Power, and Performance in Yemen* (Chicago: University of Chicago Press, 2008), photograph after p. 102; for the Iraqi president, see the cover of his novel *Rijal wa madina*.

[83] Wedeen, *Ambiguities of Domination*, pp. 28–29; Overy, *The Dictators*, pp. 115–16.

[84] Iskander, *Saddam Hussein: The Fighter, the Thinker and the Man*.

[85] See, for example, Essebsi, *Habib Bourguiba*.

[86] See, for example, Hafiz, *Hafiz al-Asad: qa'id wa umma*.

[87] A good example is a memoir about Sadat that contains many negative statements about Nasser and his policies: Mahmud Jami', *'Ariftu al-Sadat: nisf qarn min khafaya al-Sadat wa al-Ikhwan* [I knew al-Sadat: half a century of Sadat's secrets and the Brothers] (Cairo: al-Maktab al-Misri, 1998). This memoir, written by a member of the Brotherhood and a close friend of Sadat, sheds light on Sadat, Nasser, and how the peace process "negatively" affected Sadat's behavior.

described 'Ali 'Abdullah Salih, president of Yemen, as "one of the few
great people that Yemen has witnessed in its history," and then continued for almost a page describing his remarkable qualities in every
possible aspect. The author argues that the key to understanding
the Yemeni leader is his "exceptional personality,"[88] and details
'Abdullah Salih's achievements not only in war and peace, but also in
other fields such as democracy, human rights, and socioeconomic
projects.

Works written by the leaders themselves were another component of
the cult that added to their prestige and showed their capabilities. The
concept of writings by leaders goes back to the ancient kings of
Mesopotamia, who wished to be remembered as divinely inspired
purveyors of power. Saddam and Qaddafi, not unlike Evita and Juan
Perón, prided themselves on their written political testaments and
literary skills. Some employed ghostwriters, but others, such as
Saddam Hussein, used writing novels as a form of escapism.[89] From
their writings we can also learn a lot about their leadership and personalities. Saddam Hussein, more than any other leader in the region,
wrote novels that were semi-biographical, in particular *Rijal wa
madina* (Men and a city), and much information can be gleaned
about his childhood, his philosophy of life, and his attitude on many
issues.[90] Unlike Qaddafi or Nasser, Saddam Hussein did not put his
name on these books, and each stated only that it was "a novel written
by its author." Qaddafi wrote a collection of short essays with the
bizarre title of *The Village, the Village, the Land, the Land, and the
Suicide of an Astronaut*. In one essay, he attacked the city as an
unpleasant place that destroys the land and the country's agriculture,
and where residents are aggressive and push each other around and the
children living there are miserable. In another essay, an astronaut
returns to earth and cannot find a job, so he commits suicide.[91] Most

---

[88] Ahmad Muhammad al-Asbahi, *25 'aman min sirat za'im wa qa'id masirat al-
    sh'ab, 1978–2003* [25 years in the history of a leader and commander of the
    people's history, 1978–2003] (Amman: Yemen Embassy, 2004), pp. 13–14.
[89] Alberto Manguel, *The Library at Night* (New Haven: Yale University Press,
    2006), p. 94.
[90] Saddam Hussein, *Rijal wa madina*.
[91] Mu'ammar al-Qaddafi, *al-Qarya ... al-qarya, al-ard ... al-ard wa intihar ra'id
    al-fada' ma'a qisas ukhra* [The village ... the village, the land ... the land and the
    suicide of an astronaut with other stories] (Cairo: Egyptian Organization for
    Books, 1996).

of these stories fit to a certain extent Qaddafi's vision of Libya and Africa. In fact, Pierre Salinger, who was then press secretary to President John F. Kennedy and later became a journalist for the ABC network, published an English translation with a foreword. Salinger recommended the book "because it gives a very special view about an original mentality."[92] Nasser's novella, *For Freedom*, set in 1807 under the British occupation, was supposed to have been written when he was at high school in 1935. The novella is very political and was later expanded into a book by a professional writer, and added to the teaching curriculum in Egypt by the Ministry of Education.[93]

These Arab leaders have other common characteristics, even though their personality cults varied widely. One of the most important shared aspects was the strong inner belief in their destiny, and even, for some, that they were carrying a special message to their people. We may cast doubt on this, but it is certainly very hard to achieve and maintain such an elevated status for a long time without immense self-confidence and self-belief as the saviors of their countries. This is somewhat related to their sense of invincibility, which stemmed from their ability to survive countless assassination attempts and overcome the numerous internal feuds in their own camps. Fu'ad 'Allam, one of Egypt's senior intelligence officers, tells us in his memoirs that there were eleven assassination attempts against Nasser;[94] and in Iraq, there were eighteen documented assassination attempts against Saddam by the late 1980s, and probably at least a handful more by 2003.[95]

With their unerring instinct for survival, it is hardly surprising that these leaders felt invincible. The way they wrote or felt about themselves was testimony to their beliefs, and also served to build up and sustain their personality cults. Obviously, the lines between self-confidence and self-delusion blurred as time went on and they felt more comfortable in the seat of power. A few examples underpin this

---

[92] Muammar Gaddafi, *Escape to Hell and Other Stories*, with a foreword by Pierre Salinger (London: John Blake Publishing, 1999).

[93] 'Abd al-Rahim 'Ajjaj, *Fi sabil al-hurriya: qissa bada'ha al-sayyid al-ra'is Gamal 'Abd al-Nasser wa huwa talib bil-madaris al-thanawiyya, 'an ma'rakat Rashid sanat 1807* [For freedom: a continuation of the story begun by Mr. President Gamal 'Abd al-Nasser during his high school years about the battle of Rashid in 1807] (Cairo: al-Ra'id Publishing, 1970).

[94] 'Allam, *al-Ikhwan wa ana*, p. 331.

[95] For details of the plots, see the memoirs of the head of the *mukhabarat* at that time, al-Tikriti, *Muhawalat ightiyal al-ra'is Saddam Hussein*, pp. 91–161.

notion: Ahmed Ben Bella declared, "I am the sole hope of Algeria."[96] Bourguiba remarked in 1952: "If my life were taken, the people would suffer an insufferable loss."[97] Saddam Hussein wrote in his semi-autobiography, *al-Ayyam al-Tawila* (The Long Days), that he should not end up in prison as "he is capable of doing so many things" for the party.[98] Leaders outside the Arab world shared this notion of being special; François Duvalier, better known as Papa Doc, who presided over Haiti from 1957 to 1971, said in a speech that could have been delivered by any of the Arab leaders:

It is not easy to find a man who has complete confidence in himself, and in his country, and who decides to maintain its dignity and prestige; such a revolutionary is found only every 50 or 75 years ... I knew that I had to fulfill a holy mission, a mission which will be fulfilled entirely.[99]

In fact, a couple of years later Bourguiba began a speech with exactly the same message:

It is not easy to replace a man like me ... There is, between the Tunisian people and me, forty years of life passed together, of common hardships endured together, which will not exist with him who comes after me ... I have created a nation largely around myself, around my person.[100]

Charisma and eloquence were common characteristics for most, but by no means all, of these leaders. This undoubtedly inspired their citizens, which gave rise to a rather blinkered view of the leaders' capabilities. The German sociologist Max Weber argued that personality cults have parallels with "charismatic authority," one of the three types of authority defined in his famous study (the other two are traditional authority and rational–legal authority).[101] Some leaders, such as Hafiz al-Asad, lacked the charisma displayed by Nasser or Bourguiba. The balance between charisma and fear is hard to define;

---

[96] Joseph Gregory, "Ahmed Ben Bella, Revolutionary who Led Algeria after Independence, Dies at 93," *New York Times*, April 11, 2012.

[97] Lacouture, *The Demigods*, p. 152.

[98] 'Abd al-Amir Mu'alla, *al-Ayyam al-tawila* [The long days] (Baghdad: Wizarat al-I'lam, 1978), p. 136.

[99] Cited in Chirot, *Modern Tyrants*, p. 356.

[100] Habib Bourguiba, quoted in *Le Monde*, January 12, 1972, from an interview with the then British Press agency Visnews.

[101] For a discussion of Weber and charisma, see S. N. Eisenstadt, *On Charisma and Institution Building* (Chicago: University of Chicago Press, 1968), p. 48; Elias, *The Court Society*, pp. 121–26.

leaders such as Saddam Hussein and Asad utilized the fear factor, and in Syria the personality cult became an "anxiety-inducing simulacrum."[102] Lacouture posited that "there is no true charisma without eloquence."[103] Nasser was an excellent orator, and his powerful use of language undoubtedly helped to establish his cult. Almost without exception, all the leaders gave long speeches, and it was often mandatory for their supporters to listen to or read them, and in some cases this was also required of the general population. Each leader wanted to educate his people about his own vision, and show himself as the wise teacher, the loyal friend of the masses, and the father of the nation. Their speeches embraced all subjects, which in essence became state policies. This very common behavior among Arab leaders was widely shared by other tyrants and dictators across the world.[104]

Interestingly, the majority of Arab presidents were influenced by the same great world leaders: De Gaulle, Mao, and Tito.[105] Bourguiba, however was more influenced by Mustafa Kemal Atatürk, the founder of modern Turkey, and followed his example by creating a modern secular state. Saddam Hussein was impressed with Nasser's achievement in consolidating his leadership, and also admired Stalin and Nelson Mandela. Qaddafi venerated Nasser and saw him as a father figure, although one close associate argued that had Nasser lived longer, Qaddafi would have seen him as a competitor rather than a teacher.[106] Given the importance of their legacy, which was frequently expressed in speeches and interviews, it is no wonder that these presidents avidly read biographies of their favorite world leaders in the hope of learning about triumphing when faced with challenges. While most of these Arab leaders were not well educated in an academic sense, they had considerable curiosity about learning, and were well read.[107] There was also much imitation and curiosity among themselves about the intricacies of maintaining a cult: we know that Saddam Hussein was very inquisitive about how Ceauşescu ran

---

[102] Wedeen, *Ambiguities of Domination*, p. 3.
[103] Lacouture, *The Demigods*, p. 21.   [104] Chirot, *Modern Tyrants*, p. 247.
[105] See, for example, Gaddafi with Jouve, *My Vision*, p. 83.
[106] See interview with Shalqam in Sharbal, *Fi khaymat al-Qaddafi*, p. 168.
[107] For Saddam Hussein's list of reading and favorite subjects, see Sassoon, *Saddam Hussein's Ba'th Party*, p. 174. According to Shalqam, Qaddafi's favorite subjects were history and biography. He also read Machiavelli's *The Prince*, books by Michel 'Aflaq, the founder of the Ba'th Party, and writings by Nasser.

Romania using his family, and intriguingly Ceauşescu launched his own personality cult after meeting Kim Il-sung on a visit to North Korea.[108] However admired other world leaders were, and however important the predecessors of each Arab president were, each cult presented the current leader as the greatest of them all. With such an awareness of legacy and greatness, it was only natural that many of these presidents conceived grandiose projects that would radically change the lives of many people in their countries. Nasser built the Aswan Dam, Qaddafi undertook a mammoth project to create a "great artificial river" that would bring prosperity to the desert, [109] and Saddam Hussein ordered the creation of Saddam's River by digging a 350-mile canal from Baghdad to the Gulf to reduce the country's dependence on the Shatt al-Arab waterway.[110] In the same tradition, current Egyptian president 'Abd al-Fattah al-Sisi has announced an ambitious project to build a canal parallel to the Suez Canal to stimulate maritime traffic.[111] Some of the Arab dictators, such as Saddam, Qaddafi, and Ben 'Ali, used their homes to reinforce the cult of personality, and acquired or built large palaces that befitted "great men."[112] After the Arab uprising, details emerged of the palaces of Ben 'Ali and Qaddafi and how they and their families lived in the utmost luxury. Others, such as Nasser, chose to live in a modest home until the end of his life.

Without exception, these leaders were surrounded by sycophants, who by their speeches and writings reinforced the cult and affected decision making within the leadership. Overall, all "leader cults make a presumption, which never needs to be justified, to command the support and affection of their subjects."[113] Although extolling and venerating the presidents became preposterous, we do not know what percentage of people in Iraq or Syria or Tunisia believed in the cult or how seriously they took the leaders' claims. What is clear is that the

---

[108] Sassoon, *Saddam Hussein's Ba'th Party*, pp. 174–75; Chirot, *Modern Tyrants*, pp. 236–40.

[109] Gaddafi with Jouve, *My Vision*, pp. 62–63.

[110] For more details about how this river was symptomatic of Saddam's cult, see Sassoon, *Saddam Hussein's Ba'th Party*, pp. 182–83.

[111] "Sisi Reviews New Projects in Suez Canal Region," Egyptian State Information Service, November 17, 2014, available at www.sis.gov.eg/En/Templates/Articles/tmpArticleNews.aspx?ArtID=83858#.VH0VA_TF-qM.

[112] Peter York, *Dictator Style: Lifestyles of the World's Most Colorful Despots* (San Francisco: Chronicle Books, 2005).

[113] Rees, *Leader Cults*, p. 5.

cults had consequences for these countries, particularly for decision making. Because they lauded the leaders with titles and metaphors expressing their supposed superiority, each leader, for his part, assumed the role of guide, instructor, and grand teacher of his people. Bourguiba, Qaddafi, 'Ali Salih, and Saddam Hussein all loved to pontificate and instruct their populations about every aspect of life, and in many cases treated them as ignorant masses.[114] They intervened in almost all levels of state bureaucracy and saw themselves as the top experts in every field. They had views on religion and religiosity, and if their views changed, as Saddam's did in the 1990s, then the whole population was also expected to adjust its outlook.

Given that "the degree of official hero worship is staggering," the leaders rarely accepted that they made any personal errors, and refused to adapt to new circumstances if this would reduce their powers.[115] Elevating the leader to an unassailable position prevented serious discussions and debates. This meant that often no one in the inner circle would dare to tell the leader when practices or policies needed to change. In Iraq, the Ba'th archives inform us that Saddam Hussein's inner circle did not tell him the truth about many situations and events, whether during the Kuwait invasion, the 1991 uprising, or prior to the 2003 invasion. Intelligence reports sent to the president were altered, as no one was willing to inform him how the situation had gravely deteriorated in certain strategic areas. A major implication for regimes relying on a personality cult is that criticism of a revered leader indirectly questions the political system they headed.[116] Hence, it is doubtful that regimes such as Saddam's or Bashar al-Asad's engaged in an open dialogue about the consequences of their policies, because when the leader is wrong, the whole system loses its legitimacy.[117]

---

[114] Lacouture, *The Demigods*, p. 282. See also how Saddam Hussein instructed his people about cleanliness, discipline, and respect, in Sassoon, *Saddam Hussein's Ba'th Party*, pp. 42, 172.

[115] Chirot, *Modern Tyrants*, p. 248.

[116] Juan J. Linz, "The Religious Use of Politics and/or the Political Use of Religion: Ersatz Ideology versus Ersatz Religion," in Hans Maier (ed.), *Totalitarianism and Political Religions*, vol. I: *Concepts for the Comparison of Dictatorships*, translated by Jodi Bruhn (London: Routledge, 2004), p. 110.

[117] For a comparison of the decision-making process of Saddam and Bashar, see Joseph Sassoon, "Comment les tyrans prennent leur décisions" [How tyrants reach their decisions], *Le Monde Diplomatique*, no. 695 (February 2012). The article also appeared in the English version of *Le Monde Diplomatique* as "The Competence of the Tyrants," February 2012.

Discussing the cult of Stalin, Juan Linz commented, "if Stalin was not right then the whole system could not be right."[118] Archie Brown, who has published extensively on the Soviet Union, argued that leadership by a single man led to "stupid decisions or sponsoring dreadful actions," and that personal rule is more dangerous than a collective group.[119]

Becoming revered and unchallengeable had another repercussion. When a leader aged, he did not want to leave his position, in part because he believed that there was no one as qualified as himself, even when his successor would have been one of his sons. Among the eight republics, this issue was a problem for four of them: Egypt's Mubarak; Tunisia's Bourguiba; Algeria's Bouteflika; and Syria's Hafiz al-Asad. Owen discusses the psychological implications of aging by referencing the work of the psychiatrist Jerrold Post, and posits that these leaders suffered "a decline in judgment and intellectual ability, increased rigidity, a denial of physical disabilities, and a tendency toward marked fluctuations in personal behavior."[120] The Palestinian poet Mahmoud Darwish eloquently summed up the issue of aging dictators in a poem "A Speech from the Grave," part of which is:

I am in my eighties and will live for another eighty
I will keep holding my sword
I will carry your coffins when you die
It is my right to live and it is your right to die
Nothing will come after me
Who will you worship?[121]

Indeed, when one looks at Bourguiba or others, the insistence on continuing to govern in spite of serious ailments and long absences

---

[118] Discussion of Linz's article "The Religious Use of Politics," in Maier (ed.), *Concepts for the Comparison of Dictatorships*, p. 136.

[119] Archie Brown, *The Myth of the Strong Leader: Political Leadership in the Modern Age* (London: Random House, 2014), p. 254.

[120] Owen, *The Rise and Fall of Arab Presidents for Life*, p. 196.

[121] Mahmud Darwish, "Shahid 'ala zaman al-tughat: khutub al-diktatur al-mawzuna" [Witness to tyranny: metric speeches of the dictator], available at www.alkarmelj.org/userfiles/pdfs/4.pdf. Poets often gave voice to the painful episodes of tyranny, not only in the Arab world but also in other countries such as North Korea, and as a result became fugitives. See, for example, Jang Jin-sung, *Dear Leader: My Escape from North Korea*, translated by Shirley Lee (New York: Random House, 2014).

for medical treatment clearly underscores this attachment to power and the belief in being irreplaceable.

Another common factor is how these leaders created myths around their personality cults. Ben 'Ali, for example, created the myth of the "economic miracle" and everyone dutifully regurgitated how Tunisia had achieved this under his guidance. Obviously this image of a miracle maker helped Ben 'Ali both domestically and internationally. In Iraq, Saddam Hussein created the myth of "victory" against Iran after eight horrendous years of war, which allowed him to strengthen his position both internally and regionally. Another shared element, which also applied to leaders who did not develop a personality cult, was the way they manipulated their inner circles. Describing how an absolute ruler behaves, the German sociologist Norbert Elias aptly defined it:

He must carefully channel the tensions, cultivate petty jealousies and maintain, within the groups, a fragmentation in their aims and therefore the pressure they exert. He must allow opposed pressures to interpenetrate each other and hold them in equilibrium; and this requires a high degree of calculation.[122]

A successful disciple of this philosophy was Saddam Hussein, as was clearly revealed in the archives and audiotapes of meetings with his closest associates, the Revolutionary Command Council. He mastered the art of manipulating this inner group, including his own family, to the extent that they all accepted that he was their ultimate leader. Another leader who practiced this method was 'Ali Salih of Yemen, who managed to maintain his position by keeping "the constellation of networks" off balance almost permanently. By manufacturing one crisis after another, he "portrayed himself as the one indispensable figure that could ensure stability."[123]

One possible advantage of the cult pointed out by Daniel Chirot is that, however mistakenly, people in countries with strong cults "felt that if only the benign great leader knew [about an issue or problem], perhaps things would go better."[124] This hope was expressed in the numerous petitions and appeals that ordinary citizens sent to their

---

[122] Elias, *The Court Society*, p. 122.
[123] Thomas Juneau, "Yemen and the Arab Spring," in Mehran Kamrava (ed.), *Beyond the Arab Spring: The Evolving Ruling Bargain in the Middle East* (New York: Oxford University Press, 2014), p. 378.
[124] Chirot, *Modern Tyrants*, p. 228.

leaders requesting help in solving their problems. The Iraqi archives illustrate how Iraqis sent an incredible number of petitions to their leader and also requested meetings with him to appeal to his generosity.

In assessing the subject of cult, it can perhaps be seen as "a barometer of certain developments within a political system."[125] First, the existence of a cult indicates the extent to which power was personalized; second, it shows how much the political debate was controlled (see Chapter 2); third, it illustrates the level of censorship and regulation of the media (see Chapter 4); and finally, it underscores the measure of control over education and youth (Chapters 2 and 4 partially covered these points).[126] It seems that whenever a regime intensified a cult, it was symptomatic of increasing concerns about its legitimacy. In an interesting memo published by WikiLeaks, the Romanian ambassador in Tunisia told his American counterpart in late 2007 that the situation in Tunisia reminded him of the period preceding the collapse of Ceauşescu, and he suggested that "the increasing drumbeat of propaganda in favor of . . . Ben Ali" reflects "the weakness of the regime and growing concern about inchoate, but real opposition."[127]

In the Arab world, cults manifested themselves at different levels. Saddam Hussein, for instance, perfected the personality cult along the lines of Stalin and Ceauşescu, but many others utilized it to enhance their leadership in response to criticisms or challenges. Bashar al-Asad, who simply inherited the leadership from his father, was more dependent on his family, because he could not easily acquire the political and military base that his father had created over several decades.[128] Hence, Bashar could not follow his father's emphasis on the cult, but reverted to exploiting it after the civil war began. More pictures of Bashar and articles about his wise leadership spread in the Syrian media. Bashar began reflecting the image of the popular leader; he told a journalist: "I live a normal life. That's why I am popular."[129] Whatever the degree of

---

[125] Rees, "Leader Cults," p. 8.   [126] Ibid.

[127] American Embassy in Tunisia to State Department, "Finding Parallels between Ben Ali and Ceausescu," November 30, 2007, ref. 07TunisS1544, available at www.cablegatesearch.net/cable.php?id=07TUNIS1544, accessed April 11, 2012.

[128] For an interesting description of the major personalities within Bashar al-Asad's inner circle, see "Bashar al-Assad's Inner Circle," BBC News, July 30, 2012, available at www.bbc.com/news/world-middle-east-13216195, accessed July 14, 2013.

[129] Andrew Gilligan, "Interview with Bashar al-Asad," *Sunday Telegraph*, October 30, 2011.

the cult, it gave its protagonists serious leverage in controlling their society, as well as investing them with an almost divine authority. Ordinary citizens paid a heavy price for the mass adulation; apart from the lack of political freedom and dignity, culture, art, and education suffered heavily in all these countries. Writing history became simply a means for some of these regimes to control their populations; artists and writers were forced to collaborate or face destitution, and although the number of students increased, the overall quality of education dropped.

Not all artists and intellectuals conformed, of course, and some wrote about the tyranny of these leaders, but these were a small minority in the face of the intense coercion that took place against anyone or anything that seemed threatening to these regimes. Similarly, it would be wrong to assume that all citizens of these republics endorsed the cult or participated in spreading it; there was resistance in most of these countries that took many forms: demonstrations, strikes, poems, novels, etc. But overall, they were ineffective until the 2011 uprisings, as the regimes managed to control opposition. At the same time, numerous government bureaucrats and party officials realized that the cult could be exploited for their own interests as well, and they used it to enhance their own position vis-à-vis the leadership.

An important point about the cult is the issue of inheritance. Roger Owen wrote about the politics of succession and argued that in certain republics where the issue of succession was high on the agenda, as in Egypt, Libya, Tunisia, Yemen, and Syria, "the expectation of a family succession affected every part of the political process."[130] Furthermore, designating a successor with the intention of creating stability backfired in many cases, as the process took a long time and created "an atmosphere of anxiety and uncertainty."[131] Outside the Arab world, however, there are a number of successful episodes of a new leader inheriting a cult. In the Soviet Union, for example, the glorification of the top leader was a permanent element in Communist Party politics, and thus Stalin, Khrushchev, and Brezhnev all had their own cults, but to different degrees.[132] Likewise, in North

[130] Owen, *The Rise and Fall of Arab Presidents for Life*, p. 139.
[131] Ibid. For the discussion of the succession in those six republics, see pp. 140–52.
[132] Boris Korsch, *The Brezhnev Personality Cult – Continuity: The Librarian's Point of View*, Research Paper No. 65 (Jerusalem: The Hebrew University, July 1987).

Korea, the cult was passed from father to son, and now to the grandson. In the Arab world, the most successful transfer of cult took place in Tunisia. In spite of the coup that brought Ben 'Ali to power, symbols of Bourguiba's cult such as the Avenue Bourguiba were allowed to continue by that name, but in the interim, Ben 'Ali moved swiftly to establish his own cult.[133] In Syria, after the death of Hafiz al-Asad, there was very little in the methodical build-up of the cult of Bashar, but that changed when the uprising began. Similarly, one could argue that had Qusay Hussein succeeded Saddam, it would have been very difficult, at least in the first few years, to establish the same degree of cult enjoyed by his father.

Finally, although the focus has been on the Arab republics, there are plenty of personality cults in the monarchies. Perusing the daily newspapers in the Gulf and Saudi Arabia provides ample examples of a cult, and some of its consequences for decision making are not much different from what has been described here.

Future of leadership and cult in the region

A chapter has closed on the cult of personality in most of these countries. Saddam Hussein was hanged after the US-led invasion that overthrew his regime; Ben 'Ali was exiled to Saudi Arabia; Mubarak was ousted and imprisoned; Bashar al-Asad is fighting for survival; and Qaddafi was killed and his death transmitted to the world by images filmed on mobile phones.[134] In a bizarre way, Qaddafi was almost prophetic about his end in one of his short stories, appropriately titled "Escape to Hell":

How cruel people can be when they rise up together, a crushing flood that has no mercy for anything in its path ... The masses can be so compassionate when they are happy, carrying their sons upon their shoulders in the way they carried Hannibal ... Robespierre, Mussolini, and Nixon, yet how harsh they can be when they become angry.[135]

---

[133] Jerry Sorkin, "The Tunisian Model," *Middle East Quarterly* (Fall 2001), pp. 25–29.

[134] For an interesting historical perspective of the end of tyrants, see Simon Sebag Montefiore, "Dictators Get the Deaths they Deserve," *New York Times*, October 27, 2011.

[135] Gaddafi, *Escape to Hell and Other Stories*, pp. 41–42.

Once the end of these leaders was nigh, the quest for their assets began. Mubarak, Ben 'Ali, and Qaddafi, together with members of their families and their inner circles, stashed away substantial assets in different countries using a complicated structure of corporations difficult to track down. According to one report, one Libyan man, Bashir Salih Bashir, has information about the whereabouts of around $7 billion of Qaddafi's African investments. Bashir was captured by the rebels but managed (or was allowed) to escape to France, where he disappeared. Similarly, few of the assets of the Egyptian and Tunisian presidents have been recovered.[136] Scholars have argued that tyrants endure because they can "reward their cronies," and hence money becomes a critical instrument for survival.[137] Saddam Hussein was aware of the importance of this, and believed it was the reason for the collapse of the first Ba'th regime in 1963. According to his planning minister, after the nationalization of oil in 1973 he was instructed by Saddam to allocate 5 percent to the party, to be used in times of crisis to ensure that the Ba'th would have financial resources even if out of power.[138]

An interesting hypothetical question is whether the cult of personality could return to these republics after the Arab uprisings. In some cases, a cult has continued after the death of the leader; the most powerful example is that of Napoleon Bonaparte, whose cult actually gathered momentum after his death.[139] In recent history, veneration of Stalin is still plentiful, and in Italy people still pay homage to the legacy of Mussolini, whom they believed had "the most original ideas."[140] In Tunisia, there are numerous signs of nostalgia for Bourguibism. During the campaign for parliamentary elections in late 2014, the winning party, Nida', showed during its main rally a twenty-five-minute video

---

[136] Robert F. Worth, "Obstacles Mar Quest for Arab Dictators' Assets," *New York Times*, June 7, 2012.

[137] Bruce Bueno De Mesquita and Alastair Smith, "How Tyrants Endure," *New York Times*, June 9, 2011. The scholars who wrote *The Dictator's Handbook* mentioned earlier in this chapter argue that one factor in the fall of Mubarak and Ben 'Ali was that the two countries were facing serious economic problems and therefore could not ensure the continuing flow of rewards to their inner circle.

[138] Hashim, *Mudhakkirat wazir 'Iraqi ma'a al-Bakr wa Saddam*, pp. 148–49.

[139] For a fascinating study of Napoleon, see Sudhir Hazareesingh, *The Legend of Napoleon* (London: Granta Books, 2004).

[140] Elisabetta Povoledo, "A Dead Dictator who Draws Tens of Thousands in Italy," *New York Times*, November 2, 2011.

about Bourguiba. Furthermore, many party brochures carried pictures of him on their covers. There is even some wistfulness for Saddam Hussein in Iraq among certain sectors. What unites all those longing for a dictator and his cult is the desperate need for a strong man who can rule, provide security, and inspire confidence among his people. In Iraq, during the horrific civil war that erupted after the 2003 invasion, many citizens longed for the return of strong law and order.

A unique case in the Arab republics is the ex-president of Yemen, 'Ali 'Abdullah Salih. Although he was overthrown by a popular revolt, he remained in the country and continued to wield significant power. His enemies accuse him of incessant meddling in internal politics, and, more seriously, of "arranging terrorist attacks and some of the assassinations of more than 150 high-ranking officers."[141] What is intriguing is that after an interview and profile of him was published in the *New York Times*, the deposed president was not enraged about the story or the accusations. Two days later, a Yemeni newspaper that is part of Salih's media empire even carried a similar headline: "Ruler with great powers even after departing his seat."[142]

Some leaders return in different guises but wielding the same power. The classic example is Russia's Vladimir Putin, who understood the desire of large parts of the population for a strong, decisive leader. After serving as president for two terms, he could not run for a third, so he was appointed prime minister, after which he changed the rules and returned as president; in the words of one profile: "A Tsar is Reborn."[143] In the Arab republics, an example of a leader who attempted to build a cult but failed abysmally was Nuri al-Maliki. Billboards with giant photos of al-Maliki adorned Baghdad during his tenure, at the same time as he controlled the security services in the country.[144] Al-Maliki remains entrenched in Baghdad as a vice president, with strong influence over parts of the security services and the Shi'i militias. A more interesting example of a possible use of the

---

[141] Robert F. Worth, "Even Out of Office, a Wielder of Great Power in Yemen," *New York Times*, February 1, 2014. Nuri al-Maliki was allowed to stay in Iraq after he resigned as prime minister under internal and international pressure, and many argue that he is continuing to be a destabilizing factor in the country.

[142] *Al-Yaman al-yawm*, February 3, 2014. The newspaper carried a picture on the front page of 'Ali 'Abdullah Salih with Mr. Worth.

[143] Charles Clover and Catherine Belton, "A Tsar is Reborn," *Financial Times*, May 5/6, 2012.

[144] Michael Peel, "Iraq: Singular Ambition," *Financial Times*, May 7, 2012.

cult is Egypt's President Sisi. Since he took power in July 2013, there have been efforts to transform his image from a general to a statesman. Two days before he came to give a speech at the United Nations General Assembly in September 2014, *al-Ahram* informed its readers that "the whole world is waiting for 'Abd al-Fattah al-Sisi's speech" in "a historical event for a leader carrying the dreams and challenges of his people on his shoulders."[145] After the speech, the Egyptian media was flooded with praise from different personalities. The talk show host 'Umru Adib declared the speech to be a work of genius and an amazing success both within the United Nations and outside it. The imam of 'Umr Makram Mosque announced that Sisi "won by a knockout" and he saluted the president for his historic brave speech.[146] This style of sycophancy augurs the beginning of a new cult.

Conclusion

The authoritarian regimes in the Arab republics became more identified with their leaders than with the ideology or policy of the regime. With the exception of Algeria, the other seven leaderships were personalist regimes built around one man. Even in the regimes that did not create a cult of personality, decision making was centralized and the leader unassailable. It is probable that we may never understand the minds of these leaders who used wars, terror, and any other means to stay in power. They inflicted repression in all its forms without worrying about the suffering of their people, and most saw their nations as their own private domain, in which they could do whatever they wished. The sycophancy surrounding these leaders exacerbated the situation, and any criticism of the leader or his family became synonymous with betrayal.[147]

---

[145] Muhammad Fu'ad, "The World is Expecting al-Sisi's Speech at the United Nations," *al-Ahram*, September 22, 2014.

[146] "What they Said about al-Sisi's Speech at the United Nations," *al-Masrawy*, September 24, 2014, available at www.masrawy.com/News/News_Egypt/details/2014/9/24/353090/, accessed October 17, 2014.

[147] For a fascinating discussion of "criticism" and "betrayal" see the court proceedings of the Egyptian colloquial poet Ahmad Najm in 'Isa, *Sha'ir takdir al-amn*, pp. 177–202. Although Egypt had less draconian laws than Iraq in regard to offending the president, punishment was still two years imprisonment for anyone insulting the president in public.

Apart from Tunisia, which rid itself of Ben 'Ali and is currently in a state of transition (see Chapter 7), most other republics can only dream of freeing themselves of their sole leader. As an Egyptian politician who opposed Mubarak and started a new party, al-Ghad (Tomorrow), wrote in his memoirs: "We were dreaming – and still are – to free ourselves from the nightmare of the one man, the one party, the one voice, the one opinion, the one owner, the sole successor."[148] Probably no one can sum up tyranny and dictatorship in the Arab world better than Mahmoud Darwish, who wrote a poem called: "Khitab al-Jalus" (The Speech of the Rise to the Throne):

I will choose my people
I will choose my people individually
I will choose you, one by one, from my mother's lineage and my sect
I will choose you so that you are worthy of me
I will give you all the rights
I will give you the right to serve me
To raise my pictures on your walls
Because that is your right.[149]

---

[148] Nur, *Sajin al-hurriya*, p. 6. Nur ran against Mubarak in the presidential elections of 2005.
[149] Darwish, "Shahid 'ala zaman al-tughat."

7 | *Transition from authoritarianism*

The previous chapters explained how authoritarianism managed to exist for such a long time, and how deeply entrenched it became in the Arab republics. In December 2010, the first spark of popular resistance to these autocratic regimes flared up in Tunisia. By 2012, six of these republics had experienced dramatic changes, and in five of them dictatorship did not survive. In Iraq, as a result of the US-led invasion, Saddam Hussein's regime had been toppled in 2003 after more than three decades. The Arab uprisings led to the fall of Tunisia's Ben 'Ali, Egypt's Mubarak, and Yemen's 'Ali 'Abdullah Salih. With the help of an international coalition, Qaddafi's rule over Libya came to an end. In Syria, a civil war is raging with no end in sight as of late 2015, and it is unclear whether the rule of the Asad dynasty will cease.

The uprisings demonstrated that the Arab region is similar to other parts of the world where dictators were overthrown by spontaneous pressure from the streets, and the grip of tyranny unraveled in a matter of weeks. However, the same question that faced former Soviet Bloc countries now faces the Arab republics: what is the trajectory of these uprisings, and how will a transition to a more liberal system, if achieved, shape their futures? Political scientists have conducted interesting comparative research about the resilience of former Soviet republics and Arab countries that underline the importance of economic factors under dictatorship and during transition periods.[1] As Samuel Huntington indicated, countries transitioning to democracy have to cope with transitional problems such as "the legacy of authoritarianism and establishing effective control of the

---

[1] Steve Hess, "Sources of Authoritarian Resilience in Regional Protest Waves: The Post-Communist Colour Revolutions and 2011 Arab Uprisings," *Government and Opposition*, vol. 50 (2015), pp. 1–29, published online January 9, 2015: doi:10.1017/gov.2014.39.

military." Furthermore, there are specific problems "endemic to specific countries."[2]

This chapter will address some of the general burning issues that continue to confront these countries on their troubled path to post-authoritarianism. National variations notwithstanding, there are numerous common challenges that they need to tackle in order to rid themselves of tyranny. The many urgent problems can be addressed under three general sections: first, institutions, governance, and the role of religion; second, economic topics such as corruption, inequality, and the brain drain; and third, the sensitive questions of accountability, reconciliation, overhaul of the security apparatus, and the role of the military. As Tunisia is the only republic that is truly transitioning of its own accord, a fourth section is devoted to that country.

Governance and politics

Scholars have correctly argued that authoritarian regimes succeed in staying in power if they possess "at least one of the following pillars of incumbent strength": an institutionalized single ruling party; an extensive security apparatus; and state control over the economy.[3] In most of the republics under study, more than one of those factors was a key to their durability. Once the dictatorships collapsed in five of the republics, reforming governance and building institutional capacity became essential for any successful transition. It is fascinating to see how the paths of each of those five republics differed dramatically once the old regimes collapsed, or, in the case of Syria, are still resisting downfall.

In Barbara Geddes' words, "different forms of authoritarianism break down in characteristically different ways," and thus transitions, if they were to take place in the other republics, will be most likely different.[4] In theory, Iraq should have been the perfect model where the old entrenched institutions such as the single ideological party, the

---

[2] Samuel P. Huntington, *The Third Wave: Democratization in the Late Twentieth Century* (Norman: Oklahoma University Press, 1991), p. 253.

[3] Lucan Way, "Resistance to Contagion: Sources of Authoritarian Stability in the Former Soviet Union," in Valerie Bunce, Michael McFaul, and Kathryn Stoner-Weiss (eds.), *Democracy and Authoritarianism in the Postcommunist World* (New York: Cambridge University Press, 2010), p. 230.

[4] Barbara Geddes, "Authoritarian Breakdown: Empirical Test of a Game Theoretic Argument." Working Paper, annual meeting of the American Political Science Association, September 1999.

Ba'th, and the coercive state apparatus were crushed as a result of the invasion in 2003. After the fall of Baghdad, the Iraqi state collapsed, its power structures disintegrated, and there was nothing to replace them. The Office of Reconstruction and Humanitarian Assistance (ORHA) under General Garner did not fill the massive institutional void created, because its emphasis was directed toward refugee work and oilfield repair. It turned out, of course, that there was neither a refugee problem nor oilfield fires in the immediate aftermath of the 2003 war.[5]

As the old power structures disintegrated, the country was thrown into near total chaos. Essential services run by the government were halted. The looting that followed spared no bank, hospital, power station, or government office, and cost the country around $12 billion.[6] No wonder a British diplomat cabled his government in London: "Garner's outfit, ORHA, is an unbelievable mess. No leadership, no strategy, no coordination, no structure, and inaccessible to ordinary Iraqis."[7] By May 2003, ORHA was dissolved and the Coalition Provisional Authority (CPA) was established in its place under Ambassador L. Paul Bremer III. Within a week of his arrival in Baghdad, Bremer issued the de-Ba'thification decree. Overnight, almost 30,000 Iraqis – including experienced middle management in economic ministries, teachers, and doctors – were dismissed from their jobs.[8]

This was a turning point in Iraq's history: first the senior management of the country had fled or been arrested, and now middle management was kicked out. The result was a huge vacuum that the Americans could not fill. The CPA found it hard to recruit the right American

[5] L. Paul Bremer III, *My Year in Iraq: The Struggle to Build a Future of Hope* (New York: Simon & Schuster, 2006), p. 27.

[6] George Packer, *The Assassin's Gate* (New York: Farrar, Straus, & Giroux, 2005), p. 139.

[7] Peter Galbraith quotes Sir John Sawers, British ambassador to Egypt, who was in Baghdad to report to British prime minister Tony Blair, in *The End of Iraq: How American Incompetence Created a War without End* (New York: Simon & Schuster, 2006), p. 117.

[8] See Bremer's point of view in *My Year in Iraq*, pp. 39–42. See also David L. Phillips, *Losing Iraq: Inside the Postwar Reconstruction Fiasco* (New York: Basic Books, 2005), pp. 143–53. See also an account of the shortcomings of the CPA in Special Inspector General for Iraq Reconstruction (SIGIR), *October 30, 2005 Quarterly Report to Congress*, pp. 77–78, available at http://cybercemetery.unt.edu/archive/sigir/20131001095724/http://www.sigir.mil/publications/quarterlyreports/October2005.html.

personnel for the right jobs.[9] Indeed, very few of the recruits had regional knowledge or expertise in the fields they were overseeing, or any real understanding of Iraq's history and its economy. Matters were exacerbated by the CPA's reliance on a "revolving door of diplomats," resulting in a lack of continuity as most officials had brief stints in Iraq averaging six to nine months.[10] While the invasion ended Saddam Hussein's tyranny, it could not eradicate authoritarianism. New leaders such as Nuri al-Maliki exploited the new institutions set up after the invasion to co-opt different, previously excluded, segments of the population. Most importantly, one of the three basic ingredients of autocracy continued blatantly: regime control over Iraq's resources, in a country where oil revenues constitute more than 95 percent of its total revenues. This allowed the new regime to exert its influence, and, as is discussed below, corruption reached new heights across the whole system.

Iraq is also an important case study in highlighting the fact that elections do not necessarily deliver democracy or democratic institutions. The determination of the West, and in particular of the USA, to conduct elections to show the world that Iraq had become democratic succeeded up to a certain point, but did not intrinsically change the system. Indeed, relatively free elections were held in Iraq on several occasions, and allowed Iraqis for the first time in decades to cast their votes. However, once the elections were over, the government continued to dominate the state, and governance was marred by corruption and inefficiency. Voting once every four years does not in itself alter the basics of a regime, although it is undoubtedly an important transitional step. The problem in Iraq was that voting was not accompanied by building better institutions. The collapse of the Iraqi army in Mosul in summer 2014 was mostly the result of politicization of the military, corruption, lack of training, and the sectarian policy of consecutive governments, predominantly al-Maliki's.

Given their colonial past, the historical context in which institutions were created in these republics is key to our understanding of the transition. As Lisa Anderson shows in her study of state building in

---

[9] SIGIR, *October 30, 2005 Quarterly Report to Congress*, pp. 78–80.
[10] Larry Diamond, *Squandered Victory: The American Occupation and the Bungled Effort to Bring Democracy to Iraq* (New York: Times Books, 2005), p. 289. Diamond gives an example of a twenty-four-year-old Yale graduate who was in charge of reorganizing the Baghdad stock exchange.

Tunisia and Libya, their bureaucracies were a product of the encounter with the international system.[11] Algeria had to rebuild institutions from a very rudimentary base after a long colonization by France. The rest of the republics inherited various institutions, and some – such as Tunisia – developed theirs better than others. In Libya under Qaddafi, institutions were an anathema. As one of his ministers recounts, the leader reviled any kind of institution, whether it was a political party, parliament, the army, or even the diplomatic corps, which he replaced by committees to run embassies abroad.[12] As a result, when Qaddafi's reign was over, there were no institutions to run the state. The country slid into chaos, and by early 2015 it had become a failed state. As one scholar points out, to avert failure, states need "clusters of institutions and incentives that produce stability."[13] In Libya's case, and to a certain extent in Iraq after the 2003 invasion, the effectiveness of the state to carry out functions such as providing security, supplying social services, and creating job opportunities was very low indeed. Both countries exemplify many of the common processes that are the "pathways to state failure," such as tribal and ethnic conflicts, corrupt control, and management of resources by the state.[14]

Lack of institutions led to concentration of power. The issue of concentrating power is neither new nor restricted to the Arab republics. In discussing the French Revolution, Tocqueville argued that the reason "centralization did not perish in the Revolution is that it was in itself the beginning of the Revolution as well as its sign."[15] In the post-communist era, one example of concentration of power is President Islam Karimov of Uzbekistan, who "centralized power early in the transformation and has jealously guarded his prerogatives."[16] Unfortunately, as of late 2015, it seems that a number of those countries that experienced uprisings are either heading to the chaos and disintegration that Iraq endured in the years of civil war, 2005–07, or taking the path of concentrating power.

[11] Lisa Anderson, *The State and Social Transformation in Tunisia and Libya, 1830–1980* (Princeton: Princeton University Press, 1986).

[12] Sharbal, *Fi khaymat al-Qaddafi*, interview with 'Abd al-Salam al-Triki, p. 255.

[13] Jack A. Goldstone, "Pathways to State Failure," in Harvey Starr (ed.), *Dealing with Failed States: Crossing Analytic Boundaries* (New York: Routledge, 2009), p. 7.

[14] Ibid., p. 8.   [15] Tocqueville, *L'Ancien régime et la révolution*, p. 61.

[16] Timothy Frye, *Building States and Markets after Communism: The Perils of Polarized Democracy* (New York: Cambridge University Press, 2010), p. 233.

Governance and decision making in these countries are influenced by certain factors that have direct and indirect impacts on the process of transition. One is that authoritarian governments functioned without public trust, and during transition this is not swiftly restored. Whether in Eastern Europe or the Arab world, the main reason for the lack of trust between the authorities and citizens was the massive web of lies that had been created in every sphere, whether economic, social, or security related. In these societies "everything is just pretence," given that "the lack of honesty was so pervasive."[17] For almost half a century the populations of these republics were promised growth, prosperity, and jobs by the different regimes, but were utterly disillusioned by the final results. A second element was the lack of long-term planning and an unwillingness to make unpopular decisions. This continued after the Arab uprisings, as is shown in one of the rare memoirs written about the transition period by an Egyptian minister of finance, al-Biblawi. He discusses the influence of the street on the decision-making process and the cabinet's obsession with meeting the demands of the demonstrators. "The preoccupation of the government was 'complying' with the street rather than 'leading' the street."[18]

The third factor is the role of the army, which was, and is, a critical factor in governance. The involvement of the military in politics varies greatly, as discussed in Chapter 3. Tunisia was blessed by the fact that the army was kept out of politics. As cases outside the Arab region showed, when the army did not participate in national policy making, it became easier "to take a hands-off attitude to the transition," and declare its concern with protecting the country.[19] In other Arab countries such as Egypt, the army was an integral part of the regime, and the transitional government not only had to heed the "advice" of the military, but had to be sensitive to its budgetary requirements at a time when Egypt was burdened with economic difficulties. Egypt's experience with the military is comparable to that of some South American countries, in particular Brazil and Chile, where the military actually had its "autonomy enhanced during the first phases of

---

[17] Feiwel Kupferberg, *The Break-up of Communism in East Germany and Eastern Europe* (London: Macmillan, 1999), p. 31.
[18] Al-Biblawi, *Arba'at shuhur fi qafas al-hukuma*, p. 153.
[19] Guillermo O'Donnell and Philippe C. Schmitter, *Transitions from Authoritarian Rule: Tentative Conclusions about Uncertain Democracies* (Baltimore: Johns Hopkins University Press, 2013), p. 38.

democratization."[20] In all those countries, the military saw itself as the authority best equipped to "define patriotism, honor ... and to exert guardianship of the national interest."[21]

Intriguingly, one of Egypt's politicians blamed the media for "scaring the military" away from democracy after the 1952 Revolution by making negative insinuations about the role of the armed forces.[22] A totally different situation occurred in Iraq, where the army was disbanded by the USA, which led to chaos, creating a serious division in Iraqi society and even more unemployment. Later, it had to be rebuilt by the Americans at a huge cost, only to be undermined in 2014 by its failure to fight the Islamic State of Iraq and the Levant (ISIL). In some countries, while the armed forces were the main bulwark of power when the authoritarian leaders took over, other components, such as a network of family members and tribal support (in the cases of Yemen and Libya), became as important.[23]

A fourth aspect that has influenced transition in the region is the fragmentation of political actors. The regimes did not tolerate independent and organized dissent. Thus "they tend either to fragment the subaltern, especially the political class, or to subsume them under their own populist institutions."[24] As noted in Chapter 2, Islamic and religious groups were the most organized centers of power that these regimes feared and repressed. Indeed, polarization is an important characteristic of post-autocratic regimes; it emerges in countries that experience a possibility of creating new political parties or of running for the presidency without fear of retribution (for example, fifteen political parties and twenty-seven candidates came forward for Tunisia's presidential election in 2014.) In post-communism, one lesson learned was that "as polarization increases in democracy, executives have a much more difficult time conducting economic and institutional reform."[25] This is exacerbated by the tendency of politicians in these circumstances to subvert reform or carry out inconsistent

---

[20] Felipe Agüero, "The New 'Double Challenge': Democratic Control and Efficacy of Military, Police, and Intelligence," in Alfred Stepan (ed.), *Democracies in Danger* (Baltimore: Johns Hopkins University Press, 2009), p. 62.

[21] Ibid., p. 63.   [22] Muhyi al-Din, *Wa al-'an atakallam*, p. 320.

[23] For a discussion of elements of power in Yemen, see John Peterson, "Yemen on the Precipice: Governing the Ungovernable," in Kadhim (ed.), *Governance in the Middle East and North Africa*, pp. 306–11.

[24] Bayat, *Life as Politics*, p. 25.

[25] Frye, *Building States and Markets after Communism*, p. 5.

reforms. This leads to the fifth factor impacting transition: religion and religious movements.

Ethnic and religious conflicts are not a new phenomenon in the region, but they never previously reached the level we are witnessing now. In Iraq, sectarian conflict erupted after the collapse of the Ba'th regime. The uprising in Syria partly turned into a sectarian conflict as the civil war dragged on, and in Yemen the battle between Houthis and the government has also largely become sectarian driven. Religious leaders faced challenges throughout the twentieth century from secularist authoritarianism and structural problems that undermined their power. Regimes in the region found ways to coexist and to co-opt the religious authorities. In Syria, for example, "the political leadership managed to establish ambiguous, but nevertheless robust, partnerships with religious figures who had genuine credibility in the eyes of many Muslims."[26] A common feature for the countries undergoing transition is the emergence of radical Islamists, and no doubt this will continue to impact the process in the coming years. Interestingly, as Alfred Stepan points out, the four-volume series *Transition from Authoritarian Rule*, which established the field of studying transition, did not dedicate even one chapter to ethnic and religious conflicts.[27]

These conflicts are not confined to the Middle East; Yugoslavia, Nigeria, and Sri Lanka all suffered from similar struggles. What one can learn from post-communist Europe is that the high degree of violence stemming from ethnic strife was due to the tyrannical regimes' repression of the strong sentiments of the populations, and after communism, as in the Arab region, ethnic identities needed to draw attention to themselves and to express their uniqueness. Once a conflict erupted, "hate becomes self-reproducing and self-justifying."[28] Furthermore, in all these conflicted areas, poverty and lack of resources led to a more ferocious struggle between ethnic and sectarian groups.

---

[26] Thomas Pierret, *Religion and State in Syria: The Sunni Ulama from Coup to Revolution* (New York: Cambridge University Press, 2013), p. 3.

[27] Alfred Stepan, "Introduction: Undertheorized Political Problems in the Founding Democratization Literature," in Stepan (ed.), *Democracies in Danger*, p. 2.

[28] Kupferberg, *The Break-up of Communism*, p. 76. The author analyzes what he terms "the hotbed of hatred" in Europe, which has many similarities to what took place after the toppling of some of these dictatorships in the Arab world, pp. 69–97.

In spite of being repressed by the authoritarian regimes in both Egypt and Tunisia, the Islamist movements Hizb al-Huriyya wa al-'Adala (Freedom and Justice Party – FJP) in Egypt, and al-Nahda (The Renaissance) in Tunisia won the first democratic elections in their countries. This stirred the debate about their role in the uprisings and created tensions with the rest of the population, particularly in Egypt. There were, however, stark differences between these two movements: al-Nahda, unlike the FJP, which represented the Muslim Brothers, was more flexible, and willing to share power with other parties. Opponents of Islamist movements raised a spectrum of issues: compatibility of religion with democracy, women's rights, and national unity.[29] In Egypt, the enmity between the two camps came to the fore when President Morsi was ousted in a coup d'état by the army with huge popular support. In Tunisia, al-Nahda lost in the parliamentary elections of late 2014, but it remains an important player in the nascent democracy.

For the rest of the republics, sectarian strife continues unabated: in Iraq, Syria, and Yemen the issue is not about Islamist versus other movements but reflects more of the Sunni–Shi'i divide, inflamed by outside forces such as Saudi Arabia on one hand and Iran on the other. Many Arab writers are addressing the topic of Islam and politics, and they range from the extreme to the more balanced. An example of the former is al-Safi Sa'id, who argues that the "Islamic *tayyar* (movement) strives to create a theocratic country." He goes further in concocting a joint conspiracy between Zionism and Islamic movements, as they share "their hatred for the Arabic nationalist trend."[30] He argues that the Arab Spring has turned into autumn because although authoritarianism came to an end, the military men and the religious groups, both relying on oil money, are the winners of the Arab uprisings. A more moderate view is represented by Marwan Muasher, a former foreign minister of Jordan who also served as his country's ambassador to the USA. He addresses an important question of whether the

---

[29] For a comprehensive discussion of Islamist movements after the uprising, see Brynen et al., *Beyond the Arab Spring*, pp. 119–46.

[30] Al-Safi Sa'id, *Kharif al-'Arab: al-bi'r wa al-sawma'a wa al-jiniral – al-harb al-damiyya bayn al-'Aruba wa al-Islam* [The Arab autumn: the well, the hermitage, and the general – the bloody war between Arabism and Islamism] (Tunis: 'Urabia Publishing, 2012), p. 572. The title refers to three factors that, according to the author, dominated modern Arab history: the oil well, the religious man, and the military.

Islamists will embrace pluralism as an element in transition, and posits that while Islamist parties in Tunisia, Egypt, and Morocco "evolved toward moderation, their commitment to pluralism is still less than categorical."[31]

The sixth factor that will greatly influence the results of transition is the economy. Good governance and successful economic policies are closely interrelated. The desperate need by the new regimes to focus on sound economic policies and to fight corruption is vital for the future of these countries.

Economy and corruption

Economic grievances were undoubtedly important in fueling popular protests in many of these republics in 2011. Research indicates that corruption is a major source of instability as its injustice enrages and prompts extreme responses from citizens, and that the struggle to establish sustainable democracies in countries such as Afghanistan and Iraq is mostly due to the fact that their governments are mired in graft.[32] Income inequality; corruption; rising unemployment, particularly among the youth; increased food prices; drought; and an array of other economic elements all combined to produce the strong desire for regime change. According to a Gallup survey in Egypt, inflation was a high concern for those polled, followed by unemployment, food shortages, and lack of proper drinking water.[33] While there was economic growth in these republics (due mainly to oil and gas revenues) it was not shared, and opportunities shrank.[34] Transition from authoritarianism without significant economic progress is basically doomed.

---

[31] Marwan Muasher, *The Second Arab Awakening and the Battle for Pluralism* (New Haven: Yale University Press, 2014), p. 175.

[32] See, for example, Sarah Chayes, *Thieves of State: Why Corruption Threatens Global Security* (New York: Norton, 2015). The author bases her book on her experience as a journalist in Afghanistan.

[33] Daniel Byman, "Regime Change in the Middle East: Problems and Prospects," in Daniel Byman and Marylena Mantas (eds.), *Religion, Democracy, and Politics in the Middle East* (New York: Academy of Political Science, 2012), p. 63.

[34] For the economic reasons behind the Arab uprising, see Magdi Amin et al., *After the Spring: Economic Transitions in the Arab World* (New York: Oxford University Press, 2012), pp. 31–53. The book consists of discussions by fifteen authors. See also Malik and Awadallah, "The Economics of the Arab Spring."

Since 1960, there have been 103 cases of transition in the world; in 57 of them there was a successful economic transition as GDP per capita grew steadily over time, while in 46 cases GDP per capita actually declined.[35] Research on transition clearly demonstrates that the development of a middle class, economic reforms, and improving education all contribute to a higher success ratio for transition.[36]

As Chapter 5 showed, the leadership in these republics paid scant attention to economic issues, because the economy was mostly seen through the prism of regime durability and as a bastion of cronyism to reward supporters. Fundamental reforms, before and after the uprising, were delayed for fear of derailing political alliances; a case in point is Yemen, where the National Dialogue conference took ten months to reach an agreement about sharing power and transitioning the country in 2013.[37] Even when policies were introduced to improve the economy, such as privatization in Syria under Bashar al-Asad, they "generated overlapping and competing structures of authority that stand simultaneously in co-operation and conflict with one another."[38] In fact, in 2010, a Transformation Index ranked Syria at 117 out of 128 countries in terms of economic management.[39] Overall, economic liberalization before 2011 was utilized to reward the networks of support, and did not substantially change the centralization of political power. Those close to the regime amassed huge wealth, and although income inequality in the Arab region was comparatively low throughout the 1970s and most of the 1980s, no dramatic improvement took place in the following three decades.[40] Hence the perception of inequality was a dominant grievance among the demonstrators. Daron Acemoglu and James Robinson suggest that high inequality contributes to large protests since unequal dictatorships are more likely to

---

[35] Amin et al., *After the Spring*, pp. 13–14.

[36] European Bank for Reconstruction and Development, *Transition Report 2013*, p. 34, available at www.tr.ebrd.com.

[37] International Monetary Fund, *Republic of Yemen*, Staff Report for the 2014 Article IV Consultation, July 3, 2014, IMF Country Report No. 14/276. For an analysis of the conference that ended in January 2014, see Erica Gaston, "Process Learned in Yemen's National Dialogue," *United States Institute of Peace Special Report 342*, February 2014.

[38] Samer N. Abboud and Fred H. Lawson, "Antimonies of Economic Governance in Contemporary Syria," in Kadhim (ed.), *Governance in the Middle East and North Africa*, p. 340.

[39] Ibid., p. 330.   [40] Brynen et al., *Beyond the Arab Spring*, p. 227.

encounter sizeable protests when citizens place redistributive pressure on the regime.[41]

Another factor that swayed public opinion was the lack of transparency in how economic decisions were taken and implemented. Needless to say, once regimes collapse, the new governments are incapable of changing the system and becoming fully transparent. This becomes obvious in al-Biblawi's description of the way in which the Egyptian government ran its affairs after the uprising.[42] Transparency and corruption are invariably interrelated.

Although an uprising did not topple Iraq's leadership, it can still provide important lessons for the process of transition. Iraq's political economy post-2003 is somewhat unique, given the country's circumstances. The unraveling of authoritarianism was followed by a civil war, which led to the emigration of almost 2 million Iraqis, and caused a serious brain drain that impacted economic management. This was then followed by a new type of authoritarianism that came on the heels of democratic elections. The change of regime, in spite of massive help from the USA and its allies, did not change the fundamentals of Iraq's economy. One lesson from Iraq is that money is not the panacea for transition. Iraq is a wealthy country, and after the invasion oil prices rocketed to as high as $130, which was coupled with massive capital spent by the USA (roughly $60 billion) to rebuild the country. Iraq is also a pointer for countries such as Libya and Syria: the invasion shattered the state, and rebuilding it was not straightforward. In fact, after the overthrow of Saddam Hussein's regime, most of the money was spent on security and infrastructure, which in turn meant more chaos, more mismanagement of projects, and more corruption, delaying any serious attempt to restore the country economically. The fact that Iraq was once again cursed by bad leadership just exacerbated the situation. One Kurdish politician stated succinctly that Iraq was pushed to the brink under al-Maliki's regime: "His eight years in office were characterized by shortsighted governance, corruption and sectarianism that marginalized important communities and centralized power."[43]

---

[41] Daron Acemoglu and James A. Robinson, *Economic Origins of Dictatorships and Democracy* (New York: Cambridge University Press, 2006).

[42] See pp. 181–82 in Chapter 5, about the episode related to salaries and benefits of ministers.

[43] Qubad Talabani, "Saving Iraq in the Post-Maliki Era," *Wall Street Journal*, December 8, 2014.

A critical issue facing these republics is unemployment, particularly of the youth. The effect of the brain drain from Iraq after the invasion was devastating for the economy. If this were to be repeated in other countries, the long-term impact would be colossal. It has already happened in Syria as a result of the civil war, and in Libya with the collapse of the state after the fall of Qaddafi. Egypt had suffered in the past from brain drain, but this might intensify as the country possibly replaces one form of authoritarianism with another.[44]

According to an opinion poll of 18,000 youth from 20 countries in the region, 26 percent of those surveyed said they would like to permanently migrate to another country if they had the opportunity.[45] Brain drain could intensify because of soaring expectations after the uprisings for improved living standards and job opportunities. Neither the public nor the private sector is absorbing large numbers of educated youth. The public sector in these republics had grown substantially with no increase in efficiency, and there is a desperate need for modernization. On one hand, the private sector, wary of the instability, is shying away from new investments and in general has little confidence in the authorities. On the other hand, the public perceives large segments of the private sector "as synonymous with corruption."[46] Certainly, the poor state of government machinery was one of the reasons for the economic downturn in the republics that witnessed the uprising. The high turnover of ministers and senior officials in the economic ministries further aggravated the situation.

The most important lesson from Iraq is that corruption actually expanded significantly after the collapse of tyrannical rule. While corruption existed during the Saddam Hussein era, particularly during the 1990s under the Oil-For-Food program, it never reached the magnitude seen today. Corruption prevails in every sector in Iraq, and all efforts to uproot it or to create serious parliamentary committees to scrutinize business dealings either failed or were resisted by al-Maliki's government. In the 2012 Corruption Perception Index, Iraq came out as number 169 out

---

[44] According to one report, 60 percent of the highly educated Arabs who settled in the USA in the last decade originated from Egypt: see Samir al-Tannir, *al-Faqr wa al-fasad fi al-'alam al-'Arabi* [Poverty and corruption in the Arab world] (Beirut: al-Saqi, 2009), p. 79.

[45] Gallup, *The Silatech Index: Voices of Young Arabs*, January 2010, p. 26, available at www.gallup.com/poll/120758/silatech-index-voices-young-arabs .aspx.

[46] Amin et al., *After the Spring*, p. 7.

of 174 countries worldwide.[47] Iraqi corruption is ubiquitous. It is exemplified by the findings of the inspector-general of the Ministry for Higher Education in 2009, showing that as many as 4,000 of the almost 14,000 candidates in the January elections of that year had forged educational qualifications.[48]

Corruption was good for the insurgency, and remains good for the numerous militias that are spreading death and destruction almost daily in Iraq. It is estimated that corruption has added roughly 20 percent to the cost of doing business in the country. Needless to say, the poor pay a heavy price for this sorry state of affairs, as they are forced to hand over bribes for services to which they are essentially entitled. The IMF estimates that 10–20 percent of Iraqi workers are "ghosts" who receive a paycheck but rarely show up for work.[49] A recent study by the United Nations Development Programme (UNDP) indicated that an Iraqi citizen pays on average four bribes a year, the largest portion of them related to public utilities, followed by offers for recruitment and promotion.[50] There is no doubt that the tolerance of rampant corruption that occurred on both the American and Iraqi sides contributed substantially to its entrenchment. The International Crisis Group stated bluntly that al-Maliki's government "has allowed corruption to become entrenched and spread throughout its institutions. This in turn has contributed to a severe decay in public services."[51]

Corruption is not just a feature of economic activity; it has a bearing on security matters. The success of ISIL in the summer of 2014 can be directly traced to corruption. Back in 2010, a report by *The Military Balance* underlined the obstacles to better security in Iraq by pointing out that "corruption among officers is widespread, with cronyism and nepotism rampant in the assignment and promotion system."[52] Iraq is not alone in the way corruption has become rampant after the fall of a

---

[47] Transparency International, "Corruption Perceptions Index 2012," available at www.transparency.org/cpi2012.

[48] Frank B. Gunter, *The Political Economy of Iraq: Restoring Balance in a Post-Conflict Society* (Northampton, MA: Edward Elgar Publishing, 2013), p. 49.

[49] Ibid., p. 50.

[50] United Nations Development Programme (UNDP), *Corruption and Integrity: Challenges in the Public Sector in Iraq*, January 2013.

[51] International Crisis Group, "Failing Oversight: Iraq's Unchecked Government," *Middle East Report*, no. 113, September 2011.

[52] International Institute for Strategic Studies (IISS), "Chapter Five: Middle East and North Africa," *The Military Balance*, vol. 110 (2010), p. 236.

tyrannical system. As fear is reduced, and ideology weakens, corruption spreads and becomes a way of life. Weak institutions coupled with a usually inefficient and low-paid public sector push many civil servants to become corrupt. Another driver is the expansion of the hidden economy; for instance, in East–Central Europe, one in five people was engaged in the hidden economy in 2008 and received undeclared wages.[53] In the twelve countries of the former Soviet Union, corruption has become the major challenge in the process of transition, and nearly all the countries in the region are below the global average in the 2012 Transparency International Report. In Russia, corruption has become intertwined with Vladimir Putin's rule. Karen Dawisha, who researched the subject, argues that Russian elites maximized their gains by controlling the market and then depositing their profits in offshore accounts. Her conclusion could be an equally accurate portrayal of al-Maliki's Iraq and many other transitioning states: "From the beginning Putin and his circle sought to create an authoritarian regime ruled by a close-knit cabal with embedded interests, plans, and capabilities."[54] The only difference is that al-Maliki was ousted not because of his faulty management, but thanks to strong internal and external pressure after the takeover of Mosul by ISIL and the shabby performance of corrupt military officers. One commentator argued that the story of the last twenty years in Russia has not been the failure of democracy, but the "rise of a new form of authoritarianism."[55]

Kleptocracy in countries undergoing transition constitutes the most dangerous risk, and allows for the creation of a new type of authoritarianism. As Sarah Chayes posits, kleptocracy can take different forms: in Egypt it is the military–kleptocratic complex, while in Tunisia it is the bureaucratic kleptocracy.[56] Both types are entrenched and challenging to uproot given their control of the economy. During transition, all competing sides use allegations of cronyism, corruption, and nepotism as election tools in order to discredit political competitors and project the image of a new and clean

[53] Colin C. Williams, "The Hidden Economy in East–Central Europe: Lessons from a Ten-Nation Survey," *Problems of Post-Communism*, vol. 56, no. 4 (July/August 2009), pp. 15–28.

[54] Karen Dawisha, *Putin's Kleptocracy: Who Owns Russia?* (New York: Simon & Schuster, 2014), p. 8.

[55] Anne Applebaum, "How he and his Cronies Stole Russia," *New York Review of Books*, December 18, 2014, p. 26.

[56] Chayes, *Thieves of State*, pp. 79–90, 91–100.

leadership.[57] Whether in Russia or elsewhere, the focus on Putin and Russian leadership is well placed. Robert Rotberg, who studied corruption, rightly posits that "where top leaders are uncorrupted and where top leaders act effectively and decisively against corruption by punishing misbehaving colleagues and relentlessly pursuing miscreants, a governmental culture of abstinence can be created that positively rewards honesty and integrity."[58] Hence, cronyism and nepotism in these republics will hinge on the leadership's behavior and whether they would be willing to operate more open economies. As one Arabic book's title put it, *Intaha zaman al-furas al-da'i'a* (The era of missed chances is over), given that these countries lost more than three decades of economic growth and prosperity; hopefully they will not miss the next thirty years as well.[59]

Becoming democratic is not, unfortunately, a guarantee of uprooting corruption. Time and again, we have evidence that even countries that transitioned to democracy still suffer from corruption; as shown by the Petrobras case in Brazil. In a country that has enjoyed thirty years of democracy, a huge scandal erupted when it was discovered that top officials of Brazil's state-run oil company operated a kickback scheme on contracts, and had managed to embezzle more than $400 million.[60] Some Brazilians argue that the root of this corruption lies in their county's reluctance, until now, to face the dark side of its past, and that perpetrators of horrible acts of torture under the military rule were never brought to justice. The argument is that immunity from past crimes opened the door to a laxity toward powerful economic groups, who believed that their corrupt activities would go unpunished.

Accountability, reconciliation, and reform of security services

A description of the state of affairs in Eastern Europe after Stalin could easily apply to many of the republics discussed here:

---

[57] See, for example, Thomas B. Pepinsky, *Economic Crises and the Breakdown of Authoritarian Regimes: Indonesia and Malaysia in Comparative Perspectives* (New York: Cambridge University Press, 2009), p. 207.

[58] Robert I. Rotberg, "Leadership Alters Corrupt Behavior," in Rotberg (ed.), *Corruption, Global Security, and World Order*, p. 342.

[59] Anis Mansur, *Intaha zaman al-furas al-da'i'a* [The era of missed chances is over] (Cairo: al-Nahda Publishing, 1998).

[60] "Petrobras Scandal: Brazilian Oil Executives among 35 Charged," *Guardian*, December 11, 2014.

Societies for decades were composed of victims, perpetrators and bystanders, the last burdened by tacit conformity and silence in the face of flagrant illegalities and immoralities. Individuals and whole communities were profoundly affected, physically, materially and psychologically, often in ways that lie beyond historical investigation and reconstruction.[61]

In Romania, Ceaușescu's brutal reign had a lasting effect on the psyche of his people, and as one Romanian commented: "If the past was full of terrible things, the future will be full of terrible things."[62] People living under tyrannical regimes such as those in Romania or many of the Arab republics will need a fundamental change of mindset if they are to transition to a true democracy. In his first address after becoming president of the Czech Republic in December 1989, Václav Havel eloquently described life in his country in words that readily apply to the populations of the Arab republics:

The worst thing is that we live in a contaminated moral environment. We fell morally ill because we became used to saying something different from what we thought. We learned not to believe in anything, to ignore one another, to care only about ourselves... We had all become used to the totalitarian system and accepted it as an unchangeable fact and thus helped to perpetuate it.[63]

The memoirs of Arab writers inform us of similar conditions: a system of lies, fear, and sycophancy, a strong desire to protect one's family and survive under authoritarian regimes. The coercion and fear used by such regimes have serious implications. The question to be raised during the transition process is whether accountability for what happened in the past will take place. After the Arab uprisings, a "blamestorming" process began, whether in Tunisia or Egypt. In the words of one observer, "the participants apportion blame to some figures of the *ancien régime*, discredit or champion others, and in the process establish their own revolutionary credentials."[64] Libya is

---

[61] Kevin McDermott and Matthew Stibbe, "Stalinist Terror in Eastern Europe: Problems, Perspectives and Interpretations," in Kevin McDermott and Matthew Stibbe (eds.), *Stalinist Terror in Eastern Europe: Elite Purges and Mass Repression* (Manchester: Manchester University Press, 2010), p. 1.

[62] Marci Shore, *The Taste of Ashes: The Afterlife of Totalitarianism in Eastern Europe* (New York: Broadway Books, 2013), p. 87.

[63] Václav Havel, "New Year's Address to the Nation," Czechoslovakia, January 1, 1990, Czech Republic Presidential Website, Speeches, available at http://old.hrad.cz/president/Havel.speeches/.

[64] Gana, "Visions of Dissent," p. 181.

another example where memoirs of the previous regime have put all the blame on Qaddafi and his two sons for what happened in their country over four decades. Those who were in power in the beginning, but found themselves ousted by Qaddafi, argue that in addition to him, roughly twenty others should shoulder the responsibility for what took place.[65] Experts who worked in Libya after the revolution argue that a major dilemma stemming from the previous regime's legacy is "the overwhelming number of perpetrators implicated in the crimes committed" during Qaddafi's era.[66] Likewise, in the eyes of the masses, those identified with the old regime were many and had to be punished. In essence what happened in Libya was revenge by *al-thuwwar* (revolutionaries) against those suspected of being part of the security services under the previous government, and an unwillingness to allow them to be part of a post-revolutionary system. Having a large number of these *thuwwar* battalions without any chain of command exacerbated the mayhem.[67] Following the collapse of the regime, international human rights organizations reported many cases of torture and murder taking place with impunity.[68]

Obeying orders was the main justification given by members of these regimes, whether in the Arab world or in other authoritarian states. As quoted in Chapter 4, one senior Syrian security official argued that all those in the security services were mechanical robots executing orders. However, understanding the consequences of torture is pertinent to any successful transition. In many countries, torture has a deep colonial past. Some, such as Algeria and Tunisia, inherited the French system, and with the passage of time new methods were introduced, and torture expanded and became ingrained in the operations of these security

---

[65] See for instance the interview with 'Abd al-Mun'im al-Huni, who was one of the original members of the Revolutionary Command Council but from the mid 1970s opposed Qaddafi, in Sharbal, *Fi khaymat al-Qaddafi*, p. 99.

[66] Marieke Wierda, "Confronting Qadhafi's Legacy: Transitional Justice in Libya," in Peter Cole and Brian McQuinn (eds.), *The Libyan Revolution and its Aftermath* (New York: Oxford University Press, 2015), p. 158. Wierda is an international criminal lawyer and was part of the United Nations Support Mission in Libya.

[67] Ian Martin, "The United Nations' Role in the First Year of the Transition," in Cole and McQuinn (eds.), *The Libyan Revolution and its Aftermath*, p. 137. Martin was special representative of the United Nations secretary-general and head of the UN Support Mission in Libya from September 2012 to October 2013.

[68] International Crisis Group, "Trial by Error," pp. 22–31.

agencies.[69] Torture was not the only component of coercion; having informants from all walks of life instilled deep fear and distrust among citizens. Countries in Eastern Europe are still haunted by issues of betrayal and compromise committed by many citizens. Whether in Europe or the Arab world, informants operated at every level and impacted everyone in society.[70]

The problem facing the Arab world is similar to those in many other countries; whenever "a nation has experienced a dark chapter in its history, the question arises whether the past should simply be forgotten or whether it should be recalled and recorded for the benefit of the current generation."[71] With the Arab uprisings, researching and understanding the past of such regimes is critical for the future. The issue of reconciling with the past is still hovering over Eastern Europe more than twenty years after the collapse of communism. Individual complicity with the security services in countries such as Egypt, Iraq, Libya, Syria, and Tunisia will continue to overshadow these countries for many years to come. Whether in Iraq or Libya, and now in Syria, as violence expands, the long-term ramifications of complicity are becoming even more far-reaching. There is a dark heritage with every dictatorship, and when the dictatorship disappears, people have to confront the past and resolve the issues of guilt and responsibility. The regimes in the Arab republics managed for a long time to force the majority of individuals in their societies to abide by rules that ensured their survival in power for decades. As Havel aptly states: "individuals are reduced to little more than tiny cogs in

---

[69] For an interesting historical survey of torture in Tunisia, see 'Abd al-Latif al-Hanashi, "Mumarasat al-ta'dhib tijah al-wataniyyin al-Tunisiyyin zaman al-himaya al-Faransiyya" [The practice of torture toward Tunisian nationalists during the French protectorate], in al-Tamimi (ed.), *Dirasat wa shahadat hawla dahaya al-ta'dhib*, pp. 33–53.

[70] See, for example, Barbara Miller, *Narratives of Guilt and Compliance in Unified Germany: Stasi Informers and their Impact on Society* (New York: Routledge, 1999); Jan Cienski, "Informant Claims from Communist Era Haunt Czech Politics," *Financial Times*, November 29, 2013.

[71] Christian Tomuschat, "Foreword," in Daniel Rothenberg (ed.), *Memory of Silence: The Guatemalan Truth Commission Report* (New York: Palgrave Macmillan, 2012), p. xv. Tomuschat was the lead commissioner for the Commission for Historical Clarification in Guatemala. Millions of police documents were scanned chronicling the appalling ordeal of the population under military dictatorship.

an enormous mechanism and their significance is limited to their function."[72]

There is no guarantee that in post-authoritarian regimes the power of the security services will radically diminish. New organs with different names might be set up, possibly with motives not so different from those envisaged by the original authoritarian regimes. This was evident in Iraq post-Saddam Hussein, where Prime Minister al-Maliki restructured the security services to strengthen his own position and to allow him control over the security mechanism. According to one report, by mid 2009 more than 600,000 people were employed in the security apparatus. Al-Maliki followed the pattern of other authoritarian rulers by subverting the chain of command and ensuring that senior military officers and heads of security were tied to him personally.[73]

After the Arab uprisings some security agencies were significantly weakened, as in Yemen and Libya, because non-state actors stepped in to fill the power vacuum. The question became one of how power is divided between state and quasi-state agencies.[74] In Libya, for example, the chasm between the various groups and regions has been growing, supported by different countries. Security sector reform, whether in Egypt or Tunisia, is a key challenge for any transition.[75] With the return of army rule in Egypt, any talk of reform has almost disappeared, and in Tunisia, the chances of a major reform are feeble since al-Nida' won the 2014 elections. It should be noted that after the disintegration of the Soviet Union, both Gorbachev and Yeltsin promised to destroy the KGB as the most powerful organization in the country, and both failed. The lessons from other countries indicate that even when conditions prevail for "coaxing the military out of power and inducing them to tolerate a transition toward democracy," a complicated problem arises of "how to administer justice to those

---

[72] Havel et al., *The Power of the Powerless*, p. 73.
[73] International Institute for Strategic Studies, "Chapter Five." See also Peel, "Iraq: Singular Ambition."
[74] See details of an interesting symposium in Brian McQuinn, "Assessing (In) Security after the Arab Spring," *Political Science and Politics*, vol. 46 (October 2013), pp. 709–39.
[75] For a discussion of reform see Lutterbeck, "After the Fall," p. 7; Mohamed Kadry Said and Noha Bakr, "Egypt Security Sector Reforms," Arab Reform Initiative, January 2011, available at www.arab-reform.net/egypt-security-sector-reforms.

directly responsible for past acts of repression."[76] It should be noted that experts who studied the transition process have recommended that all elements of the security sector, be they military, police, or intelligence services, should be understood as essentially interrelated. A "policy [that is] consistent and persistent and works through a clear chain of command" is seen as the "most essential ingredient of success in countering thrusts to democracy."[77] However, one expert on the military in the Arab world argues that "the power of Arab militaries and militias, not the *mukhabarat*, has been dramatically enhanced in reaction to 'Middle-East revolutions'."[78]

Without question, a robust and independent judicial system is fundamental for a state undergoing transition. Trust in how the system operates is critical, and this has been missing in all those Arab republics where the independence of judges is seen as an illusion. In Tunisia during Ben 'Ali's era, lawyers were put under surveillance both by the security services and the ruling party, the RCD.[79] One member of the Nida' party pointed out that the courts are not independent either vis-à-vis the authorities or toward public opinion, as both can influence judges' decisions. He added that the constitution must address this and shore up the independence of the judicial system.[80] In Egypt, the situation is no better, and since the return of the military to power, courts have been, at the behest of the authorities, jailing members of the Muslim Brotherhood or other political opponents. Similarly, in Iraq, ten years after toppling Saddam, the courts are still struggling to find a way to act independently of pressure from the authorities or the militias, or even worse, judges are reaching decisions based on bribery.

Different countries have confronted their past in a variety of ways in order to smooth the transition. South Africa and Guatemala have published large quantities of documents from their military dictatorships detailing the horrendous acts committed. In late 2014,

[76] O'Donnell and Schmitter, *Transitions from Authoritarian Rule*, pp. 15–41.
[77] Agüero, "The New 'Double Challenge,'" p. 73.
[78] Robert Springborg, "The Role of the Militaries in the Arab Thermidor," paper presented to workshop at the London School of Economics and Political Science, *The Arab Thermidor: The Resurgence of the Security State*, October 10, 2014.
[79] Hibou, *The Force of Obedience*, pp. 119–23.
[80] Interview with Rafi' Ben Achour, Tunis, December 16, 2014. Ben Achour, a professor of law, occupied numerous important positions, including ambassador to Morocco, after the revolution.

Brazil published a report documenting two decades of government-sanctioned political killings and torture.[81] While Tunisia is currently refusing to open its archives, there is no doubt that testimonies collected and published are a step in the right direction. Furthermore, the Truth and Dignity Commission created in 2013, and non-governmental organizations (NGOs) based in Tunisia, are raising the issue of the past and attempting to deal with it. It is too early to tell whether they will succeed, but at least efforts are being made. Countries like Iraq could have benefited from knowing the contents of the archives of the intelligence and the Ba'th Party that are now available (currently only for approved researchers going to the Hoover Institute at Stanford University), but fear of retribution during the post-invasion period pushed to the margins any attempt to create a truth commission or collect testimonies of those who suffered under the previous regime. In addition, al-Maliki's attempts to recreate an autocratic system shifted the focus of human rights organizations to what was taking place under his rule. Thus, Tunisia is the only country out of those that witnessed an uprising that is undergoing a real transition.

Tunisia: a case of exceptionalism?

Five years after President Zine al-'Abidine Ben 'Ali's flight on January 14, 2011, Tunisia seems an exception in its transition achievements compared to the other Arab countries that toppled their authoritarian leaders. During the first few months of transition, Tunisia experienced waves of unrest, largely due to the rejection by demonstrators of the continuing role played by old-regime officials in the government. However, even in those circumstances, the popular uprising achieved some success, because the void left by Ben 'Ali was immediately filled when Muhammad Ghannouchi, who had been prime minister for eleven years, continued as temporary prime minister. Ghannouchi later told me that he had no inkling that Ben 'Ali was leaving the country; but immediately after the news of his departure became known, Ghannouchi told the parliament that without a president or leader mayhem would spread, and that law and order, together with the principles of the

---

[81] The 2,000-page report was published in early December 2014 and named 377 people responsible for 434 deaths and disappearances, as well as thousands of acts of torture. See Jenny Barchfield, "Brazil's Panel Details Military Regime's Brutality," Associated Press, December 10, 2014.

constitution, must be safeguarded.[82] He became acting president for a few hours, and then temporary prime minister for six weeks. The head of the Majlis al-Nuwwab (Chamber of Deputies), Fu'ad al-Mubazza', took over as temporary president. By the end of February 2011, when demonstrations became more violent, Ghannouchi resigned and Béji Caïd Essebsi was appointed prime minister in his stead.

Tunisia's exceptionalism needs to be understood. Some Tunisians argue that Ben 'Ali's despotism was as not as harsh as in countries such as Iraq and Syria, but it is doubtful that this relativity is the key to the country's different trajectory.[83] In fact, repression in Tunisia and the role of the security services was as harsh and comprehensive as in other republics. There is no doubt, however, that unlike other authoritarian regimes in the Arab world, Tunisia's institutional capacity had continued to develop in spite of the constraints of Ben 'Ali's regime. For instance, although labor unions were coopted by the regime, they were still an important voice in the country's affairs and played a significant role in the 2011 uprising.[84]

Three critical factors help to explain why Tunisia is the only country that is experiencing a proper transition. The first, and probably the most important, is the neutrality of the army; a neutrality that was preserved over almost half a century in spite of some turbulent events and the change of leadership. As mentioned, Tunisia was also the only country among the eight republics that had not engaged in a full military conflict either internally or externally. The second factor is the level of education; Tunisia had attained a high level of literacy and its universities continued to develop in spite of the obstacles imposed by Ben 'Ali's system. The third aspect is the role of women; their status had fundamentally changed since Bourguiba's days, and Tunisia was the first Arab country to ban polygamy after its independence in 1956. Furthermore, women continued to play a significant role in every sphere. Tunisians owe Bourguiba a great debt of gratitude for introducing these major changes, notwithstanding his many faults and the

---

[82] Interview with Muhammad Ghannouchi, Tunis, December 17, 2014. See also his speech to the parliament, available at www.youtube.com/watch?v=r4vv2IF-zwg.

[83] Interview with Rafi' Ben Achour.

[84] Sami Zemni, "From Socio-Economic Protest to National Revolt: The Labor Origins of the Tunisian Revolution," in Gana (ed.), *The Making of the Tunisian Revolution*, pp. 127–46.

autocratic system he developed along with a cult of personality. No wonder that Nida' Tunis Party, which won the parliamentary elections in November 2014, and Essebsi, who won the presidency elections in December 2014, have focused on Bourguiba and his ideology as a way of enlisting public support.

Tunisia suffered from many of the ailments that plagued the other Arab countries: poverty, high unemployment, and "a sense of degradation and indignity that reflected the frustration and despair felt by young men throughout Tunisia."[85] If transition continues on its current path, three important aspects need to be tackled: First, the relationship between the Islamists and secularists; second, economic difficulties; and third, dealing with the past and its remaining legacy. The gulf of mistrust between the Islamists and secularists in Tunisia is as deep as in other countries such as Egypt. Secularists argue that the Islamists, and in particular the Nahda Party, "played on the religious emotions of the individual in Tunisia."[86] Even a high official in the Nahda Party claimed that one of the reasons contributing to what she called "the destructive forces in the Arab world" is the use of religion to control the state.[87] However, as previously discussed, the Ben 'Ali regime saw in Islam and Islamists a real threat, and members of religious movements suffered tremendously in ways similar to those in Egypt, Iraq, Libya, and Syria. From the post-revolution testimonies of active members of such organizations, a bleak picture arises: during Ben 'Ali's era, the Qur'an was banned in many prisons, and prayers were forbidden to take place on time or in groups.[88] Therefore, for transition to be successful the right balance has to be found; the role and influence of religion in state and society have to be defined by the constitution and respected by all sides. The lessons from Egypt should be heeded; the Muslim Brotherhood has been banned and any religious activity is viewed with extreme suspicion by the current authorities. A great advantage for Tunisia in comparison with Egypt is that its Islamic movement, al-Nahda, is more moderate and willing to share

---

[85] Malek Sghiri, "Greetings to the Dawn: Living though the Bittersweet Revolution (Tunisia)," in Layla al-Zubaidi, Matthew Cassel, and Nemonie Craven Roderick (eds.), *Diaries of an Unfinished Revolution: Voices from Tunis to Damascus* (New York: Penguin Books, 2013), p. 18.

[86] Interview with Professor 'Abd al-Jalil al-Tamimi, Tunis, December 17, 2014.

[87] Interview with Mahrazia al-'Abaydi Ma'ayza from al-Nahda Party, Tunis, December 16, 2014.

[88] Al-Tamimi (ed.), *al-Mu'aridun al-siyasiyyun tahta al-ta'dhib fi Tunis*, p. 23.

power. Its leader, Sheikh Rached al-Ghannouchi, has emphasized *al-tawafiq* (harmony) rather than conflict, and the need for coexistence between secularists and Islamists.[89]

Economically, Tunisia has to address the challenges in a system fundamentally different from past practices of clientelism and corruption. Muhammad Ghannouchi, who was not only prime minister but also in charge of economic development during the decade before the revolution, believes that the problem of unemployment began when Tunisia was far more successful in educating its youth than in creating job opportunities for them. According to him, in 1994 the percentage of unemployment among the educated was about 4.6 percent, but by 2000 it exceeded 30 percent.[90] The failure stemmed in part from not adapting the education system to suit the needs of the country, which also happens in other countries in the region, where technical and engineering schools do not attract enough students, because most find jobs in the public sector unrelated to their degrees. Because wealth is concentrated in the capital, Tunis, and along the eastern coast, Ghannouchi admitted that his government and its predecessors had ignored the development of the hinterland. Only in 2010 was investment directed to the inland regions that suffer from high levels of poverty.

The reality was that Tunisia's economy was underperforming even before the 2011 revolution. According to one report, misguided policies led to "glaring misallocation of resources. Four-fifths of Tunisia's workforce is employed in low productivity sectors."[91] Muhammad Ghannouchi acknowledged that corruption was a major impediment, and that those close to President Ben 'Ali, such as his wife's family, took advantage of their status.[92] An interesting perspective on corruption is given by a member of al-Nahda who was a vice chair of the parliament. She maintains that one of the most damaging aspects in the Arab world is what she termed *al-ghanima* (profit or plunder) from being in authority. In her words, people around those in power expect to benefit, and even her own family was upset with her because she

---

[89] Interview with Sheikh Rached al-Ghannouchi, Tunis, December 17, 2014.

[90] According to the 2015 Budget Law, unemployment is estimated at 15.2 percent, while unemployment among those holding academic degrees is 31.4 percent. See "La semaine financière," *La Presse de Tunisie*, December 17, 2014, p. v.

[91] "Tunisia after the Revolution: Spring is Still in the Air," *Economist*, October 25, 2014.

[92] Interview with Muhammad Ghannouchi.

refused to help members of her extended family to get jobs or promotions. Their perception was, "what is the point in being a Member of Parliament or minister if your family cannot benefit?"[93]

Critics of the Islamist movement argued that al-Nahda squandered its time in power and had no experience in handling economic issues. Asked about the economic problems facing the country, al-Nahda leader Rached al-Ghannouchi emphasized that without stability, these problems cannot be addressed, and that his party focused on creating stability. Interestingly, senior members of the Nida' Party repeated to me the same theme about stability, because it would attract investment and create jobs. The problem, of course, is more of a vicious circle: no stability, no investment, and no new jobs; on the other hand, not solving economic problems creates instability and exacerbates unemployment. Ben Achour, like many others in Tunisia, is critical of al-Nahda; in his opinion the party lacks experience in managing the country, as most of its senior members were either in exile for many years or in Ben 'Ali's jails. Furthermore, al-Nahda's policy was seen as disastrous during the Troika, when al-Nahda, together with al-Takattul (Coalition) and the Congress for the Republic, ran the country after the first elections. While some of these criticisms are valid and al-Nahda was too eager to get rid of the old guard (for example, most governors were replaced), leaving a huge vacuum in managing the country, the big positive was that al-Nahda took an important step – one that the Muslim Brotherhood in Egypt shied away from – in forming a coalition with secularist parties.

Transitional justice and coping with the past are burning issues for all countries undergoing transition, as we have seen. In the words of one senior member of the Nahda Party, Mrs. Mahrazia al-'Abaydi Ma'ayza, there must be a confrontation with the past; those who committed crimes against the Tunisian people must acknowledge their crimes and ask for forgiveness. However, al-Nahda voted against *al-'azl al-siyasi* (political exclusion). As the head of the Nahda told me, his party is against the politics of vengeance, having witnessed the catastrophic consequences of de-Ba'thification in Iraq and the waves of revenge that led to Libya's collapse. Intriguingly, the Libyans after the toppling of Qaddafi were also wary of the Iraqi experience and its disastrous results.[94]

[93] Interview with Mahrazia al-'Abaydi Ma'ayza.
[94] Martin, "The United Nations' Role in the First Year of Transition," p. 129.

Rached al-Ghannouchi posited that rejection of revenge is the lesser evil, as the alternative is civil war and social chaos. Hence he strongly supports the policy of harmonization rather than revenge.[95] Interestingly, the opposition party, Nida' Tunis, agrees with this policy. As one senior member, Ben Achour, reiterated, there is "no place for rummaging into the past." In his view, anyone can rejoin the political activities of any party unless they have committed criminal offences such as embezzlement. Indeed, many of the powerful figures under Ben 'Ali have been returning home from prison, and some are finding their way back into politics.[96] The best example, of course, is Béji Caïd Essebsi, the country's president since December 2014, who was himself at one point interior minister under Ben 'Ali. Transitional justice is also intertwined with the collective memory of the past, a pertinent point for this book with its focus on memoirs and memories of the past. Research on transitional justice and changing memories in three countries from central Europe – the Czech Republic, Hungary, and Poland – show that "the past is a function of the present," and that obstacles to transition are not due to the past but more to how they are represented "by present political forces and policies."[97]

Although the two camps appear to hold similar positions, there is a fundamental gap in perception between them. Al-Nida' is willing simply to allow people from the security services and Interior Ministry to return to normal life, ideally with no discussion of the past. Al-Nahda, on the other hand, while not calling for blanket revenge, wants to see some of those who committed torture being named and their crimes discussed. In this they are not alone. A number of academics, such as 'Abd al-Jalil al-Tamimi through his foundation, have launched a series of conferences and collected dozens of testimonies of political prisoners from across the spectrum. With the help of some international organizations, such as Mémorial Berlin, these collections are a harbinger of genuine transitional justice in Tunisia. The fact that political prisoners,

---

[95] Interview with Sheikh Rached al-Ghannouchi.

[96] Carlotta Gall, "Questions of Justice in Tunisia as Ousted Leaders are Freed," *New York Times*, July 16, 2014. According to this report, the interior minister and the head of the security service have been released while the former secretary-general of the defunct governing party, RCD, has returned to politics and is actually assisting the newly elected President Essebsi.

[97] Roman David, "Transitional Justice and Changing Memories of the Past in Central Europe," *Government and Opposition*, vol. 50 (January 2015), pp. 40–41.

be they Islamists or leftists, are willing to come forward to discuss in proper forums what happened to them and to give the names of their torturers, signals real progress in healing the country from half a century of repression and torture. Another positive sign is that the screening of a recent film depicting the torture of Islamists during the 1990s initially encountered opposition, but word soon spread and newspapers began openly commenting on it and interviewing its director.[98] Consecutive governments after the revolution have refused to open any archives, even those relating to independence. Admitting the mistakes of the past must be the first step in reversing this horrendous disease of denial and refusal that has plagued Tunisia and the other authoritarian Arab countries since their independence. As one activist arrested and tortured under both Bourguiba and Ben 'Ali pleaded in his testimony:

At the end of the day, I have only one request for the torturers and those responsible for administering torture to commit to stop this repulsive method. Bourguiba used the men of France and Ben 'Ali used the men of Bourguiba, and in order that the new regime would not use the men of Ben 'Ali, let the executioners admit to their deeds. I read memoirs [of senior people] and no one admits torture, but surely they knew about it. Let the people know about it so we can build democracy and freedom based on proper principles.[99]

Another testimony echoes the view that everyone in Tunisia knew about torture, not just the security services and Ministry of Interior. It points the finger at the medical profession, whose doctors force-fed prisoners when they went on hunger strike; and the journalists who heard about what was happening in the cells but ignored it. Remarkably, the testimony indicates that the only person who was willing to admit torture publicly was Bourguiba himself. When a group of released activists and ex-prisoners met him in June 1980, he told them: "I do not want them to torture my children." But then

---

[98] *Conflit* [Conflict], directed by Moncef Barbouch (Tunisia: Quinta Distributions 2014); see also comments in *La Presse*, January 29, 2015: "À la découverte de *Conflit*, film sur l'oppression des Islamistes en Tunisie" [In Discovering *Conflit*, a film about the oppression of Islamists in Tunisia].

[99] Hama al-Hamami, "al-Ta'dhib fi 'ahday Bourguiba wa Ben 'Ali: shahada shakhsiyya" [Torture in the eras of Bourguiba and Ben 'Ali: a personal testimony,] in al-Tamimi (ed.), *Dirasat wa shahadat*, p. 130. Al-Hamami was first arrested in 1972 as a student activist.

proceeded to justify torture by informing them: "They tortured you to get information because you were very stubborn."[100]

One report summed up this central test by defining the challenge for Tunisian authorities as "how to assert control over the size and mandate of the internal security services without creating a backlash or hollowing out capacity."[101] Hence, while Tunisia has been exceptional, particularly in comparison to Iraq, Libya, Yemen, and to a large extent Egypt, a difficult path lies ahead. Economic issues, transitional justice, reconciliation with the past, and cohabitation between Islamists and secularists are all challenges for the country in the next two to three years. The role of Tunisia's neighbors, particularly Algeria, will be critical, given Algeria's powerful stance against Islamists and its economic importance to Tunisia. Finally, the chaos in Libya is another worrying aspect for Tunisia's leaders because of the porous borders between the two countries.

Conclusion

The leaders of the republics under study obstructed any potential opposition by centralizing all decisions and fermenting and exploiting divisions whenever possible. When these centralized states collapsed, there were few structures that could replace them or that could be utilized in restoring social cohesion. Thus transition became a difficult process. Destabilizing consequences for the transition and democratization process are varied: the role of the military and the security services; the political economy of inequality and corruption; and the conflict about the role of religion. Whether in Brazil, Chile, or the Arab world, each consequence will continue to influence the outcome of a successful transition.[102] European countries experiencing transitions

---

[100] Al-Sadiq Ben Mahni, "Intiba'at masirat munadil" [Impressions from the life of an activist], in al-Tamimi (ed.), *Dirasat wa shahadat*, pp. 118–19.

[101] Alex Arieff and Carla E. Humud, *Political Transition in Tunisia* (Washington: Congressional Research Service, October 22, 2014).

[102] See, for example, a comparison of seven southern European and South American countries, and why Brazil has experienced the most difficulty in consolidating democracy, in Juan J. Linz and Alfred Stepan, *Problems of Democratic Transition and Consolidation: Southern Europe, South America, and Post-Communist Europe* (Baltimore: Johns Hopkins University Press, 1996), pp. 166–89. The seven countries in southern Europe and South America

have enjoyed one huge benefit unavailable to any of these Arab countries: the possibility of future entry into the European Union and the massive aid given by Europe to integrate their new members economically and politically. Yet, even in countries like Spain, forty years after the death of the dictator Franco, people are still confronting their past, and victims argue that while they agree with the concept of reconciliation, they do not want just to turn the page on the past.[103] Tunisia has been fortunate, at least until now, that the military stayed out of politics for most of the last five decades; but its security services are powerful, and could resume their nefarious activities. Time will tell whether the post-authoritarian republics will be able to fundamentally subdue the security services whose activities have dominated the lives of the Arab peoples during the last four decades.

It should also be underscored that the emphasis on democracy by the West, and especially the United States, was always somewhat misplaced. Free voting is important, but it is only one of several essential elements in a democratic society. Iraq showed after the fall of Saddam Hussein that although its people can vote relatively freely, they are still doomed to be governed under a corrupt and quasi-authoritarian system. No real development of strong democratic institutions or an independent judiciary took place in the decade after the overthrow of the Ba'th regime.

Transitions are by nature "uncertain in their outcome," as Daniel Brumberg explains, since this is "partly a function of nonstructural or random factors such as the elite's skills and choices."[104] Therefore, we need to consider the nature of revolutions, and whether what we are witnessing in the Arab world marks the beginning of a long and arduous path until these countries become more open and free, or whether it is just a period of instability and conflict until another authoritarian regime takes over. The French Revolution and other revolutions underwent a tortuous path until their countries achieved a broad-based democracy. Although serious crises, whether social, economic, or political, plagued the great revolutions in France,

---

compared by the authors are: Spain, Portugal, Greece, Uruguay, Brazil, Argentina, and Chile.

[103] Jim Yardley, "Facing his Torturer as Spain Confronts its Past," *New York Times*, April 7, 2014.

[104] Daniel Brumberg, "Theories of Transition," in Lynch (ed.), *The Arab Uprisings Explained*, p. 35.

Russia, and China, they "culminated in fundamental and enduring social transformations."[105] In other words, "democratic transitions are often violent and lengthy."[106] State building takes a long time, and is riven by upheavals and turbulence, and thus it is possible that we might be seeing an opening chapter in these Arab uprisings.

[105] Theda Skocpol, *States and Social Revolutions: A Comparative Analysis of France, Russia, and China* (New York: Cambridge University Press, 1979), p. 161. See also James Defronzo, *Revolutions and Revolutionary Movements*, 5th edn. (Boulder, CO: Westview Press, 2015). This edition has a chapter on the Arab Revolution of 2011.

[106] "Has the Arab Spring Failed?" *Economist*, July 13, 2014.

Conclusion

The challenging question of whether dictatorship is beneficial for people economically or socially has long been argued by political economists. What is clear, as one of them observed, is that "dictators have a great capacity for *action*, good or bad."[1] Dictators can declare war, raise taxes, or introduce far-reaching social measures without much opposition. Some see strong executive power as a key reason for the economic success of Singapore and other East Asian countries. But prosperity was not the outcome in the eight republics studied here after three or four decades of authoritarian rule.

Although some dictators introduced significant social and educational reforms, such as improving the status of women, making education compulsory, and upgrading health services and infrastructure, the overall balance sheet of the "social contract" between leaders and citizens for the six decades preceding the Arab uprising was negative. Furthermore, much of the progress achieved was obliterated by military conflicts and civil wars in most of these countries, for which a heavy economic and social price was paid. National resources were diverted to the military and the security apparatus rather than toward strengthening the initial reforms. Thus, in reviewing the history of tyranny in the Arab world, it would be almost impossible to come up with a positive scorecard for the dictators' policies. On the contrary, the catalogue of almost unmitigated disasters in all spheres is probably too long to list. What is evident is that these rulers did not respect the basics of the social contract with their people, and the engine of growth in their economies was very weak compared to the vitality of many other developing countries in Latin America or South-East Asia. The progress made in these Arab republics during the last half-century was mostly thanks to oil, remittances, or aid; not a recipe for a healthy economy.

[1] Wintrobe, *The Political Economy of Dictatorship*, p. 338.

At the beginning of this book I raised several questions about the anatomy of these authoritarian regimes. The first referred to their common denominators. These regimes shared most of the principal features of other authoritarian and totalitarian regimes outside the region, which can be summed up as:

(1) politicizing all state institutions under the auspices of a ruling party, including political control of the military;
(2) consolidating power and suppressing freedoms through wars, military conflicts, and fighting terrorism (Tunisia is a key exception);
(3) utilizing elections and referendums as tools to perpetuate the regimes, rather than allowing free political participation and contestation;
(4) infringing on the daily lives of citizens by penetrating the society through a wide web of informants, and harshly repressing all opposition;
(5) managing and exploiting the economy as a vehicle for increasing support and allocating benefits;
(6) centralizing decision making, sometimes complemented by a personality cult around the leader.[2]

A second question was about the role of the coercive organizations and whether this has changed over the years. Although the security apparatus and the military in these republics underwent many changes in response to wars, internal military conflicts, and shifts in the internal opposition throughout these decades, their fundamental tenets did not alter significantly. Repression, arrests, torture, and fear underwent different cycles and fluctuated from one country to another, but overall they remained deeply entrenched in the system. This leads to the third question, about the legacy of these authoritarian regimes and their institutions. The fissures we are witnessing in 2015 across most of these republics are largely due to the divisive legacy of these regimes. Most of the leaders kept the state institutions weak while consolidating their personal hold on power. A look at countries such as Libya, Yemen, and, to a large extent, Syria confirms this finding.

---

[2] An interesting list of totalitarian characteristics was presented in a study of George Orwell's famous book *1984* in Hermann Lübbe, "The Historicity of Totalitarianism: George Orwell's Evidence," in Maier (ed.), *Concepts for the Comparison of Dictatorships*, pp. 247–52.

The fourth, a hypothetical question, was about the possible return of authoritarianism and cults of personality. Huntington argued, based on the wave of democratization in the late twentieth century that "authoritarian nostalgia" was not prevalent in harsh authoritarian regimes.[3] However, the experience of some of the Arab republics such as Iraq, Libya, and Yemen that witnessed violence and mayhem indicate that the people in these countries are actually "nostalgic" for a return to order and security, and the old-style authoritarianism provided that to a large extent. The Arab world seems desperate for strong leaders whose appeal is their supposed ability to deliver security and prosperity to their people. While Iraq's authoritarianism was not brought down by the masses, as in the other republics that experienced the Arab uprising, it soon returned with a different face. Under the cover of elections and free voting, Iraq's prime minister for eight years, Nuri al-Maliki, managed to rebuild coercive institutions and to create a loyal inner circle in return for granting them staggering economic benefits, but then he could not provide the order and security that the Iraqi people desperately desired. In fact, leaders such as al-Maliki inflamed sectarian tensions that led to even more violence. Iraq under al-Maliki meets many of the criteria to be considered a competitive authoritarian regime.[4] In Egypt it is still too early to declare whether the new president, Sisi, will reinstitute authoritarianism or a cult of personality, but the signs are far from encouraging two years after his rise to power.

In the Arab world, there is no doubt that republics and monarchies share many characteristics, and both could be called authoritarian. Neither have truly free elections. Both, with varying degrees, resort to security apparatuses to co-opt or repress their opponents, and the army is vital for their internal security. Economic patronage and corruption prevail both in monarchies and republics, although with varying intensity. Finally, both use the war on terror as a means to fight and subdue their internal opposition. The notion that monarchies have enjoyed more legitimacy for historical reasons is feeble at best. Most of the monarchies have employed their large wealth from oil and natural gas to overcome demands for reform. This is true even for less wealthy kingdoms, like Jordan, in that these demands have been "backstopped

---

[3] Huntington, *The Third Wave*, pp. 256–57.
[4] Steven Levitsky and Lucan A. Way, *Competitive Authoritarianism: Hybrid Regimes after the Cold War* (New York: Cambridge University Press, 2010).

by their wealthier allies."[5] A striking example of monarchies "purchasing" loyalty was in Saudi Arabia, where almost $32 billion was handed out in bonuses and grants to government employees and a wide range of organizations after the coronation of King Salman, the new monarch, in 2015. Another similarity is the large public sector in monarchies and republics; in Saudi Arabia it is estimated that 3 million people out of a 5.5 million workforce are government employees.[6]

As mentioned in the Introduction, this book did not include monarchies mainly for practical reasons such as the rarity of memoirs, and the overwhelming amount of material to add to a manuscript already covering eight countries. However, it should also be said that the monarchies of the Arab world exhibit a wide range of governance styles, not all of which readily lend themselves to comparison with the authoritarian republics. For example, Saudi Arabia has no ruling party or effective legislature, making its style of authoritarianism difficult to compare systematically to the republics. On the other hand, some monarchies such as Kuwait, Jordan, and Morocco have embraced a relatively more open system with their political institutions, and are somewhat less authoritarian than the countries examined in this book.[7] Other differences lie in the functionality of the key actors of the state. For instance, scholars such as Springborg have highlighted the differences in character and structure of the militaries in republics and monarchies by pointing out that republican militaries have "a greater propensity to be engaged in the productive economy either as a corporate institution or in the form of individual officers."[8]

[5] F. Gregory Gause, III, *Kings for All Seasons: How the Middle East Monarchies Survived the Arab Spring*, Brookings Doha Center Analysis Paper, Number 8, September 2013. The report discusses in detail the strategies adopted by different monarchies in response to the fallout of the uprisings in certain republics. See also Steve A. Yetiv, "Oil, Saudi Arabia, and the Spring that Has Not Come," in Mark L. Haas and David W. Lesch (eds.), *The Arab Spring: Change and Resistance in the Middle East* (Boulder, CO: Westview Press, 2013), pp. 97–115; Curtis R. Ryan, "Jordan and the Arab Spring," in Haas and Lesch (eds.), *The Arab Spring*, pp. 116–30.

[6] Ben Hubbard, "Saudi King Unleashes a Torrent as Bonuses Flow to the Masses," *New York Times*, February 20, 2015.

[7] See discussion of this topic in Michael Herb, *All in the Family: Absolutism, Revolution, and Democracy in the Middle Eastern Monarchies* (Albany: State University of New York Press, 1999).

[8] Robert Springborg "Arab Militaries," in Lynch (ed.), *The Arab Uprisings Explained*, p. 149.

What can we learn from these memoirs? The first, and probably most pertinent, revelation that emerges from studying a half-century of memoirs from these eight republics is the utter lack of accountability and the unwillingness to admit failure or bad policies. It is shocking that almost no one was, or is, willing to take responsibility for anything that happened while they were in power as senior officials. Libya in the aftermath of Qaddafi is an egregious example: none of its high-ranking officials who fled the country as the end of the regime loomed, or those who were among its inner circle, is willing to accept any blame for the violent contortions that Libya underwent. Like many other former members of Qaddafi's regime, 'Abd al-Salam Jallud, one of the leader's closest associates, blamed Qaddafi and his two sons for the disastrous path taken by the country. He shows no sign of regret, nor does he make any admission of personal failure. These former Libyan officials also do not explain why they allowed a leader whom they characterized as "irrational" to remain in power. For example, they recount that Qaddafi once stormed out of a meeting of the Revolutionary Command Council, announced his resignation, and headed to Cairo where he stayed for two weeks, threatening never to return. Rather than use this opportunity to get rid of him, they waited for him to cool down and return to the leadership two weeks later.[9] The point here is that no matter how revered a leader may be, the dynamics of leadership is such that it is impossible to stay at the top without the acquiescence and support of others.

Egyptian generals after the crushing defeat of 1967 blamed either other generals or the political leaders, even though some of them were in charge of the front. Similarly, a senior Egyptian responsible for running the state television, and who wrote his memoirs after the fall of Mubarak, either justified some of the actions of the previous regime – including during the first days of the uprising – or presented certain events in a way that leaves the reader to decide which version to accept.[10] Another facet of the lack of accountability is deflecting the blame to external powers. For instance, five years after the fall of Saddam Hussein, the Iraqi ambassador to Washington during the invasion of Kuwait still blames outside forces such as the USA and the Zionists for

---

[9] See interview with 'Abd al-Mun'im al-Huni in Sharbal, *Fi khaymat al-Qaddafi*, pp. 147–48. The incident took place in 1972.
[10] El-Manawy, *Tahrir: The Last 18 Days of Mubarak*.

"trapping Iraq into a war" that ended disastrously for his country. He refuses to discuss how he represented Iraq and its leader when they were attacking an Arab neighbor that was not threatening Iraq's security or its borders.[11] Even writers and intellectuals preferred to blame outside forces and avoid analyzing the internal situation that led to such political and economic decay.[12] A more balanced approach comes in a memoir by a Yemeni politician, who wrote:

> In spite of all the demonstrations, coups, revolutions, and sacrifices, our state of affairs in Yemen and the Arab world is bad, bad as everyone admits so. Who is responsible for that?
>
> No doubt we all made mistakes and avoided the truth. Otherwise we would not be in this situation. If everyone insists that he is correct and others are to be blamed, this is self-delusion, escapism, and avoiding finding a way out of this crisis [we live in].[13]

A second feature that emerges from these memoirs is the presence of fear, which indirectly could be an excuse or a factor in the unwillingness of senior officials to shoulder any responsibility. This fear manifests in the reluctance of authors to even hint at criticism of the leadership or the system while their president is alive. Many waited until the death of their leader to begin writing, and at the same time they assiduously avoid any analysis of the new president. This is particularly true of Egypt, and therefore we discover more interesting aspects of each president only after the death of the previous one. In Syria, where a family dynasty continued, no one dared to criticize Hafiz al-Asad after his death because his son Bashar had succeeded him. Fear is also pervasive in the writings of political prisoners and opponents who suffered immensely in all the republics, and who feared the consequences of disclosure not only for themselves but also for their families. It becomes evident from multiple recollections how these regimes directly or indirectly instilled fear into their societies, from the fear of criticizing high authorities to the fear of admitting responsibility because of the high cost of failure. Fear was also

---

[11] Al-Mashshat, *Kuntu safiran lil-'Iraq*, p. 30.

[12] See, for example, Mansur, *Intaha zaman al-furas al-da'i'a*. Although the book is really about the Camp David Accords, the author finds no fault with Egypt's leaders and maintains that the loss of so many "opportunities" was because of the Jews, Zionists, and the USA. He mocks Arab leaders for their lack of leadership, but does not refer to Mubarak.

[13] Al-'Ayni, *Khamsun 'aman fi al-rimal al-mutaharrika*, p. 11.

evident in the paralysis surrounding economic or political initiatives, in case these should fail or take the glory away from their superiors. The pronouncements by senior Libyan officials after the revolution that Qaddafi had been mentally unbalanced, sexually abusive to women and young men, and a tyrant with a monstrous ego who led his country into catastrophe make one ponder why they balked at trying to put a halt his actions or end his dominance. Was it simply fear for themselves and their families? Of course, it is hard to judge; in shifting blame from themselves, these officials were not unique. Few former regime insiders in the Arab world have ever admitted responsibility for any mistakes their governments made, as the memoirs reveal. More research is needed to understand how this fear operated in the different layers of society and bureaucracy.

As fear receded with the Arab uprisings of 2011, the glaring question is whether it could be revived or, once its hold is broken, is it hard to re-establish a climate of fear? Sadly, the history of post-revolutionary eras tells us that fear can be reintroduced, and already there are signs in Egypt that citizens are becoming more wary of criticizing the government publicly because of the threat of arrest and maltreatment.

A third facet of these memoirs is that all the regimes discussed collected a mass of information about their citizens, and particularly about their opponents, through extensive networks of informants. However, as in other authoritarian regimes, the quantity of information gathered did not necessarily lead to proper action or analysis, in part due to officials' fear of taking initiative or of delivering bad news to the leadership. As mentioned, several memoirs tell us that informants reported the plan to assassinate President Sadat a couple of hours before it took place, but an ossified and very bureaucratic security service prevented the information from reaching the higher echelons and thus saving the president's life. The security organizations, omnipresent and omniscient, looked undefeatable. But in exactly the same manner as in Eastern Europe, they collapsed because they could not fathom what was taking place on the streets. Commenting on how the structure of East Germany crumbled unexpectedly and relatively swiftly, one scholar noted: "A series of accidents, some of them mistakes, so minor that they might otherwise have been trivialities, threw off sparks into the supercharged atmosphere of the autumn of 1989."[14]

---

[14] Sarotte, *The Collapse*, p. xx.

Indeed, political scientists have already written about the unpredictable sparks to revolutions that cannot be controlled. Timur Kuran contends that people who dislike a regime keep their private opinions to themselves, intent on accruing the rewards of public support and wary of the punishments for public dissent. Once there is a surge in opposition, however, those who previously hid their beliefs come out and show strong support to the revolution.[15] What is obvious, whether in the Arab republics or in Iran under the Shah, is that these regimes, however powerful they seemed, were "much less rooted, less embedded in society" than they appeared, and fear alone could not hold back revolt after the governments had failed to deliver economic progress, justice, and social freedoms throughout the decades.[16]

A fourth issue that emerges is the politics of memory. One drawback of these memoirs is the distortion of events, both intentional and unintentional. Some authors embellished their accounts for personal and political gain; others omitted facts simply through lapse of memory, with so many memoirs being written years after the events. After the toppling of Mubarak in Egypt, many political parties and factions took credit for the revolution and carried its symbols for political advantage. A similar reaction took place in Romania, where many crucial facts about what really happened during the tumultuous days that led to the fall of the Ceaușescu regime remained unknown even decades later.[17] In countries like Chile, which transitioned successfully from authoritarianism, scholars are debating "how the politics of memory of the recent past shapes Chile's political community today."[18] Indeed, this is a critical rite of passage if these authoritarian republics are to transition to more open and free societies. The experiences of other countries tell us that collective memory is transformed in the years following the collapse of an

---

[15] Timur Kuran, "Sparks and Prairie Fires: A Theory of Unanticipated Political Revolution," *Public Choice*, vol. 61, no. 1 (April 1989), pp. 41–74.

[16] Theda Skocpol, "Rentier State and Shi'a Islam in the Iranian Revolution," *Theory and Society*, vol. 11, no. 3 (May 1982), p. 268.

[17] Grigore Pop-Eleches, "Romania Twenty Years after 1989: The Bizarre Echoes of a Contested Revolution," in Michael Bernhard and Jan Kubik (eds.), *Twenty Years after Communism: The Politics of Memory and Commemoration* (New York: Oxford University Press, 2014), p. 86.

[18] Katherine Hite, Cath Collins, and Alfredo Joignant, "The Politics of Memory in Chile," in Cath Collins, Katherine Hite, and Alfredo Joignant (eds.), *The Politics of Memory in Chile: From Pinochet to Bachelet* (Boulder, CO: Lynne Rienner, 2013), p. 1.

authoritarian regime. However, as indicated in Chapter 7, when these memories become public, the history of torture, repression, and betrayal that they reveal becomes a trauma that future generations will have to address.

A fifth tenet derived from these memoirs is the lack of attention paid by policy makers and leaders to economic development. Economic management came to the fore mostly when a financial crisis erupted or workers went on strike. Although the system of patronage and corruption existed in non-Arab dictatorships such as Argentina and the Philippines, many countries in Latin America and Asia gradually managed to transition to more open societies and their economic performance improved. In terms of economic management, the policies followed in these Arab republics, including those blessed with natural resources such as Iraq, Libya, and Sudan, were highly incompetent. They were also coupled with costly military adventures, which resulted in weak economic institutions, an enormous waste of resources, and a chronic lack of opportunities for large segments of the population. These conflicts exacted a heavy toll on the region. According to one estimate, "there was a 14 per cent loss in the AW [Arab World] output (GDP) in the immediate aftermath of the first Gulf War."[19]

Patronage had a profound effect not only on economic policies but also on building institutional capacity. In Libya, for example, patronage "made cooperation in communal goals problematic, and created an enormous sense of entitlement."[20] The issue of entitlement surfaces time and again in the recollections of politicians. Oil revenues allowed the leaders of these republics to control their countries by their policy of distributing economic benefits, the price tag of which was allegiance to the regime. This patronage system also operated in the countries not endowed with oil; a combination of remittances and aid enabled their leaders to pursue the same patronage policy. The promise of jobs to graduates was instigated in Egypt by Nasser and spread across the Arab world as an enticement to gain the support of the youth. Patronage and entitlement combined to dilute trust in

---

[19] Ali Kadri, "A Depressive Pre-Arab Uprisings Economic Performance," in Gerges (ed.), *The New Middle East*, p. 86. For a table of the military spending as a percentage of GDP for selected Arab countries, see p. 87. For a table listing selected conflicts and wars in the Arab world between 1948 and 2006, see p. 88.

[20] Dirk Vandewalle, "Libya's Uncertain Revolution," in Cole and McQuinn (eds.), *The Libyan Revolution and its Aftermath*, p. 23.

public institutions in the region, and after the uprisings of 2011, new regimes found out that it was a long haul to restore this trust after decades of abuse. Regimes attempted different policies, but these were not combined with fundamental changes in the structure of state institutions. For instance, President Sadat adopted economic liberalism in the 1970s in the belief that it would change Egypt, but it was a top-down policy, and dictatorship continued to be the method by which the country was managed.

Two topics related to economic policy are institution building and dependence on oil. Overall, the authoritarian systems prevented the development of economic institutions that could be independent, such as central banks. Although finance ministries and central banks managed to recruit a high caliber of economists and university graduates, the final say about monetary and fiscal policy usually rested in the presidential palaces or in consultations between the president and one or two ministers. Powerful interest groups influenced decision making regardless of any economic justification. Given the weakness of these independent institutions and the lack of trust in the state, corruption has increased in these republics over the last two or three decades. If other republics were to follow in Iraq's steps since the overthrow of Saddam Hussein, then one can expect corruption to expand as centralized leadership recedes and fear is relatively reduced.

An interrelated topic is the reliance on oil in some republics and the dependence on rentier income of remittances and aid in others. Unfortunately, over the four decades studied, countries endowed with natural resources have become more dependent on oil both for revenue and exports, and the sector does not provide large employment because it is capital intensive. With oil prices hovering around $45–50 in 2015, the repercussions for the region (not only for oil-exporting countries) are hard to judge, but there is no doubt that there will be cuts in spending and investment, at least in the initial stages.

This leads to one of the most complicated issues facing these republics and the region as a whole: unemployment. Widespread unemployment, poverty and inequality, combined with bulging youth populations, were partially responsible for the uprisings. Daron Acemoglu and James Robinson rightly attribute countries' poverty to the quality of leadership. Countries such as Egypt are poor "because it has been ruled by a narrow elite that have organized society for their own benefit at the expense of the vast mass of people."[21] The inner groups of leaders such as Mubarak, Ben 'Ali, and Qaddafi accumulated vast wealth and paid scant attention to the real economic development of the masses. None of these countries has seriously addressed the thorny issue of unemployment and inequality. Most reverted to expanding their public sectors and relied on heavy subsidies to appease their populations. It is becoming more obvious that this cannot continue, and with possible budgetary constraints on the horizon, new solutions need to be found. In Egypt, these problems are exacerbated by the fact that the army remains a leading economic force with its own financial interests. In other republics, where violence or a lack of stability is prevailing – such as Iraq, Syria, Libya, and Sudan – local and foreign investments have dropped significantly. Rebuilding those countries in the future would absorb a high percentage of the workforce, but the fundamentals of their economies are not changing and are patently not adapting to the demands of the twenty-first century.

Some scholars argue that one reason most Arab nations are monarchical dictatorships or authoritarian republics is "the major role oil and natural gas exports play in their economics and the world economy."[22] The argument is that the United States and Britain, in spite of their pro-democracy rhetoric, did not support democratic political systems, particularly in countries with large energy resources. While it is hard to disagree with this, the fact remains that there were other republics without natural resources that were as tyrannical as those with large reserves of oil and natural gas. First and foremost, there are historical reasons for this: all of these Arab republics were colonies that were left after independence with limited institutional capacity. Second, leadership came mostly from the military, which was not necessarily the best source of leaders who cared more about the future of the people than about staying in power. Third, these countries were strategically significant for both superpowers during the Cold War, not only for their oil but also for their geographic locations. Both the Soviet Union and the United States were intent on expanding their influence in the region at almost any cost, and military dictatorships suited their overall strategies. Military conflicts were not discouraged, as these

---

[21] Daron Acemoglu and James A. Robinson, *Why Nations Fail: The Origins of Power, Prosperity, and Poverty* (New York: Crown Publishers, 2012), p. 3.

[22] DeFronzo, *Revolutions and Revolutionary Movements*, p. 444.

allowed the two superpowers to supply arms and technical aid and thus expand their spheres of influence. Until the fall of communism, these republics engaged in multiple wars against Israel (1948, 1956, 1967, and 1973), and in a war of attrition between Egypt and Israel, mostly during 1969–70. Other wars erupted in that period: the Yemen War in the 1960s had significant political and military consequences for Egypt and Yemen. Another conflict that impacted the whole region was the eight-year Iran–Iraq War, which obliterated Iraq's development of the 1970s. Major internal conflicts, with the two world superpowers (the Soviet Union and the United States) supporting one side or another, took place during those years: Iraq against the Kurds at different times from the late 1960s to the late 1980s, and Syria's battle with Islamists in 1982. Even after the collapse of the Soviet Union, other wars were instigated, Iraq's invasion of Kuwait being the most blatant example. In essence, these conflicts served the Arab regimes by rallying their populations to their side to fight external enemies. I have argued that one of the main reasons why Tunisia is the only republic that appears to be truly transitioning in 2015 is that it was the only one of the eight not engaged in a war or military conflict, and its army stayed out of politics for almost half a century.

Conflicts with Israel undoubtedly affected these regimes, as they had to contend with public pressure to support the Palestinians, but while there was genuine support for the Palestinian cause, it was also manipulated to serve the leaders' interests. Measures toward a more liberal society were repeatedly postponed in countries such as Syria, whose leaders argued that they were in a state of war, even though a ceasefire between Israel and Syria was respected by both sides for almost four decades. Another conflict that had an immense impact on the Arab world was the invasion of Iraq in 2003 by a US-led coalition. Instability in Iraq and the spread of sectarianism across the region propelled violence to unprecedented levels. Finally, the war that these regimes launched against Islamist groups became intertwined with the "War on Terror" initiated by the USA after the 9/11 attacks. Unfortunately, the rise of extremist groups such as the Islamic State will reinforce this linkage, and in some countries fighting terror will become indistinguishable from oppressing and controlling their opponents.

To bring authoritarianism to an end in these Arab republics and deal with its roots is no easy task. The experience of other countries teaches us that it is a long process full of danger and resistance to change. This book began with the treatise on tyranny by al-Kawakibi, *Taba'i' al-istibdad*, written more than a century ago. It is only appropriate to conclude with his advice on how the successful removal of despotism is governed by certain principles; in particular:

(1) Despotism must not be fought with violence. It must be fought gradually and with gentleness.
(2) Before fighting despotism, its replacement must be ready.[23]

Elaborating further, he wrote:

A people that have been abased for so long that [it] has become like animals or worse, will absolutely not demand liberty. It might avenge itself on the despot, but this will be only with the purpose of taking revenge on him [the leader], and not in order to get rid of despotism. This will not benefit such a people for it will be exchanging one disease for another.[24]

Having emphasized that revolutions need aims and objectives beyond just getting rid of authoritarian leaders, he correctly predicted: "Otherwise confusion and a destructive civil war will result, and the victory will go to the despot. The objectives of resistance, therefore, must be made public, and the people must be won over to them." Summing up the structure of authoritarianism, al-Kawakibi concluded: "Despotism is surrounded and supported by forces of all kinds: terror, the army, especially when it is a foreign army; the power of wealth and the wealthy; foreign support; men of religion, and the inertia of the common people."[25]

Al-Kawakibi's insightful analysis can easily be applied to conditions in the eight republics studied here. In essence, three republics – Libya, Syria, and Yemen – are enduring destructive civil wars, and confusion is even more rife by late 2015. Terror, army involvement, and the intervention of foreign powers are all present, as al-Kawakibi anticipated more than a century ago. Foreign support and a lethal intertwining of religion and state are crushing the ideals of more open, free, and equal societies that inspired the uprisings five years ago. In the name of religion, and with a determination to recreate a caliphate that existed

---

[23] Al-Kawakibi, *Taba'i' al-istibdad*, p. 143. Translation of the quote is from al-Husry, *Three Reformers*, p. 67.
[24] Ibid., p. 144; translation from al-Husry, *Three Reformers*, p. 67.
[25] Ibid., p. 146; translation from al-Husry, *Three Reformers*, p. 68.

more than a thousand years ago, horrendous acts are being committed against civilian populations and minorities.

In Libya, an unraveling of the country is taking place and chaos is prevailing. Describing the state of Libya in early 2015, a seasoned journalist put it: "Two competing governments claim legitimacy. Armed militias roam the streets. The electricity is frequently out of service, and most business is at standstill; revenues from oil ... have dwindled by more than ninety percent ... What has followed the downfall of a tyrant– a downfall encouraged by NATO air strikes– is the tyranny of a dangerous and pervasive instability."[26] In Syria, the civil war continues unabated and estimates of more than 250,000 casualties were reported by mid 2015, with roughly 11 million being displaced from their homes, including 5 million people who fled the country to seek refuge, mostly in neighboring countries. In Yemen, the Houthis – Zaydis affiliated with Shi'ism – had overpowered their opponents by early 2015 and succeeded in controlling the capital, San'a'. The existing weak state ceased to function and the country is in dire straits. In March 2015, Saudi Arabia launched a war against the Houthis to reestablish the government of Mansur Hadi, who fled the capital as the Houthis advanced. Attempting to stem "the Iranian influence," the Saudis are bringing the region into a wider conflict of sectarianism. Yemen is the poorest among the eight republics and has long suffered from instability. Its population growth of 3.2 percent a year stresses its limited resources.[27] In each of these three countries, chaos has paralyzed the economy and will impact its people for years to come, even after some semblance of order is restored. A further critical factor that might exacerbate conditions and could trigger a large displacement is the scarcity of water. According to a United Nations report, Yemen could be the first country in the world that could run out of drinking water given its chronic shortages.[28] A serious aggravating factor not only in Yemen but in other countries is that more than ever across the region, "non-state actors increasingly set the agenda,

---

[26] Jon Lee Anderson, "Letter from Libya: The Unravelling," *New Yorker*, February 23 and March 2, 2015, p. 110.

[27] For background on Yemen's problems and the rise of authoritarianism of 'Ali Salih, see Isa Blumi, *Chaos in Yemen: Societal Collapse and the New Authoritarianism* (New York: Routledge, 2011).

[28] "Yemen: Time Running Out for Solution to Water Crisis," Integrated Regional Information Networks (IRIN), August 13, 2012.

challenging governments, overthrowing them or prompting them to retrench behind increasingly repressive controls."[29]

A fourth republic, Iraq, is also in the midst of a battle against the Islamic State of Iraq and the Levant (ISIL), and sectarianism still dominates the country. Violent attacks and suicide bombs have lessened from their peak of a few years ago but the toll on civilians is still high. The advance of ISIL in northern Iraq forced Prime Minister al-Maliki to resign, but he remains influential in the country given his control of parts of the security apparatus and his deep connections to some of the militias. It remains to be seen whether the new prime minister will try to reduce sectarianism. The decline in oil prices will substantially impact Iraq, which still derives 98 percent of its revenues from oil. More than a decade after the invasion, the country has not been able to diversify its sources of income or find employment for its youth outside the public sector, even with a huge cash flow from oil.

Sudan is fighting again in the south, away from world attention, and its soldiers continue their savage attacks on South Sudan. Reports of rape and displacement are flowing out, and one report described the southern Sudanese economy as in "intensive care given its grim situation."[30] Meanwhile, high internal and external deficits coupled with international sanctions continue to affect the Sudanese economy, and an oil price collapse will further cut into economic growth. In April 2015, 'Omar al-Bashir engineered another win in the presidential elections with 94 percent of the votes, and his ruling party, the National Congress, took about 76 percent of the seats in the parliament.

Algeria is relatively out of the limelight since its "elections" in 2014 that allowed Bouteflika to stay in power, as he has been since 1999. The president is not seen much in public because of his deteriorating health. Once again, the drop in oil prices will weaken the Algerian economy, given its dependence on oil revenues. Already a hiring freeze in the public sector has been announced and several large projects, including urban tramways, postponed. Yet Algeria is showing signs of relative

---

[29] "The Rule of the Gunman," *Economist*, October 11, 2014.

[30] James Copnall, "South Sudan Economy in 'Intensive Care' as Famine Looms," BBC, July 9, 2014. See also Somini Sengupta, "Soldiers from Sudan Raped Hundreds in Darfur, Human Rights Group Finds," *New York Times*, February 11, 2015.

progress: the economy grew at more than 3 percent in 2013 and official statistics of unemployment indicated a drop to under 10 percent.[31]

Egypt's story of the 2011 revolution is not over yet. Books and articles will continue to be written,[32] and memoirs about the days of revolution and their aftermath will be published. What is clear is that the dramatic overthrow of the elected president, Muhammad Morsi, and the rise of President Sisi with the full support of the army was just another chapter in the history of Egypt's revolution. The role of the military has been glorified for almost six decades, allowing it to accumulate political and economic influence. This "sacred" role of the military and its positioning as an impartial referee did not reduce authoritarianism in the country. The army resented the rise of Mubarak's son Gamal, who was from outside the military, and begrudged the corruption of his coterie. Many questions loom without definite answers in late 2015: What will be the fate of the Muslim Brotherhood, now that it has been outlawed and suppressed? Will the economic situation under Sisi, with the colossal financial support of Saudi Arabia, ameliorate the living conditions of millions of Egyptians? Will Egypt's fight against extreme groups in Sinai and Libya lead to embroilment in a new military conflict? Will fear return to the millions who demonstrated and fought against Mubarak? Time will tell. As a piece of graffiti in Cairo asks: "Do you remember the tomorrow that never came?"[33]

The sole glimmer of hope among those eight republics is Tunisia, the only country that is moving away from authoritarianism. A new coalition government was formed after the presidential elections that includes a few members of al-Nahda. The new parliament, the Assembly of the People's Representatives (ARP), comprises 69 percent men and 31 percent women, and there are 9 women out of a total of 38 ministers and state secretaries. These are positive signs for the improved status of women in governing Tunisia, and the figures are much higher than in other Arab countries. Other positive signs are the numerous publications and documentaries discussing the past and analyzing the traumas of

---

[31] Tariq Benbahmed, "Algeria 2014," available at www.africaneconomicoutlook .org, accessed February 12, 2015.

[32] See, for example, Thanassis Cambanis, *Once upon a Revolution: An Egyptian Story* (New York: Simon & Schuster, 2015).

[33] Graffiti described by Cambanis in *Once upon a Revolution*, p. vii. See also review of the book: Patrick Cockburn, "Tomorrow Never Came," *New York Times Book Review*, February 15, 2015, p. 19.

repression. Alas, such encouraging signals will have to be in tandem with boosting economic growth, not only in the more developed coastlands but also in rural areas, which have suffered neglect and low investment for the last four decades. It is hoped that Europe, in spite of its own economic difficulties, can increase its investments in Tunisia, thereby creating more job opportunities. There is no doubt that Tunisians across the political spectrum felt immensely proud in October 2015 when the Nobel Peace Prize was awarded to the National Dialogue Quartet for its role in the democratization process and the dialogue it conducted between Islamists and secular parties. The quartet, a coalition of labor union leaders, businesspeople, lawyers, and human rights activists, managed to conduct talks among the different factions in Tunisia amidst the deepening political and economic crisis in 2013.

Looking ahead, one cannot help but reflect on the spreading violence in the region, and its trajectory seems to be rising either along sectarian lines (Iraq, Syria, and Yemen), or in fighting Islamist extremists in the form of ISIL and al-Qaʿida. Violence, as Hannah Arendt indicated, has played a huge role in human affairs throughout history.[34] Violence in the Arab region has its roots in colonialism, in military conflicts, and in a widely imposed authoritarianism that has employed every means possible to stay in power. Violence was entrenched in these republics: against opposition, real or imaginary; against minorities such as the Kurds; and against Islamist groups.

It would be wrong, however, to conclude that the regimes in these eight republics endured only through repression and violence. All of them perfected the use of public sector jobs and the allocation of subsidies as core features in their strategy to obtain popular support, while enriching a small network of supporters in return for their active loyalty. It is highly likely that contestations in the region will continue, particularly with diminishing state resources as a result of depressed oil prices.[35] Labor unrest could surface again if more job opportunities do not open up, and activism for more freedom will most likely continue, aided by social media.

---

[34] Hannah Arendt, "A Special Supplement: Reflections on Violence," *New York Review of Books*, February 27, 1969.

[35] Two edited volumes are very informative about contestation and contentious politics: Beinin and Vairel (eds.), *Social Movements, Mobilization, and Contestation*; and Albrecht (ed.), *Contentious Politics*.

Delving deeper into the phenomenon of authoritarianism, its roots, mechanisms, repressive apparatus, and implications for future generations needs to continue. Already a dialogue has begun among scholars to analyze the events of the uprisings in light of studies conducted in the preceding two decades.[36] After suffering long, cruel years of tyranny, the people of these republics deserve to live in more free and equal societies, and a commitment to increasing our understanding of these regimes is another step toward that goal.

---

[36] See, for example, Marc Morjé Howard and Meir R. Walters, "Explaining the Unexpected: Political Science and the Surprises of 1989 and 2011," *Perspectives on Politics*, vol. 12, no. 12 (June 2014), pp. 394–408, and the responses of Eva Bellin, Ellen Lust, and Marc Lynch to Howard and Walters' reflections, pp. 409–16; and finally Howard and Walters' response to the three critics, pp. 417–19.

Appendix: Timeline of major events in the Arab republics

Algeria

1963: Ahmed Ben Bella becomes president following independence from France.

1965: Houari Boumediene overthrows Ahmed Ben Bella and becomes president.

1978: Boumediene dies and Chadhli Bendjedid becomes president in early 1979. He remains in office until 1992.

1992: • The Islamic Salvation Front wins electoral victories in the general election.
  • The military pressures President Bendjedid to resign, a state of emergency is declared, and the Islamic Salvation Front is forced to dissolve.
  • A military council assumes authority.
  • An insurgency begins, and fighting continues throughout the 1990s.

1994: Liamine Zeroual is elected president.

1999: 'Abd al-'Aziz Bouteflika is elected president.

2011: Small uprisings take place in Algeria in response to the large uprisings taking place in Tunisia, Egypt, Syria and elsewhere in the Arab world.

2014: Bouteflika becomes president for a fourth term at age 77 with 81 percent of the vote.

Egypt

1948: War between the new state of Israel and Arab nations (Egypt, Jordan, Syria, and Iraq).

1952:   • Egyptian Free Officers, led by Gamal 'Abd al-Nasser, overthrow the monarchy.
        • Muhammad Neguib serves as the first president.

1954:   'Abd al-Nasser puts Muhammad Neguib under house arrest and takes over as president.

1956:   'Abd al-Nasser nationalizes the Suez Canal. Britain, France, and Israel invade Egypt. The United States and the Soviet Union intervene, and a ceasefire is signed.

1958:   Syria and Egypt form a union called the United Arab Republic.

1961:   The United Arab Republic dissolves when Syria withdraws from the Union.

1962:   Egypt intervenes in the Yemeni Civil War to support the People's Democratic Republic of Yemen (South Yemen).

1967:   Israel defeats Egypt, Jordan, and Syria in the Six-Day War. Israel occupies Egypt's Sinai Peninsula.

1970:   'Abd al-Nasser dies; Anwar al-Sadat becomes president.

1973:   Syria and Egypt declare war on Israel. Egypt uses the war to begin negotiations for a peace treaty and a return of the Sinai Peninsula.

1979:   Sadat signs a peace treaty with Israel at Camp David.

1981:   Sadat assassinated by Islamists. Hosni Mubarak becomes president.

2011:   • Large-scale popular uprisings take place in Egypt. Mubarak is removed from power.
        • The Muslim Brotherhood wins a majority of parliamentary seats in elections in November.

2012:   Muhammad Morsi is elected president.

2013:   Following mass protests, the military removes Morsi from office and places him under arrest.

2014:   'Abd al-Fattah al-Sisi is elected president.

Iraq

1948:   War between the new state of Israel and Arab nations (Egypt, Jordan, Syria, and Iraq).

1958:   'Abd al-Karim Qasim overthrows the Hashemite royal family in Iraq in a coup.

1963:
- The Iraqi Ba'th Party overthrows 'Abd al-Karim Qasim in a coup.
- After nine months, the Ba'th Party is overthrown and 'Abd al-Salam 'Arif becomes president.

1966:   'Abd al-Salam 'Arif is killed in a plane crash. His brother, 'Abd al-Rahman 'Arif, becomes president.

1968:   The Iraqi Ba'th Party overthrows 'Abd al-Rahman 'Arif. Ahmad Hasan al-Bakr becomes president, and Saddam Hussein serves as vice president.

1972:   Iraq nationalizes its oil.

1979:   Bakr resigns and Saddam Hussein becomes president.

1980:   Iran–Iraq War begins, following the Islamic Revolution and the rise of Ayatollah Ruhollah Khomeini to power in Iran in 1979.

1988:
- The Iraqi government uses chemical weapons against the Kurds in Halabja in March.
- Iran and Iraq sign a ceasefire agreement in August, ending the Iran–Iraq War.

1990–91:
- Iraq invades Kuwait.
- UN imposes sanctions on Iraq, then a US-led coalition drives Iraqi forces from Kuwait in the First Gulf War.

1995:   UN Oil-For-Food program begins with the stated goal of mitigating the humanitarian impact of sanctions.

2003:   US and coalition forces invade Iraq and overthrow Saddam Hussein's regime.

2004:   US administrators return sovereignty to a transitional government.

2006:   Nuri al-Maliki is elected as prime minister. Saddam is tried and executed in December.

2014:   Maliki is forced to resign after Mosul fell into the hands of ISIL. Haidar al-'Abadi becomes the new prime minister.

Libya

1951:   Libya achieves independence from the Italians under King Idris al-Sanusi.

1969:   Mu'ammar al-Qaddafi overthrows Libyan monarchy and becomes president.

1977:   Qaddafi declares a "People's Revolution" and begins dismantling the state's institutions.
1980:   Libyan troops intervene in a civil war in northern Chad.
1986:   The US bombs Libyan military facilities and residential areas.
1992:   The UN imposes sanctions on Libya for its role in the Lockerbie bombings in 1988.
2003:   Libya agrees to halt weapons of mass destruction program.
2006:   Libya and the United States restore diplomatic relations.
2011:   • Large-scale popular uprisings take place in Libya. Mu'ammar al-Qaddafi is killed.
          • Libya descends into civil war with two rival governments claiming legitimacy.

Sudan

1955:   First Sudanese Civil War begins between the northern and southern parts of Sudan.
1956:   Sudan becomes independent under the rule of a five-member Security Council.
1958:   Ibrahim 'Abboud stages a coup and becomes president.
1964:   Islamists overthrow 'Abboud. Isma'il al-Azhari becomes president.
1969:   Ja'far al-Numayri leads a military coup against the Islamist government of Sudan.
1972:   First Sudanese Civil War ends with the signing of the Addis Ababa agreement after seventeen years of fighting.
1983:   Second Sudanese Civil War begins between northern and southern Sudan.
1985:   al-Numayri is overthrown in a military coup.
1989:   • The Sudanese government is overthrown in a military coup; the National Salvation Revolution takes power.
          • 'Omar al-Bashir becomes president.
2005:   Second Sudanese Civil War ends with the signing of a comprehensive peace agreement after twenty-two years of fighting and more than a million casualties.
2011:   • The Republic of South Sudan gains independence from Sudan through a referendum.
          • Bashir remains president despite warrants to arrest him for crimes against humanity and genocide.

2015:   Bashir wins 94 percent of the votes in elections boycotted by the opposition. Voter turnout was about 46 per cent. The leader, wanted by the International Criminal Court on war-crimes charges, begins another five-year term.

Syria

1947:   Ba'th Party is founded in Syria by Michel 'Aflaq and Salah al-Din al-Bitar.
1948:   War between the new state of Israel and Arab nations (Egypt, Jordan, Syria, and Iraq).
1949:   Syrian army officer Adib al-Shishakli installs himself as president after a series of three military coups.
1955:   Shukri al-Quwwatli is elected president.
1958:   Syria and Egypt form a union called the United Arab Republic.
1961:   Syria dissolves its union with Egypt after Syrian officers stage a coup.
1963:   Amin al-Hafiz becomes president.
1966:   Nur al-Din al-Atasi comes to power.
1967:   Israel defeats Egypt, Jordan, and Syria in the Six-Day War. Israel occupies Syria's Golan Heights.
1970:   Hafiz al-Asad overthrows President Nur al-Din al-Atasi.
1971:   Hafiz al-Asad becomes president.
1973:   Syria and Egypt declare a war on Israel, known as the "October War."
1981:   Israel annexes the Golan Heights from Syria.
1983:   Syrian military occupies southern Lebanon.
2000:   Bashar al-Asad becomes the president after his father, Hafiz al-Asad, dies.
2005:   Syria withdraws troops from Lebanon.
2011:   • Large-scale popular uprisings take place in Syria following protests in Tunisia, Egypt, and elsewhere in the Arab world.
         • A civil war begins in Syria between opponents of the regime and the government's forces. Since fighting began, at least 250,000 have been killed, 5 million civilians have fled their homes to find refuge in neighboring

countries, and another 6 million became displaced in Syria.

Tunisia

1957: Habib Bourguiba becomes president of Tunisia after independence.

1963: Neo-Destour Party (later called the Destourian Socialist Party) becomes the only legal party in Tunisia.

1981: Government permits other political parties to contest parliamentary elections.

1987: Zine al-'Abidine Ben 'Ali deposes Bourguiba in a peaceful coup to become president.

1988: The Destourian Socialist Party is re-named the Democratic Constitutional Rally.

1999: Tunisia holds multi-party presidential elections; Ben 'Ali wins.

2000: Bourguiba dies.

2004: President Ben 'Ali wins a fourth term after changing the constitution in 2002.

2009: Ben 'Ali wins a fifth term in office.

2011: Ben 'Ali is removed from power and flees to Saudi Arabia after large-scale uprisings that later spread to Egypt, Libya, Syria, Yemen, and Bahrain.

2011: • Al-Nahda Party wins the plurality of parliamentary seats.
 • Muhammad Ghannouchi serves as interim prime minister from January to February.
 • Béji Caïd Essebsi serves as prime minister from February to December.

2014: • Al-Nahda agrees to hold new elections following widespread discontentment with their government. Nida' Tunis wins a plurality of seats in the October elections.
 • Parliament passes a new constitution.
 • Béji Caïd Essebsi is elected president in December.

Yemen

1962: • Yemeni monarchy is toppled and North Yemen becomes a republic.

- Egypt intervenes in the Yemeni Civil War to support the People's Democratic Republic of Yemen in the south.

1967:   The British withdraw from Aden. The People's Democratic Republic of Yemen in the south splits off from North Yemen, beginning a civil war.

1978:   'Ali 'Abdullah Salih elected president of the Yemen Arab Republic.

1990:   - The civil war in Yemen ends, and North and South Yemen unite as the Republic of Yemen.
          - Salih becomes president of the new Republic of Yemen.

2011:   - Salih is removed from power after large-scale popular uprisings take place.
          - 'Abd Rabbuh Hadi, Salih's former vice president, becomes president.

2015:   - Houthi Rebels overtake capital city, San'a'; Hadi flees to Saudi Arabia.
          - Saudi-led coalition begins heavy bombardment of Yemen in March to restore Hadi's regime and dislodge the Houthis from power.

Bibliography

"À la découverte de *Conflit*, film sur l'oppression des Islamistes en Tunisie" [In discovering *Conflict*, a film about the oppression of Islamists in Tunisia], *La Presse*, January 29, 2015.

Abboud, Samer N. and Fred H. Lawson, "Antimonies of Economic Governance in Contemporary Syria," in Abbas Kadhim (ed.), *Governance in the Middle East and North Africa: A Handbook*, London: Routledge, 2013, pp. 330–41.

'Abd al-'Aziz, Basma, *Ighra' al-sulta al-mutlaq: masar al-'unf fi 'alaqat al-shurta bil-muwatin 'abr al-tarikh* [The temptation of absolute authority: the trajectory of violence in the police relationship with the citizen throughout history], Cairo: Safsafa Publishing, 2011.

'Abd al-'Aziz, Muhammad and Hashim Abu Ranat, *Asrar jihaz al-asrar: jihaz al-amn al-Sudani 1969–1985* [Secrets of the secret organization: the Sudanese security services 1969–1985], Khartoum: 'Izzat Publications, 2008.

'Abd al-Hamid, Barlanti, *al-Mushir wa ana* [The field marshal and I], Cairo: Madbuly Books, 1992.

'Abd al-Mut'a, 'Abd al-Basit, *al-Tabaqat al-ijtima'iyya wa mustaqbal Misr: ittijahat al-taghayyur wa al-tafa'ulat 1975–2020* [Social classes and Egypt's future: trends of changes and reactions 1975–2020], Cairo: Merit Publishing, 2002.

'Abd al-Nasser, Gamal, *The Philosophy of the Revolution*, Cairo: n.p., 1959.

Abdelnasser, Gamal, "Egypt: Succession Politics," in Volker Perthes (ed.), *Arab Elites: Negotiating the Politics of Change*, Boulder, CO: Lynne Rienner, 2004, pp. 117–39.

Abdul Aziz, Muhammad and Youssef Hussein, "The President, the Son, and the Military: The Question of Succession in Egypt," *Arab Studies Journal*, vol. 9/10, no. 2/1 (Fall/Spring 2002), pp. 73–88.

'Abidayn, Hasan, *Hayat fi al-siyasa wa al-diblumasiyya al-Sudaniyya* [My life in Sudan's politics and diplomacy], Omdurman: Mirghani Cultural Center, 2013.

Aboul-Enein, Youssef, "Syrian Defense Minister General Mustafa Talas: Memoirs, Volume Two," *Military Review*, vol. 85, no. 3 (May/June 2005), pp. 99–102.

Abrahamian, Ervand, *Tortured Confessions: Prisons and Public Recantations in Modern Iran*, Berkeley: University of California Press, 1999.

Abu 'Assaf, Amin, *Dhikrayati* [My memoirs], Damascus: n.p., 1996.

Abu Basha, Hasan, *Mudhakkirat Hasan Abu Basha fi al-amn wa al-siyasa: Yanayir 1977, Uktubir 1981, Ramadan 1987* [Memoirs of Hasan Abu Basha in security and politics: January 1977, October 1981, Ramadan 1987], Cairo: al-Hilal Publishing, 1990.

Abu 'Izz al-Din, Najib, *'Ishrun 'aman fi khidmat al-Yaman* [Twenty years in the service of Yemen], Beirut: Dar al-Bahith, 1991.

Abu Lahum, Sinan, *al-Yaman: haqa'iq wa watha'iq 'ayshtuha* [Yemen: truths and documents I lived through], vol. II: 1962–1974, San'a': al-'Afif Foundation, 2006.

Abu Shama, 'Abbas and Muhammad al-Amin al-Bushri, *al-Hayakil al-tanzimiyya li-ajhizat al-amn fi al-duwal al-'Arabiyya: dirasa tamhidiyya li-wad' haykil tanzimi muwahhad* [Organization structures of security services in the Arab world: an initial study to create a unified organizational structure], Riyadh: Naif Arab Academy for Security Studies, 1997.

Acemoglu, Daron and James A. Robinson, *Economic Origins of Dictatorships and Democracy*, New York: Cambridge University Press, 2006.

Why Nations Fail: The Origins of Power, Prosperity, and Poverty, New York: Crown Publishers, 2012.

Achour, Habib, *Ma vie politique et syndicale: enthousiasme et déceptions, 1944–1981* [My life in politics and unions: enthusiasm and deceptions, 1944–1981], Tunis: Alif, 1989.

Aclimandos, Tewfik, "Reforming the Egyptian Security Services," Arab Reform Initiative, June 2011, available at www.arab-reform.net/reforming-egyptian-security-services.

Agüero, Felipe, "The New 'Double Challenge': Democratic Control and Efficacy of Military, Police, and Intelligence," in Alfred Stepan (ed.), *Democracies in Danger*, Baltimore: Johns Hopkins University Press, 2009, pp. 59–74.

'Ajjaj, 'Abd al-Rahim, *Fi sabil al-hurriyya: qissa bada'ha al-sayyid al-ra'is Gamal 'Abd al-Nasser wa huwa talib bil-madaris al-thanawiyya, 'an ma'rakat Rashid sanat 1807* [For freedom: a continuation of the story begun by Mr. President Gamal 'Abd al-Nasser during his high school years about the battle of Rashid in 1807], Cairo: al-Ra'id Publishing, 1970.

Albats, Yevgenia, *State within a State: The KGB and its Hold on Russia – Past, Present, and Future*, New York: Farrar Straus Giroux, 1994.

Albrecht, Holger, "Political Opposition and Arab Authoritarianism: Some Conceptual Remarks," in Holger Albrecht (ed.), *Contentious Politics in the Middle East: Political Opposition under Authoritarianism*, Gainesville: University of Florida Press, 2010, pp. 17–34.

    Raging Against the Machine: Political Opposition under Authoritarianism in Egypt, Syracuse, NY: Syracuse University Press, 2013.

'Ali, Kamal Hasan, *Mashawir al-'umr: asrar wa khafaya sab'in 'aman min 'umr Misr fi al-harb wa al-mukhabarat wa al-siyasa* [Life's deliberations: secrets and mysteries of seventy years of Egypt's life in war, intelligence, and politics], Cairo: al-Shuruq Publishing, 1994.

al-'Ali, Muhammad Ibrahim, *Hayati wa al-i'dam* [My life and the execution], vol. I, Damascus: n.p., 2000.

'Allam, Fu'ad, *al-Ikhwan wa ana: min al-Manshiyya ila al-minassa* [The Brothers and I: from al-Manshiyya to the Podium], Cairo: al-Misri Publications, 1996.

American Embassy in Tunisia to State Department, "Finding Parallels between Ben Ali and Ceausescu," available at www.cablegatesearch.net/cable.php?id+07TUNIS1544, November 30, 2007.

Amin, Galal, *Egypt in the Era of Hosni Mubarak, 1981–2011*, Cairo: American University Press, 2011.

Amin, Magdi et al., *After the Spring: Economic Transitions in the Arab World*, New York: Oxford University Press, 2012.

Amnesty International, "Algeria: Torture in the 'War on Terror': A Memorandum to the Algerian President." News release, April 18, 2006, available at www.amnesty.org/en/library/asset/MDE28/008/2006/en/386174b5-d43c-11dd-8743-d305bea2b2c7/mde280082006en.pdf

    Libya: Investigation Needed into Prison Deaths, October 10, 2006.

Anderson, Jon Lee, "Letter from Libya: The Unravelling," *New Yorker*, February 23 and March 2, 2015, pp. 108–18.

Anderson, Lisa, "Authoritarian Legacies and Regime Change: Towards Understanding Political Transition in the Arab World," in Fawaz A. Gerges (ed.), *The New Middle East: Protest and Revolution in the Arab World*, New York: Cambridge University Press, 2014, pp. 41–59.

    The State and Social Transformation in Tunisia and Libya, 1830–1980, Princeton: Princeton University Press, 1986.

Angrist, Michele Penner, *Party Building in the Modern Middle East*, Seattle: University of Washington Press, 2006.

Applebaum, Anne, "How he and his Cronies Stole Russia," *New York Review of Books*, December 18, 2014.

Arendt, Hannah, "On the Nature of Totalitarianism: An Essay in Understanding," in Hannah Arendt (ed.), *Essays in Understanding, 1930–1954*, New York: Harcourt, 1994, pp. 328–60.

The Origins of Totalitarianism, New York: Harcourt, Brace & Company, 1951.

"A Special Supplement: Reflections on Violence," *New York Review of Books*, February 27, 1969.

Arieff, Alex and Carla E. Humud, *Political Transition in Tunisia*, Washington: Congressional Research Service, October 22, 2014.

Aroyan, Nubar, *Diary of a Soldier in the Egyptian Military: A Peek Inside the Egyptian Army*, Bloomington, IN: Westview Press, 2012.

Art, David, "What do we Know about Authoritarianism after Ten Years?" Review article, *Comparative Politics*, vol. 44, no. 3 (April 2012), pp. 351–73.

al-Asbahi, Ahmad Muhammad, *25 'aman min sirat za'im wa qa'id masirat al-sh'ab, 1978–2003* [25 years in the history of a leader and commander of the people's history, 1978–2003], Amman: Yemen Embassy, 2004.

al-'Ashi, Muhammad Suhail, *Fajr al-istiqlal fi Suriya: mun'ataf khatir fi tarikhihi: khawatir wa dhikrayat* [Dawn of independence in Syria: a dangerous detour in its history: reflections and memoirs], Beirut: Dar al-Nafa'is, 1999.

Ashour, Omar, "Islamist De-Radicalization in Algeria: Successes and Failure," *Middle East Institute Policy Brief*, no. 21, November 2008.

'Ashur, Radwa, *Faraj* [Relief], Cairo: al-Shuruq Publications, 2008.

As'id, Muhammad Shakir, *al-Barlaman al-Suri fi tatawwurihi al-tarikhi* [The Syrian parliament and its historical development], Damascus: al-Mada Press, 2002.

al-Atrash, Mansur Sultan, *al-Jil al-mudan: sira dhatiyya* [The condemned generation: an autobiography], Beirut: Riyad al-Rayyis Books, 2008.

al-'Ayni, Muhsin, *Khamsun 'aman fi al-rimal al-mutaharrika: qissati ma'a bina' al-dawla al-haditha fi al-Yaman* [Fifty years of shifting sands: my story in building the modern state in Yemen], Beirut: al-Nahar Publishing, 2000.

Baghat, Mirette, "Memoirs of an Egyptian Citizen," in Nasser Weddady and Sohrab Ahmari (eds.), *Arab Spring Dreams: The Next Generation Speaks Out for Freedom and Justice from North Africa to Iran*, New York: Palgrave Macmillan, 2012, pp. 53–57.

"Bahrain: How the Police Recruit Radicals," *Economist*, October 13, 2012.

Bakri, Mahmud, *Ayyam fi al-sijn* [Days in prison], Cairo: Jazirat al-Ward, 2010.

Barak, Oren and Assaf David, "The Arab Security Sector: A New Research Agenda for a Neglected Topic," *Armed Forces & Society*, vol. 36, no. 5 (2010), pp. 804–24.

Baram, Amatzia, "Saddam Husayn, the Ba'th Regime and the Iraqi Officers Corps," in Barry Rubin and Thomas A. Keaney (eds.), *Armed Forces in the Middle East: Politics and Strategy*, London: Frank Cass, 2002, pp. 206–30.

Barchfield, Jenny, "Brazil's Panel Details Military Regime's Brutality," Associated Press, December 10, 2014.

Barnes, Jessica, "Managing the Waters of the Ba'th Country: The Politics of Water Scarcity in Syria," *Geopolitics*, vol. 14, no. 3 (August 2009), pp. 15–30.

"Bashar al-Assad's Inner Circle," BBC News, July 30, 2012, available at www.bbc.com/news/world-middle-east-13216195.

Bayat, Asef, *Life as Politics: How Ordinary People Change the Middle East*, 2nd edn., Stanford: Stanford University Press, 2013.

al-Baz, Muhammad, *al-'Aqrab al-sam: 'Umar Sulayman jiniral al-mukhabarat al-ghamid* [The poisonous scorpion: 'Umar Sulayman the mysterious intelligence general], Cairo: Kanuz Publications, 2014.

Beeri, Eliezer, *Army Officers in Arab Politics and Society*, translated by Dov Ben-Abba, New York: Praeger, 1979.

Beinin, Joel and Frédéric Vairel (eds.), *Social Movements, Mobilization, and Contestation in the Middle East and North Africa*, 2nd edn., Stanford: Stanford University Press, 2013.

Belhadj, Souhaïl, *La Syrie de Bashar al-Asad: anatomie d'un régime autoritaire* [The Syria of Bashar al-Asad: anatomy of an authoritarian regime], Paris: Belin, 2013.

Bellin, Eva, "Reconsidering the Robustness of Authoritarianism in the Middle East: Lessons from the Arab Spring," *Comparative Politics*, vol. 44, no. 2 (January 2012), pp. 127–49.

"The Robustness of Authoritarianism in the Middle East: Exceptionalism in Comparative Perspective," *Comparative Politics*, vol. 36, no. 2 (2004), pp. 139–57.

Benbahmed, Tariq, "Algeria 2014," available at www.africaneconomicout look.org.

Bengio, Ofra, *Saddam's Word: Political Discourse in Iraq*, Oxford: Oxford University Press, 1998.

Ben Mahni, al-Sadiq, "Intiba'at masirat munadil" [Impressions from the life of an activist], in 'Abd al-Jalil al-Tamimi (ed.), *Dirasat wa shahadat hawla dahaya al-ta'dhib wa al-iztihad bi-anzimat al-hukm bi al-Maghrab al-Kabir, 1956–2010* [Studies and testimonies about victims of torture and repression in the Maghreb, 1956–2010], Tunis: al-Tamimi Foundation, 2013, pp. 117–21.

al-Biblawi, Hazim, *Arba'at shuhur fi qafas al-hukuma* [Four months in the government's cage], Cairo: al-Shuruq Publishing, 2012.

Bili, Ahmad, *al-Safwa al-'askariyya wa al-bina' al-siyasi fi Misr* [The military elites and the political structure in Egypt], Cairo: General Egyptian Organization for the Book, 1993.

Blaydes, Lisa, *Elections and Distributive Politics in Mubarak's Egypt*, New York: Cambridge University Press, 2011.

Blumi, Isa, *Chaos in Yemen: Societal Collapse and the New Authoritarianism*, New York: Routledge, 2011.

Booth, Marilyn, *May her Likes be Multiplied: Biography and Gender Politics in Egypt*, Berkeley: University of California Press, 2001.

Boubekeur, Amel, "Rolling Either Way? Algerian Entrepreneurs as both Agents of Change and Means of Preservation of the System," *Journal of North African Studies*, vol. 18, no. 3 (2013), pp. 469–81.

Bou Nassif, Hicham, "A Military Besieged: The Armed Forces, the Police, and the Party in Bin 'Ali's Tunisia 1987–2011," *International Journal of Middle East Studies*, vol. 47, no. 1 (February 2015), pp. 65–87.

Brand, Laurie A., *Official Stories: Politics and National Narratives in Egypt and Algeria*, Stanford: Stanford University Press, 2014.

Brehony, Noel, *Yemen Divided: The Story of a Failed State in South Arabia*, New York: I. B. Tauris, 2013.

Bremer, Paul, III, *My Year in Iraq: The Struggle to Build a Future of Hope*, New York: Simon & Schuster, 2006.

Brooker, L. Paul, *Defiant Dictatorships: Communist and Middle-Eastern Dictatorships in a Democratic Age*, New York: New York University Press, 1997.

Brown, Archie, *The Myth of the Strong Leader: Political Leadership in the Modern Age*, London: Random House, 2014.

Brown, Nathan J., "Bumpy Democratic Routes to Dictatorial Ends?" in Noureddine Jebnoun, Mehrdad Kia, and Mimi Kirk (eds.), *Modern Middle East Authoritarianism: Roots, Ramifications, and Crisis*, New York: Routledge, 2014, pp. 27–39.

Brownlee, Jason, *Authoritarianism in an Age of Democratization*, New York: Cambridge University Press, 2007.

Brumberg, Daniel, "Theories of Transition," in Marc Lynch (ed.), *The Arab Uprisings Explained: New Contentious Politics in the Middle East*, New York: Columbia University Press, 2014, pp. 29–54.

Brynen, Rex, Pete W. Moore, Bassel F. Salloukh, and Marie-Joëlle Zahar, *Beyond the Arab Spring: Authoritarianism and Democratization in the Arab World*, Boulder, CO: Lynne Rienner, 2012.

al-Burlusi, 'Abd al-Wahhab, *Kuntu waziran ma'a 'Abd al-Nasser* [I was a minister with 'Abd al-Nasser], Cairo: Arab Mustaqbal Publishing, 1992.

Byman, Daniel, "Regime Change in the Middle East: Problems and Prospects," in Daniel Byman and Marylena Mantas (eds.), *Religion, Democracy, and Politics in the Middle East*, New York: Academy of Political Science, 2012, pp. 59–80.

Cambanis, Thanassis, *Once Upon a Revolution: An Egyptian Story*, New York: Simon & Schuster, 2015.

Campbell, Joseph, *The Hero with a Thousand Faces*, 3rd edn., Novato, CA: New World Library, 2008.

Celoza, Albert F., *Ferdinand Marcos and the Philippines: The Political Economy of Authoritarianism*, Westport: Praeger, 1997.

de Châtel, Francesca, "The Role of Drought and Climate Change in the Syrian Uprising: Untangling the Triggers of the Revolution," *Middle Eastern Studies*, vol. 50, no. 4 (July 2014), pp. 521–35.

Chayes, Sarah, *Thieves of State: Why Corruption Threatens Global Security*, New York: Norton, 2015.

Chirot, Daniel, *Modern Tyrants: The Power and Prevalence of Evil in our Age*, Princeton: Princeton University Press, 1994.

Chouikha, Larbi, "L'Opposition à Ben Ali et les élections de 2004," *L'Année du Maghreb, 2004*, Paris: CNRS Édition, 2006, pp. 361–73.

Chrisafis, Angelique, "Libya Protests: Gunshots, Screams and Talk of Revolution," *Guardian*, February 20, 2011.

Cienski, Jan, "Informant Claims from Communist Era Haunt Czech Politics," *Financial Times*, November 29, 2013.

Clover, Charles and Catherine Belton, "A Tsar is Reborn," *Financial Times*, May 5/6, 2012.

Cockburn, Patrick, "Tomorrow Never Came," *New York Times Book Review*, February 15, 2015.

Conflit [Conflict], directed by Moncef Barbouch, Tunisia: Quinta distributors, 2014 [Film].

Connerton, Paul, *How Societies Remember*, New York: Cambridge University Press, 1989.

Cook, Steven A., *Ruling but not Governing: The Military and Political Development in Egypt, Algeria, and Turkey*, Baltimore: Johns Hopkins University Press, 2007.

Coolidge, Frederick L. and Daniel L. Segal, "Is Kim Jong-il like Saddam Hussein or Adolf Hitler? A Personality Disorder Evaluation," *Behavioral Sciences of Terrorism and Political Aggression*, vol. 1, no. 3 (September 2009), pp. 195–202.

Copnall, James, "South Sudan Economy in 'Intensive Care' as Famine Looms," BBC, July 9, 2014.

Cronin, Stephanie, *Armies and State-Building in the Modern Middle East: Politics, Nationalism, and Military Reform*, New York: I. B. Tauris, 2014.

Daoudy, Marwa, "Les Politiques de l'eau en Syrie: réalisations et obstacles" [The politics of water in Syria: achievements and obstacles], in Baudoin Dupret, Zouhair Ghazzal, Youssef Courbage, and Mohammed al-Dbiyat (eds.), *La Syrie au présent: reflets d'une société* [Syria today: reflections on society], Arles: Actes Sud, 2007, pp. 607–15.

Daragahi, Borzou, "In Tunisia, Ben Ali was 'Big Brother'," *Los Angeles Times*, January 15, 2011.

Darwish, Mahmud, "Shahid 'ala zaman al-tughat: khutub al-diktatur al-mawzuna" [Witness to tyranny: metric speeches of the dictator], available at www.alkarmelj.org/userfiles/pdfs/4.pdf.

David, Roman, "Transitional Justice and Changing Memories of the Past in Central Europe," *Government and Opposition*, vol. 50 (January 2015), pp. 24–44.

Dawisha, Karen, *Putin's Kleptocracy: Who Owns Russia?* New York: Simon & Schuster, 2014.

Deeb, Mary-Jane, *Libya's Foreign Policy in North Africa*, Boulder, CO: Westview Press, 1991.

DeFronzo, James, *Revolutions and Revolutionary Movements*, 5th edn., Boulder, CO: Westview Press, 2015.

Deletant, Dennis, *Ceauşescu and the Securitate: Coercion and Dissent in Romania, 1965–1989*, London: Hurst & Co., 2006.

Diamond, Larry, *Squandered Victory: The American Occupation and the Bungled Effort to Bring Democracy to Iraq*, New York: Times Books, 2005.

Disraeli, Benjamin, *Sybil, or the Two Nations*, Oxford: Oxford World's Classics, 2008.

al-Dulaymi, Khalil, *Saddam Hussein min al-zinzana al-Amrikiyya: hadha ma hadatha* [Saddam Hussein from his American cell: this is what happened] (Khartoum: al-Manbar Publishing, 2009).

Dunbar, Charles, "The Middle East Political Economy and the Arab Awakening: A Difficult Symbiosis?" in Abbas Kadhim (ed.), *Governance in the Middle East and North Africa: A Handbook*, London: Routledge, 2013, pp. 50–62.

Egerton, George (ed.), *Political Memoir: Essays on the Politics of Memory*, London: Frank Cass, 1994.

Eickelman, Dale and M. G. Dennison, "Arabizing the Omani Intelligence Services: Clash of Cultures?" *International Journal of Intelligence and Counterintelligence*, vol. 7, no. 1 (1994), pp. 1–28.

Eisenstadt, S. N., *On Charisma and Institution Building*, Chicago: University of Chicago Press, 1968.

Elgin, C. and O. Oztunah, "Shadow Economies around the World: Model Based Estimates," *Bogazici University Department of Economics Working Papers*, vol. 5 (2012), pp. 1–48.

Elias, Norbert, *The Court Society*, translated by Edmund Jephcott, New York: Pantheon Books, 1983.

Erdle, Steffan, *Ben Ali's "New Tunisia" (1987–2009): A Case Study of Authoritarian Modernization in the Arab World*, Berlin: Klaus Schwarz, 2010.

Essebsi, Béji Caïd, *Habib Bourguiba: le bon grain et l'ivraie* [Habib Bourguiba: the wheat and the chaff], Tunis: Sud Editions, 2009.

    al-Habib Bourguiba: al-muhimm wa al-ahamm [Habib Bourguiba: the important and the more important], Tunis: Dar al-Junub Publications, 2011.

European Bank for Reconstruction and Development, *Transition Report 2013*, available at www.tr.ebrd.com

Fadil, Samir, *Kuntu qadiyan li-hadath al-minassa: mudhakkirat qadi min Harb al-Yaman ila ightiyal al-Sadat* [I was a judge for the Podium Event: memoirs of a judge from the Yemen War until the assassination of Sadat], Cairo: Sphinx Publishing, 1993.

Fadl, Bilal, "al-Dawla al-Misriyya "al-mukhawwakha" kama ra'aha kahinaha al-a'zam" [The "peachy" Egyptian state as its grand priest perceived it], January 11, 2015, available at www.madamasr.com/ar/opinion/politics/.

Farah, Nadia Ramsis, *Egypt's Political Economy: Power Relations in Development*, Cairo: American University Press, 2009.

al-Faris, Nawaf, "Barnamij bila hudud" [Program without boundaries], Al-Jazeera, December 8, 2012.

Faruq, 'Abd al-Khaliq, *al-Fasad fi Misr: dirasa iqtisadiyya tahliliyya* [Corruption in Egypt: an analytical economic study], Cairo: al-'Arabi Publishing, 2006.

    Judhur al-fasad al-idari fi Misr: bi'at al-'amal wa siyasat al-ajur fi Misr 1963–2002 [The roots of administrative corruption in Egypt: work environment and policies of ranks and salaries in Egypt 1963–2003], Cairo: al-Shuruq Publishing, 2008.

al-Fathi, Sa'ad Allah, *Min burj al-takrir: akthar min dhikrayat wa aqall min tarikh* [From the tower of a refinery: more than memories and less than history], Amman: al-Ayyam Publishing, 2014.

Fawzi, Mahmud, *Asrar suqut ta'irat al-Mushir Ahmad Badawi* [The secrets of the plane crash of Field Marshal Ahmad Badawi], Cairo: al-Hadaf Publishing, 1992.

al-Fariq al-Shadhili: asrar al-sidam ma'a al-Sadat [Lieutenant-General al-Shadhili: the secrets of clashes with Sadat], Cairo: al-Watan Publishing, 1993.

al-Faysal, Yusif, *Dhikrayat wa mawaqif* [Memories and stances], Damascus: al-Takwin Publishing, 2007.

al-Fayturi, 'Ali Salim, *Mudhakkirat mudda'i 'amm: shahadat 'ala 'asr al-zalam* [Memoirs of an attorney general: testimonies about the dark era], Tarablus: al-Ruwad Publishing, 2012.

al-Fayyad, Ma'ad, *Zahira sakhina jiddan: al-qissa al-haqiqiyya li-qatl al-Sayyid 'Abd al-Majid al-Khu'i* [A very hot afternoon: the true story of the killing of Sayyid 'Abd al-Majid al-Khu'i], Baghdad: Dar al-Huda, 2007.

Federal Commissioner for the Records of the State Security Service of the former German Democratic Republic, *Stasi: The Exhibition of the GDR's State Security Exhibition*, Berlin, 2011.

Ferris, Jesse, *Nasser's Gamble: How Intervention in Yemen Caused the Six-Day War and the Decline of Egyptian Power*, Princeton: Princeton University Press, 2013.

Fikri, Amira, *al-Mushir Muhammad 'Abd al-Halim Abu Ghazala: masirat hayat* [Field Marshal Muhammad 'Abd al-Halim Abu Ghazala: a life journey], Cairo: al-Jumhuriyya Publishing, 2010.

Flood, Christopher G., *Political Myth*, New York: Routledge, 2002.

Folkenflick, Robert (ed.), *The Culture of Autobiography: Constructions of Self-Representation*, Stanford: Stanford University Press, 1993.

Foltz, William J., "Libya's Military Power," in René Lemarchand (ed.), *The Green and the Black: Qadhafi's Policies in Africa*, Bloomington: Indiana University Press, 1988, pp. 52–69.

Foucault, Michel, "Méthodologie pour la connaissance du monde: comment se débarrasser du Marxisme" [Methodology for knowing the world: how to get rid of Marxism], *Dits et écrits*, vol. III, Paris: Gallimard, 1978.

Friedman, Thomas L., "Mubarak Trying to Penetrate Egyptian Red Tape," *New York Times*, November 2, 1981.

"WikiLeaks, Drought and Syria," *New York Times*, January 21, 2014.

Friedrich, Carl J. and Zbigniew K. Brzezinski, *Totalitarian Dictatorship and Autocracy*, New York: Praeger, 1961.

Frye, Timothy, *Building States and Markets after Communism: The Perils of Polarized Democracy*, New York: Cambridge University Press, 2010.

Fu'ad, Muhammad, "The World is Expecting al-Sisi's Speech at the United Nations," *al-Ahram*, September 22, 2014.

Gaddafi, Muammar, *Escape to Hell and Other Stories*, with a foreword by Pierre Salinger, London: John Blake Publishing, 1999.

Gaddafi, Muammar with Edmond Jouve, *My Vision*, London: John Blake, 2005. [See also under Qaddafi]

Galbraith, Peter, *The End of Iraq: How American Incompetence Created a War without End*, New York: Simon & Schuster, 2006.

Gall, Carlotta, "Questions of Justice in Tunisia as Ousted Leaders are Freed," *New York Times*, July 16, 2014.

Gallup, *The Silatech Index: Voices of Young Arabs*, January 2010, available at www.gallup.com/poll/120758/silatech-index-voices-young-arabs.aspx.

Gana, Nouri, "Visions of Dissent, Voices of Discontent: Postcolonial Tunisian Film and Song," in Nouri Gana (ed.), *The Making of the Tunisian Revolution: Contexts, Architects, Prospects*, Edinburgh: Edinburgh University Press, 2013, pp. 180–203.

Gandhi, Jennifer, *Political Institutions under Dictatorship*, New York: Cambridge University Press, 2008.

Gandhi, Jennifer and Adam Przeworski, "Authoritarian Institutions and the Survival of Autocrats," *Comparative Political Studies*, vol. 40, no. 11 (September 2007), pp. 1279–301.

Garas, Felix, *Bourguiba wa mawlad umma* [Bourguiba and the birth of a nation], Tunis: Free Constitutional Party Publications, 1956.

Gaston, Erica, "Process Learned in Yemen's National Dialogue," *United States Institute of Peace Special Report 342*, February 2014.

Gause, F. Gregory, III, *Kings for All Seasons: How the Middle East Monarchies Survived the Arab Spring*, Brookings Doha Center Analysis Paper, Number 8, September 2013.

Geddes, Barbara, "Authoritarian Breakdown: Empirical Test of a Game Theoretic Argument," Working Paper, annual meeting of the American Political Science Association, September 1999.

Ghalib, Murad, *Ma'a 'Abd al-Nasser wa al-Sadat: sanawat al-intisar wa ayyam al-mihan* [With 'Abd al-Nasser and al-Sadat: years of victory and days of tribulation], Cairo: Ahram Center for Publishing, 2001.

al-Ghazali, Zainab, *Return of the Pharaoh: Memoir in Nasser's Prison*, translated by Mokrane Guezzou, Leicester: Islamic Foundation, 1994.

el-Ghobashy, Mona, "Governments and Oppositions," in Michele Penner Angrist (ed.), *Politics and Society in the Contemporary Middle East*, Boulder, CO: Lynne Rienner, 2010, pp. 29–47.

Gilligan, Andrew, "Interview with Bashar al-Asad," *Sunday Telegraph*, October 30, 2011.

Goldschmidt, Arthur, *Biographical Dictionary of Modern Egypt*, Boulder, CO: Lynne Rienner, 2002.

Goldstone, Jack A., "Pathways to State Failure," in Harvey Starr (ed.), *Dealing with Failed States: Crossing Analytic Boundaries*, New York: Routledge, 2009, pp. 5–16.

Gotowicki, Stephen H., "The Military in Egyptian Society," in Phebe Marr (ed.), *Egypt at the Crossroads: Domestic Stability and Regional Role*, Washington: National Defense University Press, 1999, pp. 105–25.

Gregory, Joseph, "Ahmed Ben Bella: Revolutionary who Led Algeria after Independence, Dies at 93," *New York Times*, April 11, 2012.

Gregory, Paul R., *Terror by Quota: State Security from Lenin to Stalin (An Archival Study)*, New Haven: Yale University Press, 2009.

Gunter, Frank B., *The Political Economy of Iraq: Restoring Balance in a Post-Conflict Society*, Northampton, MA: Edward Elgar Publishing, 2013.

Gupta, Akhil, "Narrating the State of Corruption," in Dieter Haller and Cris Shore (eds.), *Corruption: Anthropological Perspectives*, London: Pluto Press, 2005, pp. 173–93.

Gusdorf, Georges, "Conditions and Limits of Autobiography," in James Olney (ed.), *Autobiography: Essays Theoretical and Critical*, Princeton: Princeton University Press, 1980, pp. 28–48.

Hachemaoui, Mohammed, "La corruption politique en Algérie: l'envers de l'autoritarisme" [Political corruption in Algeria: the other side of authoritarianism], *Esprit*, June 2011, pp. 111–35.

Haddad, Bassam, *Business Networks in Syria: The Political Economy of Authoritarian Resilience*, Stanford: Stanford University Press, 2012.

"Syria's State Bourgeoisie: An Organic Backbone for the Regime," *Middle East Critique*, vol. 21, no. 3 (Fall 2012), pp. 231–57.

Hadid, Muhammad, *Mudhakkirati: al-sira' min ajl al-dimuqratiyya fi al-'Iraq* [My memoirs: the struggle for democracy in Iraq], Beirut: al-Saqi, 2006.

al-Hadidi, Salah, *Qabdat al-huda: Husayn Jalukhan tarikh wa rihla* [The guiding hand: Husayn Jalukhan's history and journey], 2nd edn., Karbala: al-Hadidi Center for Studies and Research, 2009.

al-Hadidi, Salah al-Din, *Shahid 'ala Harb al-Yaman* [Witness of the Yemen War], Cairo: Madbuly Publications, 1984.

Hadjadj, Djilati, "Algeria: A Future Hijacked by Corruption," *Mediterranean Politics*, vol. 12, no. 2 (September 2007), pp. 263–77.

Hafiz, 'Adil, *Hafiz al-Asad: qa'id wa umma* [Hafiz al-Asad: a leader and a nation], Damascus: al-Markaz al-Dawli Publications, 1993.

Hajji, Ahmad, *Mudhakkirat jundi Misri fi jabhat Qanat al-Suways* [Memoirs of an Egyptian soldier on the Suez Canal front], Cairo: al-Fikr Publishing, 1988.

al-Hakim, Sulayman, *'Abd al-Nasser wa al-Ikhwan: bayn al-wifaq wa al-shiqaq* ['Abd al-Nasser and the Brothers: between harmony and rift], Cairo: Jazirat al-Ward, 2010.

al-Jayyar yatadhakkar: sijil dhikrayat Mahmud al-Jayyar mudir maktab Gamal 'Abd al-Nasser [al-Jayyar remembers: record of memories of Mahmud al-Jayyar, bureau chief of Gamal 'Abd al-Nasser], Damascus: Talas Publishing, 1991.

al-Hamami, Hama, "al-Ta'dhib fi 'ahday Bourguiba wa Ben 'Ali: shahada shakhsiyya" [Torture in the eras of Bourguiba and Ben 'Ali: a personal testimony], in 'Abd al-Jalil al-Tamimi (ed.), *Dirasat wa shahadat hawla dahaya al-ta'dhib wa al-iztihad bi-anzimat al-hukm bil-Maghrab al-Kabir, 1956–2010* [Studies and testimonies about victims of torture and repression in the Maghreb, 1956–2010], Tunis: al-Tamimi Foundation, 2013, pp. 123–30.

al-Hamash, Munir, "Hizb al-Ba'th al-'Arabi al-Ishtiraki fi Suriya (1953–2005)" [The Arab Socialist Ba'th Party in Syria (1953–2005)], in Muhammad Jamal Barut (ed.), *al-Ahzab wa al-harakat wa al-tanzimat al-qawmiyy fi al-watan al-'Arabi* [Nationalist parties, movements, and organizations in the Arab world], Beirut: Center for Arab Unity Studies, 2012, pp. 88–175.

al-Hamdani, Ra'ad Majid, *Qabla an yughadiruna al-tarikh* [Before history leaves us], Beirut: Arab Scientific Publishers, 2007.

Hamdun, Walid, *Dhikrayat wa ara'* [Memories and opinions], Damascus: Walid Hamdun, 2007.

Hammad, Majdi, *al-'Askariyyun al-'Arab wa qadiyyat al-wahda* [The Arab military and the case of unity], Beirut: Center for Arab Unity Studies, 1987.

Hammuda, 'Adil, *Ightiyal ra'is: bil-watha'iq asrar ightiyal Anwar al-Sadat* [Assassination of a president: documents of the secrets of the assassination of Anwar al-Sadat], Cairo: Sina Publishing, 1986.

Hamrush, Ahmad, *Misr wa al-'askariyyun* [Egypt and the military men], 3rd edn., vol. I, Cairo: Madbuly Library, 1983.

al-Hanashi, 'Abd al-Latif, "Mumarasat al-ta'dhib tijah al-wataniyyin al-Tunisiyyin zaman al-himaya al-Faransiyya" [The practice of torture toward Tunisian nationalists during the French protectorate], in 'Abd al-Jalil al-Tamimi (ed.), *Dirasat wa shahadat hawla dahaya al-ta'dhib wa al-iztihad bi-anzimat al-hukm bil-Maghrab al-Kabir, 1956–2010* [Studies and testimonies about victims of torture and repression in the Maghreb, 1956–2010], no. 25, Tunis: al-Tamimi Foundation, 2013, pp. 33–53.

Hanna, Sami A. and George H. Gardner, *Arab Socialism: A Documentary Survey*, Salt Lake City: University of Utah Press, 1969.

"Has the Arab Spring Failed?" *Economist*, July 13, 2014.

Hashim, Jawad, *Mudhakkirat wazir 'Iraqi ma'a al-Bakr wa Saddam: dhikrayat fi al-siyasa al-'Iraqiyya, 1967–2000* [Memoirs of an Iraqi minister with al-Bakr and Saddam: reflections on Iraqi politics, 1967–2000], Beirut: al-Saqi Publishing, 2003.

Haugbolle, Sune, "The Victim's Tale in Syria: Imprisonment, Individualism, and Liberalism," in Laleh Khalili and Jillian Schwedler (eds.), *Policing and Prisons in the Middle East: Formation of Coercion*, London: Hurst, 2010, pp. 223–40.

Havel, Václav, "New Year's Address to the Nation," Czechoslovakia, January 1, 1990. Czech Republic presidential website, speeches, available at http://old.hrad.cz/president/Havel.speeches/.

Havel, Václav et al., *The Power of the Powerless: Citizens against the State in Central–Eastern Europe*, New York: M. E. Sharpe, 1990.

Haykal, Muhammad Hasanayn, *Uktubir 1973: al-silah wa al-siyasa* [October 1973: arms and politics], Cairo: al-Ahram Institute, 1993.

Hazareesingh, Sudhir, *The Legend of Napoleon*, London: Granta Books, 2004.

Hellbeck, Jochen, *Revolution on my Mind: Writing a Diary under Stalin*, Cambridge, MA: Harvard University Press, 2006.

Hennessy, Peter, *Distilling the Frenzy: Writing the History of One's Own Times*, London: Biteback Publishing, 2012.

Herb, Michael, *All in the Family: Absolutism, Revolution, and Democracy in the Middle Eastern Monarchies*, Albany: State University of New York Press, 1999.

Hess, Steve, "Sources of Authoritarian Resilience in Regional Protest Waves: The Post-Communist Colour Revolutions and 2011 Arab Uprisings," *Government and Opposition*, vol. 50 (2015), pp. 1–29, doi:10.1017/gov.2014.39.

Heydemann, Steven (ed.), *Networks of Privilege in the Middle East: The Politics of Economic Reform Revisited*, New York: Palgrave Macmillan, 2004.

Hibou, Béatrice, *The Force of Obedience: The Political Economy of Repression in Tunisia*, translated by Andrew Brown, Cambridge: Polity, 2011.

Hibou, Béatrice and John Hulsey, "Domination and Control in Tunisia: Economic Levers for the Exercise of Authoritarian Power," *Review of African Political Economy*, vol. 33, no. 108 (June 2006), pp. 185–206.

Hilsum, Lindsey, *Sandstorm: Libya in the Time of Revolution*, New York: Penguin Press, 2012.

Hinnebusch, Raymond A., "Party Activists in Syria and Egypt: Political Participation in Authoritarian Modernizing States," *International Political Science Review*, vol. 4, no. 1 (1983), pp. 84–93.

Syria: Revolution from Above, New York: Routledge, 2002.

Hite, Katherine, Cath Collins, and Alfredo Joignant, "The Politics of Memory in Chile," in Cath Collins, Katherine Hite, and Alfredo Joignant (eds.), *The Politics of Memory in Chile: From Pinochet to Bachelet*, Boulder, CO: Lynne Rienner, 2013, pp. 1–29.

Hishmat, Muhammad Jamal, *Mudhakkirat na'ib min Misr: sharaf al-niyaba 'an al-sha'b wa 'azmat al-tajriba* [Memoirs of a representative from Egypt: the honor of representing the people and the grandeur of the experience], Cairo: al-Wafa' Publishing, 2006.

Hizb al-Ba'th al-'Arabi al-Ishtiraki, *Azmat al-iqtisad al-Sudani: asbab al-azma wa tariq al-khuruj minha* [The Sudanese economic crisis: reasons for the crisis and ways to solve it], Khartoum: n.p., 1986.

al-Haraka al-Tashihiyya: min al-Mu'tamar al-Qawmi al-'Ashir al-Istithna'i ila al-Mu'tamar al-Qawmi al-Thalith 'Ashir [The Corrective Movement: from the Extraordinary National Tenth Conference to the Thirteen National Conference], Damascus: Cultural Bureau and Party Preparatory, 1983.

Hawla al-dimuqratiyya al-markaziyya [About centralized democracy], Damascus: Cultural Bureau and Party Preparatory Publications, n.d. (1970s).

Hizb al-Watani al-Dimuqrati, *al-Mu'tamar al-'Amm al-Rabi', 20–22 Yuliyu 1986* [The Fourth General Conference, July 20–22, 1986], Cairo: al-Hizb al-Watani al-Dimuqrati, 1986.

al-Mu'tamar al-Sanawi al-Rabi' [The Fourth Annual Conference], September 19–21, 2006, Cairo: n.p., 2006.

Ru'ya li-mustaqbal Misr: watha'iq al-Mu'tamar al-'Amm al-Thamin lil-Hizb al-Watani al-Dimuqrati wa tashkilat al-hizb [A vision of the future of Egypt: documents from the Eighth General Conference of the National Democratic Party and the structures of the party], September 15–17, Cairo: al-Jumhuriyya Publishing, 2002.

al-Sha'b wa al-intaj: taqrir ila al-Mu'tamar al-'Amm al-Rabi' li-Hizb al-Watan 'am 1986 [The people and production: report to the Fourth General Conference 1986], Cairo: al-Hizb al-Watani, 1986.

Hopkins, Stephen, *The Politics of Memoir and the Northern Ireland Conflict*, Liverpool: Liverpool University Press, 2013.

Howard, Marc Morjé and Meir R. Walters, "Explaining the Unexpected: Political Science and the Surprises of 1989 and 2011," *Perspectives on Politics*, vol. 12 (2014), pp. 394–408.

Hubbard, Ben, "Saudi King Unleashes a Torrent as Bonuses Flow to the Masses," *New York Times*, February 20, 2015.

Human Rights Watch, *Behind Closed Doors: Torture and Detention in Egypt*, New York: Human Rights Watch, 1992.

Huntington, Samuel P., *Political Order in Changing Societies*, New Haven: Yale University Press, 2006.

    The Third Wave: Democratization in the Late Twentieth Century, Norman: Oklahoma University Press, 1991.

Husayn, Lu'ay, *al-Fiqd: hikayat min dhakira mutakhiyyala li-sajin haqiqi* [The loss: stories from an imaginary memory of a real prisoner], Beirut: al-Furat, 2006.

al-Husayni, Hamdi, *Mudhakkirat Shams Badran: asrar al-hayat al-khassa li-Nasser wa Su'ad, al-Sadat wa Hamat* [Memoirs of Shams Badran: the secrets of the private lives of Nasser with Su'ad, Sadat with Hamat], Cairo: al-Nakhba Publishing, 2014.

Husni, Hamada, *Shams Badran: al-rajul alladhi hakama Misr* [Shams Badran: the man who ruled Egypt], Beirut: Beirut Library, 2008.

al-Husry, Khaldun S., *Three Reformers: A Study in Modern Arab Political Thought*, Beirut: Khayats, 1966.

Hussein, Saddam, *al-Mukhtarat* [The Collection], vol. III, Baghdad: Dar al-Shu'un al-Thaqafiyya, 1988.

    Nazra fi al-din wa al-turath [A glimpse into religion and tradition], Baghdad: al-Hurriyya Publishing House, 1980.

    al-Qal'a al-hasina: riwaya li-katibiha [The immune castle: a novel by its author], Baghdad: al-Huriyya Publishing House, 2001.

    Rijal wa madina: riwaya li-katibiha [Men and a city: a novel by its author], Baghdad: Ministry of Culture, n.d.

    Zabiba wa al-malik: riwaya li-katibiha [Zabiba and the king: a novel by its author], Baghdad: al-Bilad Publishing House, n.d.

Huwaydi, Amin Hamid, *al-Furas al-da'i'a: al-qararat al-hasima fi Harbay al-Istinzaf wa Uktubir: haqa'iq tunsharu li-awwal marra ma'a thamani watha'iq sirriyya* [The missed opportunities: decisive decisions in the Wars of Attrition and October: facts published for the first time with eight secret documents], Beirut: Corporation for Printing and Publishing, 1992.

    Ma'a 'Abd al-Nasser [With 'Abd al-Nasser], Cairo: al-Mustaqbal Publishing, 1985.

Ibrahim, Abu Hamid Ahmad, *Qissat kifah wa najah* [The story of struggle and success], Khartoum: 'Izzat Publishing, 2006.

Ibrahim, Hafiz Ahmad 'Abdullah, *al-Nukhab al-iqtisadiyya al-jadida fi al-Sudan* [The new economic elites in Sudan], Khartoum: al-Sudan Publishing, 2007.

Ibrahim, Hasanayn Tawfiq, *Zahirat al-ʿunf al-siyasi fi al-nuzum al-ʿArabiyya* [The phenomenon of political violence in the Arab regimes], 3rd edn., Beirut: Center for Arab Unity Studies, 2011.

Imam, ʿAbdullah, *al-Fariq Muhammad Fawzi: al-naksa, al-istinzaf, al-sijin* [Lieutenant General Muhammad Fawzi: the setback, the attrition, the prison], Cairo: Dar al-Khayyal Publishing, 2001.

International Crisis Group, "Failing Oversight: Iraq's Unchecked Government," *Middle East Report*, no. 113, September 2011.

"Trial by Error: Justice in Post-Qadhafi Libya," *Middle East/North Africa Report*, no. 140, April 17, 2013.

International Institute for Strategic Studies (IISS), "Chapter Five: Middle East and North Africa," *The Military Balance*, vol. 110 (2010), pp. 235–82.

International Monetary Fund, *Republic of Yemen*, Staff Report for the 2014 Article IV Consultation, July 3, 2014, IMF Country Report No. 14/276.

Iraq Survey Group, *Regime Strategic Intent*, vol. I: *Comprehensive Report of the Special Advisor to the Director of Central Intelligence*, September 30, 2003.

al-Iryani, ʿAbd al-Rahman ibn Yahya, *Mudhakkirat al-raʾis al-qadi* [Memoirs of the president judge], vol. II: *1962–67*, Cairo: Egyptian Association for Books, 2013.

ʿIsa, ʿAbd al-Raziq ʿAbd al-Raziq (ed.), *Mudhakkirat al-sagh Salah Salim* [Memoirs of the listener Salah Salim], Cairo: Egyptian Institution for the Book, 2013.

ʿIsa, Salah, *Shaʿir takdir al-amn al-ʿamm* [The poet who annoyed state security], 2nd edn., Cairo: al-Shuruq Publishing, 2008.

Iskander, Amir, *Saddam Hussein: The Fighter, the Thinker and the Man*, translated by Hassan Selim, Paris: Hachette Réalités, 1980.

Ismael, Tareq Y., *The Rise and Fall of the Communist Party of Iraq*, Cambridge: Cambridge University Press, 2008.

Ismaʿil, Muhammad Hafiz, *Amn Misr al-qawmi fi ʿasr al-tahadiyyat* [Egyptian national security in the era of challenges], Cairo: al-Ahram Center for Publishing, 1987.

Ismaʿil, Muhammad Sadiq, *al-Fasad al-idari fi al-ʿalam al-ʿArabi: mafhumaha wa abʿadaha al-mukhtalifa* [Administrative corruption in the Arab world: its concepts and miscellaneous ramifications], Cairo: Arab Group, 2014.

Jabi, Nasr, *al-Jazaʾir: al-dawla wa al-nukhab, dirasat fi al-nukhab, al-ahzab al-siyasiyya wa al-harakat al-ijtimaʿiyya* [Algeria: the state and the elites, a study in elites, political parties, and social movements], Algiers: al-Shihab Publications, 2008.

al-Jam'ani, Dafi, *Min al-hizb ila al-sijin 1948–1994: mudhakkirat* [From party to prison, 1948–1994: memoirs], Beirut: Riyad al-Rayyis Books, 2007.

al-Jamasi, Muhammad 'Abd al-Ghani, *Mudhakkirat al-Jamasi: Harb Uktubir 1973* [al-Jamasi's memoirs: The October 1973 War], Paris: al-Sharqiyya Publishing, 1990.

Jami', Mahmud, *'Ariftu al-Sadat: nisf qarn min khafaya al-Sadat wa al-Ikhwan* [I knew al-Sadat: half a century of Sadat's secrets and the Brothers], Cairo: al-Maktab al-Misri, 1998.

al-Janzuri, Kamal, *Misr wa al-tanmiya* [Egypt and development], Cairo: Dar al-Shuruq, 2013.

   Tariqi: sanawat al-hilm, wa al-sidam, wa al-'uzla: min al-qarya ila ria'sat majlis al-wuzara' [My path: years of dreams, confrontation, and isolation: from the village to head of the cabinet], Cairo: Dar al-Shuruq, 2013.

al-Jawadi, Muhammad Muhammad, *Mudhakkirat qadat al-mukhabarat wa al-mabahith: al-amn al-qawmi li-Misr* [Memoirs of the leaders of intelligence and security: the national security of Egypt], Cairo: Dar al-Khayyal Publishing, 1999.

   Qadat al-shurta fi al-siyasa al-Misriyya 1952–2002: dirasa tahliliyya wa mawsu'at shakhsiyyat [Police commanders in Egyptian politics 1952–2002: an analytical study and a biographical dictionary], Cairo: Madbuly Publishing, 2003.

   al-Shahid 'Abd al-Mun'im Riyad: sima' al-'askariyya al-Misriyya [The martyr 'Abd al-Mun'im Riyad: the finest of the Egyptian military], Cairo: al-Atibba' Publishing, 1984.

al-Jawhari, Las'ad, "Torture in Ben 'Ali's Era," in 'Abd al-Jalil al-Tamimi (ed.), *Dirasat wa shahadat hawla dahaya al-ta'dhib wa al-iztihad bi-anzimat al-hukm bil-Maghrab al-Kabir, 1956–2010* [Studies and testimonies about victims of torture and repression in the Maghreb, 1956–2010], no. 25, Tunis: al-Tamimi Foundation, 2013, pp. 205–10.

al-Jayyar, Sawsan, *Fathi Sarur wa al-barlaman: asrar wa i'tirafat* [Fathi Sarur and the parliament: secrets and confessions], Cairo: Arab Press and Publications, 2002.

   Majlis nuss al-layl: ru'ya suhufiyya jari'a: barlaman 1995–2000 [The midnight council: a brave journalistic insight: the parliament of 1995–2000], Cairo: Arab Agency for Media and Publications, 2000.

Jebnoun, Noureddine, "Ben Ali's Tunisia: The Authoritarian Path of a Dystopian State," in Noureddine Jebnoun, Mehrdad Kia, and Mimi Kirk (eds.), *Modern Middle East Authoritarianism*, New York: Routledge, 2014, pp. 101–22.

al-Jilad, Majdi, *Mushir al-nasr: mudhakkirat Ahmad Isma'il wazir al-harbiyya fi Ma'rakat Uktubir 1973* [The marshal of victory: memoirs of Ahmad Ismail, minister of war in the October 1973 War], Cairo: Nahdat Misr Publishing, 2013.

Jin-sung, Jang, *Dear Leader: My Escape from North Korea*, translated by Shirley Lee, New York: Random House, 2014.

Joffé, George, "Political Dynamics in North Africa," *International Affairs*, vol. 85, no. 5 (2009), pp. 931–49.

Juneau, Thomas, "Yemen and the Arab Spring," in Mehran Kamrava (ed.), *Beyond the Arab Spring: The Evolving Ruling Bargain in the Middle East*, New York: Oxford University Press, 2014, pp. 373–96.

Juwayli, Salim Salama, *Taqyim al-kifaya al-idariyya wa al-mihniyya li-umana' al-shurta* [An appraisal of the administrative and technical capabilities of deputy inspectors], Cairo: Institute for Higher Studies for Police Officers, n.d.

al-Ka'bi, al-Munji, *Mudakhalat 'udu bil-Lajna al-Markaziyya* [Interjections of a member of the Central Committee], Tunis: al-Kitab Publishing, 1986.

Kadri, Ali, "A Depressive Pre-Arab Uprisings Economic Performance," in Fawaz A. Gerges (ed.), *The New Middle East: Protest and Revolution in the Arab World*, New York: Cambridge University Press, 2014, pp. 80–106.

Kandil, Hazem, *Soldiers, Spies, and Statesmen: Egypt's Road to Revolt*, New York: Verso, 2014.

Karshenas, Massoud and Valentine M. Moghadam (eds.), *Social Policy in the Middle East: Economic, Political, and Gender Dynamics*, United Nations Research Institute for Social Development (UNRISD), New York: Palgrave Macmillan, 2006.

Kassab, Suzanne, *Contemporary Arab Thought: Cultural Critique in Comparative Perspective*, New York: Columbia University Press, 2010.

Kassem, Maye, *Egyptian Politics: The Dynamics of Authoritarian Rule*, Boulder, CO: Lynne Rienner, 2004.

Katz, Kimberly, *A Young Palestinian's Diary, 1941–1945: The Life of Sami 'Amr*, Austin: University of Texas Press, 2009.

al-Kawakibi, 'Abd al-Rahman, *Taba'i' al-istibdad wa masari' al-isti'bad* [The nature of tyranny and struggle against enslavement], Cairo: Iqra' Foundation, 2013.

Kedourie, Elie, *Arabic Political Memoirs and Other Studies*, London: Frank Cass, 1974.

Kéfi, Ridha, "Les Habits neufs de l'armée" [The new clothes of the army], *Jeune Afrique*, July 13–20, 1999, pp. 24–26.

Kennedy, Mark C. (ed.), *Twenty Years of Development in Egypt (1977–1997), Part I: Economy, Politics, Regional Relations*, Cairo Papers 20th Anniversary Symposium, vol. 21, monograph 3, Cairo: American University Press, 1998.

Kermanach, Laure and Guillaume Guichard, "La Pieuvre Ben Ali disséquée" [The octopus Ben Ali dissected], *Le Figaro*, January 21, 2011.

al-Khafaji, Isam, "State Terror and the Degradation of Politics in Iraq," *Middle East Report*, no. 176, May–June 1992, pp. 15–21.

"War as a Vehicle for the Rise and Demise of a State-Controlled Society: The Case of Ba'thist Iraq," in Steven Heydemann (ed.), *War, Institutions, and Social Change in the Middle East*, Berkeley: University of California Press, 2000, pp. 258–91.

Khalifa, Mustafa, *al-Qawqa'a: yawmiyyat mutalassis* [The shell: the diary of a voyeur], 2nd edn., Beirut: Dar al-Adab, 2010.

Khalil, Khalil Hasan, *al-Wasya: 'an qissat hayat al-jundi alladhi asbaha ustadhan lil-iqtisad al-siyasi bi al-jami'a* [al-Wasya: the life story of the soldier who became a professor of political economy at the university], Cairo: Egyptian Association for the Book, 1983.

Khalil, Mahmud, "al-Amn al-qawmi: ittijahat al-tahdid wa ab'ad al-muwajaha" [The national security: trends of threats and dimensions of confrontation], *al-Nasr*, no. 583 (January 1988), pp. 22–23.

Khalili, Laleh and Jillian Schwedler (eds.), "Introduction," in *Policing and Prisons in the Middle East: Formation of Coercion*, London: Hurst, 2010, pp. 1–40.

al-Khujli, 'Abd al-Rahman, *al-Jaysh wa al-siyasa* [The army and politics], Omdurman: Mirghani Cultural Center, 2012.

Kienle, Eberhard, *Ba'th v. Ba'th: The Conflict between Syria and Iraq 1968–1989*, London: I. B. Tauris, 1991.

"More than a Response to Islamism: The Political Deliberalization of Egypt in the 1990s," *Middle East Journal*, vol. 52, no. 2 (1998), pp. 219–35.

Kifaya, "Corruption in Egypt: A Dark Cloud that Does Not Vanish," 2006, available at https://docs.google.com/document/d/1rh6YoHyQopURU x2Pm2DdZfdHqofYS8R3AawzfPUkCxs/edit?hl=en.

el-Kikhia, Mansour O., *Libya's Qaddafi: The Politics of Contradiction*, Gainesville: University Press of Florida, 1997.

Kirkpatrick, David D., "Egypt's New Autocrat, Sisi Knows Best," *New York Times*, May 25 2014.

Korany, Baghat, "Restricted Democratization from Above: Egypt," in Baghat Korany, Rex Brynen, and Paul Noble (eds.), *Political Liberalization and Democratization in the Arab World*, vol. II: *Comparative Experiences*, Boulder, CO: Lynne Rienner, 1998, pp. 39–69.

Korsch, Boris, *The Brezhnev Personality Cult – Continuity: The Librarian's Point of View*, Research Paper No. 65, Jerusalem: The Hebrew University, 1987.

Kupferberg, Feiwel, *The Break-up of Communism in East Germany and Eastern Europe*, London: Macmillan, 1999.

Kuran, Timur, "Sparks and Prairie Fires: A Theory of Unanticipated Political Revolution," *Public Choice*, vol. 61, no. 1 (1989), pp. 41–74.

Lacouture, Jean, *The Demigods: Charismatic Leadership in the Third World*, New York: Alfred Knopf, 1970.

al-Lamushi, 'Abd al-Mun'im Yusif, *Fi 'ahd Mu'ammar al-Qaddafi: kuntu mutahaddithan rasmiyyan* [In the era of Mu'ammar al-Qaddafi: I was an official spokesman], Tripoli: al-Hadath Publishing, 2012.

Laribi, Lyes, *L'Algérie des généraux* [The generals' Algeria], Paris: Max Milo, 2007.

Dans les geôles de Nezzar [In the dungeons of Nezzar], Paris: Paris–Méditerranée, 2002.

Lesch, Ann M., "Democratization in a Fragmented Society: Sudan," in Baghat Korany, Rex Brynen, and Paul Noble (eds.), *Political Liberalization and Democratization in the Arab World, vol. II: Comparative Experiences*, Boulder, CO: Lynne Rienner, 1998, pp. 203–22.

Levinson, Charles and Margaret Coker, "Inside a Flawed Spy Machine as Gadhafi's Rule Crumbled," *Wall Street Journal*, September 2, 2011.

Levitsky, Steven and Lucan A. Way, *Competitive Authoritarianism: Hybrid Regimes after the Cold War*, New York: Cambridge University Press, 2010.

Lewis, Aidan, "Tracking down Ben Ali's Fortune," BBC News, January 31, 2011, available at www.bbc.co.uk/news/mobile/world-africa-12302659.

"Lieutenant General Salih Halbi Meets with Members of the Armed Forces," *al-Nasr*, no. 643, January 1993.

Limam, Mohammed Halim, "Detailed Analysis of the Phenomenon of Political Corruption in Algeria: Causes, Repercussions and Reform," *Contemporary Arab Affairs*, vol. 5, no. 2 (2012), pp. 252–78.

Zahirat al-fasad al-siyasi fi al-Jaza'ir: al-asbab wa al-athar wa al-islah [The political corruption phenomenon in Algeria: causes, effects, and reform], Beirut: Markaz Dirasat al-Wihda al-'Arabiyya, 2011.

Linz, Juan J., "The Religious Use of Politics and/or the Political Use of Religion: Ersatz Ideology versus Ersatz Religion," in Hans Maier (ed.), *Totalitarianism and Political Religions, vol. I: Concepts for the Comparison of Dictatorships*, translated by Jodi Bruhn, New York: Routledge, 2004, pp. 102–20.

Linz, Juan J. and Alfred Stepan, *Problems of Democratic Transition and Consolidation: Southern Europe, South America, and Post-Communist Europe*, Baltimore: Johns Hopkins University Press, 1996.

al-Lishani, Sa'id 'Isa, *Min al-dhakira: qissat kifah* [From memory: the story of a struggle], Beirut: Bissan Publishing, 2012.

Lockman, Zachary (ed.), *Workers and Working Classes in the Middle East: Struggles, History, Historiographies*, Albany: State University of New York Press, 1994.

Looney, R., "Economic Consequences of Conflict: The Rise of Iraq's Informal Economy," *Journal of Economic Issues*, vol. 4 (2006), pp. 1–17.

Lübbe, Hermann, "The Historicity of Totalitarianism: George Orwell's Evidence," in Hans Maier (ed.), *Totalitarianism and Political Religions, vol. I: Concepts for the Comparison of Dictatorships*, New York: Routledge, 2004, pp. 247–52.

Luciani, Giacomo, "Linking Economic and Political Reform in the Middle East: The Role of the Bourgeoisie," in Oliver Schlumberger (ed.), *Debating Authoritarianism: Dynamics and Durability in Nondemocratic Regimes*, Stanford: Stanford University Press, 2007, pp. 161–76.

Lust, Ellen, "*Elections,*" in Marc Lynch (ed.), *The Arab Uprisings Explained: New Contentious Politics in the Middle East*, New York: Columbia University Press, 2014, pp. 218–45.

Lust-Okar, Ellen, *Structuring Conflict in the Arab World: Incumbents, Opponents, and Institutions*, New York: Cambridge University Press, 2005.

Lutterbeck, Derek, "After the Fall: Security Sector Reform in post-Ben Ali Tunisia," Arab Reform Initiative, 2012, available at www.arab-reform .net/after-fall-security-sector-reform-post-ben-ali-tunisia.

"Arab Uprisings, Armed Forces, and Civil–Military Relations," *Armed Forces and Society*, vol. 39, no. 1 (April 2012), pp. 28–52.

Lyon, Alistair, "Analysis – Egyptian Army could hold Key to Mubarak's Fate," Reuters, January 28, 2011.

al-Madini, Tawfiq, *Suqut al-dawla al-bulisiyya fi Tunis* [The collapse of the police state in Tunisia], Beirut: Arab Scientific Publishers, 2011.

Magaloni, Beatriz, *Voting for Autocracy: Hegemonic Party Survival and its Demise in Mexico*, New York: Cambridge University Press, 2006.

el-Mahdi, Rabab, "The Democracy Movement: Cycles of Protest," in Rabab el-Mahdi and Philip Marfleet (eds.), *Egypt: The Moment of Change*, New York: Zed Books, 2009, pp. 87–102.

De Maio, Paola, "From Soldiers to Policemen: Qadhafi's Army in the New Century," *Journal of Middle Eastern Geopolitics*, vol. 2, no. 3 (2006), pp. 17–26.

al-Majdub, Taha, "al-Jaysh al-Misri ba'd Yunyu 1967" [The Egyptian army after June 1967], in Lutfi al-Khuli (ed.), *Harb Yunyu 1967: ba'd 30 sana* [The June 1967 War: 30 years later], Cairo: al-Ahram Publishing, 1997, pp. 115–42.

Makhal, Rihab, "Tarikh al-mu'tamarat al-qawmiyya" [History of the regional conferences], in Muhammad Jamal Barut (ed.), *al-Ahzab wa al-harakat wa al-tanzimat al-qawmiyy fi al-watan al-'Arabi* [Nationalist parties, movements, and organizations in the Arab world], Beirut: Center for Arab Unity Studies, 2012, pp. 898–922.

Makiya, Kanan, *Republic of Fear: The Politics of Modern Iraq*, Berkeley: University of California, 1998.

Malik, Adeel and Bassem Awadallah, "The Economics of the Arab Spring," *World Development*, vol. 45 (May 2013), pp. 296–313.

Mana'i, Ahmad, *al-Ta'dhib al-Tunisi fi al-hadiqa al-sirriyya lil-Jiniral Ben 'Ali* [The Tunisian torture in the secret garden of General Ben 'Ali], Cairo: Madbuly Bookshop, n.d.

el-Manawy, Abdel-Latif, *Tahrir: The Last 18 Days of Mubarak: An Insider's Account of the Uprising in Egypt*, London: Gilgamesh, 2012.

Mandel, Barrett J., "Full of Life Now," in James Olney (ed.), *Autobiography: Essays Theoretical and Critical*, Princeton: Princeton University Press, 1980, pp. 49–72.

Manguel, Alberto, *The Library at Night*, New Haven: Yale University Press, 2006.

Mansur, Anis, *Intaha zaman al-furas al-da'i'a* [The era of missed chances is over], Cairo: al-Nahda Publishing, 1998.

Mansur, Fawzi (ed.), *al-Haraka al-'ummaliyya fi ma'rakat al-tahawwal: dirasat fi al-intikhabat al-naqabiyya 1991* [The labor movement in the battle of change: studies in the union elections of 1991], Cairo: Markaz al-Buhuth al-'Arabiyya, 1994.

al-Marashi, Ibrahim, "Iraq's Security and Intelligence Network: A Guide and an Analysis," *Middle East Review of International Affairs*, vol. 6, no. 3 (September 2002), pp. 1–13.

al-Marashi, Ibrahim and Sammy Salama, *Iraq's Armed Forces: An Analytical History*, New York: Routledge, 2008.

Mar'i, Sayyid, *Awraq siyasiyya* [Political papers], 3 vols., Cairo: al-Maktab al-Misri al-Hadith, 1978: vol. I, *Min al-qarya ila al-islah* [From the village to reform]; vol. II, *Min azmat Mars ila al-naksa* [From the March crisis until the defeat]; vol. III, *Ma'a al-ra'is al-Sadat* [With President Sadat].

Martin, Ian, "The United Nations' Role in the First Year of the Transition," in Peter Cole and Brian McQuinn (eds.), *The Libyan Revolution and its Aftermath*, New York: Oxford University Press, 2015, pp. 127–52.

al-Mashshat, Muhammad, *Kuntu safiran lil-'Iraq fi Washintun: hikayati ma'a Saddam fi ghazu al-Kuwait* [I was Iraq's ambassador in Washington: my story with Saddam during the invasion of Kuwait], Beirut: Arab Institute for Research and Publishing, 2008.

Matar, Hisham, *Anatomy of a Disappearance: A Novel*, New York: Dial Press, 2012.

In the Country of Men, New York: Dial Press, 2006.

"The Return: A Father's Disappearance, a Journey Home," *New Yorker*, April 8, 2013.

Mattes, Hanspeter, "Challenges to Security Sector Governance in the Middle East: The Libyan Case," conference paper, Geneva Centre for the Democratic Control of Armed Forces (DCAF), July 12–13, 2004.

"Formal and Informal Authority in Libya since 1969," in Dirk Vandewalle (ed.), *Libya Since 1969: Qaddafi's Revolution Revisited*, New York: Palgrave Macmillan, 2008, pp. 55–81.

al-Mawardi, Abu al-Hasan, *The Ordinances of Government: A Translation of al-Ahkam al-Sultaniyya wa al-Wilayat al-Diniyya*, translated by Wafaa H. Wahba, Reading: Garnet Publishing, 1996.

McDermott, Kevin and Matthew Stibbe, "Stalinist Terror in Eastern Europe: Problems, Perspectives and Interpretations," in Kevin McDermott and Matthew Stibbe (eds.), *Stalinist Terror in Eastern Europe: Elite Purges and Mass Repression*, Manchester: Manchester University Press, 2010, pp. 1–18.

McQuinn, Brian, "Assessing (In)Security after the Arab Spring," *Political Science and Politics*, vol. 46 (October 2013), pp. 709–39.

de Mesquita, Bruce Bueno and Alastair Smith, *The Dictator's Handbook: Why Bad Behavior is Almost Always Good Politics*, New York: Public Affairs, 2011.

"How Tyrants Endure," *New York Times*, June 9, 2011.

Mestiri, Ahmed, *Shahada lil-tarikh: dhikrayat wa ta'mmulat wa ta'aliq hawla fatra min al-tarikh al-mu'asir li-Tunis wa al-Maghrab al-Kabir (1940–1990) wa thawrat 2010–2011* [Testimony to history: reminiscences, reflections, and commentaries about a period in the contemporary history of Tunisia and the Greater Maghreb (1940–1990) and the revolution 2010–2011], Tunis: al-Junub Publishing, 2011.

Témoignage pour l'histoire [Testimony for history], Tunis: Sud Editions, 2011.

Middle East Watch, *Syria Unmasked: The Suppression of Human Rights by the Asad Regime*, New Haven: Yale University Press, 1991.

el-Mikawy, Noha, *The Building of Consensus in Egypt's Transition Process*, Cairo: American University Press, 1999.

Miller, Barbara, *Narratives of Guilt and Compliance in Unified Germany: Stasi Informers and their Impact on Society*, New York: Routledge, 1999.

Mirak-Weissbach, Muriel, *Madmen at the Helm: Pathology and Politics in the Arab Spring*, Reading: Ithaca Press, 2012.

Mitchell, Timothy, *Rule of Experts: Egypt, Techno-Politics, Modernity*, Berkeley: University of California Press, 2002.

Mohi el-Din, Khaled, *Memories of a Revolution: Egypt 1952*, Cairo: American University of Cairo Press, 1992. (For his Arabic publications, see Muhyi al-Din, Khalid.)

de Montaigne, Michel, *Montaigne's Essays in Three Books*, vol. II: *Religion and Philosophy*, London: n.p., 1743.

Montefiore, Simon Sebag, "Dictators Get the Deaths they Deserve," *New York Times*, October 27, 2011.

Moore, Clement H., "The Single Party as a Source of Legitimacy," in Samuel P. Huntington and Clement H. Moore (eds.), *Authoritarian Politics in Modern Society: The Dynamics of Established One-Party Systems*, New York: Basic Books, 1970, pp. 48–72.

"More than 1,200 Bodies Found in Tripoli Mass Grave," BBC News, September 25, 2011.

Mu'alla, 'Abd al-Amir, *al-Ayyam al-tawila* [The long days], Baghdad: Wizarat al-I'lam, 1978.

Muasher, Marwan, *The Second Arab Awakening and the Battle for Pluralism*, New Haven: Yale University Press, 2014.

Mubarak, Zuhair Farid, *Usul al-istibdad al-'Arabi* [The origins of Arab despotism], Beirut: al-Intishar, 2010.

Muhyi al-Din, Khalid, *Wa al-'an atakallam* [Now I speak], Cairo: Ahram Center for Translations and Publications, 1992. (For his English publications, see Mohi el-Din, Khaled.)

Munif, 'Abd al-Rahman, *Sharq al-Mutawassit* [East of the Mediterranean], Beirut: al-Tali'a Publishing, 1975.

Muqayyid, Muhammad As'ad, *Masira fi al-hayat: tarikh ma lam yu'arrikh lahu al-akharun* [Journey in life: a history that was not documented by others], Damascus: al-Dhakira Publishing, 2005.

Murphy, Emma C., *Economic and Political Change in Tunisia: from Bourguiba to Ben Ali*, New York: St. Martin's Press, 1999.

Muru, Muhammad, *Sulayman Khatir, "Batal Sina'"*: *al-jundi al-Muslim alladhi dafa' 'an karamat Misr wa jayshiha* [Sulayman Khatir, "Hero of the Sinai": the Muslim soldier who defended Egypt's honor and its army], Cairo: Digest Books, 1986.

Mustafa, Hala, "Mu'asharat wa nata'ij intikhabat 1995" [Indicators and results of the 1995 elections], in Hala Mustafa (ed.), *al-Intikhabat al-barlamaniyya fi Misr, 1995* [The parliamentary elections in Egypt, 1995], Cairo: al-Ahram Political and Strategic Studies Center, 1997, pp. 35–51.

Mustafa, Muhammad, *Kuntu waziran lil-dakhiliyya* [I was a minister of the interior], Cairo: Akhbar al-Yawm, 1992.

al-Muzzafir, Zuhair, *Min al-hizb al-wahid ila hizb al-aghlabiyya* [From the single party to the majority party], Tunisia: Sanbakit, 2004.

Mzali, Mohamed, *Hadith al-fi'l* [The talk of action], Tunis: Tunisian Society for Publications, 1985.

　La Parole de l'action: conversation avec Xavière Ulysse [The talk of action: conversation with Xavière Ulysse], Paris: Publisud, 1984.

　Un premier ministre de Bourguiba témoigne [A prime minister of Bourguiba testifies], Paris: Jean Picollec, 2004.

al-Nabulsi, Shakir, *Su'ud al-mujtami' al-'askari al-'Arabi fi Misr wa al-Sham, 1948–2000* [The rise of the Arab military society in Egypt and Syria, 1948–2000], Beirut: Arab Institute for Research and Publishing, 2003.

el-Naggar, Mona, "Egypt to End the Ubiquity of Mubarak," *New York Times*, April 22, 2011.

Nasif, 'Imad, *Buyut min al-zujaj: al-malaffat al-sirriyya li-fasad al-kibar* [Glasshouses: the secret files of the corruption of the powerful], Cairo: Arab Media, 1999.

Nasir, Shihab, *'Amru Musa: al-malaffat al-sirriyya* ['Amru Musa: the secret files], Cairo: Center for Arabic Civilization, 2001.

Nasr, Salah, *Mudhakkirat Salah Nasr: thawrat 23 Yuliyu bayn al-masir wa al-masir* [The memoirs of Salah Nasr: the July 23 revolution between the journey and the destiny], vol. I, Abu Dhabi: Ittihad Publishing, 1986.

Nezzar, Khalid, *Bouteflika: al-rajul wa al-hasila* [Bouteflika: the man and the outcome], Algiers: APIC, 2003.

　Mudhakkirat al-Liwa' Khalid Nezzar [Memoirs of Major-General Khalid Nezzar], Algiers: al-Shihab Publishing, 1999.

Nordlinger, Eric, *Soldiers in Politics: Military Coups and Governments*, Englewood Cliffs, NJ: Prentice Hall, 1977.

Norton, Augustus Richard (ed.), *Civil Society in the Middle East*, vol. I, Leiden: Brill, 2005.

Nur, Ayman, *Sajin al-huriyya: Ayman Nur yaktubu min khalf al-aswar* [The prisoner of freedom: Ayman Nur writes from behind walls], Cairo: n.p., 2006.

Nur, Ayman and Majdi Shindi, *al-'Askari al-aswad, Zaki Badr* [The black policeman, Zaki Badr], Cairo: Arab International Publishing Company, 1990.

O'Donnell, Guillermo and Philippe C. Schmitter, *Transitions from Authoritarian Rule: Tentative Conclusions about Uncertain Democracies*, Baltimore: Johns Hopkins University Press, 2013.

Orzoff, Andrea, "The Husbandman: Tomáš Masaryk's Leader Cult in Interwar Czechoslovakia," *Austrian History Yearbook*, vol. 39 (2008), pp. 121–37.

Overy, Richard, *The Dictators: Hitler's Germany and Stalin's Russia*, London: Penguin, 2008.

Owen, Roger, *The Rise and Fall of Arab Presidents for Life*, Cambridge, MA: Harvard University Press, 2012.

  State, Power, and Politics in the Making of the Modern Middle East, 3rd edn., New York: Routledge, 2008.

Packer, George, *The Assassin's Gate*, New York: Farrar, Straus, & Giroux, 2005.

Pargeter, Alison, *Libya: The Rise and Fall of Qaddafi*, New Haven: Yale University Press, 2012.

Peel, Michael, "Iraq: Singular Ambition," *Financial Times*, May 7, 2012.

Pepinsky, Thomas B., *Economic Crises and the Breakdown of Authoritarian Regimes: Indonesia and Malaysia in Comparative Perspectives*, New York: Cambridge University Press, 2009.

Persak, Krzystof and Łukasz Kamiński (eds.), *A Handbook of the Communist Security Apparatus in East Central Europe 1944–1989*, Warsaw: Institute of National Remembrance, 2005.

Perthes, Volker, *The Political Economy of Syria under Asad*, London: I. B. Tauris, 1997.

  "Syria: Difficult Inheritance," in Volker Perthes (ed.), *Arab Elites: Negotiating the Politics of Change*, Boulder, CO: Lynne Rienner, 2004, pp. 87–114.

Peterson, John, "Yemen on the Precipice: Governing the Ungovernable," in Abbas Kadhim (ed.), *Governance in the Middle East and North Africa: A Handbook*, London: Routledge, 2013, pp. 306–18.

"Petrobras Scandal: Brazilian Oil Executives among 35 Charged," *Guardian*, December 11, 2014.

Phillips, David L., *Losing Iraq: Inside the Postwar Reconstruction Fiasco*, New York: Basic Books, 2005.

Picard, Elizabeth, "Arab Military in Politics: From Revolutionary Plot to Authoritarian State," in Giacomo Luciani (ed.), *The Arab State*, Berkeley: University of California Press, 1990, pp. 189–220.

Pierret, Thomas, *Religion and State in Syria: The Sunni Ulama from Coup to Revolution*, New York: Cambridge University Press, 2013.

Pop-Eleches, Grigore, "Romania Twenty Years after 1989: The Bizarre Echoes of a Contested Revolution," in Michael Berhard and Jan

Kubik (eds.), *Twenty Years after Communism: The Politics of Memory and Commemoration*, New York: Oxford University Press, 2014, pp. 85–103.

Post, Jerrold M., "Saddam Hussein of Iraq: A Political Psychology Profile," in Jerrold M. Post (ed.), *The Psychological Assessment of Political Leaders: With Profiles of Saddam Hussein and Bill Clinton*, Ann Arbor: University of Michigan Press, 2005, pp. 335–66.

Povoledo, Elisabetta, "A Dead Dictator who Draws Tens of Thousands in Italy," *New York Times*, November 2, 2011.

al-Qaddafi, Mu'ammar, *The Green Book*, Tripoli: Public Establishment for Publishing, n.d.

    al-Qarya … al-qarya, al-ard … al-ard wa intihar ra'id al-fada' ma'a qisas ukhra [The village … the village, the land … the land and the suicide of an astronaut with other stories], Cairo: Egyptian Organization for Books, 1996. [See also under Gaddafi]

Qadduri, Fakhri, *Hakadha 'ariftu al-Bakr wa Saddam: rihlat 35 'aman fi Hizb al-Ba'th* [This was the way I knew al-Bakr and Saddam: a journey of 35 years in the Ba'th Party], London: Dar al-Hikma, 2006.

Qadri, Husayn, *'Abd al-Nasser wa alladhin kanu ma'ahu* ['Abd al-Nasser and those who were with him], Cairo: al-Jumhuriyya Publishing, 2007.

Qarm, George, "al-Iqtisad al-siyasi lil-intiqal al-dimuqrati fi al-watan al-'Arabi" [The political economy of the democratic transition in the Arab world], *al-Mustaqbal al-'Arabi* [The Arab Future], no. 426 (August 2014), pp. 19–40.

al-Qayzani, Tariq, *al-Hizb al-Dimuqrati al-Taqaddumi* [The Progressive Democratic Party], Tunis: Dar Muhammad for Publishing, 2011.

al-Qiyada al-Qawmiyya, *Nidal al-Ba'th: watha'iq Hizb al-Ba'th al-'Arabi al-Ishtiraki* [The struggle of the Ba'th: documents of the Arab Socialist Ba'th Party], vol. IV: *1955–1961*, Beirut: al-Tali'a Publishing, 1964.

Quinlivan, James T., "Coup-proofing: Its Practice and Consequences in the Middle East," *International Security*, vol. 24, no. 2 (Fall 1999), pp. 131–65.

al-Qulaybi, al-Shadhili, *Adwa' min al-dhakira: al-Habib Bourguiba* [Lights from memory: Habib Bourguiba], Tunis: Dimitir, 2014.

Qutb, Shiyam 'Abd al-Hamid, *Mustaqbal al-sahafa al-hizbiyya fi Misr* [The future of the party press in Egypt], Cairo: Dar al-'Alam al-'Arabi, 2010.

Ra'fat, Muhammad 'Abd al-Rahman. *Dhikrayat dabit bahri* [Memories of a navy officer], Cairo: Egyptian Organization for the Book, 2003.

Ra'if, Ahmad, *al-Bawwaba al-sawda': safahat min tarikh al-Ikhwan al-Muslimin* [The black gate: pages from the history of the Muslim Brotherhood], Cairo: al-Zahra' Publishing, 1989.

Radwan, Fathi, *Fathi Radwan yarwi li-Dhia' al-Din Bibars asrar hukumat Yuliyu* [Fathi Radwan recounts to Dhia' al-Din Bibars the secrets of the July government], Cairo: al-Ma'rifa Publishing, 1976.

Ramadan, 'Abd al-'Azim, *Mudhakkirat al-siyasiyyin wa al-zu'ama' fi Misr, 1891–1981* [Memoirs of politicians and leaders in Egypt, 1891–1981], Cairo: al-Watan al-'Arabi, 1985.

al-Sira' al-ijtima'i wa al-siyasi fi 'asr Mubarak [The social and political clash in Mubarak's era], vol. VII, Cairo: al-Hay'a al-Misriyya lil-Kitab, 1995.

Rashid, Nura, *Rijal hawla al-ra'is: hiwar ma'a shakhsiyyat hamma* [Men around the president: dialogue with important personalities], vol. I, Cairo: Egyptian Institution for the Book, 1997.

al-Razzaz, Munif, *al-'Amal al-fikriyya wa al-siyasiyya* [Intellectual and political works], 3 vols., Beirut: Dar al-Mutawassit, 1985.

Reda, Adel, *A Reading in Assad Thinking*, Cairo: Akhbar al-Yawm, n.d.

Rees, E. A., "Leader Cults: Varieties, Preconditions and Functions," in Balázas Apor, Jan C. Behrends, Polly Jones, and E. A. Rees (eds.), *The Leader Cult in Communist Dictatorships: Stalin and the Eastern Bloc*, New York: Palgrave Macmillan, 2004, pp. 3–28.

Reynolds, Dwight F. (ed.), *Interpreting the Self: Autobiography in the Arabic Literary Tradition*, Berkeley: University of California Press, 2001.

Richards, Alan and John Waterbury, *A Political Economy of the Middle East*, 3rd edn., Boulder, CO: Westview Press, 2008.

Richardson, Catherine (ed.), *Clothing and Culture, 1350–1650*, Aldershot: Ashgate Publishing Co., 2004.

Ricoeur, Paul, *Memory, History, Forgetting*, translated by Kathleen Blamey and David Pellauer, Chicago: University of Chicago Press, 2004.

Roberts, Hugh, *The Battlefield Algeria, 1988–2002: Studies in a Broken Polity*, New York: Verso, 2003.

"Who Said Gaddafi Had to Go?" *London Review of Books*, vol. 33, no. 22, November 17, 2011, pp. 8–18.

Rogg, Margaret L., "Egyptian Policemen Fight Troops in Revolt Set off near Pyramids," *New York Times*, February 27, 1986.

Rotberg, Robert I., "How Corruption Compromises World Peace and Stability," in Robert I. Rotberg (ed.), *Corruption, Global Security, and World Order*, Baltimore: Brookings Institution Press, 2009, pp. 1–26.

"Leadership Alters Corrupt Behavior," in Robert I. Rotberg (ed.), *Corruption, Global Security, and World Order*, Baltimore: Brookings Institution Press, 2009, pp. 341–58

Rubin, Barry, "The Military in Contemporary Arab Politics," in Barry Rubin and Thomas A. Keaney (eds.), *Armed Forces in the Middle East*, London: Frank Cass, 2002, pp. 1–22.

Ryan, Curtis R., "Jordan and the Arab Spring," in Mark L. Haas and Mark W. Lesch (eds.), *The Arab Spring: Change and Resistance in the Middle East*, Boulder, CO: Westview Press, 2013, pp. 116–30.

el-Saadany, Salah, *Egypt and Libya from Inside, 1969–1976: The Qaddafi Revolution and the Eventual Break in Relations*, translated by Mohammad el-Behairy, London: McFarland & Co., 1994.

el-Saadawi, Nawal, *al-Insan: ithnay 'ashr imra'a fi zinzana* [The human: twelve women in a cell], Cairo: Madbuly Publishing, 2005.

  Memoirs from the Women's Prison, translated by Marilyn Booth, London: Women's Press, 1986.

Sachs, Jonah, *Winning the Story Wars*, Cambridge, MA: Harvard Business Review Press, 2012.

Sa'd al-Din, 'Adnan, *al-Ikhwan al-Muslimun fi Suriya, mudhakkirat wa dhikrayat: sanawat al-majazir al-mur'iba min 'am 1977 wa hatta 'am 1983* [The Muslim Brothers in Syria, memoirs and memories: the years of the terrifying massacres from 1977 until 1983], Cairo: Madbuly Bookshop, 2010.

el-Sadat, Anwar, *In Search of Identity: An Autobiography*, London: Collins, 1978.

Sadowski, Yahya M., *Political Vegetables? Businessman and Bureaucrat in the Development of Egyptian Agriculture*, Washington: Brookings Institution, 1991.

Saffar, Muhammad Bashir, "al-Nukhba al-siyasiyya fi al-Jaza'ir" [The political elites in Algeria], in *al-Nukhba al-siyasiyya fi al-'alam al-'Arabi* [The political elites in the Arab world], Papers for the Third Conference for Young Researchers, Cairo, November 11–13, 1995, Cairo: Center for Political Research and Studies, 1996, pp. 99–164.

Sa'id, 'Abd al-Mun'im, *Islah al-sasa: al-Hizb Al-Watani wa al-Ikhwan wa al-libraliyyun* [Reform of governance: the National Party and the Brothers and liberals], Cairo: Nahdat Misr Publications, 2010.

Said, Mohamed Kadry and Noha Bakr, "Egypt Security Sector Reforms," Arab Reform Initiative, 2011, available at www.arab-reform.net/egypt-security-sector-reforms.

Sa'id, al-Safi, *Kharif al-'Arab: al-bi'r wa al-sawma'a wa al-jiniral – al-harb al-damiyya bayn al-'Aruba wa al-Islam* [The Arab autumn: the well, the hermitage, and the general – the bloody war between Arabism and Islam], Tunis: 'Urabia Publishing, 2012.

Saine, Abdoulaye, "The Gambia's 'Elected Autocrat Poverty, Peripherality, and Political Instability,' 1994–2006," *Armed Forces & Society*, vol. 34, no. 3 (April 2008), pp. 450–73.

Sakinjo, Hatim al-Sirr, *al-Sudan: ra'is ma'a iqaf al-tanfidh: tajribati ma'a intikhabat 2010* [Sudan: president with no implementation: my experience with the 2010 elections], Cairo: al-Ward Library, 2011.

al-Sakri, Fathi bin Hasan, "Dirasa hawla usas wa asalib muqawamat al-fasad al-idari" [A study of the basics and means of combating administrative corruption], in Arab Organization for Administrative Development, *al-Fasad al-idari wa al-mali fi al-watan al-'Arabi* [Administrative and financial corruption in the Arab world], Cairo: Arab Organization for Administrative Development, 2008, pp. 149–67.

Saleh, Heba, "Egyptian Academics Strike in Fight of Campus Democracy," *Financial Times*, October 4, 2011.

Salih, Yasin al-Hajj, *Bilkhalas, ya shabab: 16 'aman fi al-sujun al-Suriyya* [Salvation, young men: sixteen years in the Syrian prisons], Beirut: Dar al-Saqi, 2012.

al-Salihi, Najib, *al-Zilzal: madha hadatha fi al-'Iraq ba'd al-insihab min al-Kuwait? Khafaya al-ayyam al-damiyya* [The earthquake: what happened in Iraq after the retreat from Kuwait? Mysteries of the bloody days], London: al-Rafid Publications, 1998.

al-Samarra'i, Wafiq, *Hutam al-bawwaba al-sharqiyya* [Ruins of the eastern gate], Kuwait: al-Qabas Publishing, 1997.

Samraoui, Mohammed, *Chronique des années de sang: Algérie: comment les services secrets ont manipulé les groupes islamistes* [Chronicle of the years of blood: Algeria: how the secret services manipulated the Islamist groups], Paris: Denoël Impacts, 2003.

Sarotte, Mary Elise, *The Collapse: The Accidental Opening of the Berlin Wall*, New York: Basic Books, 2014.

Sassoon, Joseph, "Comment les tyrans prennent leur décisions" [How tyrants reach their decisions], *Le Monde Diplomatique*, no. 695 (February 2012), pp. 1 and 16.

"The Competence of the Tyrants," *Le Monde Diplomatique*, English edn., no. 1202 (February 2012).

"The East German Ministry of State Security and Iraq, 1968–1989," *Journal of Cold War Studies*, vol. 16, no. 1 (Winter 2014), pp. 4–23.

"The Iraqi Ba'th Party Preparatory School and the 'Cultural' Courses of the Branches," *Middle Eastern Studies*, vol. 50, no. 1 (2014), pp. 27–42.

Saddam Hussein's Ba'th Party: Inside an Authoritarian Regime, Cambridge: Cambridge University Press, 2012.

Saydawi, Riyad, *Sira'at al-nukhab al-siyasiyya wa al-'askariyya fi al-Jaza'ir: al-hizb, al-jaysh, al-dawla* [Political and military clashes of the elites in Algeria: the party, the army, the state], Beirut: Arab Institute, 1999.

Sayigh, Yezid, "Agencies of Coercion: Armies and Internal Security Forces," *International Journal of Middle East Studies*, vol. 43, no. 3 (August 2011), pp. 403–05.

Arab Military Industry: Capability, Performance, and Impact, London: Brassey's, 1992.

al-Sayyid, Jalal, *Tajribati al-barlamaniyya* [My parliamentary experience], Egypt: n.p., n.d.

Schatzberg, Michael G., *The Dialectics of Oppression in Zaire*, Bloomington: Indiana University Press, 1988.

Schrift, Melissa, *Biography of a Chairman Mao Badge: The Creation and Mass Consumption of a Personality Cult*, New Brunswick, NJ: Rutgers University Press, 2001.

Scott, James C., "Patron–Client Politics and Political Change in Southeast Asia," *American Political Science Review*, vol. 66, no. 1 (March 1972), pp. 91–113.

Seitz, Adam C., "Ties that Bind and Divide: The 'Arab Spring' and Yemeni Civil–Military Relations," in Helen Lackner (ed.), *Why Yemen Matters: A Society in Transition*, London: Middle East Institute, SOAS, 2014, pp. 50–68.

"La Semaine financière," *La Presse de Tunisie*, December 17, 2014.

Sengupta, Somini, "Soldiers from Sudan Raped Hundreds in Darfur, Human Rights Group Finds," *New York Times*, February 11, 2015.

Sghiri, Malek, "Greetings to the Dawn: Living through the Bittersweet Revolution (Tunisia)," in Layla al-Zubaidi, Matthew Cassel, and Nemonie Craven Roderick (eds.), *Diaries of an Unfinished Revolution: Voices from Tunis to Damascus*, New York: Penguin Books, 2013, pp. 9–47.

al-Shahawi, Qadri 'Abd al-Fattah, *Jara'im al-sulta al-shurtiyya* [Crimes of the police authority], Cairo: al-Nahda Publishing, 1977.

Sharbal, Ghassan, *Fi khaymat al-Qaddafi: rifaq al-'aqid yakshufun khabaya 'ahdihi* [In Qaddafi's tent: the colonel's comrades expose the mysteries of his era], Beirut: Riyad al-Rayyis Publishing, 2013.

al-Sharif, Mahir and Qays al-Zarli, *al-Siyar al-dhatiyya fi Bilad al-Sham* [Autobiographies in the Levant countries], Damascus: Dar al-Mada, 2009.

Shaw, George Bernard, "The Sanity of Art," in *Major Critical Essays*, introduction by Michael Holroyd, Harmondsworth: Penguin, 1986, pp. 309–60.

Shore, Marci, *The Taste of Ashes: The Afterlife of Totalitarianism in Eastern Europe*, New York: Broadway Books, 2013.

Shu'aybi, Fawzi, *Shahid min al-mukhabarat al-Suriyya, 1955–1968* [Witness from the Syrian intelligence, 1955–1968], Beirut: Riyad al-Rayyis, 2008.

Singerman, Diane, "Networks, Jobs, and Everyday Life in Cairo," in Donna Lee Bowen and Evelyn A. Early (eds.), *Everyday Life in the Muslim Middle East*, Bloomington: Indiana University Press, 2002, pp. 199–208.

Sirrs, Owen L., *A History of the Egyptian Intelligence Service: A History of the Mukhabarat, 1910–2009*, New York: Routledge, 2010.

"Sisi Reviews New Projects in Suez Canal Region," Egyptian State Information Service, November 17, 2014, available at www.sis.gov.eg/En/Templates/Articles/tmpArticleNews.aspx?ArtID=83858#.VH0VA_TF-qM.

Skocpol, Theda, "Rentier State and Shi'a Islam in the Iranian Revolution," *Theory and Society*, vol. 11, no. 3 (May 1982), pp. 265–83.

States and Social Revolutions: A Comparative Analysis of France, Russia, and China, New York: Cambridge University Press, 1979.

Slackman, Michael and Mona el-Naggar, "Embattled Arab Leaders Decide it's Better to Fight than Quit," *New York Times*, April 28, 2011.

Smith, Sidonie and Julia Watson, *A Guide for Interpreting Life Narratives: Reading Autobiography*, 2nd edn., Minneapolis: University of Minnesota Press, 2010.

Smith, William C., *Authoritarianism and the Crisis of the Argentine Political Economy*, Stanford: Stanford University Press, 1991.

Snow, Shane, "Those Who Tell Stories Rule the World," TEDx Talk, August 11, 2014, available at www.youtube.com/watch?v=Asm2Ad49cyI.

Soliman, Samer, *The Autumn of Dictatorship: Fiscal Crisis and Political Change in Egypt under Mubarak*, Stanford: Stanford University Press, 2011.

Sorkin, Jerry, "The Tunisian Model," *Middle East Quarterly* (Fall 2001), pp. 25–29.

Special Inspector General for Iraq Reconstruction (SIGIR), *October 30, 2005 Quarterly Report to Congress*.

Spengemann, William C., *The Forms of Autobiography: Episodes in the History of a Literary Genre*, New Haven: Yale University Press, 1980.

Springborg, Robert, "Arab Militaries," in Marc Lynch (ed.), *The Arab Uprisings Explained: New Contentious Politics in the Middle East*, New York: Columbia University Press, 2014, pp. 142–59.

"Economic Involvement of Militaries," *International Journal of Middle East Studies*, vol. 43, no. 3 (2011), pp. 397–99.

Family, Power, and Politics in Egypt: Sayed Bey Marei – his Clan, Clients, and Cohorts, Philadelphia: University of Pennsylvania Press, 1982.

Mubarak's Egypt: Fragmentation of the Political Order, Boulder, CO: Westview Press, 1989.

"The Role of Militaries in the Arab Thermidor," Paper presented to workshop at the London School of Economics and Political Science:

The Arab Thermidor: The Resurgence of the Security State, October 10, 2014.

St. John, Ronald Bruce, "Libya's Authoritarian Tradition," in Noureddine Jebnoun, Mehrdad Kia, and Mimi Kirk (eds.), *Modern Middle East Authoritarianism: Roots, Ramifications, and Crisis*, New York: Routledge, 2014, pp. 123–41.

Stacher, Joshua A., "Conditioned Participation: The Mubarak State and Egypt's Muslim Brothers," in Noureddine Jebnoun, Mehrdad Kia, and Mimi Kirk (eds.), *Modern Middle East Authoritarianism: Roots, Ramifications, and Crisis*, New York: Routledge, 2014, pp. 183–98.

"Parties Over: The Demise of Egypt's Opposition Parties," *British Journal of Middle Eastern Studies*, vol. 31, no. 2 (November 2004), pp. 215–33.

Stepan, Alfred, "Introduction: Undertheorized Political Problems in the Founding Democratization Literature," in Alfred Stepan (ed.), *Democracies in Danger*, Baltimore: Johns Hopkins University Press, 2009, pp. 1–16.

The Military in Politics: Changing Patterns in Brazil, Princeton: Princeton University Press, 1971.

Stone, Martin, *The Agony of Algeria*, New York: Columbia University Press, 1997.

Storm, Lise, *Party Politics and the Prospects for Democracy in North Africa*, Boulder, CO: Lynne Rienner, 2013.

"Students and the Party: Rushing to Join," *Economist*, February 22, 2014.

Subh, Ahmad Isma'il, *'Ubur al-mihna: mushahadat 'ayaniyya wa dirasa nafsiyya lil-insan al-Misri fi Harb Uktubir* [The tribulation of the crossing: eye-witness accounts and a psychological study of the Egyptian individual during the October War], Cairo: Egyptian Association for the Book, 1976.

al-Suwaydi, Tawfiq, *My Memoirs: Half a Century of the History of Iraq and the Arab Cause*, translated by Nancy Roberts, Boulder, CO: Lynne Rienner, 2013.

Svolik, Milan W., *The Politics of Authoritarian Rule*, New York: Cambridge University Press, 2012.

Tait, Robert, "28 Hours in the Dark Heart of Egypt's Torture Machine," *Guardian*, February 9, 2011.

Talabani, Qubad, "Saving Iraq in the Post-Maliki Era," *Wall Street Journal*, December 8, 2014.

Talas, Mustafa, *Mir'at hayati* [Reflections of my Life], Damascus: Talas Publishing, 1991.

Tarikh al-jaysh al-'Arabi al-Suri [History of the Arab Syrian army], 3 vols., vol. II: *1949–70*, Damascus: Markaz al-Dirasat al-'Askariyya, 2002.

Tal'at, Hasan, *Fi khidmat al-amn al-siyasi, Mayu 1939–Mayu 1971* [In the service of political security, May 1939–May 1971], Cairo: al-Watan al-'Arabi, 1983.

al-Talmasani, 'Umar, *Dhikrayat la mudhakkirat* [Memories not memoirs], Cairo: Islamic Press and Publications, 1985.

al-Tamimi, 'Abd al-Jalil (ed.), *Dawr al-qasr al-ri'asi fi al-nizam al-Nufimbiri* [The role of the presidential palace in the November regime], no. 41, Tunis: al-Tamimi Foundation for Scientific Research and Information, 2014.

   al-Mu'aridun al-siyasiyyun tahta al-ta'dhib fi Tunis: 'abr sijillat al-dhakira [The political opponents under torture in Tunisia: through records of memory], no. 29, Tunis: al-Tamimi Foundation for Scientific Research and Information, 2013.

al-Tannir, Samir, *al-Faqr wa al-fasad fi al-'alam al-'Arabi* [Poverty and corruption in the Arab world], Beirut: al-Saqi, 2009.

Tantawi, Mahmud, *Makasib al-jundi al-ishtirakiyya* [The socialist achievements of the soldier], Cairo: n.p., 1961.

al-Taqrir al-istratiji al-'Arabi, 1996 [The Arabic strategic report, 1996], Cairo: al-Ahram Center for Political and Strategic Studies, 1996.

Tawafan fi bilad al-Ba'th [Flood in the Country of the Ba'th], directed by Omar Amiralay, Syria and France, 2003 [Film].

al-Tawil, Muhammad, *al-Mar'a wa al-barlaman: taqyim al-tajriba al-barlamaniyya lil-mar'a al-Misriyya* [Woman and parliament: an assessment of the parliamentary experience for the Egyptian woman], Cairo: al-Nada Publishing, 2001.

al-Tikriti, Barazan, *Muhawalat ightiyal al-ra'is Saddam Hussein* [Attempts to assassinate President Saddam Hussein], Baghdad: Arab Publishing House, 1982.

Tomasky, Michael, "How to Become Eminent in Washington," *New York Review of Books*, December 4, 2014, pp. 26–28.

Tomuschat, Christian, "Foreword," in Daniel Rothenberg (ed.), *Memory of Silence: The Guatemalan Truth Commission Report*, New York: Palgrave Macmillan, 2012, pp. xv–xviii.

de Tocqueville, Alexis, *L'Ancien régime et la révolution* [The *ancien régime* and the French Revolution], translated by Arthur Goldhammer with an introduction by Jon Elster, New York: Cambridge University Press, 2011.

Transparency International, "Corruption Perceptions Index 2010," available at www.transparency.org/cpi2010/results.

   "Corruption Perceptions Index 2012," available at www.transparency.org/cpi2012.

"The Tripoli Files," *Globus and Mail*, September 17, 2011, pp. F6–F7.

Tucker, Judith, "Biography as History: The Exemplary Life of Khayr al-Din al-Ramli," in Mary Ann Fay (ed.), *Auto/Biography and the Construction of Identity and Community in the Middle East*, New York: Palgrave, 2001, pp. 9–17.

"Tunisia after the Revolution: Spring is Still in the Air," *Economist*, October 25, 2014.

al-'Ujayli, 'Abd al-Salam, *Dhikrayat ayyam al-siyasa: al-juz' al-thani min kitab lam uktab juz'uhu al-awwal ba'd* [Memories of the days of politics: the second volume of a book whose first volume has not yet been written], Beirut: Riyad al-Rayyis, 2000.

'Ukasha, Tharwat, *Mudhakkirati fi al-siyasa wa al-thaqafa* [My memoirs in politics and culture], vol. II, Cairo: al-Hilal Publishing House, 1990.

'Umar, Nabil, *Dhi'b al-mukhabarat al-asmar: al-bab al-sirri li-Gamal 'Abd al-Nasser* [The brown wolf of the intelligence: the secret door to Gamal 'Abd al-Nasser], Cairo: Dar al-Fursan, 2000.

United Nations Development Programme (UNDP), *Corruption and Integrity: Challenges in the Public Sector in Iraq*, January 2013.

'Uthman, Hashim, *al-Muhakamat al-siyasiyya fi Suriya* [Political trials in Syria], Beirut: Riyad al-Rayyis Publishing, 2004.

'Uthman, 'Uthman Ahmad, *Safahat min tajribati* [Pages from my experience], Cairo: al-Maktab al-Misri al-Hadith, 1981.

Van Dam, Nikolaos, *The Struggle for Power in Syria: Politics and Society under Asad and the Ba'th Party*, revised 4th edn., London: I. B. Tauris, 2011.

Vandewalle, Dirk, *A History of Modern Libya*, New York: Cambridge University Press, 2006.

"Libya's Uncertain Revolution," in Peter Cole and Brian McQuinn (eds.), *The Libyan Revolution and its Aftermath*, New York: Oxford University Press, 2015, pp. 17–30.

von Clausewitz, Carl, *On War*, Princeton: Princeton University Press, 1976.

Wahid, Latif, *Military Expenditure and Economic Growth in the Middle East*, London: Palgrave Macmillan, 2009.

Way, Lucan, "Resistance to Contagion: Sources of Authoritarian Stability in the Former Soviet Union," in Valerie Bunce, Michael McFaul, and Kathryn Stoner-Weiss (eds.), *Democracy and Authoritarianism in the Postcommunist World*, New York: Cambridge University Press, 2010, pp. 229–52.

Wedeen, Lisa, *Ambiguities of Domination: Politics, Rhetoric, and Symbols in Contemporary Syria*, Chicago: University of Chicago Press, 1999.

Peripheral Visions: Publics, Power, and Performance in Yemen, Chicago: University of Chicago Press, 2008.

Weeks, Jessica L., *Dictators at War and Peace*, Ithaca, NY: Cornell University Press, 2014.

"Strongmen and Straw Men: Authoritarian Regimes and the Initiation of International Conflict," *American Political Science Review*, vol. 106, no. 2 (May 2012), pp. 326–47.

Weinberg, Carroll A., "Saddam: A Psychiatric Opinion," Middle East Council Seminar Paper, Foreign Policy Research Institute, Philadelphia, February 19, 1991.

Werenfels, Isabelle, "Algeria: System Continuity through Elite Change," in Volker Perthes (ed.), *Arab Elites: Negotiating the Politics of Change*, Boulder, CO: Lynne Rienner, 2004, pp. 173–205.

Managing Instability in Algeria: Elites and Political Change since 1995, London: Routledge, 2007.

"What they Said about al-Sisi's Speech at the United Nations," *al-Masrawy*, 2014, available at www.masrawy.com/News/News_Egypt/details/2014/9/24/353090/.

Wierda, Marieke, "Confronting Qadhafi's Legacy: Transitional Justice in Libya," in Peter Cole and Brian McQuinn (eds.), *The Libyan Revolution and its Aftermath*, New York: Oxford University Press, 2015, pp. 153–74.

Williams, Colin C., "The Hidden Economy in East–Central Europe: Lessons from a Ten-Nation Survey," *Problems of Post-Communism*, vol. 56, no. 4 (July/August 2009), pp. 15–28.

Willis, Michael J., "Political Parties in the Maghrib: Ideology and Identification, a Suggested Typology," *Journal of North African Studies*, vol. 7, no. 3 (2002), pp. 1–28.

"Political Parties in the Maghrib: The Illusion of Significance?" *Journal of North African Studies*, vol. 7, no. 2 (2002), pp. 1–22.

Politics and Power in the Maghreb: Algeria, Tunisia and Morocco from Independence to the Arab Spring, New York: Columbia University Press, 2012.

Wintrobe, Ronald, *The Political Economy of Dictatorship*, New York: Cambridge University Press, 1998.

Wizarat al-Maliyya wa al-Iqtisad al-Watani [Ministry of Finance and National Economy], *Khitab wazir al-maliyya wa al-iqtisad al-watani, mashru' al-muwazana al-'amma li-'am 1998* [Speech of the minister of finance and national economy, budget proposal 1998], Khartoum: n.p., n.d.

Woods, Kevin M. and James Lacey, *Iraqi Perspectives Project: Saddam and Terrorism, Emerging Insights from Captured Iraqi Documents*, vol. V, Alexandria, VA: Institute for Defense Analysis, 2007.

Worth, Robert F., "Even Out of Office, a Wielder of Great Power in Yemen," *New York Times*, February 1, 2014.

"Obstacles Mar Quest for Arab Dictators' Assets," *New York Times*, June 7, 2012.

Yardley, Jim, "Facing his Torturer as Spain Confronts its Past," *New York Times*, April 7, 2014.

"Yemen: Time Running Out for Solution to Water Crisis," Integrated Regional Information Network (IRIN), August 13, 2012.

Yetiv, Steve A., "Oil, Saudi Arabia, and the Spring that Has Not Come," in Mark L. Haas and David W. Lesch (eds.), *The Arab Spring: Change and Resistance in the Middle East*, Boulder, CO: Westview Press, 2013, pp. 97–115.

York, Peter, *Dictator Style: Lifestyles of the World's Most Colorful Despots*, San Francisco: Chronicle Books, 2005.

Zemni, Sami, "From Socio-Economic Protest to National Revolt: The Labor Origins of the Tunisian Revolution," in Nouri Gana (ed.), *The Making of the Tunisian Revolution: Contexts, Architects, Prospects*, Edinburgh: Edinburgh University Press, 2013, pp. 127–46.

Zisser, Eyal, "The Syrian Army on the Domestic and External Fronts," in Barry Rubin and Thomas A. Keaney (eds.), *Armed Forces in the Middle East*, London: Frank Cass, 2002, pp. 113–29.

Žižek, Slavoj, *Did Somebody say Totalitarianism: Five Interventions in the (Mis)Use of a Notion*, New York: Verso, 2001.

Index

CPSIA information can be obtained
at www.ICGtesting.com
Printed in the USA
LVHW01s1730130518
577033LV00011B/116/P

9 781107 618312